Oracle
Desk Reference

ISBN 0-13-013294-2

9 780130 132949

90000

PRENTICE HALL ORACLE SERIES

O **THE INDEPENDENT VOICE ON ORACLE**
ther books in this series

Building Intelligent Databases with Oracle PL/SQL, Triggers, and Stored Procedures, 2/e / **Kevin T. Owens**

Data Warehousing with Oracle: An Administrator's Handbook / **Sima Yazdani and Shirley Wong**

Developing Oracle Forms Applications / **Albert Lulushi**

Inside Oracle Designer/2000 / **Albert Lulushi**

Oracle8 and UNIX Performance Tuning / **Ahmed Alomari**

Oracle8 Database Administration on Windows NT / **Lynnwood Brown**

Oracle Database Administration on UNIX Systems / **Lynnwood Brown**

Oracle: A Database Developer's Guide, 2/e / **Ulka Rodgers**

Oracle DBA Reference Library / **Ahmed Alomari, Lynnwood Brown, and Guy Harrison**

Oracle Designer: A Template for Developing An Enterprise Standards Document / **Mark Kramm and Kent Graziano**

Oracle Desk Reference / **Guy Harrison**

Oracle Developer's Resource Library / **Lulushi and Stowe**

Oracle Developer/2000 Forms / **Albert Lulushi**

Oracle Developer/2000 Handbook, 2/e / **Michael Stowe**

Oracle SQL High-Performance Tuning / **Guy Harrison**

Software Engineering with Oracle / **Elio Bonazzi**

Coming Soon

The Complete Oracle DBA Training Course / **Lynnwood Brown**

Oracle
Desk Reference

Guy Harrison

Prentice Hall PTR
Upper Saddle River, NJ 07458
http://www.phptr.com

Library of Congress Cataloging-in-Publication Data

Harrison, Guy
    Oracle desk reference / by Guy Harrison
       p. cm.-- The Prentice Hall PTR Oracle series)
    Includes bibliographic references.
    ISBN 0-13-013294-2 (alk. paper)
    1. Oracle (Computer file) 2. Relational databases. I. Title.
  II. Series.
    QA76.9.D3H365153   1999
    005.75'65--dc21   99-38904
                                                CIP

Editorial/production supervision: *Kathleen M. Caren*
Cover design director: *Jerry Votta*
Cover designer: *Talar Agasyan*
Series interior design: *Gail Cocker-Bogusz*
Manufacturing manager: *Alexis R. Heydt*
Acquisitions editor: *Tim Moore*
Editorial assistant: *Bart Blanken*
Marketing manager: *Bryan Gambrel*

© 2000 by Prentice Hall PTR
Prentice-Hall, Inc.
Upper Saddle River, New Jersey 07458

Prentice Hall books are widely used by corporations and government agencies for training, marketing, and resale.

The publisher offers discounts on this book when ordered in bulk quantities. For more information, contact Corporate Sales Department, Phone: 800-382-3419; FAX: 201- 236-7141; E-mail: corpsales@prenhall.com
Or write: Prentice Hall PTR, Corporate Sales Dept., One Lake Street, Upper Saddle River, NJ 07458.

Printed in the United States of America
10 9 8 7 6 5 4 3 2 1

ISBN 0-13-013294-2

Prentice-Hall International (UK) Limited, *London*
Prentice-Hall of Australia Pty. Limited, *Sydney*
Prentice-Hall Canada Inc., *Toronto*
Prentice-Hall Hispanoamericana, S.A., *Mexico*
Prentice-Hall of India Private Limited, *New Delhi*
Prentice-Hall of Japan, Inc., *Tokyo*
Prentice-Hall (Singapore) Pte. Ltd., *Singapore*
Editora Prentice-Hall do Brasil, Ltda., *Rio de Janeiro*

Contents

Chapter 2
SQL Expressions and Functions   19

Chapter 3
Data Manipulation and Transaction Control 55

Chapter 4
Data Definition Language (DDL)   69

Chapter 5
PL/SQL Language   163

Chapter 6
Oracle-Supplied PL/SQL Packages 207

Chapter 7
Oracle Java   281

Chapter 8
Command Line Utilities   351

Chapter 9
SQL*PLUS   387

Chapter 10
Initialization Parameters   419

Chapter 11
Terms, Acronyms, and Jargon   461

Appendix A
Internet Resources   481

Preface

Oracle Desktop Reference Template

How do I use SUBSTR to get trailing characters from a string? How do I create my own exceptions in PL/SQL? How do I create a read-only transaction? How do I add a new log file to my database? What's the syntax for publishing a Java-stored program in PL/SQL?

Oracle administrators and developers face questions like these every day. With the ever-expanding scope of the Oracle product line, finding the answers involves an increasingly difficult struggle through the massive and often inconvenient Oracle on-line documentation set. The aim of this book is to improve your productivity by placing essential Oracle information at your fingertips.

When I started administering and developing applications with Oracle databases in the 1980s, every developer and DBA on my team had a set of manuals, which could comfortably fit on a desk. Now—in the last year of the twentieth century—the full documentation set requires several shelves in a large bookcase. Luckily, the dilemma of finding space for printed documentation almost never arises because printed manuals have virtually disappeared from the workplace. Oracle Corporation literally gives away electronic documentation, while charging extravagant prices for the printed versions. The result has been the almost total elimination of printed Oracle documentation in the average office.

I'm a real fan of on-line documentation, but the process of locating snippets of information in the Oracle on-line documentation set just takes too long. Suppose you had the Oracle documentation set on CD-ROM and you wanted to find the exact syntax for the SELECT statement. Here's what you would do:

- If you didn't have the Oracle on-line documentation installed on your hard disk, you would have to put the CD in your CD drive and wait a few seconds for your system to recognize it.
- Next, you must fire up your Web browser and load the Oracle documentation set home page.
- Then you have to locate the correct document, in this case, the Oracle SQL reference.
- When the document is found, you must open the Index page for the document and locate the SELECT entry.
- And finally, you have to navigate to the page containing the Select documentation, which is large and takes a few moments to load .

I found that this involved process was consuming too much of my time. What I needed was a quick reference to all the frequently needed information—SQL commands, PL/SQL syntax, built-in packages, API calls, configuration parameters, and command line arguments—in a package small enough to fit on my desk. Because no such reference existed, I decided to write one, and this book is the result.

How to Use this Book, and How Not to Use It!

This book was designed to be kept close at hand and used to determine the syntax or usage of some aspect of Oracle for which you are already broadly familiar. For instance, you may recall that the MOD function calculates a remainder, but you may have forgotten the order of the arguments. You may be creating a table, but need to refresh your memory on storage parameters. Or, you may be a DBA who needs to check the options of an INIT.ORA parameter.

However, I don't recommend that you use this book as your only reference to the Oracle database. There is only limited introductory and tutorial material in this book. If you need to learn about some Oracle facility from

---

1.   Actually, if you try this with the Oracle 8.1.5 documentation, you'll find that the Select index entry doesn't point to the syntax description of the SELECT statement, but to a general discourse about queries in Chapter 5. If you want the syntax of the SELECT statement, you need to page through the Table of Contents.

scratch, or if you are looking for in-depth coverage of a topic, you should consult the Oracle documentation set, other third-party books, or Internet resources. For instance, if you are new to PL/SQL, you should not use this book to teach yourself the PL/SQL language. However, once you have learned PL/SQL—and even *while* you are learning it—you will find the PL/SQL chapters of the book a very useful reference.

Structure

This book is arranged into a couple of major sections:

The first four chapters cover the SQL language, which is the basis for all data manipulation and retrieval in Oracle. These chapters cover:

- The SELECT statement, which is the basis for all data retrieval.
- SQL functions, expressions, hints, and operators.
- The Data Manipulation Language (DML) statements: UPDATE, DELETE, and INSERT, and statements related to transaction control and locking.
- Data Definition Language (DDL) statements that create, modify, and delete database objects such as tables, indexes, and views.

The next three chapters cover PL/SQL and Java. PL/SQL implements Oracle's proprietary procedural extensions to the SQL language. It also implements many of Oracle's advanced features such as advanced queuing and large object support. In Oracle8i, a Java Virtual Machine (JVM) has been introduced and developers can now choose to develop stored procedures and triggers in Java. These three chapters cover:

- The PL/SQL language syntax and usage.
- Oracle-supplied PL/SQL packages, which extend the PL/SQL language, or which provide new Oracle functionality.
- Oracle Java, including JDBC, SQLJ, and the Oracle8i JServer environment.

The final chapters cover utilities, administration options, terms and jargon, and a brief list of Internet resources. These chapters are:

- Command line utilities provided with the Oracle server.
- The SQL*PLUS program.
- Oracle server configuration parameters.
- Jargons, terms, and acronyms.

Operating System and Oracle Version-Specific Information

This reference attempts to cover syntax for Oracle versions 7.3^2, 8.0, and 8.1^3 (also referred to as Oracle8i). It also covers command line utilities available in the UNIX and NT operating systems. To minimize confusion, the following symbols may appear in the margin to indicate that a feature is specific to an operating system or Oracle version:

7.3	The feature is specific to Oracle 7.3.
8.0+	The feature is available in Oracle 8.0 and 8i.
8i	The feature is available in Oracle8i only.
UNIX	The feature is only available in UNIX operating system variants.
NT	The feature is only available under Windows NT.

Conventions

This book employs the following conventions:

BOLD CAPITALS	Denote a command or function name.
SMALL CAPITALS	Used for argument names or fixed arguments values. These values must be provided to the command or function exactly as shown.

2. The majority of material in this book is also compatible with earlier versions of Oracle. However, there has been no attempt to document compatibility with these earlier versions.

3. Specifically, the first production release of Oracle8i, release 8.1.5.

italics	In syntax, are used for arguments, parameters, and options. The values should be replaced with the appropriate values provided by the user.
	In text, are used to indicate defined terms, usually the first time they occur in the book. Italics are also used for filenames and directories.
Underlined	In syntax, used to indicate the default value from among mutually exclusive alternatives.
Fixed width	Used for code examples and for syntax where case is significant.
CAPITALS	In code examples, SQL and PL/SQL keywords are capitalized.
[ ]	Used to enclose optional arguments.
{*itemA* | *itemB*}	In syntax, braces { } and a vertical bar (|)indicate a choice between two or more items. If all of the options are enclosed in square brackets [ ], you do not need to choose any of the options.
...	In syntax, "..." indicates that the previous argument may be repeated.

Feedback

While every effort has been made to ensure that this book is accurate and timely, there is no doubt that some errors will be found or that information in this book will be overtaken by subsequent releases of Oracle. If you find anything in need of correction, please let me know at gharriso@mira.net. I will ensure that the necessary corrections are made in future releases or in errata. You might also wish to visit my home page at http:// werple.net.au/~gharriso/; I'll post anything there that I think will be of general interest to the readers of this book.

Acknowledgments

Most importantly, I want to thank my wife, Jenni, for her patience and support. Writing a book puts as much burden on your partner as yourself and I couldn't have started—let alone completed—this book without Jenni's support. My children, Christopher, Katherine, Michael, and William, also deserve thanks for putting up with a frequently inattentive and over-stressed dad and for their encouragement. Little Willie (18 months) has my gratitude for constantly reminding me of the things that really matter.

A lot of people at Quest Software contributed either directly or indirectly to this book. In particular, Vadim Loevski and Gerrard Hocks contributed invaluable suggestions and technical review. I work with a tremendously talented and amiable group of software developers at Quest who help to make my job enjoyable and rewarding. I'd particularly like to thank John Symington for creating such an agreeable and exciting development environment. Having such a positive working environment helped give me the focus needed to put in the long hours necessary to complete this book.

At Prentice Hall, Mark Taub and Tim Moore provided editorial support for this book. Both provided invaluable direction and encouragement. Many others at Prentice Hall made very important contributions as well, and I thank you all.

The SELECT Statement

Introduction

Since the logical purpose of a database is to store data with an intention to subsequently retrieve that data, the SELECT statement is arguably the most commonly used and single most significant statement in the SQL language. The SELECT statement forms the basis of all data retrieval statements, as well as being the basis of CREATE VIEW, EXPLAIN PLAN, and certain CREATE TABLE statements. As a subquery, SELECT can be used within the WHERE clause of DML statements such as INSERT, DELETE, and UPDATE.

This chapter summarizes the syntax of the SELECT statement. It should be read in conjunction with Chapter 2, "SQL Expressions and Functions," which describes SQL functions and operators that are frequently used in SELECT statements and in other SQL statements.

Reference

The primary reference for SELECT statement syntax is the *Oracle SQL Reference*.

General Form

The following syntax diagram shows the basic form of the SELECT statement. Each element is described in more detail in the "Select Statement Reference" table below.

1

```
SELECT [{DISTINCT|ALL}] column_definition
   [column_definition, ...]
    FROM table_specifications
  [WHERE conditions]
  [START WITH expression CONNECT BY expression ]
  [GROUP BY column_definition [column_definition, ...] ]
  [ORDER BY column_definition [column_definition, ...] ]
```

Subqueries

A subquery is a SELECT statement that occurs within another SQL statement. Such a "nested" SELECT statement can be used in a wide variety of SQL contexts, including SELECT, DELETE, UPDATE, and INSERT statements.

The following statement uses a subquery to count the number of employees who share the minimum salary:

```
SELECT   count(*)
  FROM   employees
 WHERE   salary=(SELECT MIN(salary)
                    FROM employees)
```

Subqueries may also be used in the FROM clause wherever a table or view definition could appear.

```
SELECT   count(*)
  FROM   (SELECT * FROM employees
 WHERE   department_id=12)
```

Correlated Subquery

A correlated subquery is one in which the subquery refers to values in the parent query. A correlated subquery can return the same results as a join, but can be used where a join cannot, such as in an UPDATE, INSERT, and DELETE statement. For instance, the following statement assigns a sale representative for a customer who is also an employee to the employee's manager. Note the reference in the subquery to the CUSTOMERS table—this is the *correlated* part of the subquery.

```
UPDATE customers
   SET sales_rep_id=(SELECT manager_id
               FROM employees
               WHERE surname=customers.contact_surname
               AND firstname=customers.contact_firstname
               AND date_of_birth=customers.date_of_birth)
```

```
    WHERE
(contact_surname,contact_firstname,date_of_birth) IN
      (SELECT surname,firstname,date_of_birth
       FROM employees)
```

FROM Clause Table Specifications

Table specifications in the FROM clause may take many forms.

Simple Table Specification

This form of the table specification refers to an existing table, view, or snap-shot. It has the following form:

[*schema.*]*table_or_view_name*[*@dblink*] [*alias*]

Schema specifies the name of the schema that contains the object; *table_or_view_name* names an existing table or view; *dblink* specifies a database link to the database that contains the object; and *alias* specifies a table alias, which can be used to qualify column references elsewhere in the SELECT statement.

Subquery

A subquery may be used in place of a table or view name. These subqueries are sometimes referred to as *in-line views*. For instance:

```
SELECT COUNT(*)
    FROM (SELECT *
          FROM sales
          WHERE department_id=2)
```

Partition Specification

A FROM clause may nominate a specific partition. In Oracle 8.0, the PARTI-   **8.0+**
TION keyword specifies the partition concerned. In Oracle8i, the SUBPARTI-
TION clause may also restrict an operation to a sub-partition.

For instance, the following query counts the number of rows in the partition q1_98 within the partitioned table sales_part:

```
SELECT COUNT(*)
    FROM sales_part PARTITION(q1_98)
```

Collection Specification

8.0+   In Oracle 8.0 and later, a FROM clause may include a *collection* specification. This will generally be used to expand a nested table or varray into a relational table representation.

In Oracle 8.0, the THE keyword is used to identify a collection expression. For instance, in the following example, the subjects_nt_scores table contains a nested table column test_score. The query expands the nested table column for a particular subject_id, and then selects the appropriate item_number:

```
SELECT s.score
   FROM THE ( SELECT test_score
                FROM subjects_nt_scores
                WHERE subject_id=10) s
   WHERE s.item_number=1;
```

In Oracle8i, the TABLE keyword provides a similar functionality.

```
SELECT s.score
   FROM TABLE ( SELECT test_score
                  FROM subjects_nt_scores
                  WHERE subject_id=10) s
   WHERE s.item_number=1;
```

Sampling

8i   Oracle8i allows a random sample of rows to be selected. The SAMPLE clause has the following form:

```
FROM table [SAMPLE [BLOCK] percent]
```

SAMPLE returns a random selection of rows, amounting to *percent* of the table's row count. The BLOCK keyword causes the sampling to be based on a random sample of blocks rather than a random sample of rows.

Joins

The *join* operation allows the results from two or more tables to be merged based on some common column values.

Inner Join

The *inner join* is the most common type of join operation. In this join, rows from one table are joined to rows from another table based on some common ("key") values. Rows that have no match in the tables are not included in the results. For instance, the following query links details from the employee and department tables:

```
SELECT   department_name,surname,salary
  FROM   employees e,
         departments d
 WHERE   e.department_id=d.department_id
```

Note that a department without employees would not be returned in the *result set*.

Equi-joins and Theta Joins

An *equi-join* is one in which the equals operator is used to directly relate two values. This is very commonly used to look up a unique key or to join master and detail tables—such as in our previous inner join example. A join that uses an operator other than the equals operator (such as >, BETWEEN, or !=) is called a *theta join*. The previous query is an example of an equi-join. The following query is an example of a theta join.

```
SELECT   customer_id,regionname
  FROM   customers c,
         Salesregion s
 WHERE   c.phoneno BETWEEN s.lowphoneno AND
s.highphoneno
```

Outer Join

The *outer join* allows rows to be included even if they have no match in the other table. Rows which are not found in the outer join table are represented by null values. In Oracle, the outer join operator is "(+)". The following query illustrates an outer join – it will return department names even if a department has no employees:

```
SELECT department_name,surname
  FROM departments    d,
       employees      e
 WHERE d.department_id=e.department_id(+);
```

Although there can be more than one outer join in a query, each table may be outer joined to only one other table (although this outer join table may itself be outer joined to a third table).

Anti-join

Often times you need to select all rows from a table that do not have a matching row in some other result set. This is typically implemented using a subquery and the IN or EXISTS clause. The following examples illustrate the *anti-join* using the EXISTS and IN operators. Each example selects employees who are not also customers.

```
SELECT surname,firstname,date_of_birth
   FROM employees
  WHERE (surname,firstname,date_of_birth) NOT IN
        (SELECT
contact_surname,contact_firstname,date_of_birth
        FROM customers)

SELECT surname,firstname,date_of_birth
   FROM employees
  WHERE NOT EXISTS
        (SELECT *
           FROM customers
          WHERE contact_surname=employees.surname
          AND contact_firstname=employees.firstname
          AND date_of_birth=employees.date_of_birth)
```

Self-join

In a *self-join*, a table is joined to itself. This is performed in exactly the same manner as any other join. The following example shows the employ-ees table in a self-join to link employees with their manager:

```
SELECT m.surname manager,e.surname employee
   FROM employees m,
        employees e
  WHERE e.manager_id=m.employee_id
```

Set Operations

SQL implements a number of operations that deal directly with result sets. These operations, collectively referred to as "set operations," allow result sets to be concatenated, subtracted, or overlaid.

The most common of these operations is the UNION operator, which returns the sum of two result sets. By default, duplicates in each result set are eliminated. By contrast, the UNION ALL operation returns the sum of two result sets, including any duplicates. The following example returns a list of customers and employees. Employees who are also customers are only listed once.

```
SELECT
contact_surname,contact_firstname,date_of_birth
   FROM customers
   UNION
SELECT surname,firstname,date_of_birth
   FROM employees
```

MINUS returns all rows in the first result set that do not appear in the second result set. The following example returns all customers who are not also employees:

```
SELECT contact_surname,contact_firstname,date_of_birth
   FROM customers
   MINUS
SELECT surname,firstname,date_of_birth
   FROM employees
```

INTERSECT returns only the rows that appear in both result sets. The following example returns customers who are also employees:

```
SELECT contact_surname,contact_firstname,date_of_birth
   FROM customers
   INTERSECT
SELECT surname,firstname,date_of_birth
   FROM employees
```

All set operations require that the component queries return the same number of columns, and that those columns are of a compatible datatype.

Group Operations

Aggregate operations allow for summary information to be generated, typically by grouping rows. Rows can be grouped using the GROUP BY operator. If this is done, the SELECT list must consist only of columns contained within the GROUP BY clause and *aggregate functions*.

Some of the aggregate functions are:

AVG	Calculate the average value for the group.
COUNT	Return the number of rows in the group.
MAX	Return the maximum value in the group.
MIN	Return the minimum value in the group.
STDDEV	Return the standard deviation for the group.
SUM	Return the total of all values for the group.

The following example generates summary salary information for each department:

```
SELECT department_id, SUM(salary)
   FROM employees
  GROUP BY department_id
```

Hierarchical Queries

A *hierarchical query* is one in which parent and child rows exist in the same table. This is sometimes referred to as an "explosion of parts" query. In a simple self-join, a child row is joined to a parent row. In a hierarchical query, the child is joined to the parent row, the parent row is joined to its parent row, and so on, until the entire hierarchy is exposed.

For instance, in the employees table, the column manager_id points to an employee_id of an employee's manager. We can easily display the manager for each employee by issuing a self-join as follows:

```
SELECT e.surname employee,m.surname manager
   FROM employees e,
        employees m
  WHERE e.manager_id=m.employee_id;
```

```
EMPLOYEE            MANAGER
---------------     ---------------
RAMPTON             EVANS
STOKES              MILLS
NUTTALL             LEE
LEE                 MCDOWELL
......
```

To display the employees in the organizational hierarchy, we can use the hierarchical operators CONNECT BY and START WITH (the RPAD function indents each level of the hierarchy):

```
SELECT RPAD(' ',LEVEL*3)||surname employee
   FROM employees
  START WITH manager_id=0
CONNECT BY PRIOR employee_id=manager_id;


EMPLOYEE
------------------------------
   REID
      GOSLEY
```

```
        POOLE
      KEYWORTH
        WALKER
        FRYER
        MILLS
            STOKES
            BURNS
........
```

This query shows that REID is the senior employee in the hierarchy. WALKER reports to KEYWORTH, who reports to REID, and so on.

Locking

The FOR UPDATE clause allows rows retrieved to be locked, and thereby prevents the specified rows from being modified until the transaction is terminated by a COMMIT or ROLLBACK statement. If the NOWAIT modifier is used, an error will be returned if the rows cannot be locked immediately.

SELECT Statement Reference

This section provides an alphabetic reference to the statements and clauses that can be used in the SELECT statement.

Select Clause	Description
(+)	See OUTER JOIN.
ALL	See DISTINCT.
AS	See COLUMN SPECIFICATION.
COLUMN SPECIFICATION	SELECT [*schema.*][*object.*]*expression* [[AS] *alias*] [,...] A COLUMN SPECIFICATION defines the columns to be returned by a query. It consists of a comma-separated list of expressions. An expression may consist of any combination of columns belonging to tables listed in the WHERE clause, SQL constants, functions, and operators (see Chapter 2 for details concerning SQL expressions).

Select Clause	Description *(Continued)*
COLUMN SPECIFICATION (CONT.)	*Schema* specifications need not be qualified if the column name is unique among the tables specified in the FROM clause; otherwise, column expressions can be qualified with the schema and/or actual table name or with a table alias specified in the FROM clause. Each *expression* may be assigned an *alias* that redefines the column name in the output result set or assigns a name to the *expression*. The *expression* must be named if it is to be used in views and certain subqueries. The *alias* may immediately follow the *expression* or the optional AS clause can be used.
CONNECT BY	[START WITH *start_expression*] **CONNECT BY** *connect_by_expression* [AND ...] CONNECT BY implements a hierarchical query (see "Hierarchical Queries" above). START WITH identifies the starting point for the hierarchal expansion, that is, the top level of the hierarchy. CONNECT BY describes how the hierarchy is navigated. The syntax of the *connect_by_expression* is similar to a join condition, but adds the PRIOR keyword to identify the column that identifies the next level in the hierarchy. *Connect_by_expression* can take the following form: PRIOR *columna* = *columnb*. where *columnb* contains the value that *columna* will have in a parent row. For instance: PRIOR employee_id = manager_id Queries that include the CONNECT BY operation are prohibited from implementing a join, using a view that includes a join, or including an ORDER BY clause.

Select Clause	Description *(Continued)*
CUBE 8i	See GROUP BY.
DISTINCT	SELECT {DISTINCT|<u>ALL</u>} *column_list* FROM ... The DISTINCT clause eliminates any duplicate rows from the result set. This is equivalent to adding a GROUP BY clause, which contains every row in the SELECT list. ALL is the opposite of DISTINCT, and instructs that all rows be returned, including duplicates. ALL represents the default behavior.
FOR UPDATE	FOR UPDATE [OF { [*schema*.][*object*.]*column*] [,...] }] [NOWAIT] FOR UPDATE locks rows returned from the query. Row-level locks are applied to each row returned. These locks prevent the rows from being deleted or updated by other sessions until a COMMIT or ROLLBACK statement is issued. The OF clause specifies columns that might be updated. This is sometimes used as a form of documentation, but more significantly, it can restrict which rows from a multi-table join are locked. The NOWAIT clause causes Oracle to return an error if the rows cannot be locked immediately due to existing locks held by other sessions.
FROM	FROM {*table_name* [{PARTITION|SUBPARTITION}(*partition_id*)]| *subquery*|*collection_expression*} [*alias*] [,*table_name*...] The FROM clause defines the database objects (table, view, partition, snapshot) and subqueries from which the result set will be derived.

The Select Statement

Select Clause	Description *(Continued)*
FROM (CONT.)	Each data source may optionally be associated with an *alias*, which can be used to qualify column definitions elsewhere in the SELECT statement.
8.0+	In the case of a partitioned table, a specific partition or subpartition may be specified as follows (the SUBPARTITION clause is specific to Oracle8i): FROM *partitioned_table* [{PARTITION|SUBPARITION} *(identifier)*]
8i	The SAMPLE clause allows a subset of rows that match the WHERE clause to be returned. SAMPLE has the following syntax: FROM *table* [SAMPLE [BLOCK] *percent*] SAMPLE returns a random selection of rows amounting to *percent* of the table's row count. The BLOCK keyword causes the sampling to be based on a random sample of blocks rather than a random sample of rows.
8.0+	A *collection expression* is a subquery that returns a collection datatype from a single table row. This collection can then be dealt with as a relational table. In Oracle 8.0, the THE keyword identifies the subquery as a collection expression. In Oracle8i, the TABLE keyword has the same effect. See "Collection Specification" above.
GROUP BY	GROUP BY [{CUBE|ROLLUP}] [( ] *group_by_expression* [ )] [HAVING *having_condition*] GROUP BY aggregates rows satisfying the WHERE clause, returning one row for each unique combination of columns and expressions in the *group_by_expression*. Only columns in the *group_by_expression*, together with aggregate functions such as COUNT or SUM, may be present in the SELECT list.

Select Clause	Description *(Continued)*
GROUP BY (CONT.)	*Group_by_expression* is a comma-separated list of any columns from data sources specified in the FROM clause.

The HAVING clause allows rows to be eliminated from the final result set on the basis of the values of an aggregate function; for instance:

HAVING COUNT(*)>0

HAVING can be used to eliminate rows based on non-aggregate conditions, but this sort of elimination is usually more efficiently implemented using the WHERE clause.

8i	ROLLUP causes subtotals (super-aggregates) for each grouping level to be included in the result set. ROLLUP returns an extra row for each combination of GROUP BY columns and for each leading combination of columns. For instance, if columns A,B, and C are specified in the ROLLUP clause, subtotals will be generated for each combination of A+B+C, A+B, and A. You can use the GROUPING function (see Chapter 2) to distinguish between these super-aggregate rows and ordinary aggregate rows.
8i	CUBE is similar in implementation to ROLLUP. It also generates subtotals for trailing and intermediate columns. This sort of grouping is sometimes referred to as cross-tabulation. If the grouping is A,B,C, then subtotals will be created for each combination of A+B+C, A+B, A+C, B+C, A, B, and C. You can use the GROUPING function (see Chapter 2) to distinguish between these super-aggregate rows and ordinary aggregate rows.

HAVING	See GROUP BY.
INTERSECT	query1
	INTERSECT
	query2

The Select Statement

Select Clause	Description *(Continued)*
INTERSECT (CONT.)	INTERSECT is a set operation that returns rows which are common to two queries. The columns and datatypes of each query must be identical. Only rows that appear in both queries will be returned.

MINUS	query1
	MINUS
	query2
	MINUS is a set operation that returns all rows in *query1* which do not appear in *query2*. The columns and datatypes of each query must be identical.

ORDER BY	ORDER BY [*column_spec* [,*column_spec*…]]
	ORDER BY controls the ordering of rows in the result set. Each *column_spec* has the following format:
	{*column_name*|*column_number*|*expression*}[{ASC|DESC}]
	ORDER BY arguments consist of a comma-separated list of items which appear in, or could legally be specified in, the SELECT list. Alternately, a single number may be specified, which refers to the corresponding column number within the SELECT list.
	By default, ordering is performed in an ascending sequence. The DESC keyword causes ordering to be performed in descending order.

OUTER JOIN	WHERE {*table_alias.*}*column_name* (**+**) = [*table_alias.*]*column_name*} [AND …]
	In an **OUTER JOIN**, rows are returned from one of the tables, the *inner table*, even if there are no matching rows in the other, *outer*, table. Values for "missing" rows are represented by nulls.

Select Clause	Description *(Continued)*
OUTER JOIN (CONT.)	In Oracle, an OUTER JOIN is indicated by affixing the "(+)" operator to join columns from the outer table. It may help to think of the "(+)" operator as "adding un-matched rows." To avoid unexpected result sets, you should add the "(+)" operator to any non-join conditions in the WHERE clause that reference outer table columns.
PARTITION	See FROM.
ROLLUP	See GROUP BY.
SAMPLE	See FROM.
START WITH	See CONNECT BY.
SUBPARTITION	See FROM.
TABLE	TABLE(*collection_expression*)
8i	TABLE is used in Oracle8i to make a collection expression—most typically a single nested table column available in table format. This allows the values of a nested table to be accessed or modified. In Oracle 8.0, the THE keyword implements similar functionality.
THE	THE (*subquery*)
8.0+	THE is used in Oracle 8.0 to access a nested table. The *subquery* must return a single row and a single column. The column returned must be a nested table. A "THE" subquery can be used in place of a table or view name. In Oracle8i, THE is depreciated in favor of the TABLE keyword.

Select Clause	Description *(Continued)*

| UNION | *query1*
UNION *[*ALL*]*
query2 |

UNION returns rows from both of the queries specified. *Query1* and *query2* must return the same number of columns, and the columns must be of compatible datatypes.

If ALL is specified, all rows are returned from the two queries, even if the columns are duplicates. If ALL is not specified, duplicate rows are eliminated.

| WHERE | WHERE *where_conditions* |

The WHERE clause implements join and selection criteria.

Join conditions can be any criteria that associate two tables. Examples of join conditions are provided earlier in this chapter.

Selection criteria are conditions that restrict the rows which are returned in the result set. These conditions can include any legal SQL expressions, including subqueries.

Columns in a WHERE clause may be grouped by parentheses. This allows one group of columns to be compared with another group—possibly from a subquery. For instance:

(column1,column2)=(SELECT *column3,column4* FROM ....)

Select Clause	Description *(Continued)*
WITH	**WITH** [READ ONLY] [CHECK OPTION [CONSTRAINT *constraint_name*]]

WITH is an expression that can be applied to subqueries that restrict the operations that can be performed on the subquery. These restrictions are meaningful for subqueries that define views or that are included within UPDATE, INSERT, or DELETE statements.

READ ONLY prevents updates or deletes from being applied to the view or subquery.

CHECK OPTION prevents the subquery or view from being updated in a way that would be incompatible with the WHERE clause provided in the subquery. In other words, the subquery may not be updated in a way that would prevent the new or modified row from being visible in the subquery.

The CONSTRAINT clause allows you to explicitly name the CONSTRAINT created by the CHECK OPTION clause.

The Select Statement

2

SQL Expressions and Functions

Introduction

This chapter describes SQL expressions and their constituent elements such as functions, operators, and pseudo-columns. Additional elements of SQL such as format masks and hints are also described.

SQL expressions are combinations of columns, operators, functions, and literals. SQL expressions can be included in a SELECT list, can be provided as values to be INSERTed or UPDATEd, or they can be included in WHERE clause conditions.

References

The primary reference for SQL expressions and functions is the *Oracle SQL Reference*.

Hints are documented in the *Oracle Tuning Manual*.

Identifiers

Literals

Literals in SQL expressions may consist of numbers or strings enclosed in single quotes. Numbers may not include format information such as commas or currency symbols, but they may contain decimal places or may be expressed in scientific notation (e.g., 1e6, 100000, 10000.01).

Column and Object Names

Names for Oracle database objects, schemas, and columns may be up to 30 characters in length. Database links may be up to 128 characters in length. Object names cannot contain quotes.

Unless surrounded by double quotes, an object name is case-insensitive, consists of only alpha-numeric characters and the special characters "$","#","_", must start with an alphabetic character, and cannot include spaces.

Object names surrounded by double quotes can include spaces and special characters, and they can be case-sensitive. However, using double quotes in this way is generally a risky practice.

Bind Variables

Bind variables represent variables that are defined outside of the SQL environment. They can be used in place of literals and are prefixed by ":".

Operators

Operators combine or compare multiple expressions to create a new value. Arithmetic operators perform mathematic operations and return a result. Comparison operators compare two expressions and return true, false, or null, depending on the values of the input expressions.

Oracle supports the following operators.

SQL Operators

-	*expression1—expression2*
	Subtracts *expression2* from *expression1*.
!=	*expression1* != *expression2*
	Returns false if *expression1* and *expression2* are identical. Returns null if either expression is null, and true otherwise.
(,)	Parentheses change the association of operators so that expressions within them are performed before operations outside them. Use parentheses to ensure the intended order of operations.

SQL Operators *(Continued)*

*	*expression1 * expression2* Returns the product (multiplication) of *expression1* and *expression2*.
/	*expression1 / expression2* Divides *expression1* by *expression2*.
||	*string1 || string2* Returns the concatenation of *string1* with *string2*.
+	*expression1 + expression2* Returns the sum of *expression1* and *expression2*.
<	*expression1 < expression2* Returns true if *expression1* is less than *expression2*.
<=	*expression1 <= expression2* Returns true if *expression1* is less than or equal to *expression2*.
<>	See !=.
=	*expression1 = expression2* Returns true if *expression1* and *expression2* are identical. Returns null if either expression is null, and false otherwise.
>	*expression1 > expression2* Returns true if *expression1* is greater than *expression2*.
>=	*expression1 >= expression2* Returns true if *expression1* is greater than or equal to *expression2*.

SQL Expressions and Functions

SQL Operators *(Continued)*

ALL	*expression operator* ALL *(list)*
	Returns true if *expression* is true for all values of *list*. Operator should be an operation which could be true for multiple values such as ">", "!=", etc.
AND	*expression1* AND *expression2*
	Returns true if both *expression1* and *expression2* are true. If both are null, returns null.
ANY	*expression* = ANY *(list)*
	Equivalent to "IN", but must be preceded by "=".
BETWEEN	*testvalue* IS [NOT] BETWEEN *low_value* and *high_value*
	Returns true if *testvalue* falls between *low_value* and *high_value*.
CAST	CAST(*expression* AS *type*)
8.0+	CAST converts *expression* into the nominated datatype. *Type* is frequently a collection type, and CAST is often used in conjunction with MULTISET to convert a subquery to a collection. It can also be used as an alternative to TO_CHAR, TO_DATE, and TO_NUMBER functions (although these offer some additional formatting options).
EXISTS	EXISTS *(subquery)*
	Returns true if the subquery returns at least one row.
IN	*expression* [NOT] IN *(list)*
	Returns true if the operand matches any item in *list*. *List* may be defined by a subquery. NOT reverses the return value, returning true if the expression is not included in *list*.

SQL Operators *(Continued)*

IS NULL	*expression* **IS NULL**
	Returns true if *expression* equates to null.
LIKE	*string1* [NOT] **LIKE** *string2* [ESCAPE '*escape_character*']
	Performs a wildcard comparison. The pattern may include the wildcards "%" and "_", which match any string or single character, respectively. However, if the wildcard characters are preceded by *escape_character*, the wildcard evaluation is not performed.
MULTISET	**MULTISET**(*subquery*)
8.0+	MULTISET converts *subquery* into a collection format. It is typically used in conjunction with a CAST operation to convert a subquery result set into a specified collection type. For instance:
	CAST(MULTISET(*select*....) AS *some_collection_type*)
NOT	NOT *expression*
	Logical negation. If the expression evaluates to true, then NOT returns false, and vice versa. This can be used with operations such as EXISTS, LIKE, and IN.
OR	*expression1* OR *expression2*
	Returns true if either *expression1* or *expression2* is true.
SOME	Equivalent to ANY.

SQL Expressions and Functions

User-Defined Operators

Oracle8i allows user-defined operators to be created. These operators are based on PL/SQL functions and can be used in SQL expressions in the same way as built-in operators. For more details, see the CREATE OPERATOR command in Chapter 4, "Data Definition Language (DDL)."

Functions

This section provides a brief description of SQL functions. In general, functions are shown as they would appear in a PL/SQL program, e.g.:

```
result_type:=FUNCTION(arguments)
```

This notation provides a convenient means of showing the return value of functions, but does not in itself imply that the function can or should be used within PL/SQL programs. PL/SQL functions are covered in Chapter 5, "PL/SQL Language."

SQL Functions

ABS	*number*:=ABS(*number*)
	ABS returns the absolute value of *number.* The absolute value of a number disregards the sign of the number, effectively translating negative numbers to their positive equivalents.
ACOS	*number*:=ACOS(*number*)
	ACOS returns the arc cosine of *number,* which is supplied in radians.
ADD_MONTHS	*end_date*:=ADD_MONTHS(*start_date,number_of_months*)
	ADD_MONTHS adds *number_of_months* months to *start_date* and returns the result.
ASCII	*ascii_number*:=ASCII(*character*)
	ASCII returns the ASCII code corresponding to the supplied character.
ASIN	*number*:=ASIN(*number*)
	ASIN returns the arc sin of *number* in radians.
ATAN	*number*:=ATAN(*number*)
	ATAN returns the arc tangent of *number* in radians.

SQL Functions *(Continued)*

ATAN2	number:=**ATAN2**(number1,number2)
	ATAN2 returns the arc tangent of *number1* and *number2* in radians.

AVG	number:=**AVG**([DISTINCT] numeric_expression)
	AVG returns the average value of *numeric_expression*.
	AVG is a group function—it generates a single result from all rows in a result set or, if the query contains a GROUP BY, for each group of rows. If DISTINCT is specified, only DISTINCT values of *numeric_expression* are used to calculate the result.

BFILENAME	bfile_locator:=**BFILENAME**(directory,filename)
8.0+	BFILENAME returns a *bfile_locator* for the file *filename* within *directory*. *Directory* is a directory name created by the CREATE DIRECTORY command. *Filename* is a file within that directory. The *bfile_locator* may be used in subsequent *bfile* operations, for instance, those included within the DBMS_LOB package.

BITAND	number:=**BITAND**(number1,number2)
	BITAND returns a number derived from a bitwise AND operation on the two numeric arguments. The result is a number that has only the bits that are present in both of the numeric arguments.

CEIL	number:=**CEIL**(number)
	CEIL returns the smallest integer *number*, which is greater than or equal to the numeric argument.

CHARTOROWID	rowid:=**CHARTOROWID**(varchar2)
	CHARTOROWID returns a rowid datatype from its string equivalent. The input string may be obtained using the ROWIDTOCHAR function.

SQL Expressions and Functions

SQL Functions *(Continued)*

CHR	*character*:=CHR(*ascii_number*) CHR returns the character corresponding to the supplied *ascii_number*.
CONCAT	*result_string*:=CONCAT(*string1*, *string2*) CONCAT returns the concatenation of *string1* and *string2*. It is equivalent to the concatenation operator ("||").
CONVERT	*output_varchar*:=(CONVERT(*input_varchar*, *destination_character_set* [,*source_character_set*]) CONVERT converts the *input_varchar* string into the *NLS* (National Language Support) character set. If the *input_varchar* is not already in the default character set for the database, *source_character_set* can be used to specify the input character set.
COS	*number*:=COS(*radian_value*) COS returns the cosine of the input value.
COSH	*number*:=COSH(*radian_value*) COSH returns the hyperbolic cosine of the input value.
COUNT	*number*:=COUNT([DISTINCT] *expression*) COUNT returns the number of rows returned by the query or, if the query contains a GROUP BY clause, for each aggregate row returned by the query. If DISTINCT is specified, COUNT returns the number of unique values of *expression*; otherwise, it returns the total number of rows for which *expression* is not null.
DANGLING 8.0+	*object_ref* IS [NOT] DANGLING IS DANGLING returns true if *object_ref* (see REF) points to a non-existent object. This can occur if the object row is deleted.

SQL Functions *(Continued)*

SQL Expressions and Functions

| DECODE | *result*:=DECODE(*expression*,
            comparison1,result1,
            comparison2,result2,
            ....
            default_result) |

DECODE allows an expression to be replaced (or decoded) with an alternate value. In some respects, it's similar to an embedded IF statement. The value of *expression* is compared to each *comparison* value. If the *expression* matches the *comparison* value, then the corresponding *result* is returned. If no *comparison* matches the *expression*, then *default_result* is returned.

| DEREF | *object*:=DEREF(*object_ref*) |

8.0+

DEREF returns the object referred to by *object_ref*. An *object_ref* can be created using the REF function, or from a column of the REF datatype.

| DUMP | *varchar2*:=
     DUMP(*expression*[,*format*[,*start_position*[,*length*]]]) |

DUMP returns Oracle's internal representation of *expression* in the default database character set. *Format* may refer to any of the following codes:

1008 Octal.

1010 Decimal.

1016 Hexadecimal.

1017 Single characters.

Start_position and *length* allow a substring of *expression* to be dumped.

SQL Functions *(Continued)*

EMPTY_BLOB	*blob_locator*:=EMPTY_BLOB()
8.0+	EMPTY_BLOB returns a *BLOB* locator that has not yet been associated with LOB data. It is often used to create rows that include a LOB column prior to populating the LOB value.

EMPTY_CLOB	*Clob_locator*:=EMPTY_CLOB()
8.0+	EMPTY_CLOB is equivalent to EMPTY_BLOB, but it provides a CLOB locator.

EXISTS	EXISTS(*subquery*)
	EXISTS returns true if *subquery* returns at least one row. The *subquery* is typically a *correlated subquery* (see Chapter 1, "The Select Statement"), which tests some condition under which parent rows are to be fetched or modified.

EXP	*number*:=EXP(*power*)
	EXP returns the mathematical constant *e* (approximately 2.718), raised to the power of *power*.

FLOOR	*result_number*:=FLOOR(*number*)
	FLOOR returns the largest integer less than or equal to *number*.

GLB	*mlslabel*:=GLB(*label*)
	GLB is available only in Oracle trusted server. It returns the upper bound of an operating system *label*.

GREATEST	*number*:=GREATEST(*expression1,expression2,...,expressionN*)
	GREATEST returns the *expression* with the greatest numerical value or sort sequence. Any number of expressions of any type may be specified.

SQL Functions *(Continued)*

GROUPING	*number*:=GROUPING(*expression*)

8i

GROUPING is used in conjunction with the CUBE or ROLLUP clause of GROUP BY. GROUPING returns 1 if the current row is a super-aggregate of the given *expression*. *Expression* consists of one of the columns from the GROUP BY clause.

If the row is not a super-aggregate of the expression concerned, then GROUPING returns 0.

HEXTORAW	*raw_value*:=HEXTORAW(*character*)

HEXTORAW converts a string containing hexidecimal characters into a RAW value.

INITCAP	*output_string*:=INITCAP(*input_string*)

INITCAP capitalizes the first character in each word of *input_string*.

INSTR	*position*:=INSTR(*string*, *search_string* [, *start_position*] [, *occurrence*])

INSTR searches for *search_string* within *string*. If *search_string* is found, INSTR returns the *position* of *search_string* within *string*. Otherwise, INSTR returns 0.

If *start_position* is specified and is positive, then the search is started at *start_position* characters from the start of the string. If *start_position* is specified and is negative, then the search is started at *start_position* characters from the end of the string.

If *occurrence* is specified, then INSTR returns the position of the specified *occurrence* of the *search_string*.

SQL Expressions and Functions

SQL Functions *(Continued)*

INSTRB	*position*:=INSTRB(*string, search_string* [, *start_position*] [, *occurrence*])

INSTRB has the same functionality as INSTR, except that *position* and *start_position* are expressed in bytes rather than characters. This distinction is only meaningful if the database uses a multi-byte character set.

LAST_DAY	*output_date*:=LAST_DAY(*input_date*)

LAST_DAY returns the date of the last day in the month containing *input_date*.

LEAST	*number*:=LEAST(*expression1,expression2,...,expressionN*)

LEAST returns the *expression* that has the least numerical value or sorting sequence. Any number of expressions of any type may be specified.

LENGTH	*number*:=LENGTH(*string*)

LENGTH returns the number of characters in *string*.

LENGTHB	*number*:=LENGTHB(*string*)

LENGTHB returns the number of bytes in *string*. This function will return the same result as LENGTH in a database with a single-byte character set, but will return a different value for a multi-byte character set.

LIKE	*expression* LIKE *pattern*

LIKE returns true if *expression* matches *pattern*. *Pattern* is a string expression that can include the wildcard expressions "%" (match any sub-string) and "_" (match any single character).

LN	*number*:=LN(*number*)

LN returns the natural logarithm of *number*.

SQL Functions *(Continued)*

LOG	*number*:=**LOG**(*number,base*)
	LOG returns the logarithm of *number* in the specified *base*.
LOWER	*string*:=**LOWER**(*string*)
	LOWER returns a lowercase representation of *string*.
LPAD	*out_string*:=**LPAD**(*in_string,length,*[*pad_character*])
	LPAD returns *in_string*, left-padded to *length*. If *pad_character* is specified, then enough *pad_characters* will be appended to the left of *in_string* to make the string *length* characters long. If *pad_character* is not specified, then space characters (' ') will be appended.
LTRIM	*out_string*:=**LTRIM**(*in_string* [*,trim_characters*])
	LTRIM returns *in_string*, removing the left-most characters in *trim_characters*. If *trim_characters* is not specified, all left-most blanks are removed.
MAKE_REF 8.0+	*ref_column*:=**MAKE_REF**(*object_view, primary_key*)
	MAKE_REF creates a REF value for a row within *object_view*. *Object_view* defines the view. *Primary_key* consists of one or more values, which constitute the primary key of *object_view*.
MAX	*number*:=**MAX**([DISTINCT] *numeric_expression*)
	MAX returns the maximum value of *numeric_expression*.
	MAX is a group function—it generates a single result from all rows in a result set or, if the query contains a GROUP BY, for each group of rows. If DISTINCT is specified, only distinct values of *numeric_expression* are used to calculate the result.

SQL Expressions and Functions

SQL Functions *(Continued)*

MIN	*number:=*MIN([DISTINCT] *numeric_expression*) MIN returns the minimum value of *numeric_expression*. MIN is a group function—it generates a single result from all rows in a result set or, if the query contains a GROUP BY, for each group of rows. If DISTINCT is specified, only distinct values of *numeric_expression* are used to calculate the result.
MOD	*number:=*MOD(*number,divisor*) MOD returns the remainder of the division of *number* by *divisor*. This is the mathematical modulus operation.
MONTHS_ BETWEEN	*number:=*MONTHS_BETWEEN(*date1,date2*) MONTHS_BETWEEN returns the number of months between two dates. The number returned may be fractional.
NEW_TIME	*date:=*NEW_TIME(*input_date, timezone1, timezone2*) NEW_TIME returns the date (including time) in *timezone2* when the date in *timezone1* is *input_date*.
NEXT_DAY	*output_date:=*NEXT_DAY(*input_date,dayofweek*) NEXT_DAY returns the next date following *input_date*, which is the day of the week specified by *dayofweek*.
NLS_CHARSET_ DECL_LEN	*width:=*NLS_CHARSET_DECL_LEN(*bytes,character_set*) NLS_CHARSET_DECL_LEN returns the width of an nchar column, which consumes *bytes* of storage in *character_set*.
NLS_ CHARSET_ID	*Char_set_id:=*NLS_CHARSET_ID(*char_set_name*) NLS_CHARSET_ID returns the character set ID of *char_set_name*.

SQL Functions *(Continued)*

NLS_ CHARSET_NAME	*Char_set_name*:=**NLS_CHARSET_NAME**(*char_set_id*)
	NLS_CHARSET_NAME returns the character set name of *char_set_id*.
NLS_INITCAP	*string*:=**NLS_INITCAP**(*instring*, 'NLS_SORT = *sort_lang*")
	NLS_INITCAP acts the same as INITCAP, but uses character set-specific rules for case conversions.
NLS_LOWER	*string*:=**NLS_LOWER**(*instring*, 'NLS_SORT = *sort_lang*')
	NLS_LOWER acts the same as LOWER, but uses character set-specific rules for case conversions.
NLS_UPPER	*string*:=**NLS_UPPER**(*instring*, 'NLS_SORT = *sort_lang*')
	NLS_UPPER acts the same as UPPER, but uses character set-specific rules for case conversions.
NLSSORT	*Sort_sequence*:=**NLSSORT**(*instring*, 'NLS_SORT = *sort_lang*')
	NLSSORT returns the relative sort sequence of *instring* using the specified sort sequence or language.
NULL	*expression* IS [NOT] **NULL**
	IS NULL returns true if *expression* is null.
NVL	*return_value*:=**NVL**(*expression*, *value_if_null*)
	NVL returns *expression* unless *expression* is null, in which case, it returns *value_if_null*.
POWER	*in_number*:=**POWER**(*in_number*, *power*)
	POWER returns *in_number* raised to power of *power*.
RAWTOHEX	*hex_string*:=**RAWTOHEX**(*raw_value*)
	RAWTOHEX translates a RAW expression into hexidecimal.

SQL Functions *(Continued)*

REF	*object_ref*:=REF(*object_identifier*)

8.0+

REF returns an object reference, which points to the nominated object. The *object_identifier* would most commonly refer to a row in an object table, and REF would return the object identifier for that row.

Object_ref can be used to DEREF a specified object row, or may be used within a WHERE clause to identify a particular row.

REFTOHEX	*string*:=REFTOHEX(*ref_column*)

REFTOHEX translates a column of type REF to a hexidecimal representation.

REPLACE	*string*:=REPLACE(*in_string*, *search_string* [,*replace_string*])

REPLACE returns *in_string* with all occurrences of *search_string* replaced with *replace_string*. If *replace_string* is not specified, all occurrences of *search_string* are removed.

ROUND	*out_number*:=ROUND(*in_value*, *round_factor*)

ROUND rounds the supplied number to the specified number of decimal places. If the number of decimal places is not supplied, a value of 0 is used—this causes *in_value* to be rounded to the nearest integer value.

ROUND can also be applied to dates, in which case, *round_factor* will be a date format mask specifying the level of rounding. For instance, 'YYYY' will cause the date to be rounded to the nearest year.

ROWIDTOCHAR	*string*:=ROWIDTOCHAR(*rowid_value*)

ROWIDTOCHAR returns a string representation of a ROWID.

SQL Functions *(Continued)*

RPAD	*out_string*:=RPAD(*in_string, length,* [*pad_character*])

RPAD returns *in_string*, right-padded to *length*. If *pad_character* is specified, then enough pad characters will be appended to the right of *in_string* to make the string *length* characters long. If *pad_character* is not specified, then space characters (' ') will be appended.

RTRIM	*out_string*:=RTRIM(*in_string* [,*trim_characters*])

RTRIM returns *in_string*, removing the right-most characters in *trim_characters*. If *trim_characters* is not specified, then all right-most blanks are removed.

SIGN	*out_number*:=SIGN(*in_number*)

SIGN returns -1 if *in_number* is less than 0, +1 if *in_number* is greater than 0, and 0 if *in_number* is equal to 0.

SIN	*out_number*:=SIN(*in_number*)

SIN returns the sine value of *in_number,* which is expressed in radians.

SINH	*out_number*:=SINH(*in_number*)

SINH returns the hyperbolic sine of *in_number*.

SOUNDEX	*out_string*:=SOUNDEX(*in_string*)

SOUNDEX returns the soundex translation of *in_string*. Words with identical pronunciations but different spellings may have identical soundex values.

SQRT	*out_number*:=SQRT(*in_number*)

SQRT returns the square root of *in_number*.

SQL Expressions and Functions

SQL Functions *(Continued)*

STDDEV	*number:*=STDDEV([DISTINCT] *numeric_expression*)
	STDDEV returns the standard deviation value of *numeric_expression*.
	STDDEV is a group function—it generates a single result from all rows in a result set or, if the query contains a GROUP BY, for each group of rows. If DISTINCT is specified, only distinct values of *numeric_expression* are used to calculate the result.
SUBSTR	*out_string:*=SUBSTR(*in_string, start_position* [, *length*])
	SUBSTR returns a substring of *length* from *in_string*. The substring starts at the *start_position* character. If *start_position* is negative, the substring starts at *start_position* characters from the end of *in_string*. If *length* is not specified, SUBSTR returns the characters from *start_position* to the end of the string.
SUBSTRB	*out_string:*=SUBSTRB(*in_string, start_position* [, *length*])
	SUBSTRB has the same functionality as SUBSTR, except that *start_position* and *length* are measured in bytes rather than characters. SUBSTRB behaves the same as SUBSTR for a single-byte character set, but will return a different result in a multi-byte character set.
SUM	*number:*=SUM([DISTINCT] *numeric_expression*)
	SUM returns the sum of values of *numeric_expression*.
	SUM is a group function—it generates a single result from all rows in a result set or, if the query contains a GROUP BY, for each group of rows. If DISTINCT is specified, only distinct values of *numeric_expression* are used to calculate the result.

SQL Functions *(Continued)*

SYS_CONTEXT

8i

attribute_value:=SYS_CONTEXT(*namespace,*
    attribute_name)

SYS_CONTEXT returns the *attribute_value* for
attribute_name in *namespace*, which is created by the
CREATE CONTEXT command.

SYS_GUID

8i

string:=SYS_GUID()

SYS_GUID returns a globally unique identifier
constructed from the host ID and thread or process ID.

SYSDATE

date:=SYSDATE

SYSDATE returns the current date and time.

TAN

out_number:=TAN(*in_number*)

TAN returns the tangent of *in_number,* which is
expressed in radians.

TANH

out_number:=TANH(*in_number*)

TANH returns the hyperbolic tangent of *in_number.*

TO_CHAR

out_string:=TO_CHAR(*input_value* [,*format*] [,
    nls_parameters])

TO_CHAR returns a string representation of *input_value,*
which is a number or date. If *format* is not specified,
then a default format will be used. In the case of dates,
the default format is the value of the initialization
parameter NLS_DATE_FORMAT (see Chapter 10,
"Initialization Parameters").

TO_CHAR formats are described later in this chapter.

Nls_parameters is a string containing multiple National
Language Support (NLS) parameters that can affect
the formatting of numbers and dates.

SQL Functions *(Continued)*

TO_DATE	*date*:=**TO_DATE**(*in_string* [,*date_format*] [, *nls_parameters*])

TO_DATE returns a date value from *in_string*. If *in_string* is in the default date format for the database, then no *date_format* value is necessary. Otherwise, *date_format* describes the format of the string.

The default date format is the value of the initialization parameter NLS_DATE_FORMAT (see Chapter 10).

Date format patterns are described later in this chapter.

Nls_parameters is a string containing multiple National Language Support (NLS) parameters that can affect the formatting of numbers and dates.

TO_LOB	**TO_LOB**(*long_column*)
8i	

TO_LOB converts a column of datatype long to a LOB datatype. The target of TO_LOB must be a LOB column within a table.

TO_MULTI_BYTE	*out_string*:=**TO_MULTI_BYTE**(*in_string*)

TO_MULTI_BYTE returns a string of single-byte characters into a string of multi-byte characters for databases that support both single and multi-byte character sets.

TO_NUMBER	*number*:=**TO_NUMBER**(*string* [,*format*] [,*nls_parameters*])

TO_NUMBER converts *string* into numeric format. If *string* contains numeric formatting characters (for instance, commas or currency notation), then *format* should provide the appropriate numeric format model (see "*Numeric Masks*" in this chapter for details of these models).

Nls_parameters is a string containing multiple National Language Support (NLS) parameters that can affect the formatting of numbers and dates.

SQL Functions *(Continued)*

TRANSLATE	*out_string*:=TRANSLATE(*in_string*, *search_string*,*destination_string*)

TRANSLATE returns *in_string* with each character in *search_string* replaced with the corresponding character in *replace_string*. If *replace_string* is shorter than *search_string*, the excess characters are removed.

TRIM **8i**	*result_string*:=TRIM([{LEADING|TRAILING|BOTH}] [*character* FROM *input_string*)

TRIM strips leading and/or trailing occurrences of *character* from *input_string*. If *character* is not specified, then blank spaces are trimmed.

If LEADING, TRAILING, or BOTH is not specified, then both leading and trailing characters are trimmed.

TRUNC	*out_number*:=TRUNC(*in_number* [,*decimal_places*])

out_date:=TRUNC(*in_date* [,*date_formats*])

In the first form, TRUNC removes all figures beyond *decimal_places*. If *decimal_places* is not specified, then TRUNC removes all non-integer figures. TRUNC differs from ROUND in that no rounding occurs. For instance, ROUND(1.9)=2, whereas TRUNC(1.9)=1.

In the second form, TRUNC removes all date information of lesser magnitude than *date_format*. For instance, if *date_format* is 'HH,' then minutes and seconds are discarded. If no date format is specified, then 'DD' is assumed, e.g., hour, minutes, and seconds are discarded.

UID	*number*:=UID()

UID returns the user ID of the current user.

SQL Expressions and Functions

SQL Functions *(Continued)*

UPPER	*out_string*:=**UPPER**(*in_string*)

UPPER returns *in_string* with all characters translated to upper-case.

USER	*varchar2*:=**USER**()

USER returns the username of the current user.

USERENV	*string*:=**USERENV**(*'option'*)

USERENV returns information about the current session. The information returned is based on *option*, which can take one of the following values:

ISDBA   Returns true if the session has DBA authority.

LANGUAGE Returns the NLS character set, language, and territory.

TERMINAL Returns the terminal or client machine identifier for the session.

SESSIONID Returns the auditing session identifier. This corresponds to the audsid column in V$SESSION.

ENTRYID   Returns the auditing entry identifier.

LANG   Returns the abbreviated NLS language name.

INSTANCE Returns the instance identifier— generally useful only in Oracle parallel server environments.

VARIANCE	*number*:=**VARIANCE**([DISTINCT] *numeric_expression*)

VARIANCE returns the statistical variance of *numeric_expression*.

SQL Functions *(Continued)*

VARIANCE (CONT.)	VARIANCE is a group function—it generates a single result from all rows in a result set or, if the query contains a GROUP BY, for each group of rows. If DISTINCT is specified, only distinct values of *numeric_expression* are used to calculate the result.
VSIZE	*number*:=VSIZE(*expression*) VSIZE returns the number of bytes of storage required to hold *expression*.

User-Defined Functions

Stored functions, or functions within a stored package, may be called from SQL under well-defined circumstances. Functions called from SQL must restrict their accesses to the database and to packaged variables, particularly functions used in GROUP functions. The "restrict references" pragma is used in versions of Oracle prior to Oracle8i to enforce these restrictions.

User-defined functions are described in detail in Chapter 5, "PL/SQL Language."

Date and Numeric Format Masks

The functions TO_DATE and TO_CHAR can take a format mask that defines the format of input or output values. For instance, TO_CHAR can format a date as a string in a wide variety of formats:

```
SQL> SELECT TO_CHAR(sysdate,
    'DD-Mon-yyyy:hh24:mi:ss') FROM dual;
```

```
06-Dec-1998:21:17:37
```

```
SQL> SELECT TO_CHAR(sysdate,'fmDay ddTH Month YYYY')
    FROM dual;
```

```
Sunday 6th December 1998
```

In a similar way, format masks can be applied to numeric data, for instance, to format a number as a currency string. Input format masks can also be used in the TO_DATE function to specify the format of the string that is being converted to a date.

Date Format Masks

Date format strings can be used in TO_CHAR and TO_DATE functions. The format masks can be combined in multiple ways to display a date in almost any conceivable format.

Table 2–1 Date Format Masks

Mask	Description
AD	Returns "AD" or "BC" as appropriate.
AM	Returns "AM" or "PM" as appropriate.
BC	Returns "AD" or "BC" as appropriate.
CC	Returns the century number. If the year is 2000, then CC will return 21 (the 21st century).
D	Day of the week in numeric format (1-7).
DAY	Name of the day.
DD	Day of the month (1-31).
DDD	Day of the year (1-366).
DY	Short name of the day, for instance, "MON".
E	Abbreviated era name (only available with suitable NLS calendar settings).
EE	Full era name (only available with suitable NLS calendar settings).
FM	FM suppresses blank- and zero-padding for a format mask.
FX	FX is a format mask modifier that requires format masks to match exactly. Normally, differences in terms of blank spaces and leading zeros are ignored. When FX is specified, the format mask must match exactly.
HH	Hour of the day in 12-hour format.
HH24	Hour of the day in 24-hour format.

Table 2–1 Date Format Masks

Mask	Description
I	As a prefix to Y, YY, or YYY, specifies that the year should be formatted according to ISO standards.
IW	Week of the year (ISO format).
J	Julian date. The number of days since 01-JAN-4712BC.
LITERALS	Certain characters may be used within format masks and will be present in the output string without modification. These characters can be supplied without quoting:—/ , . ; : Additionally, any string contained within double quotes will be included in the output format.
MI	The minute within the hour.
MM	Month number, zero-prefixed. For instance, June="06".
MON	Short month name. For instance, DEC, SEP.
MONTH	Full name of the month.
PM	Returns "AM" or "PM", as appropriate.
Q	Returns the quarter of the year as an integer.
RM	Returns the number of the month as a Roman numeral.
RR	As an input to TO_DATE, RR returns a date in the next century if the year is <50 and the current year if >50. Otherwise, RR returns a year in this century.
RRRR	Accepts a year in two-digit or four-digit format. If two-digit, the year conversion mechanisms of RR are applied.
SS	Second within the minute (0-59).
SSSSS	Second of the day, e.g., the number of seconds past midnight.
W	Week of the month as a number.
WW	Week of the year in numeric format.

SQL Expressions and Functions

Table 2–1 Date Format Masks

Mask	Description
YEAR	Year spelled out as a string. For instance, "Nineteen Ninety-Nine".
YY	Two-digit year.
YYYY	Four-digit year.

Numeric Format Masks

Numeric masks can appear in TO_NUMBER and TO_CHAR functions. Numeric masks are used to convert formatted numbers to and from Oracle numbers.

Table 2–2 Numeric Format Masks

Mask	Description
$	Prefixes the number with a dollar sign.
,	Prints a comma at the specified location.
.	Prints a decimal point at the specified location.
0	Denotes a numeric placeholder. If the location is unused—for instance, the number is of a magnitude less than that allowed for—a zero will be printed.
9	Denotes a numeric placeholder. If the location is unused—for instance, the number is of a magnitude less than that allowed for—a blank will be printed.
9.99EEEE	Returns the number in scientific notation. The number of digits after the decimal point specifies the precision of the number returned.
B	Returns blanks instead of zeroes in the integral portion of a number if the number is less than one. This overrides any '0' format masks which may have been set.
C	Returns the ISO currency symbol as defined by NLS_ISO_CURRENCY.

Table 2–2 Numeric Format Masks

Mask	Description
D	Returns the decimal separator specified by NLS_NUMERIC_CHARACTER.
FM	This format mask modifies other masks to suppress leading or trailing blanks.
G	Returns the character defined by NLS_NUMERIC_CHAACTER in the specified position. This character—often ","—is used to mark magnitudes of one thousand (1,000), one million (1,000,000), etc.
L	Returns the local currency symbol defined by NLS_CURRENCY.
MI	Returns a trailing negative sign for negative numbers.
PR	Causes negative values to be enclosed in "<>".
RM	Returns the number in Roman numerals.
S	Prints a plus or minus sign, depending on the value supplied.
TM	Returns the number with the minimum number of characters consistent with retaining maximum precision. May be followed by an "e" or "9" to indicate scientific or fixed notation, respectively. Without arguments, returns fixed notation unless the output is greater than 64 characters, in which case, scientific notation is used.
U	Returns the currency symbol defined by NLS_UNION_CURRENCY.
V	Returns the number multiplied by 10^n, where n is the number of nines following the 'V'.
X	Returns the integer part of the input number formatted in hexidecimal.

Pseudo-Columns

Psuedo-columns are attributes of a result set that act like table columns, but don't have any underlying storage in the database.

Psuedo-Columns

LEVEL	In a hierarchical query (see Chapter 1, "The Select Statement") using a CONNECT BY clause, LEVEL defines the level of the current row within the hierarchy. For instance, in a hierarchical query involving an organizational tree, the president would have a LEVEL of 1, the vice-president a LEVEL of 2, direct reports to the vice-president would have a LEVEL of 3, and their immediate juniors a LEVEL of 4.
CURRVAL	*Sequence_name*.CURRVAL
	Returns the current value for the named sequence. This value must have been obtained previously through the NEXTVAL pseudo-column.
NEXTVAL	*Sequence_name*.NEXTVAL
	Increments the named sequence and returns the next value.
ROWNUM	Returns the sequence of the current row within the result set. ROWNUMs are assigned prior to any sorting required by an ORDER BY clause, so ROWNUMs may actually be returned out of sequence.
ROWID	ROWID returns the physical address of the row within the database. ROWID can be used to efficiently locate a row or determine the physical location of a row within the database.

Hints

The optimizer is the part of Oracle that determines how the SQL will be executed. Among other things, the optimizer may decide in which order to join tables, whether to use an index, and so on. Hints are instructions which you can include in your SQL statement to instruct or "guide" the Oracle query optimizer. Using hints, you can specify join orders, types of access paths, indexes to be used, the optimization goal, and other directives.

An optimizer hint appears as a comment following the first word of the SQL statement (e.g., SELECT, INSERT, DELETE, or UPDATE). A hint is differentiated from other comments by the presence of the plus sign ("+") following the opening comment delimiter ("/°"). For instance, the FULL hint in the following example tells the optimizer to perform a full table scan when resolving the query:

```
SELECT /*+ FULL(E) */ *
FROM employee e
WHERE salary > 1000000
```

Hints

ALL_ROWS	ALL_ROWS
	Uses the cost-based optimizer and optimizes for the retrieval of all rows.
AND_EQUAL	AND_EQUAL(*table_name index_name index_name ....*)
	Retrieves rows from the specified table, using each of the specified indexes, and merges the results.
APPEND	APPEND
8.0+	Invokes a direct load insert. Only valid for INSERT ... SELECT FROM statements.
BITMAP	BITMAP(*table_name index_name*)
	Retrieves rows from the specified table using the specified bitmap index.
CACHE	CACHE(*table_name*)
	Encourages rows retrieved by a full table scan to remain in the buffer cache of the SGA.
CHOOSE	CHOOSE
	If statistics have been collected for any table involved in the SQL statement, uses cost-based/all-rows optimization, otherwise uses rule-based optimization.

SQL Expressions and Functions

Hints *(Continued)*

CLUSTER	CLUSTER(*table_name*)
	Uses a cluster scan to retrieve table rows.
DRIVING_SITE	DRIVING_SITE(*table_name*)
	For a distributed SQL statement, causes the site at which the specified table resides to be the driving site.
FIRST_ROWS	FIRST_ROWS
	Specifies that the cost-based optimizer should optimize the statement to reduce the cost of retrieving the first row only.
FULL	FULL(*table_name*)
	Uses a full table scan to retrieve rows from the specified table.
HASH	HASH(*table_name*)
	Uses a hash scan to retrieve rows from the specified table. The table must be stored in a hash cluster.
HASH_AJ	HASH_AJ
	Performs an anti-join using hash join methodology. This hint must appear after the SELECT statement of a NOT IN subquery.
HASH_SJ	HASH_SJ
8.0+	Appears within an EXISTS subquery. Invokes a hash semi-join.
INDEX	INDEX(*table_name [index_name]*)
	Uses the specified index to retrieve rows from the table or, if no index is specified, uses any index.

Hints *(Continued)*

INDEX_ASC

INDEX_ASC(*table_name* [*index_name*])

Specifies an ascending index range scan using the specified index or, if no index is specified, uses any suitable index.

INDEX_COMBINE

INDEX_COMBINE(*table_name* [*index_name*...])

Instructs the optimizer to combine the specified bitmap indexes. If no bitmap indexes are specified, chooses suitable bitmap indexes.

INDEX_DESC

INDEX_DESC(*table_name* [*index_name*])

Specifies a descending index range scan using the specified index or, if no index is specified, uses any suitable index.

INDEX_FFS

INDEX_FFS(*table_name* [*index_name*])

Invokes a fast full index scan using the specified index or, if no index is specified, uses any suitable index. A fast full scan reads all the indexes in block order using multi-block reads and possibly parallel query.

MERGE

MERGE

Instructs the optimizer to perform complex view merging when resolving a query based on a view or which includes a subquery in the WHERE clause.

MERGE_AJ

MERGE_AJ

Performs an anti-join using the sort-merge join method. This hint must appear after the SELECT statement of a NOT IN subquery.

MERGE_SJ

MERGE_SJ

8.0+

Appears within an EXISTS subquery. Invokes a sort-merge semi-join.

SQL Expressions and Functions

Hints *(Continued)*

NO_EXPAND	NO_EXPAND(*table_name*)
	Oracle will sometimes expand statements with OR conditions into multiple SQL statements combined by a union operation. This hint instructs the optimizer not to do this, even if it calculates that such a transformation would be beneficial.
NO_INDEX	No_INDEX(*table_name* [*index_name*])
	Suppresses the use of the named INDEX or, if no indexes are specified, suppresses all indexes on the nominated table.
NO_MERGE	No_MERGE
	Instructs the optimizer not to perform complex view merging when resolving a query based on a view or which includes a subquery in the WHERE clause.
NO_PUSH_PRED	No_PUSH_PRED
	Does not push join conditions from the WHERE clause into a view or subquery.
NOAPPEND 8.0+	NOAPPEND
	Suppresses direct load insert in an INSERT ... SELECT FROM ... statement.
NOCACHE	NOCACHE(*table_name*)
	Discourages Oracle from keeping rows retrieved by a full table scan in the buffer cache of the SGA. Overrides the cache setting on the CREATE or ALTER TABLE statement.
NOPARALLEL	NOPARALLEL(*table_name*)
	Doesn't use parallel processing for the SQL statement. Overrides the parallel setting on the CREATE or ALTER TABLE statement

Hints *(Continued)*

NOPARALLEL_ INDEX	NOPARALLEL_INDEX(*table_name index_name*) Suppresses parallelism in fast full index scans or in partitioned index access.
NOREWRITE 8i	NOREWRITE Prevents the SQL statement from being "re-written" to take advantage of materialized views. Overrides the server parameter QUERY_REWRITE_ENABLED.
ORDERED	ORDERED Instructs the optimizer to join the tables in exactly the left to right order specified in the FROM clause.
ORDERED_ PREDICATES 8i	ORDERED_PREDICATES Causes predicates in the WHERE clause to be evaluated in the order in which they appear in the WHERE clause.
PARALLEL	PARALLEL(*table_name, degree_of_parallelism*) Instructs the optimizer to perform parallel scans on the nominated table. If no degree of parallelism is specified, the default will be used.
PARALLEL_ INDEX	PARALLEL_INDEX(*table_name* [*index_name*]) Parallelizes a fast full index scan or an index scan against a partitioned index.
PQ_DISTRIBUTE	PQ_DISTRIBUTE(*table_name outer_distribution inner_distribution*) Determines how a parallel join using *table_name* will be executed. Valid options for *outer_distribution* and *inner_distribution* are (not all combinations are valid): HASH, BROADCAST, NONE, and PARTITION.

SQL Expressions and Functions

Hints *(Continued)*

PUSH_JOIN_ PRED	PUSH_JOIN_PRED

Pushes conditions from the WHERE clause into a view or subquery. |
| **PUSH_SUBQ** | PUSH_SUBQ

Causes subqueries to be processed earlier in the execution plan. Normally, subqueries are processed last unless the SQL statement is transformed into a join. |
| **REWRITE**

8i | REWRITE(*view_name* [*view_name*...])

Restricts query rewrites to only those materialized views specified in the hint. |
| **ROWID** | ROWID(*table_name*)

Performs a ROWID access. |
| **RULE** | RULE

Uses rule-based optimization. |
| **STAR** | STAR

Considers the STAR join methodology in preference to other methods. |
| **STAR_ TRANSFORMATION**

8.0+ | STAR_TRANSFORMATION

Requests that the STAR transformation optimization be performed. This transforms a STAR query into a alternate form which can take advantage of bitmap indexes. |

Hints *(Continued)*

USE_CONCAT	USE_CONCAT
	Oracle will sometimes expand statements with OR conditions into multiple SQL statements combined by UNION ALL. This hint instructs the optimizer to do this, even if it calculates that such a transformation would not be beneficial.
USE_HASH	USE_HASH(*table_name*)
	When joining to this table, uses the hash join method.
USE_MERGE	USE_MERGE(*table_name*)
	When joining to this table, uses the sort-merge join method.
USE_NL	USE_NL(*table_name*)
	When joining to this table, uses the nested-loops join method.

SQL Expressions and Functions

Data Manipulation and Transaction Control

Introduction

The data manipulation statements, INSERT, UPDATE, and DELETE, allow us to add, modify, and remove rows from a relational table, including Oracle8 collections. Because the purpose of a database is to hold data, and because the contents of a database almost always change, DML statements are usually the second most frequently used class of SQL statement (after, of course, the SELECT statement).

Other statements such as COMMIT and ROLLBACK provide transactional control and are also described in this chapter.

The INSERT Statement

The INSERT statement allows rows to be added to a table. Its basic form is:

```
INSERT INTO table_expression
    [(column_list)]
    {VALUES(value_list)
      [RETURNING expression INTO variable] |
    subquery}
```

Table_expression specifies the table, partition, view, subquery, or table collection into which rows will be inserted. For more information, see the "Table Specifications" section later in this chapter.

Column_list provides an optional list of columns into which data can be inserted. *Column_list* is only optional if the VALUES clause or subquery contains data for all columns in the same order in which they appear in the table definition. Omitting the column list is generally bad practice.

The VALUES clause contains a list of literals or variables containing the data to be inserted. The variables may be array bind variables, in which case, multiple rows may be inserted in a single operation. If the VALUES clause is not specified, then a subquery that returns the data to be inserted may be specified. The subquery may return multiple rows.

8i   The RETURNING keyword is only available in Oracle8i. It returns the values inserted into bind or PL/SQL variables.

Direct Mode Insert

8.0+   Direct mode insert allows data blocks to be constructed in memory and inserted directly into the database files—bypassing the Oracle buffer cache. To invoke the direct load insert, use the APPEND hint (see Chapter 2, "SQL Expressions and Functions").

Direct mode insert may use space inefficiently and improves performance only in specific circumstances. Therefore, use it with caution. Direct mode insert applies a full table lock to the table. A COMMIT or ROLLBACK must immediately follow the direct mode insert.

Parallel Insert

8.0+   In Oracle 8.0 and higher, an insert based on a subquery may be processed in parallel. This is invoked by using the PARALLEL hint (see Chapter 2). Unlike other parallel DML operations, parallel insert can be used on a non-partitioned table. Parallel insert will use direct mode insert by default, although this can be suppressed using the NOAPPEND hint.

Inserting REF Data

8i   In release 8.0, if a relational table or object table contains REF-type columns, there is no simple way of inserting a relational row or row object into the table. First nulls must be inserted into the columns and then an UPDATE statement must be issued to set their values. This inefficiency is resolved in release 8.1, by allowing a VALUE subquery expression in the INSERT VALUES list. Only REFs may be inserted using this method, and the subquery may return only a single REF. A VALUE subquery expression may also be used as an argument to a function or type constructor.

Unlogged Inserts

Unlogged inserts do not generate and redo log information. Unlogged inserts may proceed at a faster rate than normal inserts, but the data inserted cannot be recovered from a "roll-forward" of the redo logs during media recovery. Only direct mode inserts (see above) can be unlogged.

8.0+

Unlogged inserts occur when the NOLOGGING keyword is specified in CREATE TABLE, CREATE INDEX, ALTER TABLE, or ALTER INDEX statements. Once NOLOGGING is associated with a table, any direct mode insert will automatically be performed without logging.

Array Insert

Multiple rows may inserted into a table in a single operation. These array inserts are generally much more efficient than inserting a single row at a time. Array inserts can be performed as follows:

- Any insert based on a subquery may insert multiple rows in a single operation.
- The VALUES clause may refer to bind variables, which are arrays. The contents of the array can be inserted in a single operation. Individual APIs may implement this facility in different ways.
- In Oracle8i PL/SQL, the FORALL statement allows multiple elements in a collection to be inserted in a single operation. See Chapter 5, "PL/SQL Language," for details of the FORALL clause.

8i

The UPDATE Statement

The UPDATE statement modifies existing data within a database table. It has the following basic form:

```
UPDATE table_expression
        SET [()column_expression=value_expression
            [,column_expression=value_expression…] ()]
WHERE where_condition
        [RETURNING expression_list INTO variable_list]
```

Table_expression specifies the table, partition, view, subquery, or table collection into which rows will be inserted. For more information, see the "Table Specifications" section later in this chapter.

Data Manipulation and Transaction Control

Column_expression may be a single column name or a list of columns enclosed in parentheses. Using a column list is convenient when setting multiple columns to the values returned by a subquery. For instance:

```
UPDATE employes c
    SET (manager_id,department_id)
         =(SELECT manager_id,department_id
            FROM departments
            WHERE department_name='BOSTON')
WHERE employee_id=1234
```

The *where_condition* is a standard WHERE clause, as described in Chapter 1, "The SELECT Statement." It may include subqueries.

The RETURNING keyword is only available in Oracle8i. It returns the values inserted into bind or PL/SQL variables.

8i

Correlated Updates

A correlated update is one which includes a subquery that contains references to columns in the table being updated. The query is evaluated for each row that is eligible for update. The correlated update is very similar to the correlated subquery described in Chapter 1. The following statement executes a correlated update: The subquery within the SELECT statement is executed once for each row in CUSTOMERS, which satisfies the WHERE clause:

```
UPDATE customers c
  SET sales_rep_id=(SELECT manager_id
                    FROM employees
                    WHERE surname=c.contact_surname
                    AND firstname=c.contact_firstname
                    AND date_of_birth=c.date_of_birth)
  WHERE
(contact_surname,contact_firstname,date_of_birth) in
    (SELECT surname,firstname,date_of_birth
      FROM employees)
```

The DELETE Statement

The DELETE statement removes rows from a database table. It has the following form:

```
DELETE [FROM] table_expression
[WHERE where_condition]
[RETURNING expression_list INTO variable_list]
```

Table_expression specifies the table, partition, view, subquery, or table collection into which rows will be inserted. For more information, see "Table Specifications" later in this chapter.

The *where_condition* is a standard WHERE clause, as described in Chapter 1. It may include subqueries.

The RETURNING keyword is only available in Oracle8i. It returns the values updated into bind or PL/SQL variables.

Table Specifications

As with the SELECT statement, DML statements may act on views, subqueries, and collection expressions. See the "Table Specifications" section of Chapter 1 for more details.

Transactions

Transactions are indivisible units of work that must either be applied to the database in their entirety or not at all. A transaction implicitly commences when a DML statement or transaction control statement (such as SET TRANSACTION) is issued to the database. The following events terminate a transaction:

- A COMMIT or ROLLBACK statement.

- Program termination. Normal termination generates an implicit COMMIT. Abnormal termination generates an implicit ROLLBACK.

- Data Definition Language (DDL) statements (such as CREATE TABLE) generate an implicit COMMIT. This restricts the use of DDL statements within transactional entities such as triggers.

Savepoints

Savepoints are named rollback points that allow a transaction to be partially undone. Savepoints are created with the SAVEPOINT command and can be specified within the ROLLBACK command.

Locks

Locks are applied during a transaction implicitly when a row is modified, or explicitly by the LOCK TABLE statement or the FOR UPDATE clause (see Chapter 1). Locks are released when the transaction terminates.

Autonomous Transactions

8i In Oracle8i, a PL/SQL program unit may execute within an *autonomous transaction*. Autonomous transactions operate outside the scope of any transaction which may be current. A COMMIT or ROLLBACK within the autonomous transaction has no effect on the status of the parent transaction.

Triggers

Triggers are stored PL/SQL programs that are initiated when specified DML activities occur (and in Oracle8i, on specified DDL or database events). The syntax of the CREATE TRIGGER command is shown in Chapter 4, "Data Definition Language (DDL)". Triggers can affect DML operations in the following ways:

- Triggers can cause otherwise valid DML operations to fail. For instance, a trigger might implement a business rule that prevents updating salaries outside of guidelines.
- Triggers can themselves issue DML statements.
8i
- INSTEAD OF triggers can be defined on views. These triggers will fire instead of the DML statement on the view. See "DML Statements on Views" below.

DML Statements on Views

DML statements can be performed on views, but some fairly strict rules govern their use:

- The view must not use set operations such as UNION, MINUS, and DISTINCT.
- The view should not include a GROUP BY clause, use group functions, or use the DISTINCT keyword.
- The view should not include a collection expression in the SELECT list.

- If the WITH CHECK OPTION is specified, the DML statement cannot create or modify rows such that the rows concerned would no longer appear in the view.

- The view must not have been created with the WITH READ ONLY option.

- If the view contains a join, only columns belonging to a table whose primary key can uniquely identify every row returned by the query can be updated. If there is only one such table in the view, then a DELETE can succeed against the view.

Oracle8i allows "instead of" triggers to be defined against views. These triggers will fire <u>instead of</u> the specified DML statement. Oracle developed "instead of" triggers primarily to allow application developers to define complex logic which would control how multi-table views would be updated.

8i

Data Manipulation and Transaction Control

DML Reference

DML Reference Statements	Description
COMMIT	COMMIT [WORK] [COMMENT *comment_text*] [FORCE *transaction_id* [,*system_change_number*]]

COMMIT terminates a transaction and makes all transaction changes permanent.

The WORK keyword has no effect and is provided for compatibility only.

The COMMENT keyword associates *comment_text* with the transaction. This can be used to identify *distributed transactions*, which may be "in-doubt".

The FORCE keyword is used to commit an in-doubt distributed transaction. The *transaction_id* identifies the transaction to be committed. This can be found in the database table DBA_2PC_PENDING. If *system_change_number* is specified, the transaction will be marked as having been completed at the specified system change number (SCN). If omitted, the transaction will be stamped with the current SCN.

DML Reference Statements	**Description** *(Continued)*

DELETE

DELETE [FROM] *table_expression*
    [WHERE *where_condition*]
    [RETURNING *expression_list* INTO *variable_list*]

Table_expression specifies the table, partition, view, subquery, or table collection into which rows will be inserted.

The *where_condition* is a standard WHERE clause, as described in Chapter 1. It may include subqueries.

8i

The RETURNING keyword is only available in Oracle8i. It returns the values deleted into bind or PL/SQL variables.

EXPLAIN PLAN

EXPLAIN PLAN
    [SET STATEMENT_ID='*statement_identifier*']
    [INTO *plan_table_name*]
    FOR *sql_statement*

EXPLAIN PLAN generates information about the optimizer's execution plan for *sql_statement*. The statement is stored in a database "plan table".

SET STATEMENT_ID causes the specified *statement_identifier* to be stored in the plan table. This allows multiple execution plans to be stored in a single table.

INTO specifies the name of the plan table. If not specified, the name 'plan_table' is assumed. A plan table is created by the script *utlxplan.sql*, which is included in the Oracle distribution.

The execution plan can be retrieved from the plan table using a SQL statement such as the following:

DML Reference Statements   Description *(Continued)*

EXPLAIN PLAN (CONT.)	```SELECT rtrim(lpad(' ',2*level)||```
	``` rtrim(operation)||' '||```
	``` rtrim(options)||' '||```
	``` object_name) query_plan```
	``` FROM plan_table```
	``` WHERE statement_id='statement_id'```
	```CONNECT BY prior id=parent_id```
	``` START with id=0;```

INSERT

INSERT INTO *table_expression*

   [*(column_list)*]

   {VALUES(value_list)

     [RETURNING *expression* INTO *variable*]

   | *subquery*}

Table_expression specifies the table, partition, view, subquery, or table collection into which rows will be inserted.

Column_list provides an optional list of columns into which data can be inserted.

The VALUES clause contains a list of literals or variables containing the data to be inserted. The variables may be array bind variables, in which case, multiple rows may be inserted in a single operation. If the VALUES clause is not specified, then a subquery that returns the data to be inserted may be specified. The subquery may return multiple rows.

8i   The RETURNING keyword is only available in Oracle8i. It returns the values inserted into bind or PL/SQL variables.

LOCK TABLE

LOCK TABLE *table_expression* IN *mode* [NOWAIT]

LOCK TABLE applies a lock to the entire *table_expression*. Locks restrict the types of DML activities that can be performed on the table, but do not restrict query access.

Data Manipulation and Transaction Control

DML Reference Statements	**Description** (Continued)
LOCK TABLE (CONT.)	*Table_expression* may be a table, view, partition, or sub-partition.

Mode may be one of the following:

ROW SHAREP	revents concurrent EXCLUSIVE locks.
ROW EXCLUSIVE	Prevents concurrent EXCLUSIVE or SHARE locks.
SHARE UPDATE	Same as ROW SHARE.
SHARE	Prohibits concurrent updates.
SHARE ROW EXCLUSIVE	Prevents concurrent SHARE locks or updates.
EXCLUSIVE	Prohibits any concurrent DML or lock activity on the table.

NOWAIT causes the lock table operation to fail with an error if the lock cannot be obtained immediately. If NOWAIT is not specified, then the session will wait indefinitely for the lock to be obtained.

RETURNING	RETURNING *column_expression* INTO *variable_list*
8i	RETURNING allows the values affected by the DML statement to be stored in local variables. *Column_expression* is a list of columns whose values are to be returned. *Variable_list* is a list of PL/SQL or bind variables that will accept the modified values.
ROLLBACK	ROLLBACK [WORK] [TO [SAVEPOINT] *savepoint_name*] [FORCE *transaction_id*] ROLLBACK revokes work done by the current transaction. The WORK keyword has no effect and is provided for compatibility only. If a *savepoint_name* is specified, then only work performed after the nominated savepoint will be undone.

DML Reference Statements   Description *(Continued)*

ROLLBACK (CONT.)	The FORCE keyword is used to commit an in-doubt distributed transaction. The *transaction_id* identifies the transaction to be committed. This can be found in the database table DBA_2PC_PENDING.
SAVEPOINT	SAVEPOINT *savepoint_name* SAVEPOINT nominates a named rollback point, which allows a transaction to be partially undone. The *savepoint_name* may be specified in a ROLLBACK statement, in which case, only work performed after the SAVEPOINT is subject to the rollback.
SET CONSTRAINT 8.0+	SET CONSTRAINT {*constraint_list*|ALL} {IMMEDIATE|DEFERRED} SET CONSTRAINT specifies when constraint checking is to occur. It can be applied to a list of constraints (*constraint_list*) or to all constraints (ALL). If set to IMMEDIATE, constraints are checked as each DML statement is executed; if set to DEFERRED, constraints are checked only when the transaction commits.
SET TRANSACTION	SET TRANSACTION [{READ ONLY|READ WRITE}] [ISOLATION LEVEL {SERIALIZABLE|READ COMMITTED}] [USE ROLLBACK SEGMENT *rollback_segment*] SET TRANSACTION controls various transaction-level processing options. READ ONLY specifies that the transaction will perform no modifications to the database and will require read consistency across SQL statements. In a read-only transaction, only changes committed before the transaction began are visible. READ WRITE represents default behavior, in which changes to the database that occurred after the transaction began will be visible.

Data Manipulation and Transaction Control

DML Reference Statements   **Description** *(Continued)*

SET TRANSACTION (CONT.)	ISOLATION LEVEL controls how the transaction deals with changes made by other transactions. The default behavior, READ COMMITTED, allows transactions to view changes made by other transactions, and transactions may update rows which have been changed by concurrent transactions once the concurrent transaction commits. The SERIALIZABLE isolation level requires that transactions execute as if they had been processed in serial. In SERIALIZABLE, no interaction between transactions is possible and an error will be generated if the transaction attempts to update rows changed by a concurrent transaction. USE ROLLBACK SEGMENT specifies the rollback segment that the transaction should use. This can be used to specify a large rollback segment, when it is known that the transaction will affect large amounts of data.

UPDATE	UPDATE *table_expression*
	    SET [(]*column_expression=value_expression*
	      [,*column_expression=value_expression*...] [)]
	    [WHERE *where_condition*]
	    [RETURNING *expression_list* INTO *variable_list*]
	
	Table_expression specifies the table, partition, view, subquery, or table collection into which rows will be inserted.
	
	Column_expression may be a single column name or a list of columns enclosed in parentheses. The *where_condition* is a standard WHERE clause, as described in Chapter 1. It may include subqueries.

8i	The RETURNING keyword is only available in Oracle8i. It returns the values updated into bind or PL/SQL variables.
VALUES	See INSERT.
WHERE	See the description of the WHERE clause in Chapter 1.

DML Reference Statements Description *(Continued)*

WHERE CURRENT OF	WHERE CURRENT OF *cursor_name*
	WHERE CURRENT OF is a special form of the WHERE clause. It is valid only in UPDATE and DELETE statements. In PL/SQL and other programmatic interfaces, cursors provide per-record access to the contents of a result set. If the cursor is based on a SELECT that includes the FOR UPDATE clause (see Chapter 1), then WHERE CURRENT OF can be used to make the UPDATE or DELETE statement operate on the last record retrieved by the cursor.

4

Data Definition Language (DDL)

Introduction

This chapter summarizes the Oracle Data Definition Language (DDL). Also included are statements that allow session and system control.

The Data Definition Language is used to create, alter, and drop database objects such as tables, indexes, views, and other schema objects. DDL also encompasses commands to control access to these objects and commands to administer the database and database sessions.

DDL statements to create stored program objects, such as stored procedures, are discussed in Chapter 5, "PL/SQL Language."

References

The primary reference for SQL expressions and functions is the *Oracle SQL Reference*.

Addition information on datatypes can be found in *Oracle Concepts*.

Many guidelines for administering database objects can be found in the *Oracle Administrator's Guide*.

Database Objects and Datatypes

Types of Database Objects

Table 4-1 describes the various types of Oracle database objects that are maintained by Oracle DDL statements.

Table 4–1 Oracle Database Objects

Object	Description
CLUSTER	An Oracle cluster stores one or more tables in a single segment. In an index cluster, rows that share a common key value are stored together. In a hash cluster, the physical location of a row is dependent on a mathematical manipulation (hash function) of its key value.
CONTEXT 8i	Contexts provide a mechanism for generating application-specific security attributes. These application-specific security attributes are controlled by a packaged procedure associated with the context.
CONTROL FILE	A control file is a small operating system file or partition that stores information critical to database startup and operation.
DATABASE	An Oracle database is composed of a shared memory segment (UNIX) or single process (NT), together with background processes (UNIX) or threads (NT), data files, redo logs, and control files. The term "database" is often used synonymously with the term *"instance."*
DATABASE LINK	A database link contains connection information for a remote database schema. The database link can be used to perform remote operations and execute distributed queries.
DATAFILE	A data file is an operating system file or raw partition that contains the data which is stored in the database.
DIMENSION 8i	A dimension defines relationships between columns in a table, which can be used to facilitate rewriting a query to take advantage of materialized views.
DIRECTORY	A directory provides an interface to an operating system directory, which may contain *BFILE* data or which may be accessed using the PL/SQL UTL_FILE package.
INDEX	Indexes exist to optimize access to data within a database. Oracle supports two index types: B°-tree (the default) and bitmapped.

Table 4–1 Oracle Database Objects *(Continued)*

Object	Description
INDEX TYPE 8i	An Oracle index type is a definition for a user-defined indexing scheme. Index types are typically used when developing Oracle data cartridges.
LIBRARY	An Oracle library is an interface to an operating system shared program library that contains routines written in a 3GL. Routines in the shared library can be called from PL/SQL and SQL.
MATERIALIZED VIEW 8i	An Oracle8i materialized view is equivalent to a snapshot, but allows queries to be dynamically and transparently rewritten to use the materialized view.
OPERATOR 8i	A user-defined operator includes methods for performing operations on specified datatypes. User-defined operators can be used in Oracle index types.
OUTLINE 8i	An outline is a set of optimizer directives that determine how a query will be executed.
PACKAGE	A package is a collection of program units, variables, and cursors which share common or related functions and which are stored in a single stored unit.
PROCEDURE FUNCTION	A procedure is a stand-alone stored program that may take parameters but that does have a return value. A function is a procedure that returns a value.
PROFILE	A profile is a set of database resource limits that can be applied to a user.
ROLE	A role is a set of privileges that can be assigned to a user in a single operation.
ROLLBACK SEGMENT	A rollback segment stores before-image data from a segment that is being altered. The rollback data is used to support the ROLLBACK command and to provide read consistency.
SEGMENT	A segment is a database object that requires a storage allocation in the database. Examples of segments are tables, indexes, clusters, etc.
SEQUENCE	A sequence is a high-performance, low-contention number generator that can be used to generate unique numbers.

Data Definition Language (DDL)

Table 4–1 Oracle Database Objects *(Continued)*

Object	Description
SNAPSHOT	A snapshot is a segment that contains the results of a query. The snapshot typically contains local copies of remote objects.
TABLE	A table is the primary data storage unit in a relational database.
TABLESPACE	A tablespace is a collection of data files that stores objects of related purposes or storage requirements. A segment will usually belong to a single tablespace.
TYPE **8.0+**	An Oracle8 object type is a user-defined, complex datatype that can be associated with methods (member functions and procedures).
USER SCHEMA	A user schema is a database account through which the database is accessed. User accounts also provide a domain in which segments exist. Database objects belonging to a single user account are often referred to as a *schema*.
VIEW	A view is a SQL query that defines a "virtual" table which can be used in many of the same operations as a standard table.

Datatypes

Table 4-2 lists the Oracle datatypes that can be specified in CREATE TABLE and ALTER TABLE statements.

Table 4–2 Oracle Datatypes

Datatype	Description
BFILE **8.0+**	The BFILE datatype is a large object locator that points to a binary file stored outside the database. The data in this file can be accessed in read-only mode using the DBMS_LOB package.
BLOB **8.0+**	The BLOB type is a binary large object which can be up to 4GB in size.
CHAR	The CHAR datatype stores fixed-length character data.
	In Oracle7, the maximum string length is 255 bytes. In Oracle8, the limit is 2,000 bytes.

Table 4–2 Oracle Datatypes *(Continued)*

Datatype	Description
CHAR VARYING	An alias for VARCHAR2.
CHARACTER	An alias for VARCHAR2.
CHARACTER VARYING	An alias for VARCHAR2.
CLOB 8.0+	The CLOB type is a character large object which can be up to 4GB in size.
DATE	The DATE datatype stores a date and time. The precision of the datatype is measured in seconds. The unit of the DATE datatype is days: Each integer value represents a single day.
DECIMAL *(precision, scale)*	An alias for NUMBER.
DOUBLE PRECISION	An alias for NUMBER.
FLOAT *(size)*	An alias for NUMBER.
INT	An alias for NUMBER.
INTEGER	An alias for NUMBER.
LONG	Character data of variable length, up to about 2 GB.
LONG RAW	Raw binary data of variable length, up to 2 GB.
NATIONAL CHAR *(size)*	Alias for NCHAR.
NCHAR *(size)*	Similar to CHAR, but stores either the specified number of characters or bytes, depending on the characteristics of the National Character Set (NCS) in effect.
NCLOB 8.0+	Similar to CLOB, but may contain multi-byte characters, depending on the National Character Set in effect.

Table 4–2 Oracle Datatypes *(Continued)*

Datatype	Description
NUMBER *(precision, scale)*	NUMBER is the fundamental Oracle numeric datatype. If no precision or scale is specified, NUMBER can store numbers of virtually any magnitude or precision. *Precision* determines the number of significant digits that NUMBER can contain. *Scale* determines the number of digits to the right of the decimal point.
NUMERIC *(precision, scale)*	Alias for NUMBER.
NVARCHAR2 *(size)*	Similar to VARCHAR2, but stores either the specified number of characters or bytes, depending on the characteristics of the NCS in effect.
RAW *(size)*	RAW stores raw binary data of up to 2000 bytes.
REAL	Alias for NUMBER.
REF 8.0+	The REF datatype stores an object ID (OID) that "points" to a row in an object table. The REF datatype can be used to retrieve the data held in the object row.
ROWID	The ROWID datatype can be used to store a ROWID value, which represents the physical location of a row within the Oracle database.
SMALLINT	Alias for NUMBER.
UROWID [*(size)*] 8.0+	UROWID can be used to store the address of a row in an index-organized table.
VARCHAR2 *(size)*	VARCHAR2 stores variable-length character string data. In Oracle8, the maximum size of VARCHAR2 is 4000; in Oracle7, the maximum size is 2000.

System Privileges

Table 4-3 lists the system privileges that may appear in the GRANT statement.

Table 4-3 System Privileges

ADMINISTER RESOURCE MANAGER	ALTER ANY CLUSTER	ALTER ANY DIMENSION
ALTER ANY INDEX	ALTER ANY INDEXTYPE	ALTER ANY LIBRARY
ALTER ANY OUTLINE	ALTER ANY PROCEDURE	ALTER ANY ROLE
ALTER ANY SEQUENCE	ALTER ANY SNAPSHOT	ALTER ANY TABLE
ALTER ANY TRIGGER	ALTER ANY TYPE	ALTER DATABASE
ALTER OPERATOR	ALTER PROFILE	ALTER RESOURCE COST
ALTER ROLLBACK SEGMENT	ALTER SESSION	ALTER SYSTEM
ALTER TABLESPACE	ALTER USER	ANALYZE ANY
AUDIT ANY	AUDIT SYSTEM	BACKUP ANY TABLE
BECOME USER	COMMENT ANY TABLE	CREATE ANY CLUSTER
CREATE ANY CONTEXT	CREATE ANY DIMENSION	CREATE ANY DIRECTORY
CREATE ANY INDEX	CREATE ANY INDEXTYPE	CREATE ANY LIBRARY
CREATE ANY OPERATOR	CREATE ANY OUTLINE	CREATE ANY PROCEDURE
CREATE ANY SEQUENCE	CREATE ANY SNAPSHOT	CREATE ANY SYNONYM
CREATE ANY TABLE	CREATE ANY TRIGGER	CREATE ANY TYPE
CREATE ANY VIEW	CREATE CLUSTER	CREATE DATABASE LINK
CREATE DIMENSION	CREATE INDEXTYPE	CREATE LIBRARY

Table 4–3 System Privileges *(Continued)*

CREATE OPERATOR	CREATE PROCEDURE	CREATE PROFILE
CREATE PUBLIC DATABASE LINK	CREATE PUBLIC SYNONYM	CREATE ROLE
CREATE ROLLBACK SEGMENT	CREATE SEQUENCE	CREATE SESSION
CREATE SNAPSHOT	CREATE SYNONYM	CREATE TABLE
CREATE TABLESPACE	CREATE TRIGGER	CREATE TYPE
CREATE USER	CREATE VIEW	DELETE ANY TABLE
DEQUEUE ANY QUEUE	DROP ANY CLUSTER	DROP ANY CONTEXT
DROP ANY DIMENSION	DROP ANY DIRECTORY	DROP ANY INDEX
DROP ANY INDEXTYPE	DROP ANY LIBRARY	DROP ANY OPERATOR
DROP ANY OUTLINE	DROP ANY PROCEDURE	DROP ANY ROLE
DROP ANY SEQUENCE	DROP ANY SNAPSHOT	DROP ANY SYNONYM
DROP ANY TABLE	DROP ANY TRIGGER	DROP ANY TYPE
DROP ANY VIEW	DROP PROFILE	DROP PUBLIC DATABASE LINK
DROP PUBLIC SYNONYM	DROP ROLLBACK SEGMENT	DROP TABLESPACE
DROP USER	ENQUEUE ANY QUEUE	EXECUTE ANY LIBRARY
EXECUTE ANY PROCEDURE	EXECUTE ANY TYPE	EXECUTE OPERATOR
FORCE ANY TRANSACTION	FORCE TRANSACTION	GLOBAL REWRITE
GRANT ANY PRIVILEGE	GRANT ANY ROLE	

Data Definition
Language (DDL)

Table 4–3 System Privileges *(Continued)*

INSERT ANY TABLE	JAVASYSPRIV	JAVAUSERPRIV
LOCK ANY TABLE	MANAGE ANY QUEUE	MANAGE TABLESPACE
RESTRICTED SESSION	REWRITE	SELECT ANY SEQUENCE
SELECT ANY TABLE	UNLIMITED TABLESPACE	UPDATE ANY TABLE

Audit Options

Table 4-4 lists auditing options that may appear in the AUDIT and NOAUDIT statements.

Table 4–4 Auditing Options

ALTER	ALTER DIMENSION	ALTER INDEX
ALTER MATERIALIZED VIEW	ALTER PROFILE	ALTER ROLE
ALTER ROLLBACK SEGMENT	ALTER SEQUENCE	ALTER SEQUENCE
ALTER TABLE	ALTER TABLE	ALTER TABLE
ALTER TABLESPACE	ALTER TRIGGER	ALTER TYPE
ALTER USER	AUDIT	AUDIT
AUDIT CLUSTER	CALL	CLUSTER
COMMENT	COMMENT TABLE	CONTEXT
CREATE CLUSTER	CREATE CONTEXT	CREATE DATABASE LINK
CREATE DIMENSION	CREATE DIRECTORY	CREATE FUNCTION
CREATE INDEX	CREATE LIBRARY	CREATE MATERIALIZED VIEW
CREATE PACKAGE	CREATE PACKAGE BODY	CREATE PROCEDURE
CREATE PROFILE	CREATE PUBLIC DATABASE LINK	CREATE PUBLIC SYNONYM

Table 4–4 Auditing Options *(Continued)*

CREATE ROLE	CREATE ROLLBACK SEGMENT	CREATE SEQUENCE
CREATE SYNONYM	CREATE TABLE	CREATE TABLESPACE
CREATE TRIGGER	CREATE TYPE	CREATE TYPE BODY
CREATE USER	CREATE VIEW	DATABASE LINK
DELETE	DELETE TABLE	DIMENSION
DIRECTORY	DROP CLUSTER	DROP CONTEXT
DROP DATABASE LINK	DROP DIMENSION	DROP DIRECTORY
DROP FUNCTION	DROP INDEX	DROP LIBRARY
DROP MATERIALIZED VIEW	DROP PACKAGE	DROP PROCEDURE
DROP PROFILE	DROP PUBLIC DATABASE LINK	DROP PUBLIC SYNONYM
DROP ROLE	DROP ROLLBACK SEGMENT	DROP SEQUENCE
DROP SYNONYM	DROP TABLE	DROP TABLESPACE
DROP TRIGGER	DROP TYPE	DROP TYPE BODY
DROP USER	DROP VIEW	EXECUTE
EXECUTE PROCEDURE	GRANT	GRANT
GRANT DIRECTORY	GRANT PROCEDURE	GRANT SEQUENCE
GRANT TABLE	GRANT TYPE	INDEX
INDEX	INSERT	INSERT TABLE
LOCK	LOCK TABLE	MATERIALIZED VIEW
NOAUDIT	NOT EXISTS	PROCEDURE

Table 4–4 Auditing Options *(Continued)*

PROFILE	PUBLIC DATABASE LINK	PUBLIC SYNONYM
READ	RENAME	REVOKE
ROLE	ROLLBACK STATEMENT	SELECT
SELECT SEQUENCE	SELECT TABLE	SEQUENCE
SESSION	SET ROLE	SYNONYM
SYSTEM AUDIT	SYSTEM GRANT	TABLE
TABLESPACE	TRIGGER	TRUNCATE CLUSTER
TRUNCATE TABLE	TYPE	UPDATE
UPDATE TABLE	USER	VIEW

DDL Language Reference

DDL Clause Description

ADD PARTITION	*See* PARTITION MAINTENANCE CLAUSES.
ALLOCATE EXTENT	ALLOCATE EXTENT [( ] [SIZE *extent_size* {K|M}] [DATAFILE *datafile_name*] [INSTANCE *instance_number*] [ )]

The ALLOCATE EXTENT clause can be used in the ALTER INDEX, ALTER TABLE, and ALTER CLUSTER statements to add a new extent to the object concerned.

SIZE specifies the size of the new extent. If not specified, normal extent sizing rules are used.

DATAFILE specifies the data file in which the extent is to be created. If not specified, then Oracle picks an appropriate data file.

Data Definition Language (DDL)

DDL Clause Description *(Continued)*

ALLOCATE EXTENT (CONT.)	INSTANCE is an Oracle Parallel Server option that makes the extent available to the specified instance only.

ALTER CLUSTER	ALTER CLUSTER *cluster_name*
	    [*Physical attributes*]
	    [SIZE cluster_size {K|M}]
	    [*Allocate_extent_clause*]
	    [*deallocate_unused_clause*]
	
	ALTER CLUSTER changes properties of the specified cluster. See entries in this chapter on CREATE CLUSTER, PHYSICAL ATTRIBUTES, ALLOCATE EXTENT, and DEALLOCATE UNUSED for more information.

ALTER DATABASE	ALTER DATABASE [*database_name*]
	    MOUNT [{STANDBY|CLONE} DATABASE]]
	    [{ARCHIVELOG|NOARCHIVELOG}]
	    [OPEN [{READ WRITE|READ ONLY}]
	    [RESETLOGS|NORESETLOGS]]
	    [CONVERT]
	    [ACTIVATE STANDBY DATABASE]
	    [RECOVER [[MANAGED] STANDBY] DATABASE
	        [AUTOMATIC [FROM *location*]]
	        [UNTIL {CANCEL|TIME *time_spec*|CHANGE *scn_number*}]
	        [USING BACKUP CONTROLFILE]
	        [[STANDBY] TABLESPACE *tablespace_list*
	        [UNTIL CONTROLFILE]]
	        [[STANDBY] DATAFILE *datafile_list* [UNTIL CONTROLFILE]]
	        [LOGFILE *logfile_name*]
	        [CONTINUE [DEFAULT]]
	        [CANCEL [IMMEDIATE]]
	        [TIMEOUT *timeout_minutes*]]

DDL Clause Description *(Continued)*

ALTER DATABASE (CONT.)	[RENAME GLOBAL_NAME TO *new_name*]
	[RESET COMPATIBILITY]
	[ENABLE [PUBLIC] thread *thread_number*]
	[DISABLE THREAD *thread_number*]
	[RENAME FILE *filename_list* TO *new_filename_list*]
	[CREATE DATAFILE *file_name_list* AS *new_filespec_list*]
	[{DATAFILE|TEMPFILE} *file_name_list*
	{ONLINE|OFFLINE [DROP]	
	RESIZE *new_size* {K|M}	
	AUTOEXTEND {OFF|ON NEXT *next_size* {K|M}
	MAXSIZE {UNLIMITED|max_size {K|M}}}|
	END BACKUP }]
	[ADD LOGFILE [THREAD *thread_number*] [GROUP *group_id*]
	(*logfile_name logfile_size* {K|M} [,*logfile_name* ...])
	[, [GROUP *group_id*] *logfile_name*...]
	[ADD LOGFILE MEMBER *filename_list* [REUSE]
	[TO] {GROUP *group_id*|logfile_list*]
	[DROP LOGFILE {GROUP *group_id*|logfile_list*}]
	[DROP LOGFILE MEMBER *file_list*]
	[CLEAR [UNARCHIVED] LOGFILE {GROUP *group_id*|logfile_list*}
	[UNRECOVERABLE DATAFILE]]
	[CREATE STANDBY CONTROLFILE AS *filename* [REUSE]]
	[BACKUP CONTROLFILE TO
	{*filename* [REUSE]	
	TRACE [{RESETLOGS|NORESETLOGS}]]
	ALTER DATABASE performs administrative actions on the database.
	MOUNT mounts the database, reading the control file, but not opening database or redo log files. The STANDBY clause causes the *standby database* to be opened.

Data Definition Language (DDL)

DDL Clause Description *(Continued)*

ALTER DATABASE (CONT.)	The CLONE clause causes the clone database—used for tablespace point-in-time recovery—to be mounted.
	ARCHIVE LOG indicates that redo logs will be copied to an archive destination when they are full.
8.0+	OPEN makes the database available for normal use. RESETLOGS is used following a media recovery to discard data in existing redo logs.
8i	The READ ONLY qualifier of the OPEN clause makes the database available for reading only.
8.0+	CONVERT migrates an Oracle7 data dictionary to Oracle8 format.
	ACTIVATE STANDBY DATABASE causes a standby database to become the active database.
	The RECOVER clause controls database media recovery. The STANDBY clause indicates that the standby database will be recovered.
8i	RECOVER MANAGED invokes the continual recovery of the standby database. Only CANCEL and TIMEOUT clauses are valid when MANAGED is specified.
	The AUTOMATIC clause causes the automatic generation of the archive log filenames needed for recovery. FROM overrides the default log file location with the location specified.
	UNTIL determines to what point the database will be recovered. CANCEL indicates that the recovery will continue until cancelled by the operator, TIME specifies a date and time to recover to, and CHANGE indicates that the database should be recovered up to the specified *System Change Number* (SCN).

DDL Clause Description *(Continued)*

ALTER DATABASE (CONT.)	USING BACKUP CONTROL FILE informs Oracle that the control file supplied for the recovery is a backup copy generated by the BACKUP CONTROLFILE clause.
	TABLESPACE and DATAFILE keywords indicate that only the specified tablespaces or data files should be recovered.
8i	The STANDBY clause may precede the TABLESPACE or DATAFILE clauses to indicate that recovery should occur in the standby database. UNTIL CONTROLFILE indicates that the recovery should use the current standby control file.
	The LOGFILE clause applies the specified log file to the database being recovered.
	CONTINUE causes the recovery to continue automatically, using log filenames generated by Oracle.
	CANCEL terminates the recovery.
	TIMEOUT applies to managed recovery only. If a required archived log does not become available after *timeout_minutes*, the sustained recovery terminates with one or more errors.
	RENAME GLOBAL_NAME changes the database's global name.
	RESET COMPATIBILITY prepares the database to be downgraded to a previous release of Oracle.
	ENABLE is an Oracle parallel server clause. It enables a thread of redo log file groups. DISABLE disables such a thread.

Data Definition Language (DDL)

DDL Clause Description *(Continued)*

ALTER DATABASE (CONT.)	RENAME FILE informs Oracle that files specified by *filename_list* have been renamed at the operating system level to the filenames specified in *new_filename_list*. CREATE DATAFILE creates an empty data file—replacing a data file that was lost due to media failure or other causes—in preparation for recovering the data file from redo log information. The DATAFILE clause allows management of data files. ONLINE and OFFLINE clauses take data files on- or off-line. The DROP clause is required to take a data file off-line in NOARCHIVELOG mode. RESIZE attempts to change the size of the data file. AUTOEXTEND changes data file auto-extend attributes—see the DATAFILE entry in this chapter for more details. END BACKUP is used to prevent media recovery on a data file after an aborted on-line backup.
8i	The TEMPFILE clause may be used in place of the DATAFILE clause to apply the operations specified to *temporary data files*. ADD LOGFILE adds a new *redo log group*. GROUP allows the new group ID to be specified. One or more *logfile_names* are specified as members—or copies—within the group. ADD LOGFILE MEMBER add new members to an existing redo log group. The group may be specified either by the GROUP clause or by listing the existing members of the group in *logfile_list*. DROP LOGFILE drops a redo log group. The group may be specified either by the GROUP clause or by listing the existing members of the group in *logfile_list*. The DROP LOGFILE MEMBER drops the redo log members in *file_list*.

DDL Clause Description *(Continued)*

ALTER DATABASE (CONT.)	CLEAR LOGFILE is used to recreate specified redo log members. UNARCHIVED allows log files that have not been archived to be cleared. UNRECOVERABLE allows the redo logs required by off-line data files to be cleared. CREATE STANDBY CONTROLFILE creates the control file needed by a standby database. BACKUP CONTROLFILE creates a backup of the existing control file. The trace options cause CREATE CONTROLFILE statements that are sufficient to rebuild the control file to be written to the current trace file.

ALTER DIMENSION	ALTER DIMENSION *dimension_name*
	  [ADD { LEVEL *level_name* IS (*level_column_list*) |
	    HIERARCHY *heirarchy_name*
	      (*child_level_name* CHILD OF *parent_level_name*
	       [CHILD OF …]
	      [JOIN KEY *column_list* REFERENCES *level_name*
	       [JOIN KEY …]]) |
	    ATTRIBUTE *level_name*
	      DETERMINES (*dependent_column_list*) }
	    [ADD …]]
	  [DROP {LEVEL *level_name* [{<u>RESTRICT</u>|CASCADE}] |
	    HIERARCHY *hierarchy_name* |
	    ATTRIBUTE *level_name*
	      DETERMINES (*dependent_column_list*) }
	    [DROP …]]
	  [COMPILE]
	
	The ALTER DIMENSION command alters the characteristics of a dimension created by the CREATE DIMENSION command.
	
	ADD adds a new level, hierarchy, or attribute to the dimension. The usage of the LEVEL, HIERARCHY, and ATTRIBUTE clauses is identical to their usage in the CREATE DIMENSION command. Multiple ADD clauses may be specified.

Data Definition Language (DDL)

DDL Clause Description *(Continued)*

ALTER DIMENSION (CONT.)	DROP removes a level, hierarchy, or attribute. RESTRICT prevents a level from being dropped if it is referenced by a hierarchy, or attribute. CASCADE causes any hierarchies or attributes which reference the level to be deleted. COMPILE revalidates an invalidated dimension.
ALTER FUNCTION	ALTER FUNCTION *function_name* COMPILE ALTER FUNCTION allows a stored function to be recompiled.

ALTER INDEX	ALTER INDEX *index_name*
	    [*Physical attributes*]
	    [ALLOCATE EXTENT *Allocate_extent_clause*]
	    [DEALLOCATE UNUSED *deallocate_unused_clause*]
	    [PARALLEL *parallel_clause*]
	    [LOGGING|NOLOGGING]
	    [REBUILD [{PARTITION|SUBPARTITON} *partition_name*]
	        [REVERSE|NOREVERSE]
	        [PARAMETERS domain_parameters]
	        [PARALLEL parallel_clause]
	        [*new_physical_attributes*]
	        [ONLINE]
	        [COMPUTE STATISTICS]
	        [COMPRESS {*compress_columns*|NOCOMPRESS}]
	        [LOGGING|NOLOGGING]]
	    [UNUSABLE]
	    [RENAME TO *new_index_name*]
	    [COALESCE]
	    [*Partition maintenance clauses*]
	ALTER INDEX alters or rebuilds the named index.
	
	ALLOCATE EXTENT adds a new index extent—see the ALLOCATE EXTENT entry for details. DEALLOCATE UNUSED removes unused space within the index– see the DELETE UNUSED entry for details.

DDL Clause Description *(Continued)*

ALTER INDEX (CONT.)	REBUILD recreates the index. PARTITION or SUBPARTITION can be specified to restrict the rebuild to a specific partition or sub-partition. Qualifiers to REBUILD function in the same manner as in CREATE INDEX.
	UNUSABLE marks the index as unusable.
8i	COALESCE instructs Oracle to merge, where possible, index leaf blocks.
8.0+	*Partition_maintenance_clauses* allow the configuration of partitions and sub-partitions in a partitioned index to be changed. See PARTITION MAINTENANCE CLAUSES in this chapter for details.
	Other clauses in the ALTER INDEX statement function exactly as they do in the CREATE INDEX statement. See the entry for CREATE INDEX for more details.
ALTER JAVA **8i**	ALTER JAVA {SOURCE|CLASS} *java_object_name* [RESOLVER((*pattern, schema*|-) (*pattern, schema*|-) ...)] [{COMPILE|RESOLVE}] [AUTHID {CURRENT_USER | <u>DEFINER</u>}]
	ALTER JAVA alters the properties of an Oracle8i JServer Java source or class.
	RESOLVER determines how names in the Java source or class should be resolved. It is somewhat analogous to CLASSPATH in external JVMs. The RESOLVER clause consists of a series of wildcards and schema identifiers. If a name in the Java program matches the wildcard, then *schema* is examined for the appropriate object. If "-" is specified as *schema*, then the name is not resolved.
	COMPILE and RESOLVE are synonymous and indicate that the objects in a class should be resolved and that sources should be compiled.

Data Definition Language (DDL)

DDL Clause Description *(Continued)*

ALTER JAVA (CONT.)	AUTHID determines whether the module runs with the privileges of the user who defined the module (DEFINER) or the permissions of the user running the module (CURRENT_USER).

ALTER MATERIALIZED VIEW

8i

ALTER MATERIALIZED VIEW *materialized_view_name*
    [Physical attributes]
    [Lob_storage]
    [{LOGGING|NOLOGGING}]
    [{CACHE|NOCACHE}]
    [partition_maintenance_clauses]
    [PARALLEL *parallel_clause*]
    [[NEVER] REFRESH {FAST|COMPLETE|FORCE}
        [ON {DEMAND|COMMIT}]
        [START WITH START_DATE]
        [WITH {PRIMARY KEY|ROWID}]
        [USING [DEFAULT] [{MASTER|LOCAL}]
        ROLLBACK SEGMENT[*rollback_segment*]]]
    [{ENABLE|DISABLE} QUERY REWRITE]
    [COMPILE]

ALTER MATERIALIZED VIEW alters the properties of an Oracle8i *materialized view.*

Partition_maintenance_clauses allow partitioning specifications to be amended. *See* PARTITION MAINTENANCE CLAUSES in this chapter for more details.

COMPILE revalidates a materialized view that may have been invalidated by a change to a master table.

Other clauses of ALTER MATERIALIZED VIEW have the same usages as in the CREATE MATERIALIZED VIEW statement, which is also defined in this chapter.

DDL Clause Description *(Continued)*

ALTER MATERIALIZED VIEW LOG	ALTER MATERIALIZED VIEW LOG ON *table_name*
	  [*Partition_maintenance_clauses*]
	  [PARTITION *partition_clause*]
	  [LOGGING|NOLOGGING] [CACHE|NOCACHE]
	  [PARALLEL *parallel_clause*]
	  [ADD [ROWID] [,] [PRIMARY KEY] [*(filter_columns)*]]
	  [{INCLUDING|EXCLUDING} NEW VALUES]
	
	ALTER MATERIALIZED VIEW changes the properties of a materialized view log.
	
	Partition_maintenance_clauses allow partitioning details to be amended. *See* PARTITION MAINTENANCE CLAUSES in this chapter for details.
	
	The ADD clause behaves like the WITH clause in the CREATE MATERIALIZED VIEW command. It causes the primary key, rowid, or other columns to be recorded in the log.
	
	Other clauses have the same usages as in the CREATE MATERIALIZED VIEW log command.

ALTER OUTLINE	ALTER OUTLINE *outline_name*
	  [REBUILD]
	  [RENAME TO *new_outline_name*]
	  [CHANGE CATEGORY TO *new_category_name*]
	
	ALTER OUTLINE modifies an outline created by the CREATE OUTLINE command.
	
	REBUILD re-optimizes the SQL statement associated with the outline and stores the new plan.
	
	RENAME changes the name of an outline.
	
	CHANGE CATEGORY changes the category associated with the outline.

Data Definition Language (DDL)

DDL Clause Description *(Continued)*

ALTER PACKAGE	ALTER PACKAGE *package_name* COMPILE {PACKAGE|BODY} ALTER PACKAGE recompiles a package header or body.
ALTER PROCEDURE	ALTER PROCEDURE *procedure_name* COMPILE ALTER PROCEDURE recompiles a PL/SQL stored procedure.

ALTER PROFILE	ALTER PROFILE *profile_name* LIMIT
	  [SESSIONS_PER_USER {*value*|UNLIMITED|DEFAULT}]
	  [CPU_PER_SESSION {*value*|UNLIMITED|DEFAULT}]
	  [CPU_PER_CALL {*value*|UNLIMITED|DEFAULT}]
	  [CONNECT_TIME {*value*|UNLIMITED|DEFAULT}]
	  [IDLE_TIME {*value*|UNLIMITED|DEFAULT}]
	  [LOGICAL_READS_PER_SESSION {*value*|UNLIMITED|DEFAULT}]
	  [LOGICAL_READS_PER_CALL {*value*|UNLIMITED|DEFAULT}]
	  [COMPOSITE_LIMIT {*value*|UNLIMITED|DEFAULT}]
	  [PRIVATE_SGA {*value* {K|M}|UNLIMITED|DEFAULT}]
	  [FAILED_LOGIN_ATTEMPTS {*value*|UNLIMITED|DEFAULT}]
	  [PASSWORD_LIFE_TIME {*value*|UNLIMITED|DEFAULT}]
	  [PASSWORD_REUSE_TIME {*value*|UNLIMITED|DEFAULT}]
	  [PASSWORD_REUSE_MAX {*value*|UNLIMITED|DEFAULT}]
	  [PASSWORD_LOCK_TIME {*value*|UNLIMITED|DEFAULT}]
	  [PASSWORD_GRACE_TIME {*value*|UNLIMITED|DEFAULT}]
	  [PASSWORD_VERIFY_FUNCTION {*function*|NULL|DEFAULT}]
	
	ALTER PROFILE changes the property of a user profile. ALTER PROFILE clauses have the same usages as in CREATE PROFILE, which is also defined in this chapter.

ALTER RESOURCE COST	ALTER RESOURCE COST
	  [CPU_PER_SESSION *weight*]
	  [CONNECT_TIME *weight*]
	  [LOGICAL_READS_PER_SESSION *weight*]
	  [PRIVATE_SGA *weight*]
	
	ALTER RESOURCE COST changes the definition of the resource aggregate calculation used by the COMPOSITE_LIMIT clause of the CREATE PROFILE command.

DDL Clause Description *(Continued)*

ALTER RESOURCE COST (CONT.)	Each of the clauses of the ALTER RESOURCE command specifies a relative weighting for a resource. The value supplied to COMPOSITE_LIMIT is the aggregate of the value each resource specified, multiplied by its *weight*.
ALTER ROLE	ALTER ROLE {NOT IDENTIFIED| IDENTIFIED {BY *password*|EXTERNALLY|GLOBALLY} } ALTER ROLE changes the authorization method for a role. Clauses in ALTER ROLE have the same usage as in CREATE ROLE, which is also described in this chapter.

ALTER ROLLBACK SEGMENT	ALTER ROLLBACK SEGMENT *rollback_segment_name*
	  {ONLINE | OFFILE |
	  STORAGE *storage_clause* |
	  SHRINK [TO *size* {K|M}]}
	
	ALTER ROLLBACK SEGMENT performs maintenance activities against the nominated rollback segment.
	
	ONLINE and OFFLINE change the availability of the rollback segment.
	
	The STORAGE clause can be used to change some storage properties of the rollback segment.
	
	SHRINK attempts to reduce the size of the rollback segment. If TO *size* is not specified, the target size will be that specified by the OPTIMAL setting in the STORAGE clause. Otherwise, the target size will be that specified by TO *size*.

ALTER SEQUENCE	ALTER SEQUENCE *sequence_name*
	  [INCREMENT BY increment_by]
	  [{MAXVALUE max_value|NOMAXVALUE}]
	  [{MINVALUE min_value|NOMINVALUE}]
	  [{CYCLE|NOCYCLE}]
	  [{CACHE cache_size|NOCACHE}]
	  [{ORDER|NOORDER}]

Data Definition Language (DDL)

DDL Clause Description *(Continued)*

ALTER SEQUENCE (CONT.)	ALTER SEQUENCE alters the characteristics of the named sequence. Clauses in ALTER SEQUENCE have the same usage as in CREATE SEQUENCE, which is also described in this chapter.

ALTER SESSION	ALTER SESSION
	    [ADVISE {COMMIT|ROLLBACK|NOTHING}]
	    [CLOSE DATABASE LINK *database_link_name*]
	    [{ENABLE|DISABLE} COMMIT IN PROCEDURE]
	    [ENABLE|DISABLE|FORCE} PARALLEL DML]
	    [SET parameter_name=value [,parameter_name=value…]
	    [SET EVENTS *'event_string'*]]
	
	ALTER SESSION modifies the state of the current session.
	
	The ADVISE clause causes advice to be forwarded to remote databases for each subsequent distributed DML statement. The advice appears in the remote data dictionary table, DBA_2PC_PENDING.
	
	CLOSE DATABASE LINK causes all remote sessions allocated through the specified database link to be closed.
	
	ENABLE COMMIT IN PROCEDURE enables COMMIT statements to be issued in stored PL/SQL programs. DISABLE prevents such commits.

8.0+	ENABLE PARALLEL DML allows PARALLEL hints or clauses to cause parallel DML to be invoked, DISABLE prevents parallel DML, and FORCE causes parallel DML to occur even in the absence of a PARALLEL hint or clause. SET allows a session configuration parameter to be changed. Any Oracle server parameter listed in the table V$PARAMETER, where ISSYS_MODIFIABLE='TRUE' can be set, together with the following special parameters: SET EVENTS sets database debugging and diagnostic flags. These are normally set on the advice of Oracle support services.

DDL Clause Description *(Continued)*

ALTER SESSION (CONT.)	CONSTRAINTS

This specifies when constraints will be validated. Values are IMMEDIATE, DEFERRED, and DEFAULT. Only constraints that are created with the DEFERRABLE option may be deferred—see CONSTRAINT.

SQL_TRACE

If true, a trace file is generated containing SQL execution statistics. False terminates the tracing.

8i

USE_STORED_OUTLINES

If true, then outlines created by CREATE OUTLINE will be used by the optimizer when generating execution plans. Other options are false, or an outline category name. If a category name is specified, only outlines associated with that category will be used.

ALTER SNAPSHOT

7.3,8.0

ALTER SNAPSHOT *snapshot_name*
    [*Physical_attributes*]
    [*lob_storage*]
    [{LOGGING|NOLOGGING}]
    [{CACHE|NOCACHE}]
    [*partition_maintenance _clauses*]
    [USING INDEX *index_physical_attributes*]
    [REFRESH [FAST|COMPLETE|FORCE] [START WITH *start_date*]
        [NEXT *next_date*]]
    [WITH {PRIMARY KEY|ROWID}]
    [USING [DEFAULT] [{MASTER|LOCAL}]
        ROLLBACK SEGMENT[*rollback_segment*]]

ALTER SNAPSHOT alters the properties of a snapshot.

8.0+

Partition_maintenance_clauses allow partitioning details to be amended. See "Partition Maintenance Clauses" in this chapter for details.

Other clauses have the same uses as in the CREATE SNAPSHOT command.

DDL Clause Description *(Continued)*

ALTER SNAPSHOT LOG
 	
7.3, 8.0
	ALTER SNAPSHOT LOG ON *table_name*
	    [*Physical_attributes*]
	    [*Partition_maintenance_clauses*]
	    [LOGGING|NOLOGGING] [CACHE|NOCACHE]
	    [PARALLEL *parallel_clause*]
	    [ADD [ROWID] [,] [PRIMARY KEY] [(*filter_columns*)]]
	
	ALTER SNAPSHOT LOG alters the properties of a snapshot log.

8.0+	*Partition_maintenance_clauses* allow partitioning details to be amended. See "Partition Maintenance Clauses" in this chapter for details.
8.0+	The ADD clause behaves like the WITH clause in the CREATE SNAPSHOT command. It causes primary key, rowid, or other columns to be recorded in the log. Other clauses have the same uses as in the CREATE SNAPSHOT log command.

ALTER SYSTEM	ALTER SYSTEM
	    [ARCHIVE LOG [THREAD *thread_id*]
	        {SEQUENCE *log_id*|
	        CHANGE *scn_id*|
	        CURRENT|NEXT|ALL|START|
	        GROUP *group_id*|
	        LOGFILE *logfile_name*|
	        }
	        [TO *archive_destination*]
	        [STOP]]
	    [SWITCH LOGFILE]
	    [CHECKPOINT {GLOBAL|LOCAL}]
	    [CHECK DATAFILES {GLOBAL|LOCAL}]
	    [DISCONNECT SESSION '*sid,serial#*' POST_TRANSACTION]
	    [KILL SESSION '*sid,serial#*']
	    [{ENABLE|DISABLE} DISTRIBUTED RECOVERY]
	    [{ENABLE|DISABLE} RESTRICTED SESSION]
	    [FLUSH SHARED_POOL]
	    [{SUSPEND|RESUME}]
	    [SET PARAMETER=*value* [,PARAMETER=*value*...]]

DDL Clause Description *(Continued)*

ALTER SYSTEM (CONT.)	ALTER SYSTEM changes the settings of the running instance and controls system activities such as archive logging.

The ARCHIVE LOG clause controls archive logging. In Oracle parallel server, a specific redo log thread may be specified. START commences automatic archiving of redo logs; STOP ceases automatic archiving. SEQUENCE, CHANGE, GROUP, and LOGFILE clauses result in automatic archiving of redo logs matching a log sequence, SCN, redo log group or redo log filename. CURRENT, NEXT, and ALL request archiving of the current log, next log due for archiving, or all logs due for archiving. The TO clause changes the archive log destination.

SWITCH LOGFILE causes the current redo log file to be closed and the next redo log file to become current.

CHECKPOINT initiates a database checkpoint. In an Oracle parallel server environment, GLOBAL will cause all instances to checkpoint.

CHECK DATAFILES checks that all data files are available. In an Oracle parallel server environment, GLOBAL will cause all instances to check data files.

KILL SESSION causes the session to be terminated immediately. *Sid* and *serial#* correspond to the equivalent columns in the V$SESSION table.

8.0+   DISCONNECT SESSION causes the session to be disconnected when all active transactions are completed. *Sid* and *serial#* correspond to the equivalent columns in the V$SESSION table.

ENABLE DISTRIBUTED RECOVERY allows the recovery of failed distributed transactions to occur automatically. This is the default behavior.

ENABLE RESTRICTED SESSION restricts database access to those accounts with the RESTRICTED SESSION privilege; DISABLE allows normal access.

Data Definition Language (DDL)

DDL Clause Description *(Continued)*

ALTER SYSTEM (CONT.)	FLUSH SHARED_POOL removes cached object definitions, SQL statements, session structures, and other data from the shared pool.
8i	SUSPEND suspends all database I/O; RESUME resumes normal database I/O.
	SET allows dynamic initialization parameters to be adjusted. Parameters that may be adjusted are those in V$PARAMETER, where the ISSYS_MODIFIABLE column is not "FALSE".

ALTER TABLE	ALTER TABLE *table_name*
	    [*physical attributes*]
	    [{ADD|MODIFY} *column_specification*]
	    [MODIFY {NESTED TABLE|VARRAY} *nested_table_column*
	        RETURN AS {LOCATOR|VALUE}]
	    [{ADD|MODIFY} CONSTRAINT
	        constraint_name constraint_properties]
	    [MOVE [ONLINE]
	        [PARTITION *partition_name*] *new_physical_attributes*]
	    [{<u>LOGGING</u>|NOLOGGING}]
	    [{CACHE|<u>NOCACHE</u>}]
	    [PARALLEL *parallel_clause*]
	    [DROP {PRIMARY KEY|
	        UNIQUE (*column_list*)|
	        CONSTRAINT *contraint_name*} [CASCADE]]
	    [SET UNUSED {COLUMN *column_name*|*column_list*}
	        [{CASCADE|INVALIDATE} CONSTRAINTS]]
	    [DROP {COLUMN *column_name*|*column_list*|
	        UNUSED COLUMNS|COLUMNS CONTINUE }
	        [{CASCADE|INVALIDATE} CONSTRAINTS]
	            [CHECKPOINT *checkpoint_rows*]]
	    [ALLOCATE EXTENT *allocate_extent_clause*]
	    [DEALLOCATE UNUSED [KEEP *keep_size* [{K|M}]]]
	    [RENAME TO *new_table_name*]
	    [{MINIMIZE|<u>NOMINIMIZE</u>} RECORDS_PER_BLOCK]
	    [{PCTTHRESHOLD *pct_threshold* |INCLUDING *column_name*}]
	    [OVERFLOW [*physical_attributes*]
	        [ALLOCATE EXTENT *allocate_extent_clause*]
	        [DEALLOCATE UNUSED *dellocate_unused_clause*]]
	    [*partition_maintenance_clauses*]

DDL Clause Description *(Continued)*

ALTER TABLE (CONT.)	ALTER TABLE changes table storage attributes, and adds, modifies, or removes columns.
	Physical attributes specify new storage attributes for the table. See the PHYSICAL ATTRIBUTES entry in this table for more details.
	The ADD clause can be used to add a column to a table. MODIFY can be used to modify the definition of an existing column. See the COLUMN SPECIFICATION entry in this table for column specification syntax.
8i	MODIFY NESTED TABLE and MODIFY VARRAY clauses determine how Oracle returns a query against a collection. LOCATOR specifies that a pointer to the collection is returned; VALUE indicates that the collection itself is returned.
	ADD CONSTRAINT and MODIFY CONSTRAINT clauses allow a table constraint to be added or amended. See the CONSTRAINT entry in this table for more details.
8i	MOVE allows a partition to be moved to a newly created segment, or the index tree of an index-organized table to be rebuilt. See PHYSICAL ATTRIBUTES for details concerning segment attributes. ONLINE indicates that DML is permitted against the table or partition while it is being moved.
8.0+	NOLOGGING indicates that rows added to the table by the direct load method or rows loaded when the table is created (if the table is created from a subquery) will not be recorded in the redo logs. LOGGING is the default.
	CACHE defines how blocks read from full table scans should be cached. CACHE encourages these blocks to stay in the buffer cache. The default behavior, NOCACHE, results in the blocks being immediately recycled.

Data Definition Language (DDL)

DDL Clause Description *(Continued)*

ALTER TABLE (CONT.)	The PARALLEL clause defines the default level of parallel processing for operations against the table. It also defines the parallelism of the table's creation if it is being created from a query.
8i	SET UNUSED marks a column or columns as unused. Unused columns cannot be queried or modified, but are not physically removed from the table. CASCADE CONSTRAINTS removes any constraints that are dependent on the unused column.
	DROP can be used to drop a primary key, or a unique or named constraint.
8i	DROP may also be used to drop a column. This physically removes the column data from a table. The columns to be dropped may be identified by name, or all unused columns may be dropped by specifying the UNUSED COLUMNS clause. Should a DROP COLUMN operation be aborted, it may be subsequently continued by a COLUMNS CONTINUE clause. CASCADE CONSTRAINTS removes any constraints that are dependent on the dropped column. CHECKPOINT causes a database checkpoint to be generated after every *checkpoint_rows* rows are processed.
	ALLOCATE EXTENT allocates a new extent. See the ALLOCATE EXTENT entry in this table for more details.
	DEALLOCATE UNUSED frees unused space within the table. See the DEALLOCATE UNUSED entry in this table for more details.
	RENAME TO renames the table.
8i	MINIMIZE RECORDS PER BLOCK reduces the number of rows stored in each database block to optimize bitmap index storage.

DDL Clause Description *(Continued)*

ALTER TABLE (CONT.) 8.0+	The PCTTHRESHOLD and INCLUDING clauses control the split of rows between the index and overflow segments of an index-organized table. See CREATE TABLE for more details.
8.0+	OVERFLOW changes the storage characteristics of the overflow segment of an index-organized table.
8.0+	*Partition_maintenance_clauses* allow management of partition storage. See "Partition Maintenance Clauses" in this chapter for more details.

ALTER TABLESPACE 8.0+	ALTER TABLESPACE *tablespace_name*
	  [{LOGGING|NOLOGGING}]
	  [ADD {DATAFILE|TEMPFILE} *datafile_specs*]
	  [RENAME DATAFILE *old_filename* TO *new_filename*]
	  [DEFAULT STORAGE *storage_clause*]
	  [MINIMUM EXTENT *extent_size* [{K|M}]]
	  [ONLINE]
	  [OFFLINE {NORMAL|TEMPORARY|IMMEDIATE|FOR RECOVER}]
	  [{BEGIN|END} BACKUP]
	  [{READ ONLY |READ WRITE}]
	  [{PERMANENT|TEMPORARY}]
	  [COALESCE]
	
	ALTER TABLESPACE alters the configuration or status of a tablespace.

8.0+	NOLOGGING specifies that objects created within the tablespace will have the NOLOGGING attribute set by default, which prevents redo logging for direct mode inserts.
	ADD DATAFILE adds a new data file to the tablespace.
8i	ADD TEMPFILE takes the same arguments as ADD DATAFILE, but creates temporary data files for *locally managed temporary tablespaces*.

Data Definition Language (DDL)

DDL Clause Description *(Continued)*

ALTER TABLESPACE (CONT.)	RENAME informs Oracle that the data file has been renamed (tablespace must be off-line).
	DEFAULT STORAGE specifies the default storage attributes for objects created in the tablespace. See the STORAGE entry in this table for more details.
8.0+	MINIMUM EXTENT ensures that extents in the tablespace can be no smaller than the specified size.
	ONLINE brings an off-line tablespace back on-line.
	OFFLINE takes a tablespace off-line. NORMAL writes all modified cached blocks from the tablespace to disk (*checkpoint*) before closing the tablespace. IMMEDIATE does not perform a checkpoint, and the tablespace may require media recovery when it is brought on-line. TEMPORARY performs a checkpoint for all on-line files, and the tablespace may require media recovery when it is brought on-line.
8.0+	OFFLINE FOR RECOVER is used to take a tablespace off-line in preparation for tablespace point-in-time recovery.
	BEGIN BACKUP and END BACKUP clauses mark the beginning and end of an on-line backup of the tablespace.
	READ ONLY prevents all DML activity against the tablespace. READ WRITE restores DML capability.
	TEMPORARY converts the tablespace to a *temporary tablespace*. PERMANENT converts a temporary tablespace to a permanent tablespace.
	COALESCE merges all adjacent unused extents, reducing "honeycomb" fragmentation.

DDL Clause Description *(Continued)*

ALTER TRIGGER	ALTER TRIGGER *trigger_name* [{ENABLE|DISABLE|COMPILE [DEBUG]}]

ALTER TRIGGER enables, disables, or recompiles a database trigger.

ENABLE and DISABLE clauses enable or disable the trigger, respectively. A disabled trigger does not execute when its triggering event occurs.

COMPILE recompiles the trigger. The DEBUG option causes debug information to be stored in the compiled trigger.

ALTER TYPE
 	
8.0+
	ALTER TYPE *type_name*
	[COMPILE {SPECIFICATION|BODY}]
	[REPLACE AS OBJECT (*attributes*)
	 [MAP|ORDER MEMBER *function_specification*]
	 [MEMBER *procedure_specification*|
	  function_specification …]
	 [PRAGMA RESTRICT_REFERENCES
	  (*module_name, restrictions*) …]]

ALTER TYPE recompiles an object type or changes an object type definition.

The COMPILE keyword, together with the SPECIFICATION or BODY clause, indicates that either the type specification or type body should be recompiled.

REPLACE AS OBJECT specifies new definitions for the object type. The new definition must include all attributes and methods from the existing type, but may add new member functions. See CREATE TYPE in Chapter 5, "PL/SQL Language," for a description of MAP, ORDER, MEMBER, and PRAGMA clauses.

Data Definition Language (DDL)

DDL Clause Description *(Continued)*

| ALTER USER | ALTER USER *username*
    IDENTIFIED {BY *password*\|
          EXTERNALLY\|
          GLOBALLY AS *external_name*}
    [DEFAULT TABLESPACE *tablespace_name*]
    [TEMPORARY TABLESPACE *tablespace_name*]
    [QUOTA {*quota_size* {K\|M}\|UNLIMITED}
          ON *tablespace_name* [,QUOTA…]]
    [PROFILE *profile_name*]
    [DEFAULT ROLE {*role_list*\|all [except {*role_list*}]\|NONE}]
    [PASSWORD EXPIRE]
    [ACCOUNT {LOCK\|UNLOCK}]
    [{GRANT\|REVOKE} CONNECT THROUGH *proxy_name*
          [WITH {NONE\|ROLE {*role_list*\|all except *role_list*} }]] |

ALTER USER changes the configuration and permissions for the user.

GRANT CONNECT THROUGH *proxy* allows a proxy connection to be established using the specified account. The WITH ROLE clause specifies the roles that are available to the proxy.

The remaining clauses of ALTER USER have the same usage as in the CREATE USER statement, that is also described in this table.

| ALTER VIEW | ALTER VIEW *view_name* COMPILE |

ALTER VIEW allows the nominated view to be recompiled.

DDL Clause Description *(Continued)*

___

ANALYZE	ANALYZE {TABLE|INDEX|CLUSTER} *segment_specification*
	[{COMPUTE STATISTICS |
	   ESTIMATE STATISTICS}
	    [FOR { TABLE |
	       ALL [INDEXED] COLUMNS
	              [SIZE *histogram_size*] |
	        column_list [SIZE *histogram_size*] |
	       ALL [LOCAL] INDEXES] } ...]
	    SAMPLE *sample_size* [ROWS|PERCENT]]
	[DELETE STATISTICS]
	[VALIDATE REF UPDATE [SET DANGLING TO NULL]]
	[VALIDATE STRUCTURE [CASCADE] [INTO *table_spec*]]
	[LIST CHAINED ROWS [INTO *table_spec*]]

ANALYZE examines and/or validates the storage and data distribution of a table, index, partition, or cluster. This information can be stored in the data dictionary and may be used by the Oracle optimizer to determine SQL execution plans. Alternately, inefficiencies or errors in object storage or structure may be revealed.

8i

In Oracle8i, the DBMS_STATS package can perform some of the functions of the ANALYZE command with greater efficiency.

Segment_specification specifies a table, index, cluster, partition, or sub-partition to be analyzed.

COMPUTE STATISTICS indicates that every block allocated to the segment should be examined to calculate statistics.

ESTIMATE STATISTICS indicates that a random sample of segment entries should be examined to calculate statistics. The SAMPLE clause specifies the percentage or absolute number of rows to examine.

The FOR clause determines if table indexes and/or *column histograms* will be created. Multiple FOR clauses may be specified.

*Data Definition
Language (DDL)*

DDL Clause Description *(Continued)*

ANALYZE (CONT.)	FOR TABLE indicates that the table should be analyzed.

FOR ALL COLUMNS indicates that histograms should be generated for each column in the table.

FOR ALL INDEXED COLUMNS indicates that histograms should be generated for each column in the table that is included in an index.

FOR *column_list* indicates that the specified list of columns should have histograms generated.

FOR ALL INDEXES indicates that all indexes associated with the table should be analyzed. The LOCAL clause, when used with a partitioned table, restricts ANALYZE to *local indexes* only.

DELETE STATISTICS causes all statistics for the nominated object to be removed.

VALIDATE REF UPDATE checks the validity of ref datatypes. If a ref contains a rowid, ANALYZE will check that the rowid of the relevant object row to which the ref column refers is correct and will correct the rowid if it is incorrect. If SET DANGLING TO NULL is specified, then any ref that points to an object row that no longer exists will be set to null.

8.0+   VALIDATE STRUCTURE validates the structure of the object. If CASCADE is specified, then any indexes belonging to the object will also be checked. If the INTO clause is specified, then rowids for rows that are in an incorrect partition will be stored in the specified table. By default, this table is called INVALID_ROWS and is created by the script *utlvalid.sql*.

LIST CHAINED ROWS finds any rows that have been migrated into chained blocks and stores them in the specified table. The default table name is CHAINED_ROWS and is created by the script *utlchain1.sql*, which is included in the Oracle distribution.

DDL Clause Description *(Continued)*

ASSOCIATE STATISTICS
 	
8i
	ASSOCIATE STATISTICS WITH
	     {COLUMNS *column_list* |
	     FUNCTIONS *function_list* |
	     PACKAGES *package_list* |
	     TYPES *type_list* |
	     INDEXES *index_list* |
	     INDEXTYPES *index_type_list*}
	  USING {*statistics_object_type* |
	     DEFAULT COST (*cpu_cost,io_cost,network_cost*) |
	     DEFAULT SELECTIVITY *selectivity_pct*}
	
	ASSOCIATE STATISTICS allows user-defined optimizer cost statistics to be associated with specific columns, PL/SQL stored programs, object types, and *domain indexes*.
	
	The COLUMNs clause defines a list of columns to be associated. Each column must be qualified with the column's table name.
	
	FUNCTIONS and PACKAGES clauses specify lists of PL/SQL stored programs to be associated. TYPES allow a list of Oracle object types to be associated. INDEXES and INDEXTYPES clauses allow *domain indexes* to be associated.
	
	USING associates the object with a *statistics_object_type*, a DEFAULT COST, or SELECTIVITY. A *statistics_object_type* is a user-defined type defined in accordance with the system type *ODCIStats*. This type contains methods that define how statistics for the object should be collected and how optimizer costs for the object should be calculated.
	
	DEFAULT COST defines the optimizer CPU, I/O, and network costs for a single execution or access of the specified object. This option is not valid in conjunction with the COLUMNs clause.
	
	DEFAULT SELECTIVITY defines the percentage of rows expected to satisfy conditions involving the object being associated.

Data Definition Language (DDL)

DDL Clause Description *(Continued)*

AUDIT	AUDIT {*audit_options*}
	    [ON {*object_name*|DIRECTORY *directory_name*|DEFAULT}]
	    [BY {*user_list*|*proxy_name*
	        [ON BEHALF OF {ANY|*user_list*}]}]
	    [BY {SESSION|ACCESS} [WHENEVER [NOT] SUCCESSFUL]

The AUDIT command causes details of selected user activities to be recorded in the Oracle audit table. Auditing must be enabled with the AUDIT_TRAIL parameter (see Chapter 10, "Initialization Parameters") or the statement to take effect.

Audit_options specify the type of auditing to be performed. A full list of audit options can be found in Table 4-4. *Audit_options* is a list of actions from one of the following categories:

- A database activity, such as SELECT TABLE or ALTER SEQUENCE.

- A system privilege, such as DELETE ANY TABLE.

- A DML operation, such as UPDATE, INSERT, RENAME, etc. These options are associated with the ON clause to record specific operations against nominated tables.

The ON clause can be specified together with DML *audit_options* to audit specified accesses to a nominated object. *Object_name* must be the name of a table, view, sequence, stored program object, snapshot, or library. The DIRECTORY clause allows a directory created with CREATE DIRECTORY to be audited. The DEFAULT clause causes the options specified to become the default for all objects subsequently created.

BY *user_list* specifies a list of users to be audited. This option is not valid if an ON *object* clause has been specified. If the username is a *proxy,* then the ON BEHALF OF clause allows auditing only for selected users of the proxy.

DDL Clause Description *(Continued)*

AUDIT (CONT.)	BY SESSION indicates that only a single entry should be written to the audit log for each unique audit activity for each session, even if the session performs the same auditable event many times. BY ACCESS indicates that a separate entry should be written to the audit log for each auditable activity. The WHENEVER clause allows the auditing to be restricted to successful or unsuccessful commands only.
CACHE	CACHE|NOCACHE The CACHE clause controls the caching of data blocks read into the buffer cache from full scans of the specified segment. CACHE encourages caching of blocks read in by full table scan; NOCACHE discourages such caching. CACHE can be included in ALTER or CREATE TABLE, SNAPSHOT, SNAPSHOT LOG, MATERIALIZED VIEW, and MATERIALIZED VIEW LOG.

COLUMN
SPECIFICATION
	column_name datatype
	    [DEFAULT *default_value*] [NOT NULL]
	    [SCOPE IS *table_name*}
	    [WITH ROWID]
	    [*constraint_clause* [,*constraint_clause*…]]
	    [OBJECT ID {SYSTEM GENERATED|PRIMARY KEY}]
	
	COLUMN SPECIFICATIONs can be used in CREATE and ALTER TABLE statements to define column names and properties.
	
	Each column must be of one of the *datatypes* specified in Table 4-2.
	
	The DEFAULT clause supplies a default value, which is applied to the column if a value is not provided in an INSERT statement.

8.0+	The SCOPE clause restricts a column of the ref datatype to reference rows only in the specified table.

Data Definition Language (DDL)

DDL Clause Description *(Continued)*

COLUMN SPECIFICATION (CONT.) 8.0+	WITH ROWID indicates that a column of the ref datatype will store the rowid of the referenced row, as well as its object ID.

Constraint_clauses specify column constraints, which can include PRIMARY KEY, CHECK, and other clauses, as specified in the CONSTRAINT entry in this table. |
| **8i** | OBJECT ID determines whether the object IDs created for rows of object tables are SYSTEM GENERATED or based on the table's PRIMARY KEY. |
| **COMMENT** | COMMENT ON {TABLE *table_name*|COLUMN *table.column_name*} is *comment_text*

COMMENT associates a comment string with a table or column. The text can be retrieved from the data dictionary views ALL_TAB_COMMENTS and ALL_COL_COMMENTS. Table comments can also be added for views or snapshots. |
| **CONSTRAINT** | [CONSTRAINT *contraint_name*]
  { {UNIQUE|PRIMARY KEY} [(*column_list*)] |
  [NOT NULL] |
  [FOREIGN KEY (*fk_column_list*) REFERENCES *pk_table*
      [ON DELETE {CASCADE|SET NULL}]] |
  CHECK (*check_condition*) }
  {[[NOT] DEFERRABLE] [INITIALLY {IMMEDIATE|DEFERRED}]
  [RELY|NORELY]
  [{ENABLE [VALIDATE|NOVALIDATE] |DISABLE}]
  [EXCEPTIONS INTO *exceptions_table*]
  [USING INDEX *Physical_storage*
      [TABLESPACE *tablespace_name*]
      [NOSORT] [LOGGING|NOLOGGING]]

The CONSTRAINT clause specifies conditions that must be satisfied by all rows within a table. In most circumstances, the CONSTRAINT keyword may be omitted, for instance, when defining a column constraint or specific constraint types such as PRIMARY KEY or FOREIGN KEY. |

DDL Clause Description *(Continued)*

CONSTRAINT (CONT.)	A CONSTRAINT may be associated with a specific column or with an entire table. If associated with a table, then FOREIGN KEY, UNIQUE, and PRIMARY KEY constraints must specify column lists.

UNIQUE requires all values for a column or *column_list* to be unique. PRIMARY KEY implements a set of columns that must be unique and that can also be the subject of a FOREIGN KEY or REFERENCES constraint. Both PRIMARY KEY and UNIQUE constraints require the creation of an implicit index. If desired, physical storage characteristics of the index can be specified in the USING INDEX clause. The options of the USING INDEX clause have the same uses as in the CREATE INDEX statement.

NOT NULL indicates that the column in question may not be null. This option is only available for column constraints, but the same effect can be obtained with a table CHECK constraint.

The FOREIGN KEY and REFERENCES clauses define a set of foreign key constraints that must match the value of the primary key of *pk_table*. ON DELETE defines the behavior when a row in the primary key table is deleted. If set to CASCADE, then the matching row in the foreign key table (i.e., the table to which the foreign key constraint is being applied) will be deleted. If set to SET NULL, then the foreign key columns will be set to null (Oracle8i only).

CHECK defines an expression that must evaluate to true for every row in the table.

8.0+

DEFERRABLE indicates that constraint checking may be deferred (by the SET CONSTRAINT command) until the end of a transaction. NOT DEFERRABLE is the default. The INITIALLY clause determines if constraint checking will be deferred when the constraint is first created.

Data Definition Language (DDL)

DDL Clause Description *(Continued)*

CONSTRAINT (CONT.) 8i	RELY applies only to *materialized views*, and it indicates that the materialized view may be used in a *query rewrite*, even if the constraint in question has not been validated. NORELY is the default, and it suppresses query rewrite on the materialized view unless the constraint is validated.
	ENABLE indicates that the constraint should become active; DISABLE indicates that the constraint should be disabled. If NOVALIDATE is specified in conjunction with ENABLE, then existing table data will not be checked for conformity with the constraint. VALIDATE indicates that existing data should be checked.
	EXCEPTIONS INTO defines a table that will receive the ROWIDS of rows that violate the constraint when the constraint is first created or when it is enabled. This table must conform to the structure defined by the script *utlexcpt.sql*, which is included in the Oracle distribution.

CREATE CLUSTER	CREATE CLUSTER *cluster_name* (*cluster_key_definition*)
	    [*Physical_attributes*]
	    [SIZE *cluster_size* {K|M}]
	    [INDEX|
	    [SINGLE TABLE] HASHKEYS *hash_keys*
	        [HASH IS *hash_expression*]]
	    [PARALLEL *Parallel_clause*]
	    [CACHE|NOCACHE]

	CREATE CLUSTER creates an empty Oracle cluster. When a table is stored in an Oracle cluster, the rows in the table are physically stored in a location determined by the value of the cluster key or by a mathematical manipulation (hash) of the cluster key.

DDL Clause Description *(Continued)*

CREATE CLUSTER (CONT.)	The *cluster_key_definition* defines the names and datatypes of the cluster or hash key. Tables being added to the cluster will specify matching columns in the CLUSTER clause of the CREATE TABLE statement.

The SIZE clause specifies the amount of space to be reserved for each unique value of the cluster key. The default is one data block.

The INDEX clause specifies that the cluster will be an index cluster. In an index cluster, rows from multiple tables that share the same cluster key values will be stored in contiguous storage, possibly optimizing joins of these tables. An index cluster will be created if neither INDEX nor HASHKEYS is specified.

HASHKEYS specifies that the cluster is to be a hash cluster, and specifies the number of unique hash keys to generate. A hash value is generated mathematically from the cluster key using a formula which will, at most, generate *hash_keys* unique values. |
| **8i** | SINGLE TABLE specifies that a hash cluster will contain only a single table.

HASH IS provides an expression to be used in place of the internal hash function. The expression should reference the cluster key columns and yield a positive number. |
| **CREATE CONTEXT** | CREATE [OR REPLACE] CONTEXT *context_namespace* USING *package_name*

CREATE CONTEXT creates an application security context namespace and associates the namespace with a PL/SQL package. Context attributes can be retrieved by the SYS_CONTEXT function (see Chapter 2, "SQL Expressions and Functions"). |

Data Definition Language (DDL)

DDL Clause Description *(Continued)*

CREATE CONTROLFILE	CREATE CONTROLFILE [REUSE] [SET] DATABASE *database_name*
	    LOGFILE *logfile_specification*
	    {RESET|NORESETLOGS}
	    DATAFILE *datafile_specification*
	    [MAXLOGFILES *maxlogfiles_value*]
	    [MAXLOGMEMBERS *maxlogmembers_value*]
	    [MAXLOGHISTORY *maxloghistory_value*]
	    [MAXDATAFILES *maxdatafiles_value*]
	    [MAXINSTANCES *maxinstances_value*]
	    [{ARCHIVELOG|NOARCHIVELOG}]
	    [CHARACTER SET *character_set_value*]

CREATE CONTROLFILE creates or recreates an Oracle control file. This may be necessary if all existing control files have been lost or damaged, or if it is required to change the database name or any of the limits that were specified in the CREATE DATABASE command.

The control files will be created in the locations specified by the initialization parameter CONTROL_FILES. The REUSE clause indicates that these files may be overwritten.

DATABASE specifies the name of the database. If the name of the database is to be changed, then the SET clause must also be specified.

LOGFILE *logfile_specification* specifies the locations and sizes of existing redo logs. See the LOGFILE entry in this table for complete syntax. RESETLOGS indicates that the contents of the log files will not be applied. The log files do not have to exist in this case. NORESETLOGS indicates that the log files exist and contain valid data.

DATAFILE *datafile_specification* provides a list of all the data files in the instance. The sizes of the data files need not be specified.

DDL Clause Description *(Continued)*

CREATE CONTROLFILE (CONT.)	MAXLOGFILES specifies the maximum number of *redo log groups* that can ever be configured. MAXLOGMEMBERS specifies the maximum number of *redo log members* (copies) that can be included in a redo log group. MAXLOGHISTORY (Oracle parallel server) specifies the amount of archived log history information that will be kept. MAXDATAFILES stipulates the maximum number of data files that can ever be added to the instance. MAXINSTANCES (Oracle parallel server) specifies the maximum number of Oracle instances that can simultaneously access the database. ARCHIVELOG indicates that the redo logs will be archived before reuse; NOARCHIVELOG suppresses redo log archiving. CHARACTER SET specifies the NLS character set for the database.

CREATE DATABASE	CREATE DATABASE *database_name*
	  [CONTROLFILE REUSE]
	  [LOGFILE *logfile_spec*]
	  [MAXLOGFILES *maxlogfiles_value*]
	  [MAXLOGMEMBERS *maxlogmembers_value*]
	  [MAXLOGHISTORY *maxloghistory_value*]
	  [MAXDATAFILES *maxdatafiles_value*]
	  [MAXINSTANCES *maxinstances_value*]
	  [{ARCHIVELOG|NOARCHIVELOG}]
	  [CHARACTER SET *character_set_value*]
	  [NATIONAL CHARACTER SET *character_set_value*]
	  [DATAFILE *datafiles_clause*]
	
	CREATE DATABASE initializes the control files, redo log files, and data files that comprise an Oracle database.

Data Definition Language (DDL)

DDL Clause Description *(Continued)*

CREATE DATABASE (CONT.)	CONTROLFILE REUSE indicates that existing control files found in the locations defined by the CONTROL_FILES initialization parameter may be overwritten.
	LOGFILE specifies the names and sizes of the redo log files to be initialized. See the LOGFILE entry in this table for complete syntax.
	MAXLOGFILES specifies the maximum number of *redo log groups* that may ever be configured in the database.
	MAXLOGMEMBERS specifies the maximum number of *redo log members* (copies) that can be included in a redo log group.
	MAXLOGHISTORY (Oracle parallel server) specifies the amount of archived log history information that will be kept.
	MAXDATAFILES stipulates the maximum number of data files that can ever be added to the instance.
	MAXINSTANCES (Oracle parallel server) specifies the maximum number of Oracle instances that can simultaneously access the database.
	ARCHIVELOG indicates that the redo logs will be archived before reuse; NOARCHIVELOG suppresses redo log archiving.
	CHARACTER SET specifies the NLS character set for the database.
	NATIONAL CHARACTER SET specifies the character set for columns of nchar, nclob, and nvarchar2 datatypes.

DDL Clause Description *(Continued)*

CREATE DATABASE LINK	CREATE [SHARED] [PUBLIC] DATABASE LINK *db_link_name* [CONNECT TO { CURRENT_USER| *username* IDENTIFIED BY *password*}] [AUTHENTICATED BY *username* IDENTIFIED BY *password*] USING '*sqlnet_alias*' CREATE DATABASE LINK creates a link to a remote database. This link can be used to query or modify data in the remote database. *Db_link_name* specifies the name of the database link. If the initialization parameter GLOBAL_NAMES is true, then the link name must match the name of the remote database. The *db_link_name* may also include the remote domain as specified by the configuration parameter DB_DOMAIN. SHARED indicates that the database link may support multiple local sessions through a single network connection. This option requires the attachment of local sessions to a *multi-threaded server*, and the specification of the AUTHENTICATED clause. PUBLIC indicates that the database link will be available to all users. CONNECT TO provides the connection details at the remote database. If omitted and if the initialization parameter GLOBAL_NAMES is set to true, then the current username and password will be used. This is the behavior indicated by the CURRENT_USER keyword. USING specifies a SQL*NET service name, which is used to establish a connection to the remote database.

Data Definition Language (DDL)

DDL Clause Description *(Continued)*

CREATE DIMENSION
 	
8i
	CREATE [FORCE|<u>NOFORCE</u>] DIMENSION *dimension_name*
	   LEVEL *level_name* IS (*level_column_list*)
	     [LEVEL *level_name* IS ...]
	   [HIERARCHY *heirarchy_name*
	      (*child_level_name* CHILD OF *parent_level_name*
	       [CHILD OF ...]
	       [JOIN KEY *column_list* REFERENCES *level_name*
	        [JOIN KEY ...]])
	      [HIERARCHY *heirarchy_name* ...]]
	   [ATTRIBUTE *level_name*
	     DETERMINES (*dependent_column_list*)
	   [ATTRIBUTE ...]]
	
	CREATE DIMENSION creates a dimension that defines hierarchical relationships between columns in one or more tables. The optimizer can use these relationships to facilitate *query rewrite*.
	
	FORCE allows the dimension to be created, even if tables or columns referred to in the dimension do not exist.
	
	LEVEL identifies one or more columns from a single table as a level that can be used in HIERARCHY and ATTRIBUTE clauses.
	
	The HIERARCHY clause defines parent-child relationship between levels. For instance, a *department* level might be identified as being a child of a *faculty* level.
	
	The JOIN KEY clause identifies foreign key relationships between levels that are contained in multiple tables.
	
	The ATTRIBUTE clause identifies columns in a table whose values are dependent on the values of the specified level. For instance, the *job_category* level might determine the value of the *max_salary* column.

DDL Clause Description *(Continued)*

CREATE DIRECTORY **8.0+**	CREATE [OR REPLACE] DIRECTORY *directory_name* AS *'path'* CREATE DIRECTORY identifies an operating system directory to be used by the UTL_FILE package (see Chapter 6, "Oracle-Supplied PL/SQL Packages") or to be used to store BFILE data. *Directory_name* specifies the name that will be used within the database to refer to the directory path. *Path* identifies the operating system directory path.
CREATE FUNCTION	See Chapter 5, "PL/SQL language." CREATE FUNCTION creates a PL/SQL stored program function and is described in Chapter 5.

CREATE INDEX	CREATE [UNIQUE|BITMAP] INDEX *index_name*
	    ON {*table_name* (*indexed_column_list*)
	        |CLUSTER *cluster_name*}
	    [*physical_attributes*]
	    [{LOGGING|NOLOGGING}]
	    [{RECOVERABLE|UNRECOVERABLE}]
	    [ONLINE]
	    [COMPUTE STATISTICS]
	    [{COMPRESS *number_of_columns*|NOCOMPRESS}]
	    [REVERSE|NOSORT]
	    [PARALLEL *parallel_clause*]
	    [INDEXTYPE IS *index_type*
	        [PARAMETERS (*parameter_string*)]]
	    [GLOBAL PARTITION *partition_clause*]
	    [LOCAL [(PARTITION partition_name
	        [SUBPARTITION subpartition_name [,...]] [,...])]
	    [STORE IN (*tablespace_list*)]

Data Definition Language (DDL)

DDL Clause Description *(Continued)*

CREATE INDEX (CONT.)	CREATE INDEX creates an index on a table or cluster.
	UNIQUE indicates that the index should implement a unique constraint (i.e., no duplicates) on the columns in *indexed_column_list*.
	BITMAP indicates that the index will be a *bitmap index*.
	The ON clause identifies the table and columns to be indexed. If the CLUSTER keyword is present, then an index is to be created on the cluster key of the specified cluster. Otherwise, the *indexed_column_list* identifies a list of columns to be indexed. Each column in the list may be followed by the ASC or DESC keyword, which determines whether column values are added to the index in ascending or descending order.
8i	Entries in the *indexed_column_list* can include functions on table columns. These functions may be SQL functions, or user functions written in PL/SQL.
	Physical_attributes define physical storage options—see the PHYSICAL ATTRIBUTES entry in this table.
8.0+	NOLOGGING indicates that the creation of the index will not be recorded in the redo logs and that subsequent direct load (append mode) inserts will also not be logged. The default is LOGGING.
7.3	UNRECOVERABLE indicates that the creation of the index will not be recorded in the redo logs. The default is RECOVERABLE.
8i	ONLINE permits DML operations to proceed on the indexed table during the index build.
8i	COMPUTE STATISTICS collects optimizer statistics during index creation.

DDL Clause Description *(Continued)*

CREATE INDEX (CONT.) 8i	COMPRESS requests that duplicated column entries not be stored within the index, thus saving space. *Number_of_columns* specifies the number of columns to be compressed and must be at least one less than the number of key columns.
8.0+	REVERSE specifies that column key values be stored in the index in reverse alphanumeric sequence.
	NOSORT indicates that the rows are already in ascending index key order and that Oracle can therefore omit sorting the row when building the index.
	PARALLEL indicates that the index should be built in parallel. See the PARALLEL entry in this table for more details.
8i	The INDEXTYPE clause specifies that a *domain index* of the specified index type (see CREATE INDEXTYPE) should be created.
8.0+	GLOBAL indicates that the index is a *global index* on a partitioned table. See the PARTITION entry in this table for more details on specifying partitions.
8.0+	LOCAL indicates that the index is a *local index* on a partitioned table. The PARTITION and SUBPARTITION clauses define the index partitions. The STORE IN clause specifies the tablespace for each partition.
CREATE INDEXTYPE 8i	CREATE [OR REPLACE] INDEXTYPE *index_type_name* FOR *operator_name(argument_list)* [*,operator_name* ...] USING *implementation_object_type*
	CREATE INDEXTYPE creates a user-defined index type, which can be used to create application-specific *domain indexes*.
	The FOR clause specifies an operator—created by the CREATE OPERATOR command—that is supported by the index type. More than one operator can be supported.

Data Definition Language (DDL)

DDL Clause Description *(Continued)*

CREATE INDEXTYPE (CONT.)	USING defines the Oracle object type that implements the methods of the *ODCIIndex* system type. This type contains methods for creating and maintaining indexes based on the index type.

CREATE JAVA
 	
8i
	CREATE [OR REPLACE] [AND {RESOLVE|COMPILE}] [NOFORCE] JAVA
	    {CLASS [SCHEMA *schema_name*]|
	        {SOURCE|RESOURCE} NAMED *java_name* }
	    [AUTHID {CURRENT_USER | <u>DEFINER</u>}]
	    [RESOLVER((*pattern, schema*|-) (*pattern, schema*|-) ...
	    )]
	    { USING {BFILE (*directory, file*) |
	            {CLOB|BLOB|BFILE} *subquery* } |
	        AS *java_source*
	    }
	
	CREATE JAVA creates an Oracle8i JServer Java source, class, or resource.
	
	RESOLVE and COMPILE are synonymous, and indicate that a Java source or class should be resolved and compiled.
	
	If NOFORCE is provided, then failed compilations cause the CREATE JAVA statement to be rolled back. Otherwise, the object is created but marked invalid.
	
	CLASS, RESOURCE, and SOURCE indicate the type of Java object to be loaded.
	
	For a Java class, the SCHEMA keyword can be used to specify a schema other than the current schema in which the object should be created.
	
	AUTHID determines whether the module runs with the privileges of the user who defined the module (DEFINER) or the permissions of the user running the module (CURRENT_USER).

DDL Clause Description *(Continued)*

CREATE JAVA (CONT.)	RESOLVER determines how names in the Java source or class should be resolved. It is somewhat analogous to CLASSPATH in external JVMs. The RESOLVER clause consists of a series of wildcards and schema identifiers. If a name in the Java program matches the wildcard, then the specified *schema* is examined for the appropriate object. If "-" is specified as the *schema*, then the name is not resolved.
	Java source can be obtained in a number of ways:
	BFILE, together with a *directory* and *filename*, defines an operating system file containing the data.
	CLOB, BLOB, and BFILE, together with a *subquery*, define a *lob_locator* that identifies a LOB (CLOB, BLOB, or BFILE datatype) which contains the data.
	As supplies the Java source code directly within the CREATE JAVA statement.
	See Chapter 7, "Oracle Java," for examples of using CREATE JAVA.

Data Definition Language (DDL)

CREATE LIBRARY 8.0+	CREATE [OR REPLACE] LIBRARY *library_name* AS *filespecification* CREATE LIBRARY identifies an operating system shared program library whose routines may be called from within PL/SQL. *Filespecification* denotes the fully-qualified location of the program library.

CREATE MATERIALIZED VIEW
 	
8i
	CREATE {MATERIALIZED VIEW|SNAPSHOT} *mview_name*
	    [*Physical attributes*]
	    [*Lob_storage*]
	    [{LOGGING|NOLOGGING}]
	    [{CACHE|NOCACHE}]
	    [PARTITION *partition_clause*]
	    [PARALLEL *parallel_clause*]
	    [CLUSTER *cluster_name* (*cluster_columns*)]
	    [USING INDEX *index_physical_attributes*]

DDL Clause Description *(Continued)*

CREATE
MATERIALIZED
VIEW
(CONT.)
	[{ BUILD {IMMEDIATE|DEFERRED} |
	    ON PREBUILT TABLE [{WITH|WITHOUT}
	        REDUCED PRECISION] }]
	[[NEVER] REFRESH {FAST|COMPLETE|FORCE}
	        [ON {DEMAND|COMMIT}]
	        [START WITH *start_date*]
	        [WITH {PRIMARY KEY|ROWID}]
	        [USING [DEFAULT] [{MASTER|LOCAL}]
	        ROLLBACK SEGMENT[*rollback_segment*]]]
	[FOR UPDATE]
	[{ENABLE|DISABLE} QUERY REWRITE]
	as *query*

CREATE MATERIALIZED VIEW creates an Oracle8i materialized view. Materialized views supersede snapshots in Oracle8i, and the keyword SNAPSHOT may be used in place of MATERIALIZED VIEW, if desired.

The *physical attributes* clause defines database storage attributes. See the PHYSICAL ATTRIBUTES entry in this table for more details.

Lob_storage defines any special storage requirements for log columns. See the LOB clause in this table for more details.

NOLOGGING indicates that the creation and maintenance of the materialized view will not be recorded in redo logs.

CACHE prevents blocks read into the buffer cache from a full table scan from being immediately recycled; NOCACHE is the default.

CLUSTER indicates that the materialized view is to be stored in the nominated cluster and identifies the columns corresponding to the cluster key.

USING INDEX allows definition of the storage parameters for an automatically created index on the materialized view's primary key. See PHYSICAL ATTRIBUTES in this table for details.

DDL Clause Description *(Continued)*

CREATE MATERIALIZED VIEW (CONT.)	REFRESH determines the default refresh method. NEVER indicates that the materialized view may not be refreshed. COMPLETE deletes all materialized view rows and re-executes the materialized view query to completely repopulate the materialized view. FAST uses a materialized view log (see CREATE MATERIALIZED VIEW LOG) on the *master table* to propagate only changed rows. FORCE uses the FAST method, if possible, and otherwise uses the COMPLETE method.
	ON COMMIT ensures that the materialized view is refreshed whenever a transaction commits on the master table. REFRESH ON DEMAND indicates that the materialized view will be updated using the DBMS_MVIEW package (see Chapter 6, "Oracle-Supplied PL/SQL Packages").
	The WITH ROWID clause creates a materialized view that is compatible with an Oracle 7.3 master table. The default behavior is WITH PRIMARY KEY.
	START WITH specifies the date and time for the first automatic refresh. NEXT specifies a date expression involving SYSDATE, which determines the interval between refreshes.
	USING ... ROLLBACK SEGMENT determines the rollback segment to be used during transactions on the master table or local materialized views. DEFAULT causes Oracle to pick a rollback segment using the standard algorithm.
	ENABLE QUERY REWRITE permits *query rewrites* to use the materialized view; DISABLE QUERY REWRITE prevents query rewrites using the materialized view.
	FOR UPDATE indicates that a simple materialized view can be updated.

Data Definition Language (DDL)

DDL Clause Description *(Continued)*

CREATE MATERIALIZED VIEW LOG
 	
8i
	CREATE MATERIALIZED VIEW LOG ON *table_name*
	  [*Physical_attributes*]
	  [PARTITION *partition_clause*]
	  [LOGGING|NOLOGGING] [CACHE|NOCACHE]
	  [PARALLEL *parallel_clause*]
	  [WITH [ROWID] [,] [PRIMARY KEY] [(*filter_columns*)]
	  [{INCLUDING|EXCLUDING} NEW VALUES]
	
	CREATE MATERIALIZED VIEW LOG creates a log table on a materialized view master table, which can then be used to facilitate a fast refresh. *Physical_attributes* specify the physical storage parameters for the object. See the PHYSICAL_ATTRIBUTES entry in this table for more details.
	
	In Oracle8i, CREATE MATERIALIZED VIEW LOG supersedes CREATE SNAPSHOT LOG. However, the SNAPSHOT keyword can still be used in place of the MATERIALIZED VIEW keyword.
	
	The PARTITION clause can be used to partition the log table. See the PARTITION entry in this table for details.
	
	NOLOGGING prevents changes to the snapshot log from being saved to the redo logs.
	
	NOCACHE reduces the time which materialized view log blocks spend in the buffer cache. See the CACHE entry in this table for more details.
	
	The PARALLEL clause specifies the default parallelism for log table accesses. See the PARALLEL entry in this table for more details.
	
	The WITH clause determines whether the primary key and/or rowid of a modified row is stored in the materialized view log. The *filter_columns* clause can be used to specify additional column values from the master table, which will be stored in the log.
	
	The INCLUDING NEW VALUES clause causes both old and new values for columns specified in the WITH clause to be stored in the log. This allows faster refreshes for certain types of materialized views.

DDL Clause Description *(Continued)*

CREATE OPERATOR 8i	CREATE [OR REPLACE] OPERATOR *operator_name* 　　BINDING (*parameter_type_list*) RETURN *return_type* 　　[ANCILLARY TO *primary_operator*(*parameter_type_list*) 　　　[,*primary_operator*...]] 　　[WITH INDEX CONTEXT, SCAN CONTEXT 　　　*implementation_object_type* 　　　[COMPUTE ANCILLARY DATA]] 　　USING *function_name* 　　　[BINDING ... USING *function_name*]

CREATE OPERATOR creates a user-defined operator. The BINDING clause specifies a *parameter_type_list*, which—together with the *return_type*—should correspond to one of the implementations of the function *function_name*. Multiple bindings can be defined, which allow for the operator to act on multiple datatypes.

The ANCILLARY TO clause indicates that this function can receive ancillary data created by *primary_operator*. The definition of *primary_operator* should include the COMPUTE ANCILLARY DATA clause. More than one *primary_operator* can be defined.

WITH INDEX CONTEXT allows domain indexes based on an operator to use other domain indexes as data sources. SCAN CONTEXT defines an argument of the function *function_name*, which holds context information during index scans. COMPUTE ANCILLARY DATA indicates that the operator—when used in a WHERE clause—should compute any additional data that may be required elsewhere in an SQL query.

CREATE OUTLINE 8i	CREATE [OR REPLACE] OUTLINE *outline_name* 　　FOR CATEGORY *category_type* ON *sql_statement*

CREATE OUTLINE stores an *execution plan outline* for the specified *sql_statement*. In the future, this outline may be used to determine the query's execution plan if the ALTER SESSION parameter USE_STORED_OUTLINES is set to true.

CATEGORY specifies a user-defined category label that can be used to organize or group outlines.

Data Definition Language (DDL)

DDL Clause Description *(Continued)*

CREATE PACKAGE	See Chapter 5, "PL/SQL Language."
	CREATE PACKAGE creates a PL/SQL stored package header and is described in Chapter 5.

CREATE PACKAGE BODY	See Chapter 5, "PL/SQL Language."
	CREATE PACKAGE BODY creates a PL/SQL stored package body and is described in Chapter 5.

CREATE PROCEDURE	See Chapter 5, "PL/SQL Language."
	CREATE PROCEDURE creates a PL/SQL stored procedure and is described in Chapter 5.

CREATE PROFILE

```
CREATE PROFILE profile_name LIMIT
        [SESSIONS_PER_USER            {value|UNLIMITED|DEFAULT}]
        [CPU_PER_SESSION              {value|UNLIMITED|DEFAULT}]
        [CPU_PER_CALL                 {value|UNLIMITED|DEFAULT}]
        [CONNECT_TIME                 {value|UNLIMITED|DEFAULT}]
        [IDLE_TIME                    {value|UNLIMITED|DEFAULT}]
        [LOGICAL_READS_PER_SESSION {value|UNLIMITED|DEFAULT}]
        [LOGICAL_READS_PER_CALL {value|UNLIMITED|DEFAULT}]
        [COMPOSITE_LIMIT              {value|UNLIMITED|DEFAULT}]
        [PRIVATE_SGA          {value {K|M}|UNLIMITED|DEFAULT}]
        [FAILED_LOGIN_ATTEMPTS  {value|UNLIMITED|DEFAULT}]
        [PASSWORD_LIFE_TIME      {value|UNLIMITED|DEFAULT}]
        [PASSWORD_REUSE_TIME     {value|UNLIMITED|DEFAULT}]
        [PASSWORD_REUSE_MAX      {value|UNLIMITED|DEFAULT}]
        [PASSWORD_LOCK_TIME      {value|UNLIMITED|DEFAULT}]
        [PASSWORD_GRACE_TIME     {value|UNLIMITED|DEFAULT}]
        [PASSWORD_VERIFY_FUNCTION{function|NULL|DEFAULT}]
```

CREATE PROFILE creates a user profile that specifies resource limits and security restrictions that may be applied to a user.

SESSIONS_PER_USER restricts the number of simultaneous logins that can be established by the specified user account.

DDL Clause Description *(Continued)*

CREATE PROFILE (CONT.)	CPU_PER_SESSION limits the amount of server CPU time (in 1/100ths of a second) that a session can consume.
	CPU_PER_CALL limits the amount of server CPU time (in 1/100ths of a second) that can be consumed by a single SQL call (parse, execute, fetch).
	CONNECT_TIME limits the duration of a session in minutes.
	IDLE_TIME forces a session disconnect after the specified number of idle minutes.
	LOGICAL_READS_PER_SESSION limits the number of logical database reads that the session can perform.
	LOGICAL_READS_PER_CALL limits the number of logical database reads that a single SQL call (parse, execute, fetch) can consume.
	COMPOSITE_LIMIT limits the composite aggregate of certain resources for the session. See the ALTER RESOURCE entry in this table for details on defining the composite limit.
	PRIVATE_SGA limits the amount of private memory the session may allocate in the SGA (System Global Area).
8.0+	FAILED_LOGIN_ATTEMPTS defines the number of consecutive failed login attempts allowed before the account is disabled.
8.0+	PASSWORD_LIFE_TIME defines the number of days before a password change is required.
8.0+	PASSWORD_REUSE_TIME defines the number of days that must elapse before a password can be reused.
8.0+	PASSWORD_REUSE_MAX time defines the number of password changes that must occur before a password can be reused.

DDL Clause Description *(Continued)*

· CREATE PROFILE (CONT.) 8.0+	PASSWORD_LOCK_TIME defines the number of days for which an account will be disabled after exceeding FAILED_LOGIN_ATTEMPTS.
8.0+	PASSWORD_GRACE_TIME defines the number of days after PASSWORD_REUSE_TIME has occurred that a warning will be issued and login permitted on the old password.
8.0+	PASSWORD_VERIFY_FUNCTION defines a PL/SQL function that will be used to validate any new passwords.

CREATE ROLE	CREATE ROLE *role_name* 　　[{NOT IDENTIFIED | 　　　　IDENTIFIED {by *password*| 　　　　　　EXTERNALLY 　　　　　　GLOBALLY} }] CREATE ROLE creates a named database role. Privileges can be granted to the role and the role can then be granted to users or to other roles. If a role is defined as NOT IDENTIFIED (the default), the role must be explicitly granted to users. If the IDENTIFIED clause is specified, then the role can be invoked by the SET ROLE command. If IDENTIFIED BY *password*, then the user must provide the specified *password* when invoking the role. If IDENTIFIED EXTERNALLY, then the user is authenticated by the operating system; If IDENTIFIED GLOBALLY, then the user is authenticated by an Oracle security server.

CREATE ROLLBACK SEGMENT	CREATE [PUBLIC] ROLLBACK SEGMENT *rollback_segment_name* 　　[TABLESPACE *tablespace_name*] 　　[STORAGE *storage_clause*] CREATE ROLLBACK SEGMENT creates a rollback segment that stores before images of database blocks to support the ROLLBACK command and read consistency. The PUBLIC clause indicates that the rollback segment is available to all instances that mount the database.

DDL Clause Description *(Continued)*

CREATE ROLLBACK SEGMENT (CONT.)	The TABLESPACE and STORAGE clauses specify the location and storage parameters for the rollback segment.

Note that when created, a rollback segment is off-line. Use the ALTER ROLLBACK SEGMENT command to bring it on-line. |
| **CREATE SCHEMA** | CREATE SCHEMA AUTHORIZATION *schema_owner*
    DDL_commands

CREATE SCHEMA creates multiple tables, views, and grants in a single transaction.

Schema_owner is the owner of the schema—usually the name of the current user.

DDL_commands are limited to CREATE TABLE, CREATE VIEW, and GRANT statements. |
| **CREATE SEQUENCE** | CREATE SEQUENCE *sequence_name*
    [START WITH *start_with*]
    [INCREMENT BY *increment_by*]
    [{MAXVALUE *max_value*|NOMAXVALUE}]
    [{MINVALUE *min_value*|NOMINVALUE}]
    [{CYCLE|NOCYCLE}]
    [{CACHE *cache_size*|NOCACHE}]
    [{ORDER|NOORDER}]

CREATE SEQUENCE creates an Oracle sequence, which provides a fast and non-blocking way of creating unique sequence numbers.

START WITH specifies the first number to be returned by the sequence. The default is 1.

INCREMENT BY specifies the increment between successive numbers. The default is 1.

MAXVALUE specifies an upper limit for the sequence. The default is NOMAXVALUE (which is actually a number in the vicinity of 10^{27}). |

Data Definition Language (DDL)

DDL Clause Description *(Continued)*

CREATE SEQUENCE (CONT.)	MINVALUE specifies a lower bound for the sequence. The default is NOMINVALUE, which for a descending sequence is -10^{26}. CYCLE indicates that the sequence should cycle from MAXVALUE to MINVALUE (or vice versa for a descending sequence). NOCYCLE is the default. CACHE specifies the number of sequence numbers that will be stored in the SGA. Cached sequence numbers can be issued very rapidly, but numbers that are cached may be "lost" if the database experiences an instance failure. ORDER indicates that numbers should always be generated in an exact sequence. This setting is primarily intended for parallel server instances and can cause severe performance degradation.

CREATE SNAPSHOT
 	
7.3, 8.0
	CREATE SNAPSHOT *snapshot_name*
	  [*Physical_attributes*]
	  [*lob_storage*] [{<u>LOGGING</u>|NOLOGGING}] [{<u>CACHE</u>|NOCACHE}]
	  [CLUSTER *cluster_name* (*cluster_columns*)]
	  [PARTITION partition clause]
	  [USING INDEX *index_physical_attributes*]
	  [REFRESH [FAST|COMPLETE|<u>FORCE</u>] [START WITH start_date]
	     [NEXT *next_date*]]
	  [WITH {PRIMARY KEY|ROWID}]
	  [USING [DEFAULT] [{MASTER|LOCAL}]
	     ROLLBACK SEGMENT[*rollback_segment*]]
	  [FOR UPDATE]
	  AS *query*
	
	CREATE SNAPSHOT creates a snapshot based on the specified *query*. In Oracle8i, CREATE SNAPSHOT has been depreciated in favor of CREATE MATERIALIZED VIEW.
	
	The *physical attributes* clause defines database storage attributes. See the PHYSICAL ATTRIBUTES entry in this table for more details.

DDL Clause Description *(Continued)*

CREATE SNAPSHOT (CONT.) 8.0+	*Lob_storage* defines any special storage requirements for LOB columns. See the LOB clause in this table for more details.
8.0+	NOLOGGING indicates that the creation and maintenance of the snapshot will not be recorded in redo logs.
	CACHE prevents blocks read into the buffer cache from a full table scan from being immediately recycled; NOCACHE is the default.
	CLUSTER indicates that the snapshot is to be stored in the nominated cluster, and identifies the columns corresponding to the cluster key.
8.0+	The PARTITION clause allows the snapshot to be partitioned. See PARTITION in this table for more details.
	USING INDEX allows the storage parameters for the automatically created index on the snapshot's primary key to be defined. See PHYSICAL ATTRIBUTES in this table for details.
	REFRESH determines the default refresh method. COMPLETE deletes all snapshot rows and re-executes the snapshot query to completely repopulate the snapshot. FAST uses a snapshot log (see CREATE SNAPSHOT LOG) on the *master table* to propagate only changed rows. FORCE uses the FAST method if possible, and otherwise uses the COMPLETE method.
	START WITH specifies the date and time for the first automatic refresh. NEXT specifies a date expression involving SYSDATE, which determines the interval between refreshes.
	The WITH ROWID clause creates a snapshot that is compatible with an Oracle 7.3 master table.

DDL Clause Description *(Continued)*

CREATE SNAPSHOT (CONT.) 8.0+	USING ... ROLLBACK SEGMENT determines the rollback segment to be used during transactions on the master table or local snapshot. DEFAULT causes Oracle to pick a rollback segment using the standard algorithm. FOR UPDATE indicates that a simple snaphot can be updated.

CREATE SNAPSHOT LOG
 	
7.3, 8.0
	CREATE SNAPSHOT LOG ON *table_name*
	    [*Physical_attributes*]
	    [PARTITION *partition_clause*]
	    [LOGGING|NOLOGGING] [CACHE|NOCACHE]
	    [PARALLEL *parallel_clause*]
	    [WITH [ROWID] [,] [PRIMARY KEY] [(*filter_columns*)]
	
	CREATE SNAPSHOT LOG creates a log table on a snapshot master table, which can be used to facilitate a fast refresh. *Physical_attributes* specifies the physical storage parameters for the object. See the PHYSICAL_ATTRIBUTES entry in this table for more details.
	
	In Oracle8i, CREATE SNAPSHOT LOG has been depreciated in favor of CREATE MATERIALIZED VIEW LOG.

8.0+	The PARTITION clause can be used to partition the log table. See the PARTITION entry in this table for details.
8.0+	NOLOGGING prevents changes to the snapshot log from being saved to the redo logs.
8.0+	NOCACHE reduces the length of time snapshot log data blocks are held in the buffer cache.
8.0+	The PARALLEL clause specifies the default parallelism for log table accesses. See the PARALLEL entry in this table for more details.
8.0+	The WITH clause determines whether primary key and/ or rowids of modified rows are stored in the snapshot log. The *filter_columns* clause can be used to specify additional column values from the master table which will be stored in the log.

DDL Clause Description *(Continued)*

CREATE SYNONYM	CREATE [PUBLIC] SYNONYM *synonym_name* FOR *object_specification*

CREATE SYNONYM creates a synonym or alias to a database object.

PUBLIC indicates that the synonym will be available to all accounts in the current instance. Otherwise, the synonym will be available to the creating user only.

Object_specification may be a fully- or partially-qualified identifier, referring to a table, view, snapshot, materialized view, procedure, function, package, or synonym. The specification may be qualified with schema and/or database link name.

CREATE TABLE	CREATE [GLOBAL TEMPORARY] TABLE *table_name*

```
[{  (column_specification [,column_specification...]
    [ SCOPE FOR (ref_columns) IS table_name ]
    [ REF(ref_columns) WITH ROWID ]
    constraint_clauses
 ) |
 OF object_type [(column_properties)]
    [OBJECT ID {SYSTEM GENERATED|PRIMARY KEY}]
    [OIDINDEX index_name index_physical_attributes]
}]
[ON COMMIT {DELETE|PRESERVE} ROWS]
[physical_attributes]
[LOGGING|NOLOGGING]
[RECOVERABLE|UNRECOVERABLE]
[{ENABLE|DISABLE} ROW MOVEMENT]
[ORGANIZATION
    {HEAP |
    INDEX   [PCTTHRESHOLD pct_thold]
            [INCLUDING including_colname]
            [OVERFLOW overflow_physical_attributes]
            [{COMPRESS comp_columns|NOCOMPRESS}]
    }]
```

DDL Clause Description *(Continued)*

CREATE TABLE **(CONT.)**	[LOB *lob_storage*] [PARTITION *partition_clause*] [PARALLEL *parallel_clause*] [CACHE|NOCACHE] [AS *query* [ORDER BY *order_by_clause*]]

CREATE TABLE creates a database table.

8i

The GLOBAL TEMPORARY clause indicates that the table contains temporary data. Data placed in the table will not persist beyond the life of either the session or transaction, depending on the value of the ON COMMIT clause (see below).

Column_specifications define the columns that comprise the table. These specifications are required, unless the table is defined as being OF *object_type* or AS *query*. See the COLUMN SPECIFICATION entry in this table for more details.

8.0+

SCOPE FOR defines the scope of selected columns that are of the ref datatype. The ref columns specified in this way may refer only to object rows in the specified table.

8.0+

The REF ... WITH ROWID clause specifies that the REF columns listed are to store the rowid of the referenced row. This optimizes DEREF operations (see the DEREF operator in Chapter 2, "SQL Expressions and Functions").

The *constraint_clauses* specify any table constraints, such as primary or foreign key, that are not included within individual column specifications. See the CONSTRAINT entry in this table for more details.

8.0+

OF *object_type* indicates that the table is an object table whose attributes are derived from the specified *object_type* (see CREATE TYPE).

DDL Clause Description *(Continued)*

CREATE TABLE (CONT.) 8i	OBJECT ID indicates the format of the *object identifier* (OID), which is associated with each row in an object table. SYSTEM GENERATED creates a globally unique system-generated OID, while PRIMARY KEY bases the OID on the row's primary key.
8i	ON COMMIT is applicable only for a global temporary table. If DELETE, then rows in the table are automatically removed when the transaction commits. If PRESERVE, rows remain in the table until the session terminates.
	Physical attributes describe the physical storage location and configuration. See the PHYSICAL ATTRIBUTES entry in this table.
8.0+	NOLOGGING indicates that rows added to the table by the direct load method, or rows loaded when the table is created (if the table is created from a subquery), will not be recorded in the redo logs. LOGGING is the default.
7.3	UNRECOVERABLE indicates that rows loaded when the table is created (if the table is created from a subquery) will not be recorded in the redo logs. RECOVERABLE is the default.
8i	ENABLE ROW MOVEMENT indicates that updates to a partitioned table may relocate the row into another partition if appropriate. DISABLE ROW MOVEMENT suppresses such movement—generating an error if a row is updated in such a way that it belongs in a different partition.
8.0+	ORGANIZATION defines the organization of rows in the table. HEAP indicates that the rows of the table may be in any order—this is the default. INDEX indicates that the table is organized as a b*-tree, similar to the structure of standard Oracle indexes and based on the primary key of the table. Such a table is known as an *index-organized table*.

Data Definition Language (DDL)

DDL Clause Description *(Continued)*

CREATE TABLE (CONT.)	PCTTHRESHOLD specifies the percentage of the row that is stored within the index-organized table itself. The rest of the row is stored in the segment defined by the OVERFLOW clause. See PHYSICAL ATTRIBUTES in this table for details of the items that can be stored in the OVERFLOW clause.
	The INCLUDING clause provides another way of splitting a table into index and overflow sections. Columns following that specified in the INCLUDING clause will be stored in the overflow segment.
	COMPRESS requests that duplicated column entries not be stored within the index portion of an index-organized table. *Number_of_columns* specifies the number of columns to be compressed, and must be at least one less than the number of key columns.
8.0+	The LOB clause can be used to define storage for LOB columns within the table. See the LOB entry in this table for more details.
8.0+	The PARTITION clause defines how the table is to be partitioned. See the PARTITION entry in this table for more details.
	The PARALLEL clause defines the default level of parallel processing for operations against the table. It also defines the parallelism of the table creation, if it is being created from a query.
	CACHE defines how blocks read from full table scans should be cached. CACHE encourages these blocks to stay in the buffer cache. The default behavior, NOCACHE, results in the blocks being immediately recycled.

DDL Clause Description *(Continued)*

CREATE
TABLESPACE
	CREATE [TEMPORARY] TABLESPACE
	   DATAFILE *datafile* [*,datafile*…]
	   [MINIMUM EXTENT *min_ext_size* {K|M}]
	   [{<u>LOGGING</u>|NOLOGGING}]
	   [DEFAULT STORAGE *default_storage_clause*]
	   [{ONLINE|OFFLINE}]
	   [{<u>PERMANENT</u>|TEMPORARY}]
	   [EXTENT MANAGEMENT
	      {<u>DICTIONARY</u>|LOCAL
	      [{AUTOALLOCATE|UNIFORM} [*size* {K|M}]] }]

The CREATE TABLESPACE command creates a *tablespace*.

The TEMPORARY keyword, which can appear either before the tablespace keyword or elsewhere within the CREATE TABLESPACE statement, indicates that the tablespace will be used to store temporary and intermediate result sets generated to resolve large sorts, joins, and other activities.

The DATAFILE keyword defines the data files that will initially comprise the tablespace. See the DATAFILE entry in this table for more details.

8.0+ The MINIMUM EXTENT clause specifies the minimum size for any *extent* created in the tablespace.

8.0+ NOLOGGING indicates that objects created in the tablespace will, by default, have the NOLOGGING attribute (see CREATE TABLE).

The DEFAULT STORAGE clause specifies the default storage characteristics of objects created in the tablespace. See the STORAGE entry in this table for more details.

OFFLINE specifies that the tablespace will not be available for use when first created.

Data Definition
Language (DDL)

DDL Clause Description *(Continued)*

CREATE TABLESPACE (CONT.) 8i	The EXTENT MANAGEMENT clause specifies policies to be used in the tablespace. DICTIONARY is the default, and it requires that extent allocations follow global policies and be recorded in the data dictionary. LOCAL indicates that the extent map will be stored in the tablespace itself. AUTOALLOCATE indicates that the size of extents will be determined by Oracle. UNIFORM indicates that all extents will be of the same size and sets that size. AUTOALLOCATE and UNIFORM are only applicable for EXTENT MANAGEMENT LOCAL tablespaces. EXTENT MANAGEMENT LOCAL tablespaces cannot be TEMPORARY or specify DEFAULT STORAGE.
CREATE TRIGGER	See Chapter 5, "PL/SQL Language." CREATE TRIGGER creates a PL/SQL stored program function and is described in Chapter 5.
CREATE TYPE	See Chapter 5, "PL/SQL Language." CREATE TYPE creates a PL/SQL stored program function and is described in Chapter 5.
CREATE TYPE BODY	See Chapter 5, "PL/SQL Language." CREATE TYPE BODY creates a PL/SQL stored program function and is described in Chapter 5.

CREATE USER	CREATE USER *username*
	    IDENTIFIED {by *password*|
	          EXTERNALLY|
	          GLOBALLY as *external_name*}
	    [DEFAULT TABLESPACE *tablespace_name*]
	    [TEMPORARY TABLESPACE *tablespace_name*]
	    [QUOTA {*quota_size* {K|M}|UNLIMITED}
	       ON *tablespace_name* [,QUOTA…]]

DDL Clause Description *(Continued)*

CREATE USER (CONT.)	[PROFILE *profile_name*] [DEFAULT ROLE {*role_list*|all [EXCEPT {*role_list*}]|NONE}] [PASSWORD EXPIRE] [ACCOUNT {LOCK|UNLOCK}]

CREATE USER creates an Oracle user account.

IDENTIFIED BY specifies how the user will be authenticated to the database. BY *password* indicates that the user will be authenticated by password; EXTERNALLY indicates that the user will be authenticated by the operating system; and GLOBALLY indicates that the user will be authenticated by an Oracle security service.

The DEFAULT TABLESPACE clause specifies the tablespace in which objects created by the user will be placed by default.

The TEMPORARY TABLESPACE clause specifies the tablespace in which temporary segments generated during certain SQL calls will be stored.

The QUOTA clauses specify the maximum space utilization allowed within the nominated tablespaces.

PROFILE specifies a profile—created by the CREATE PROFILE statement—that is to be applied to the user.

8.0+   DEFAULT ROLE nominates certain roles—created by the CREATE ROLE command —that are active for the user by default. Other roles may need to be activated by the SET ROLE command.

8.0+   PASSWORD EXPIRE indicates that the user will be created with an expired password. The password will need to be changed before the user can log in.

8.0+   ACCOUNT LOCK creates the account in a locked or disabled state. It must be activated by the ALTER USER statement before the user can log in.

Data Definition Language (DDL)

DDL Clause Description *(Continued)*

CREATE VIEW	CREATE [OR REPLACE] [[NO] FORCE] VIEW *view_name*
	 [(*column_aliases*)]
	 [OF *object_type*
	     [WITH OBJECT OID {<u>DEFAULT</u>|(*attribute*)}]]
	 AS *query*
	 [WITH {READ ONLY|CHECK OPTION
	         [CONSTRAINT *constraint_name*]}]

CREATE VIEW creates a database view based on the specified *query*.

FORCE indicates that the *query* should be created even if there are errors in it.

Column_aliases specify the names of the columns in the resulting view. If not specified, then column names are taken from the names of columns in the *query*.

8.0+   OF *object_type* defines the view as an object view, that takes the appearance of an object table. WITH OBJECT OID defines the source of the *object identifier* (OID), which will be defined for each row of the view. DEFAULT indicates that the OID will be based on the OID of the object table or object view used in the query. *Attribute* nominates a particular column in the query whose row will be used as the source of the OID.

WITH READ ONLY stipulates that the view may not be modified. WITH CHECK OPTION stipulates that the view may be modified but only such that modified, or new rows would still be eligible to appear in the view. CONSTRAINT names the constraint that is created to support the CHECK OPTION.

DATAFILE	DATAFILE *filename filesize* [REUSE]
	         [AUTOEXTEND {<u>OFF</u>|ON [NEXT *next_size*]
	         [MAXSIZE {UNLIMITED |*max_size*}] }]
	 [, *filename*....]

DDL Clause Description *(Continued)*

DATAFILE (CONT.)	The DATAFILE clause is used in the CREATE DATABASE, CREATE CONTROLFILE, and ALTER DATABASE statements to define one or more data files to be added to the database.

Filename specifies the path and name of the data file to be added. *Filesize* indicates the size of the file, suffixed by "M" or "K," to indicate megabytes or kilobytes.

REUSE indicates that an existing file may be reused.

AUTOEXTEND controls the ability of files to expand past their initial size if additional space is required. The default is OFF, in which case data files do not extend. If set to ON, then files will extend by the NEXT size until MAXSIZE is reached or—if UNLIMITED is specified—indefinitely. |
| **DEALLOCATE UNUSED** | DEALLOCATE UNUSED [KEEP *keep_size* {K\|M}]

DEALLOCATE UNUSED can be specified in the ALTER INDEX, ALTER TABLE, ALTER SNAPSHOT, ALTER MATERIALIZED VIEW, ALTER CLUSTER, and partition maintenance statements to remove unused segment space above the high-water mark.

The KEEP clause specifies the amount of storage above the high-water mark that should not be deallocated. |
| **DISASSOCIATE STATISTICS**

8i | DISASSOCIATE STATISTICS FROM
{COLUMNS *column_list*\|
FUNCTIONS *function_list*\|
PACKAGES *package_list*\|
TYPES *type_list*\|
INDEXES *index_list*\|
INDEXTYPES *index_type_list*}
[FORCE] |

Data Definition Language (DDL)

DDL Clause Description *(Continued)*

DISASSOCIATE STATISTICS (CONT.)	DISASSOCIATE STATISTICS removes the association between user-defined optimizer statistics and the specified objects. See ASSOCIATE STATISTICS for more details.
	FORCE allows the disassociation to succeed even if optimizer statistics have been collected since the ASSOCIATE STATISTICS command was issued.
DROP CLUSTER	DROP CLUSTER *cluster_name* [INCLUDING TABLES] [CASCADE CONSTRAINTS]
	DROP CLUSTER drops a cluster created by the CREATE CLUSTER statement.
	INCLUDING TABLES drops any tables contained in the cluster.
	CASCADE CONSTRAINTS drops any constraints that refer to tables in the cluster.
DROP CONTEXT 8i	DROP CONTEXT *context_namespace*
	DROP CONTEXT drops a namespace created by the CREATE CONTEXT command.
DROP DATABASE LINK	DROP [PUBLIC] DATABASE LINK *database_link_name*
	DROP DATABASE LINK drops a database link created by the CREATE DATABASE LINK statement.
DROP DIMENSION 8i	DROP DIMENSION *dimension_name*
	DROP DIMENSION drops a dimension created by the CREATE DIMENSION command.
DROP DIRECTORY 8.0+	DROP DIRECTORY *directory_name*
	DROP DIRECTORY drops a directory created by the CREATE DIRECTORY statement.

DDL Clause Description *(Continued)*

DROP FUNCTION	DROP FUNCTION *function_name* [FORCE]
8i	DROP FUNCTION drops a function created by the CREATE FUNCTION statement.
	FORCE allows the function to be dropped even if there are dependent *functional indexes* that rely on the function. The function must have been created with the DETERMINISTIC option.
DROP INDEX	DROP INDEX *index_name* [FORCE]
8i	DROP INDEX drops an index created by the CREATE INDEX statement.
	FORCE allows a domain index to be dropped, even if its index type is invalid or the index is marked for loading.
DROP INDEXTYPE	DROP INDEXTYPE *indextype_name* [FORCE].
	DROP INDEXTYPE drops an index type created by the CREATE INDEXTYPE command.
8i	FORCE allows the index type to be dropped even if there are dependent domain indexes.
DROP LIBRARY	DROP LIBRARY *library_name*
8.0+	DROP LIBRARY drops a library created by the CREATE LIBRARY statement.
DROP MATERIALIZED VIEW	DROP MATERIALIZED VIEW *materialized_view*
	DROP MATERIALIZED VIEW drops a materialized view created by the CREATE MATERIALIZED VIEW statement.
8i	
DROP MATERIALIZED VIEW LOG	DROP MATERIALIZED VIEW LOG ON *table_name*
	DROP MATERIALIZED VIEW LOG drops a materialized view log created by the CREATE MATERIALIZED VIEW LOG statement.
8i	

Data Definition Language (DDL)

DDL Clause Description *(Continued)*

DROP OPERATOR	DROP OPERATOR *operator_name* [FORCE]
8i	DROP OPERATOR drops an operator created by the CREATE OPERATOR command.
	FORCE allows the operator to be dropped even if there are dependent objects that reference the operator.
DROP OUTLINE	DROP OUTLINE *outline_name*
	DROP OUTLINE drops an outline created by the CREATE OUTLINE command.
DROP PACKAGE	DROP PACKAGE [BODY] *package_name* [FORCE]
8i	DROP PACKAGE drops a package header or body.
	BODY indicates that the package body is to be dropped. Otherwise, the package header is dropped.
	FORCE allows the packages to be dropped even if there are dependent *functional indexes* that rely on functions in the package. The function must have been created with the DETERMINISTIC pragma.
DROP PROCEDURE 8i	DROP PROCEDURE *procedure_name* [FORCE] DROP PROCEDURE drops a procedure created by the CREATE PROCEDURE statement.
	FORCE allows the function to be dropped even if there are dependent *functional indexes* that rely on the procedure. The procedure must have been created with the DETERMINISTIC pragma.
DROP PROFILE	DROP PROFILE *profile_name* [CASCADE]
	DROP PROFILE drops a profile created by the CREATE PROFILE statement.
	CASCADE allows the profile to be dropped even if it is currently assigned to users.

DDL Clause Description *(Continued)*

DROP ROLE	DROP ROLE *role_name*
	DROP ROLE drops a role created by the CREATE ROLE statement.
DROP ROLLBACK SEGMENT	DROP ROLLBACK SEGMENT *rollback_segment_name*
	DROP ROLLBACK SEGMENT drops a rollback segment created by the CREATE ROLLBACK SEGMENT statement.
DROP SEQUENCE	DROP SEQUENCE *sequence_name*
	DROP SEQUENCE drops a sequence created by the CREATE SEQUENCE statement.
DROP SNAPSHOT	DROP SNAPSHOT *snapshot_name*
	DROP SNAPSHOT drops a snapshot created by the CREATE SNAPSHOT statement.
DROP SNAPSHOT LOG	DROP SNAPSHOT LOG ON *table_name*
	DROP SNAPSHOT LOG drops a snapshot log created by the CREATE SNAPSHOT LOG statement.
DROP SYNONYM	DROP [PUBLIC] SYNONYM *synonym_name*
	DROP SYNONYM drops a synonym created by the CREATE SYNONYM statement.
DROP TABLE	DROP TABLE *table_name* [CASCADE CONSTRAINTS]
	DROP TABLE drops a table created by the CREATE TABLE statement.
	CASCADE CONSTRAINTS causes any constraints that reference the table to be deleted.

Data Definition Language (DDL)

DDL Clause Description *(Continued)*

DROP TABLESPACE	DROP TABLESPACE *tablespace_name* [INCLUDING CONTENTS] [CASCADE CONSTRAINTS] DROP TABLESPACE drops a tablespace created by the CREATE TABLESPACE statement. INCLUDING CONTENTS allows the tablespace to be dropped even if objects still exist in the tablespace. CASCADE CONSTRAINTS causes any constraints that reference the tablespace to be deleted as a result of INCLUDING CONTENTS.
DROP TRIGGER	DROP TRIGGER *trigger_name* DROP TRIGGER drops a trigger created by the CREATE TRIGGER statement.
DROP TYPE 8.0+	DROP TYPE [BODY] *type_name* [FORCE] DROP TYPE drops a type or type body created by the CREATE TYPE or CREATE TYPE BODY statement. BODY indicates that the type body will be dropped. FORCE allows the type to be dropped, providing the type was created with the REPEATABLE pragma.
DROP USER	DROP USER *user_name* [CASCADE] DROP USER drops a user created by the CREATE USER statement. CASCADE drops all objects owned by the user before dropping the user. This allows a user to be dropped even if it owns objects.
DROP VIEW	DROP VIEW *view_name* DROP VIEW drops a view created by the CREATE VIEW statement.

DDL Clause Description *(Continued)*

EXCHANGE PARTITION
 	
8.0+
	EXCHANGE PARTITION *partition_name* WITH TABLE *table_name*
	  [{INCLUDING|EXCLUDING} INDEXES]
	  [{WITH|WITHOUT } VALIDATION]
	  [EXCEPTIONS INTO *exceptions_table*]
	
	EXCHANGE PARTITION transfers the rows in *table_name* into *partition_name* and vice versa. This clause may be specified in ALTER TABLE, ALTER INDEX, ALTER MATERIALIZED VIEW, and ALTER SNAPSHOT statements.
	
	INCLUDING INDEXES indicates that indexes on the partition and table are also to be converted. EXCLUDING INDEXES causes the indexes to be marked as unusable.
	
	WITH VALIDATION indicates that Oracle should check that the rows being transferred from table to partition match the range restriction for that partition.
	
	EXCEPTIONS indicates that any rows violating a unique constraint within the partition should be stored in the specified *exceptions_table*, which is created with the UTLEXCPT1.SQL script, which is included in the Oracle distribution.

EXCHANGE SUBPARTITION
 	
8i
	EXCHANGE SUBPARTITION *subpartition_name*
	  WITH TABLE *table_name*
	  [{INCLUDING|EXCLUDING} indexes]
	  [{WITH|WITHOUT } VALIDATION]
	  [EXCEPTIONS INTO *exceptions_table*]
	
	EXCHANGE SUBPARTITION transfers the rows in *table_name* into *subpartition_name* and vice versa. This clause may be specified in ALTER TABLE, ALTER INDEX, ALTER MATERIALIZED VIEW, and ALTER SNAPSHOT statements.
	
	INCLUDING INDEXES indicates that indexes on the sub-partition and table are also to be converted. EXCLUDING INDEXES causes these indexes to be marked as unusable.
	
	WITH VALIDATION indicates that Oracle should check that the rows being transferred from table to sub-partition match the any range restriction that exists for the partition that contains the sub-partition concerned.

Data Definition Language (DDL)

DDL Clause Description *(Continued)*

GRANT	GRANT { {*system_privileges*|*role_names*} | {*Object_privileges*|ALL} ON { [DIRECTORY] *object_name*} } TO {*users*|*roles*|PUBLIC} [WITH ADMIN OPTION]

The GRANT statement endows a user or role with the specified *system_privileges*, which are privileges associated with a role, or privileges on a nominated object.

System_privileges is a comma-separated list of system privileges as specified in Table 4-3. *Role_names* is a comma-separated list of roles as created by the CREATE ROLE statement.

If used in conjunction with the ON clause, GRANT confers the specified *object_privileges* on the specified object. The object may be a table, view, materialized view, snapshot, stored PL/SQL program, library, directory, or a synonym of any of these. If the object is a directory, then the DIRECTORY keyword must be specified.

Object_privileges define a list of object privileges that can be any of the following: ALTER, DELETE, EXECUTE, INDEX, INSERT, REFERENCES, SELECT, and UPDATE.

The WITH ADMIN OPTION clause allows the recipient of the grant to grant the privilege to others.

INITRANS	INITRANS *initrans_value*

INITRANS specifies the number of transaction slots to be created in each new data block. The number of transaction slots can limit the number of row-level locks that can be applied within a block. Values higher than default values can be appropriate for large block sizes, especially if the block is likely to approach PCTFREE during the initial data load. INITRANS may be specified for tables, snapshots, materialized views, and clusters.

DDL Clause Description *(Continued)*

LOB 8.0+	**LOB** (*lob_list*) STORE AS ([*segment_name*] [TABLESPACE *tablespace_name*] [{ENABLE|DISABLE} STORAGE IN ROW] [STORAGE *storage_clause*] [CHUNK *chunk_size*] [PCTVERSION *pct_version_percent*] [{CACHE | NOCACHE {LOGGING|NOLOGGING}] [INDEX *index_name physical_attributes*] The LOB clause is used to define storage for large objects (LOBs) in tables and partitions. *Lob_list* may name one or more LOB columns. *Segment_name* defines the name of the segment in which the LOB data will be stored. This can only be specified if *lob_list* contains a single item only. TABLESPACE defines the tablespace that contains the LOB data. DISABLE STORAGE IN ROW indicates that LOB data should always be stored outside the table or partition containing the LOB. This clause only applies to LOBs under 4K, since LOBs over 4K are always stored outside the table. STORAGE specifies storage attributes for the LOB segment. See the PHYSICAL ATTRIBUTES entry in this table for more details. CHUNK specifies the minimum size of LOB reads and writes. The value should be a multiple of the block size and less than the initial or next extent size. PCTVERSION specifies the percentage of LOB storage to be maintained for read consistency purposes.

Data Definition Language (DDL)

DDL Clause Description *(Continued)*

LOB (CONT.)	CACHE|NOCACHE determines if LOB data will be cached in Oracle shared memory. If NOCACHE is specified, then NOLOGGING—which suppresses redo logging of LOB modifications—may also be specified.

INDEX allows the name and storage characteristics of the automatically created LOB index to be specified. |
| **LOGFILE** | LOGFILE [GROUP *group_no* ( ]
  filename filesize [REUSE] [*,filename* ...] [)] [*filesize*]
  [GROUP ....]

The LOGFILE clause is used in the CREATE DATABASE, CREATE CONTROLFILE, and ALTER DATABASE statements to define one or more *redo log members* or *redo log groups* to be added to the database.

The GROUP keyword allows multiple identical redo logs to be defined. Oracle will ensure that each redo log file in a group is an exact copy of the other redo log file. If GROUP is omitted, each *filename* specified implicitly creates a group with a single member.

Filename specifies the path and name of the redo log file to be created. *Filesize* specifies the size of each file, suffixed by M or K to indicate megabytes or kilobytes. Since all redo logs in a redo log group must be the same size, the *filesize* is specified after the GROUP clause, if one is specified.

REUSE indicates that an existing file may be reused. |
| **MAXTRANS** | MAXTRANS *maxtrans_value*

MAXTRANS specifies the maximum number of transaction slots that can exist in a data block. The number of transaction slots can limit the number of row-level locks that can be applied within the block. MAXTRANS may be specified for tables, snapshots, materialized views, and clusters. |

DDL Clause Description *(Continued)*

MERGE PARTITIONS	MERGE PARTITIONS *partition1, partition2*
	INTO PARTITION *new_partition_name*
8.0+	*new_partition_attributes*
	MERGE PARTITIONS creates a new partition that has all rows from and replaces *partition1* and *partition2*. If the partitions are range-based partitions, then they must be adjacent.
	See the PARTITION entry in this table for partition specifications.
MODIFY DEFAULT ATTRIBUTES	MODIFY DEFAULT ATTRIBUTES
	[FOR PARTITION *partition_name*]
	[*physical_attributes*]
	[{LOGGING|NOLOGGING}]
8.0+	[COMPRESS *compress_columns*]
	[LOB *lob_storage*]
	[PCTTHRESHOLD *pct_thold*]
	[OVERFLOW *overflow_physical_attributes*]
	MODIFY DEFAULT ATTRIBUTES modifies the default attributes that apply to a partitioned table or index.
8i	FOR PARTITION applies the defaults to sub-partitions of the specified partition.
	Physical_attributes specifies storage location and configuration (see the PHYSICAL ATTRIBUTES entry in this table).
	LOGGING determines whether direct mode insert into the partition will be recorded in the redo logs.
	COMPRESS defines index key compression for indexes and index-only tables. See CREATE INDEX for more details.
	LOB defines LOB storage for the partition. See the LOB clause in this table for more details.
	PCTTHRESHOLD and OVERFLOW apply to index-organized tables. See CREATE TABLE for more details.

Data Definition Language (DDL)

DDL Clause Description *(Continued)*

MODIFY PARTITION
 	
8.0+
	MODIFY PARTITION *partition_name*
	    [*physical_attributes*]
	    [{LOGGING|NOLOGGING}]
	    [ALLOCATE EXTENT *Allocate_extent_clause*]
	    [DEALLOCATE UNUSED *deallocate_unused_clause*]
	    [COALESCE [SUBPARTITION] [*parallel_clause*]]
	    [[REBUILD] UNUSABLE LOCAL INDEXES]
	    [ADD SUBPARTITION *subpartition_name*
	        [TABLESPACE tablespace_name]
	        [*lob_storage_clause*]
	        [PARALLEL *parallel_clause*]]
	    [UNUSABLE]]

MODIFY PARTITION changes the attributes of the named partition.

Physical_attributes specifies storage location and configuration (see the PHYSICAL ATTRIBUTES entry in this table).

NOLOGGING specifies that direct mode insert operations into the partition will not be recorded in the redo logs.

The ALLOCATE EXTENT clause adds a new extent to the partition (see ALLOCATE EXTENT).

The DEALLOCATE UNUSED clause frees unused storage (see DEALLOCATE UNUSED).

8i   If the partition belongs to an index, COALESCE causes Oracle to merge index leaf blocks where possible. If the SUBPARTITION clause is specified, Oracle will merge one sub-partition with the remaining partitions.

8i   ADD SUBPARTITION adds a new hash sub-partition to the partition. The TABLESPACE and LOB storage details (see the LOB entry in this table) may be specified. The redistribution of hash values may be performed in parallel by specifying the PARALLEL clause.

DDL Clause Description *(Continued)*

MODIFY PARTITION (CONT.) 8i	UNUSABLE LOCAL INDEXES makes all local indexes of the partition unusable. If REBUILD is specified, the unusable indexes are rebuilt.
8i	The UNUSABLE clause marks the partition as unavailable.

MODIFY SUBPARTITION 8i	MODIFY SUBPARTITION *subpartition_name*
	    [ALLOCATE EXTENT *allocate_extent_clause*]
	    [DELETE UNUSED *delete_unused_clause*]
	    [LOB *lob_storage_parameters*]
	    [[REBUILD] UNUSABLE LOCAL INDEXES]
	
	MODIFY SUBPARTITION modifies the characteristics of the named sub-partition. It may be included in ALTER TABLE, ALTER INDEX, ALTER MATERIALIZED VIEW, and ALTER SNAPSHOT statements.
	
	The ALLOCATE EXTENT clause adds a new extent to the sub-partition (see ALLOCATE EXTENT).
	
	The DEALLOCATE UNUSED clause frees unused storage (see the DEALLOCATE UNUSED entry in this table).
	
	The LOB clause alters LOB storage details (see the LOB entry in this table for details).
	
	UNUSABLE LOCAL INDEXES makes all local indexes of the sub-partition unusable. If REBUILD is specified, the unusable indexes are rebuilt.

NOAUDIT	NOAUDIT {*audit_options*}
	    [ON {*object_name*|DIRECTORY *directory_name*|DEFAULT}]
	    [BY {*user_list*|*proxy_clause*}]
	    [BY {<u>SESSION</u>|ACCESS} [WHENEVER [NOT] SUCCESSFUL]
	
	NOAUDIT suppresses auditing that was enabled by the AUDIT statement. See the AUDIT statement for a description of clauses and options.

Data Definition Language (DDL)

DDL Clause Description *(Continued)*

PARALLEL	{NOPARALLEL|PARALLEL([*degree_of_parallelism*])}

The PARALLEL clause specifies the default level of parallel processing for an object. The default, NOPARALLEL, prevents any default parallel processing of the object (although parallelism can still be invoked via a hint). PARALLEL without a *degree_of_parallelism* indicates that parallel processing should take place using the default *degree_of_parallelism*. Otherwise, *degree_of_parallelism* can be used to specify a particular level of parallelism.

PARTITION
 	
8.0+
	PARTITION [BY RANGE (*partition_column_list*)]
	 [(PARTITION *partition_name*
	   VALUES LESS THAN *value*
	    [*physical_attributes*]
	    [*lob_storage*] [*varray_storage*]
	    [SUBPARTITIONS *subpartition_number*
	     [STORE IN (*tablespace_list*)]]
	    [(SUBPARTITION *subpartition_name*
	      TABLESPACE *tablespace_name*
	      [*lob_storage*]
	      [,SUBPARTITION *subpartition_name* ...])]
	   [PARTITION *partition_name* ...])]
	 [SUBPARTITION BY HASH (*column_list*)]
	   [SUBPARTITIONS *subpartition_number*
	     [STORE IN (*tablespace_list*)]]
	  [BY HASH (*partition_column_list*)
	   {PARTITIONS *partition_count*
	     [STORE IN (*tablespace_list*)] |
	    (PARTITION *partition_name*
	      [TABLESPACE *tablespace_name*]
	      [*lob_storage*] [,PARTITION *partition_name* ...])}

The PARTITION clause is used to define the partitioning of tables and indexes.

BY RANGE indicates that partitioning will be based on value ranges of the *partition_column_list*.

DDL Clause Description *(Continued)*

PARTITION (CONT.)	The PARTITION *partition_name* VALUE LESS THAN clause identifies the value ranges and storage details for an individual partition. Each partition may be assigned a tablespace and distinct physical attributes (see the PHYSICAL ATTRIBUTES entry in this table).
8i	Each partition may specify distinct storage for LOB and VARRAY datatypes. See the LOB and VARRAY entries in this table for more details.
8i	The STORE IN clause can be used to assign a list of tablespaces to a PARTITION or SUBPARTITION clause. This removes the necessity to specify individual partition or sub-partition details.
8i	BY HASH indicates that the object is to be partitioned by the hash value of the *partition_column_list*. This should either be accompanied by a PARTITION *partition_count* clause to specify the number of partitions, or by a list of PARTITION clauses which define each partition.
8i	BY RANGE partitions in Oracle8i may be sub-partitioned BY HASH. Sub-partitions may be created for all partitions by including a SUBPARTITION BY HASH clause together with a SUBPARTITION *subpartition_number* clause to define the number of sub-partitions in each partition. Alternately, sub-partition clauses may be included within individual partition clauses to apply specific sub-partitioning schemes to individual partitions.

PARTITION MAINTENANCE CLAUSES **8.0+**	[DROP PARTITION *partition_name*]
	    [MODIFY DEFAULT ATTRIBUTES *default_attribute_clause*]
	    [MODIFY PARTITION *partition_name*
	        partition_modifications]
	    [MODIFY SUBPARTITION *subpartition_name*
	        subpartition_modifications]
	    [RENAME {PARTITION|SUBPARTITION} *partition_name*
	    TO *new_partition_name*]
	    [SPLIT PARTITION *partition_name split_definition*]
	    [ADD PARTITION *partition_name partition_properties*]

Data Definition Language (DDL)

DDL Clause Description *(Continued)*

PARTITION MAINTENANCE CLAUSES (CONT.)	[TRUNCATE {PARTITION|SUBPARTITON} *name* [{DROP|REUSE} STORAGE] [MERGE PARTITIONS *merge_defintion*] [COALESCE PARTITION [PARALLEL *parallel_clause*]] [MOVE {PARTITION|SUBPARTITION} *partition_name partition_specifications*] [EXCHANGE {PARTITION|SUBPARTITION} *exchange_clause*] [{ENABLE|DISABLE} ROW MOVEMENT]

Partition maintenance clauses allow the configuration of partitions and sub-partitions to be altered. They can be specified in ALTER TABLE, ALTER INDEX, ALTER SNAPSHOT, and ALTER MATERIALIZED VIEW commands.

DROP PARTITION drops the specified partition.

MODIFY DEFAULT ATTRIBUTES changes the default attributes for new partitions and/or sub-partitions. See MODIFY DEFAULT ATTRIBUTES.

MODIFY PARTITION modifies the configuration of an exiting partition. See MODIFY PARTITION.

MODIFY SUBPARTITION modifies the configuration of an exiting sub-partition. See MODIFY SUBPARTITION.

RENAME PARTITION renames the partition.

SPLIT PARTITION splits an existing partition into two new partitions. See SPLIT PARTITION.

ADD PARTITION adds a range or hash partition to a partitioned table. For a range-based partition, the range specified must be above all currently specified ranges. See the PARTITION entry in this table for partition specifications.

DDL Clause Description *(Continued)*

PARTITION MAINTENANCE CLAUSES (CONT.)	TRUNCATE PARTITION and TRUNCATE SUBPARTITION remove all rows from the specified partition or sub-partition. DROP STORAGE indicates that all but the first extent allocated to the partition should be released. REUSE STORAGE indicates that all extents should be retained.
	MERGE PARTITION merges two existing partitions into a single new partition. See MERGE PARTITION.
	COALESCE PARTITION causes one partition of a hash-partitioned table to have its rows allocated to the remaining hash partitions and then deleted. This operation can be performed in parallel if the PARALLEL clause is specified.
	MOVE PARTITION and MOVE SUBPARTITION move the specified partition or sub-partition into a new segment. See the PARTITION entry in this table for a description of partition and sub-partition specifications.
	EXCHANGE PARTITION exchanges partitions or sub-partitions and tables. See EXCHANGE PARTITION and EXCHANGE SUBPARTITION.
	ENABLE ROW MOVEMENT permits updated rows to be relocated into another range-based partition, if appropriate. DISABLE ROW MOVEMENT causes updates that would cause rows to move to fail with an error.
PCTFREE	PCTFREE *pctfree_value*
	PCTFREE specifies the amount of space to reserve within a segments block for updates. *Pctfree_value* is expressed as a percentage. When a data or index block is *pctfree_value* full, no new rows will be added to the block. This ensures that some space is available to expand existing rows. In the case of a data block, rows may again be added when used space drops (by way of DELETEs) to PCTUSED. PCTFREE may be specified for tables, snapshots, materialized views, indexes, and clusters.

Data Definition Language (DDL)

DDL Clause Description *(Continued)*

PCTUSED	PCTUSED *pctused_value*
	PCTUSED specifies a threshold below which a data block will become eligible for inserts after having reached PCTFREE. PCTUSED may be specified for tables, snapshots, materialized views, and clusters.

PHYSICAL ATTRIBUTES	[PCTFREE *pctfree_value*]
	    [PCTUSED *pctused_value*]
	    [INITRANS *initrans_value*]
	    [MAXTRANS *maxtrans_value*]
	    [TABLESPACE *tablespace_name*]
	    [STORAGE (
	        [INITIAL *initial_size*]
	        [NEXT *next_size*]
	        [MINEXTENTS *minextents*]
	        [MAXEXTENTS {*max_extent_number*|UNLIMITED}]
	        [PCTINCREASE *pct_increase_amt*]
	        [FREELISTS *freelist_number*]
	        [FREELIST GROUPS *freelist_group_nbr*]
	        OPTIMAL *optimal_size*
	        BUFFER_POOL {KEEP|RECYCLE|DEFAULT})]

	PHYSICAL ATTRIBUTES is an expression for a group of clauses that define how a database object will be physically stored within the database. It can be included within CREATE or ALTER statements pertaining to tables, materialized views, snapshots, indexes, clusters, and rollback segments.
	Not all clauses are valid in all contexts. For instance, OPTIMAL is valid only for rollback segments, and TABLESPACE is usually only valid in CREATE statements and not in ALTER statements.
	Each clause is defined separately within this chapter.
RENAME	RENAME *old_object_name* TO *new_object_name*
	RENAME changes the name of a table, view, sequence, or private synonym.

DDL Clause Description *(Continued)*

REVOKE	REVOKE { {*system_privileges*|*role_names*}	{*Object_privileges*|all} ON { [DIRECTORY] *object_name*} } FROM {*users*|*roles*|PUBLIC} [CASCADE CONSTRAINTS] [FORCE]

REVOKE removes a permission previously conferred by the GRANT command. Most options are the same as those defined in the GRANT entry in this table.

CASCADE CONSTRAINTS drops any constraints that may have been created under the authority of a REFERENCES privilege.

FORCE allows a privilege to be revoked, even if this would invalidate stored programs or types that are dependent on the privilege. |
| **SET ROLE** | SET ROLE {*role_name* [IDENTIFIED BY *password*] [, *role_name*...] | ALL EXCEPT *role_list*| NONE }

SET ROLE controls the activation of roles for a session.

If one or more *role_names* are specified, then these will be activated. IDENTIFIED BY allows passwords for the roles to be provided, if necessary.

ALL EXCEPT activates all roles except those specified.

NONE disables all roles. |
| **SPLIT PARTITION**

8.0+ | SPLIT PARTITION *partition_name* AT (*split_value* [,*split_value*...]) INTO (*partition_specification, partition_specification*) [PARALLEL *parallel_clause*]

SPLIT PARTITION can be used in ALTER TABLE or ALTER INDEX statements to split a partition into two new partitions. |

Data Definition
Language (DDL)

DDL Clause Description *(Continued)*

SPLIT PARTITION (CONT.)	AT specifies the values of the partitioning columns, thus defining the point at which the partition will be split. A value should be provided for each of the partitioning columns. INTO defines the new partitions to be created. See the PARTITION entry in this table for the format of a partition specification.
STORAGE **8.0+**	STORAGE ([INITIAL *initial_size*] [NEXT *next_size*] [MINEXTENTS *minextents*] [MAXEXTENTS {*max_extent_number*|UNLIMITED}] [PCTINCREASE *pct_increase_amt*] [FREELISTS *freelist_number*] [FREELIST GROUPS *freelist_group_nbr*] OPTIMAL *optimal_size* BUFFER_POOL {KEEP|RECYCLE|DEFAULT}) The STORAGE clause is used to define disk storage characteristics for tables, materialized views, snapshots, indexes, clusters, and rollback segments. It can be included in ALTER or CREATE statements for these objects, and may appear in the DEFAULT STORAGE clause of a CREATE or ALTER TABLESPACE statement. INITIAL specifies the size of the initial (first) extent allocated to the segment. If no qualifier is specified, then the specified number of database blocks will be allocated. Otherwise, K or M may be used to denote kilobytes or megabytes. NEXT specifies the size of the second and subsequent extent. If no qualifier is specified, then the specified number of database blocks will be allocated. Otherwise, K or M may be used to denote kilobytes or megabytes. MINEXTENTS specifies the number of extents to be allocated to the object at creation.

DDL Clause Description *(Continued)*

STORAGE (CONT.)	MAXEXTENTS specifies the maximum number of extents to be allocated to the segment. The keyword UNLIMITED may be used to denote that there is no limit.

PCTINCREASE specifies the percentage by which the extent size is increased at each extent allocation. A value of 0 means that each extent allocation will be the same size. Other values cause each extent to be 100+*pct_increase_amt* percent larger than the previous extent.

FREELISTS specifies the number of *free lists* allocated to the segment. Free lists contain lists of blocks eligible for insert. Multiple free lists optimize concurrent inserts.

FREELIST GROUPS specify the number of free list groups to be allocated to the segment. Free list groups are used in Oracle parallel server to implement data segregation.

OPTIMAL specifies the optimal size for a rollback segment. Rollback segments may extend past this size if required, but will tend to shrink back toward the optimal value.

The BUFFER_POOL clause specifies which buffer pool within the *buffer cache* will be used to cache blocks read from this segment. |
| **SUBPARTITION** | See PARTITION. |
| **TABLESPACE** | TABLESPACE {*tablespace_name*|DEFAULT}

The TABLESPACE clause determines in which tablespace an object will be stored. The DEFAULT keyword indicates that the user's default tablespace should be used. |

Data Definition Language (DDL)

DDL Clause Description *(Continued)*

VARRAY	**VARRAY** *varray_name* STORE AS LOB *lob_storage_clause*
8i	The VARRAY clause specifies that varray data is to be stored in a LOB segment outside of the table containing the varray column.
	The VARRAY clause may appear in CREATE and ALTER statements for any segment that may contain a VARRAY type.
	See the LOB entry in this chapter for details of the *lob_storage_clause*.

5

PL/SQL Language

Introduction

The PL/SQL language implements Oracle's procedural extensions to the SQL language. PL/SQL is based on the ADA language, and implements looping, flow control, exception handling, modularity, and other features of a modern programming language. PL/SQL also supports object-oriented programming features such as encapsulation, overloading, and complex types. PL/SQL programs can be stored in the database, executed as stand-alone blocks, or associated with object methods.

This section provides an overview of PL/SQL program structure, datatypes, operators, functions, and keywords.

References

The *Oracle PL/SQL User's Guide and Reference* is the primary source of information for the PL/SQL language.

The *Oracle SQL Language Reference* contains details of the DDL statements used to create stored PL/SQL objects.

PL/SQL Block Structure

PL/SQL is a block-structured language. A PL/SQL block defines a unit of processing, which can include its own local variables, SQL statements, cursors, and exception handles. Blocks can be nested.

The simplest type of PL/SQL block is the *anonymous block,* which may be submitted to the PL/SQL engine from any client:

```
[DECLARE
     variable declarations ]
BEGIN
        program statements
[EXCEPTION
        WHEN exception THEN
             program statements .... ]
END;
```

Operators

PL/SQL supports the operators shown in Table 5-1.

Table 5–1 PL/SQL Operators

Operator	Description
:=	Assignment; assign an expression to a PL/SQL variable.
**	Exponentiation (raise to the power of).
NOT	Logical not.
*	Multiplication.
/	Division.
+	Addition.
-	Subtraction.
||	Concatenation.
IS NULL	Test for null value.
LIKE	Wildcard string comparison. Wildcards supported are "%" (match any string) and "_" (match any character).
BETWEEN	Test if a value is within a range.

Table 5–1 PL/SQL Operators *(Continued)*

Operator	Description
IN	Test if a value is included in a list of values.
AND	Logical and.
OR	Logical or.
=	Equals (comparison only; cannot be used to assign values).
<>, !=, ~=	Not equal to.
<	Less than.
>	Greater than.
<=	Less than or equal to.
>=	Greater than or equal to.

PL/SQL Functions

PL/SQL supports all the standard SQL functions (see Chapter 2, "SQL Expressions and Functions"), except for those noted below.

These functions may not be used in PL/SQL programs (but may be used within SQL statements that appear in PL/SQL programs):

- DECODE.
- VSIZE.
- DUMP.
- Group functions such as MIN, MAX, AVERAGE, SUM, and COUNT.

In addition, the following functions are available only in PL/SQL (these are described in the PL/SQL language reference within this chapter):

- SQLCODE and SQLERRM.
- Collection methods: COUNT, DELETE, EXISTS, EXTEND, FIRST, LAST, LIMIT, NEXT, PRIOR, and TRIM.

PL/SQL Language

PL/SQL Variables and Datatypes

PL/SQL supports the standard Oracle SQL datatypes, which were defined in Chapter 4, "Data Definition Language (DDL)." However, some standard datatypes behave differently within the PL/SQL environment:

- LONG datatypes in PL/SQL are limited to 32KB, whereas in Oracle, up to 2GB may be stored.
- In PL/SQL, CHAR, VARCHAR, and VARCHAR2 datatypes can store up to 32KB of information, whereas within the database, CHAR and VARCHAR types are limited to 255 and 2000 bytes, respectively.

PL/SQL also supports the following additional *scalar* (e.g., single-value) datatypes:

- The BINARY_INTEGER datatype is used to store signed 32-bit numbers (–2147483647 to 2147483647).
- PLS_INTEGER is similar to BINARY_INTEGER, but it allows for more efficient arithmetic.
- The BOOLEAN datatype accepts only true, false, or null values.

RecordTypes

PL/SQL supports composite datatypes, known as records. Records are an aggregation of named fields that may be of dissimilar datatypes. A record is defined as a type that contains multiple named fields, as follows:

```
TYPE type_name IS RECORD
    (field_declaration [,field_declaration]...);
```

Following the type definition, a variable of the record type may be defined. For instance, the following code declares a record type and a variable implementing the record:

```
TYPE my_record_type IS RECORD
    (mynumber NUMBER, myvarchar VARCHAR2(20), mydate DATE);
my_recode_variable my_record_type;
```

%TYPE and %ROWTYPE

A variable may be defined as being of the same datatype as a specific column. This is done by using the %TYPE keyword. For instance, the following example defines a variable as being of the same type as the column AMOUNT in the table SALES:

```
sales_amount    sales.amount%TYPE;
```

You can also define a record as being constructed of the same combination of column names and datatypes as a specific table. For instance, the following example defines a record that has fields that match the columns from the table SALES:

```
sales_record    sales%ROWTYPE;
```

Cursors

PL/SQL cursors are used to define SQL queries that will return more than one row. A PL/SQL cursor is a named query that may take parameters, as in the following example:

```
CURSOR dept_emp_csr (cp_dept_id NUMBER) IS
        SELECT *
          FROM EMPLOYEES
         WHERE department_id=cp_dept_id;
```

Cursors can be manipulated by the OPEN, FETCH, and CLOSE statements. A cursor FOR loop is also implemented, which automatically handles OPEN, FETCH, and CLOSE operations, performs an end-of-data check, and declares an implicit record to receive the cursor results. See FOR in the PL/SQL language reference in this chapter for more details.

Cursor Variables

A cursor variable is a pointer to a cursor result set. This variable is typically used to pass result sets as parameters between PL/SQL modules, or between PL/SQL modules and programs written in other languages such as OCI or JDBC.

A cursor variable is based on a REF CURSOR type, which is defined as follows:

```
TYPE CursorVariableType IS REF CURSOR
    [RETURN {table_or_cursor%ROWTYPE |
        table_or_cursor.column_name%TYPE |
        user_defined_record_type}];
```

If the RETURN keyword is specified, then the cursor variable may be associated only with a cursor that exactly matches the table, cursor, column, or record type specified (a "strongly-typed" cursor variable). Otherwise, if the RETURN keyword is omitted, then the cursor variable may be associated with a cursor of any type (a "weakly-typed" cursor variable).

PL/SQL Language

Once associated with a cursor variable type, a cursor variable becomes associated with a SQL statement through the OPEN ... FOR syntax, e.g.:

```
TYPE myCVtype IS REF CURSOR;

myCvar myCVtype;

OPEN myCvar FOR SELECT * FROM sales;
```

Cursor variables can be passed as parameters to procedures, which may then execute cursors against objects that they would not normally be able to access.

Collections and PL/SQL Tables

PL/SQL collections and tables allow for repeating groups of individual or composite datatypes. They are comparable to array structures in other languages.

Index-by tables are one-dimensional collections, each of which consists of a single PL/SQL datatype or record. Index-by tables are indexed by the datatype BINARY_INTEGER, which allows for 2^{32}, or approximately four billion elements . No limit on the number of elements is established when the table is created. Index-by tables are *sparse*: Elements may be allocated in any order, and unallocated elements do not consume storage.

Tables are created in two steps. First, TYPE is used to create the appropriate type. A variable is then declared as being of the specified type:

```
TYPE my_table_type IS TABLE OF NUMBER INDEXED BY BINARY_INTEGER;
my_table_variable my_table_type;
```

8.0+   Oracle8 collections—*nested tables* and varrays—have many properties in common with PL/SQL tables. However, nested tables and varrays can be stored in a database and can have member functions (methods).

Varrays consist of a fixed number of elements of a specific datatype. Unlike index-by tables, they are both *bounded* and *dense*. *Bounded* means that the number of elements that the varray can hold is limited by the maximum size declared when the varray type was defined. *Dense* means that all elements of the varray are initialized—even if an element is not used.

Varrays are created by using the CREATE TYPE statement, which can then be used in a variable declaration or CREATE TABLE statement.

---

1. However, because BINARY_INTEGER maps to a signed 32-bit number, half of the numbers are negative. The index range varies between -2147483647 and 2147483647.

```
CREATE OR REPLACE TYPE my varray_type AS VARRAY(100) OF NUMBER;
```

Oracle8 nested tables resemble traditional tables, but they can be stored within an Oracle8 column and used to create a PL/SQL datatype. Nested tables are *unbounded*—there is no limit to the number of elements that can be stored. When rows are initially added to the nested table, the nested table will be *dense*—there will be no gaps in nested table subscripts. However, if rows are deleted, gaps may appear in element subscripts and the table may become *sparse*.

Nested table types are created in two steps. The first statement defines a type that defines the nested table structure—this statement cannot be included in a PL/SQL program. The second statement creates a nested table from this type.

```
CREATE TYPE my_object_table_type as OBJECT
(
    item_number NUMBER,
    score NUMBER
);
CREATE TYPE my_nested_table_type AS TABLE OF my_object_table_type;
```

Scoping

PL/SQL identifiers can be referenced anywhere from within the block in which they are defined and from within any sub-block defined within the block. Sub-blocks may, however, define a local identifier of the same name as an identifier defined in the parent block, in which case, the local variable obscures the parent block's declaration.

Exceptions and Error Handling

Exceptions

Each PL/SQL block may contain an EXCEPTION section that defines actions to be taken should an error be encountered within the block. When an error is encountered and there is a corresponding exception handler defined in the current block, then the actions defined by the exception handler will be processed. If there is no appropriate handler defined within the block, then each enclosing block will be checked for an appropriate handler. If no enclosing block contains an appropriate exception handler, then the *unhandled exception* error will be raised.

Standard exceptions correspond to Oracle error codes, which are represented by the SQLCODE variable within PL/SQL. A full list of these codes can be found in the *Oracle Server Error Messages* manual. A number of pre-defined exceptions are provided by PL/SQL. Exceptions declared by the STANDARD package are defined in Table 5-2. Other supplied packages will define their own exceptions (using the EXCEPTION_INIT pragma).

Table 5–2 PL/SQL Built-in Exceptions

Exception Name	Sqlcode	Sqlerrm
DUP_VAL_ON_INDEX	0001	Unique constraint (*constraint_name*) violated
TIMEOUT_ON_RESOURCE	0051	Timeout occurred while waiting for resource
NO_DATA_FOUND	100	No data found
INVALID_CURSOR	1001	Invalid cursor
NOT_LOGGED_ON	1012	Not logged on
LOGIN_DENIED	1017	Invalid username/password; logon denied
SYS_INVALID_ROWID	1410	Invalid ROWID
TOO_MANY_ROWS	1422	Exact fetch returns more than requested number of rows
ZERO_DIVIDE	1476	Divisor is equal to zero
INVALID_NUMBER	1722	Invalid number
STORAGE_ERROR	6500	PL/SQL: storage error
PROGRAM_ERROR	6501	PL/SQL: program error
VALUE_ERROR	6502	PL/SQL: numeric or value error
ROWTYPE_MISMATCH	6504	PL/SQL: Return types of result set variables or query do not match

Table 5–2 PL/SQL Built-in Exceptions *(Continued)*

Exception Name	Sqlcode	Sqlerrm
CURSOR_ALREADY_OPEN	6511	PL/SQL: cursor already open
ACCESS_INTO_NULL	6530	Reference to uninitialized composite
COLLECTION_IS_NULL	6531	Reference to uninitialized collection
SUBSCRIPT_OUTSIDE_LIMIT	6532	Subscript outside of limit
SUBSCRIPT_BEYOND_COUNT	6533	Subscript beyond count

User-defined exceptions that associate a user-named exception with a specific Oracle error condition may be defined by using the EXCEPTION_INIT pragma. User-defined exceptions that are not associated with an Oracle error condition are created by the EXCEPTION keyword. These exceptions will only be raised explicitly if an appropriate RAISE command is issued.

Raise_application_error

PL/SQL programs may also raise exceptions that are not associated with Oracle error codes by use of the RAISE_APPLICATION_ERROR procedure. This procedure, which is actually part of the DBMS_STANDARD package, allows the user to indicate an application error, assign a SQLCODE of between –20000 and –20999, and generate an application-specific error message.

For example:

```
IF new_salary > max_salary THEN
        RAISE_APPLICATION_ERROR(-20101,
             'New salary exceeds maximum salary');
END IF;
```

PL/SQL Stored Objects

PL/SQL programs may be stored in the database in the following forms:

- A *stored procedure* is a named PL/SQL block that is stored in the database. The procedure may take arguments, but returns no value.
- A *stored function* is identical to a stored procedure except that it returns a value on completion.

PL/SQL Language

- A *package* is a group of one or more stored programs that are grouped together and usually share some common function or purpose. A *package specification* defines the public interface to these stored programs and to publicly accessible variables. The *package body* defines the internal logic of these public functions, as well as private variables and internal procedures and functions.
- A *member procedure* or *member function* is a PL/SQL procedure or function that implements a method for an Oracle8 object type.
- A *trigger* is a stored program that is executed when specific events occur. Prior to Oracle8i, these events were always DML on database tables, but from Oracle8i onward, triggers can also fire on DDL events or database-wide events such as startup or shutdown.

Stored programs are created by the CREATE PROCEDURE, CREATE FUNCTION, CREATE PACKAGE, and CREATE TYPE statements, which are defined in the PL/SQL language reference within this chapter.

Stored Procedure Parameters

A parameter declaration in PL/SQL consists of one or more specifications in the following format, separated by commas:

```
parameter_name [{IN|OUT|IN OUT}] [NOCOPY] datatype
[DEFAULT default_value]
```

The clauses IN, OUT, and IN OUT determine whether a value is passed into the stored program, out of the stored program, or can be passed both into and out of the stored program. OUT and IN OUT types allow the procedure to pass values back to the calling routine (as does the RETURN statement in a stored function).

8i   The NOCOPY keyword indicates that the return values for OUT and IN OUT parameters should be passed by reference (e.g., as a pointer to a memory location), rather than as copies of the relevant procedure variables. This improves performance for parameters that may be large structures or collections.

The DEFAULT clause assigns a default value to a parameter that is used if no value is specified when the stored program is called. This allows IN parameters to be omitted when the program is invoked.

When calling stored programs, parameters may be specified using *positional notation* or *named notation*. When using positional notation, parameters are specified in the order in which they appear in the program definition. When using named notation, parameters are specified in the format *"parameter_name => parameter_value,"* and may be specified in any order.

For example, given a procedure definition as follows:

```
create myproc( parm1 varchar2, parm2 varchar2)
```

the following calls illustrate positional notation and named notation, respectively:

```
myproc(parm1_value, parm2_value)

myproc(parm2 => parm1_value, parm1 => parm2_value)
```

Packages

Packages allow procedures, functions, variables, and cursors that share common or related functions to be stored in a single unit. Furthermore, packages allow encapsulation of internal subroutines and variables, and allow for the public interface to remain stable even if the underlying implementation changes.

The *package specification,* created by the CREATE PACKAGE statement, declares procedures, functions, cursors, and variables that are available to external routines. The *package body*—created by the CREATE PACKAGE BODY statement—contains the implementation of the public procedures and functions, together with internal and private programs and variables.

The "PL/SQL Language Reference" in this chapter contains details of the CREATE PACKAGE and CREATE PACKAGE BODY statements.

Triggers

Triggers are stored programs that are initiated when specified events occur within the database.

The following categories of triggers exist:

- DML triggers fire when an INSERT, UPDATE, or DELETE statement is executed against the nominated table.
- "Instead of" triggers fire when DML statements are executed against views.   **8.0+**
- DDL triggers fire when CREATE, ALTER, or DROP statements are executed against a schema.   **8i**

PL/SQL Language

8i

- Database event triggers fire whenever specified database events occur. These include startup, shutdown, server error, logon, and logoff.

Object Types

Object types are user-defined datatypes that may consist of composite datatypes or collections such as repeating groups or complex record types. Object types may be associated with member functions and procedures that are implemented in PL/SQL These modules implement the methods of the object type.

Although object types are created using DDL statements and cannot be declared within PL/SQL, the methods are implemented in PL/SQL and may invoke Java procedures or external C routines.

Forward Declarations

All modules must be declared before being referenced in packages. If necessary, a forward declaration of a procedure or function, which defines the arguments and return values but omits the implementation details, may precede the full definition of the module.

Overloading

Procedures or functions may be defined which share a common name, but that have argument lists that differ in the number or types of parameters. This technique, known as overloading, allows functions that share a common purpose, but that must operate on a range of datatypes, to be defined.

Execution Privileges

Prior to Oracle8i, stored program units would always be executed with the permissions of the user who created the program unit. This allowed stored procedures to bestow privileges to a user beyond those which were available through native SQL.

8i

Oracle8i allows stored programs to be executed either with the privileges of the program's creator or with those of the invoking user. This is controlled through the AUTHID clause of the CREATE PACKAGE, CREATE PROCEDURE, or CREATE FUNCTION statement.

PL/SQL Functions in SQL statements

Stored functions may be included within Oracle SQL statements, and are subject to the following certain restrictions:

- Functions in SQL statements cannot issue DDL or DML.

- Functions in DML statements cannot read the table being modified by the DML.

- Functions included within the WHERE clause cannot change package variables. Functions being executed in parallel or in remote SQL cannot read or modify package variables.

- Functions in SQL statements must not create or terminate transactions.

For stored functions that are not part of a package, these restrictions are checked at run-time. In Oracle7 and Oracle 8.0, functions that are part of a package should declare their compliance with these restrictions by using the RESTRICT_REFERENCES pragma (see the "PL/SQL Language Reference" in this chapter for details). In Oracle8i, the use of RESTRICT_REFERENCES is not necessary.

Transactions

PL/SQL programs follow the normal rules for Oracle transaction handling. A transaction is implicitly started by a DML or SET TRANSACTION statement. Transactions terminate when the COMMIT or ROLLBACK statement is encountered.

Autonomous Transactions

A PL/SQL program unit—other than a nested block—may execute within an *autonomous transaction*. An autonomous transaction executes independently of any transaction which may be in progress when the autonomous transaction program unit starts. A program unit is marked as being within the scope of an autonomous transaction by the AUTONOMOUS_TRANSACTION pragma.

PL/SQL Language

8i

SQL Statements

PL/SQL supports the following embedded SQL statements:

- SELECT statements that include the INTO keyword, or are defined within PL/SQL cursors.
- DML statements such as UPDATE, INSERT, DELETE, and LOCK.

Other SQL statements, in particular DDL statements such as CREATE, ALTER, GRANT, and others, are not directly available in PL/SQL. However, DDL statements may be executed indirectly in PL/SQL using one of the following options:

7.3+
- The DBMS_SQL package allows dynamic execution of any SQL statement. See Chapter 6, "Oracle-Supplied PL/SQL Packages," for details of DBMS_SQL.

8.0+
- The DBMS_UTILITY.EXEC_DDL_STATEMENT procedure allows any DDL statement to be executed dynamically.

8i
- The EXECUTE IMMEDIATE statement can be used to execute DDL and other dynamic SQL statements that are not queries.

PL/SQL language reference

This section defines PL/SQL language elements. In addition to the standard commands and clauses defined here, the STANDARD and DBMS_STANDARD packages define a number of procedures and functions that do not need to be qualified and which therefore may appear to be built-in. For instance, RAISE_APPLICATION_ERROR is not actually a PL/SQL built-in command, but rather a procedure in the DBMS_STANDARD package.

PL/SQL Language Elements

%FOUND	*cursorname*%FOUND
	%FOUND is a cursor attribute and must be appended to a cursor name. It returns true if the previous fetch against the cursor returned a row, false if the fetch returned no rows, and null if no fetch against the cursor occurred.

PL/SQL Language Elements *(Continued)*

%ISOPEN	*cursorname*%ISOPEN

%ISOPEN is a cursor attribute and must be appended to a cursor name. It returns true if the specified cursor is open and false otherwise.

%NOTFOUND	*cursorname*%NOTFOUND

%NOTFOUND is a cursor attribute and must be appended to a cursor name. It returns true if the previous fetch against the cursor returned a row, false if the fetch returned no rows, and null if no fetch against the cursor occurred.

%ROWCOUNT	*cursorname*%ROWCOUNT

%ROWCOUNT is a cursor attribute and must be appended to a cursor name. It returns the number of rows fetched from a cursor since the cursor was opened.

%ROWTYPE	*record_name cursor_or_table_name*%ROWTYPE

%ROWTYPE is used to define a record that conforms to the structure of a cursor or database table.

Record_name declares the record being defined. *Cursor_or_table_name* references the cursor or table from which the record will inherit its structure.

%TYPE	*variable_name* *cursor_or_table_name.column_name*%TYPE

%TYPE is used to define a record that conforms to the datatype of a cursor or table column.

Variable_name declares the variable being defined.

Cursor_or_table_name declares the table or cursor that contains the column.

Column_name declares the column within the table or cursor.

PL/SQL Language

PL/SQL Language Elements *(Continued)*

| AUTHID 8i | [CREATE OR REPLACE] {FUNCTION\|PROCEDURE\|PACKAGE} *object_name* [AUTHID {CURRENT_USER \| DEFINER}] IS ...

AUTHID is a clause used in the definition of a package, procedure, or function. It determines whether the module runs with the privileges of the user who defined the module or the permissions of the user who is running the module.

The default behavior (DEFINER) allows procedures to confer privileges to users which would otherwise not be available. The CURRENT_USER setting ensures that a procedure may only perform actions that the executing user is authorized to perform. |
| --- | --- |
| AUTONOMOUS_ TRANSACTION 8i | PRAGMA AUTONOMOUS_TRANSACTION

The AUTONOMOUS_TRANSACTION pragma indicates that a PL/SQL program unit (stored program, method, anonymous block, packaged module) will execute within an *autonomous transaction*. Autonomous transactions operate outside the scope of the parent transaction.

The AUTONOMOUS_TRANSACTION pragma is included in the declaration section of the PL/SQL program unit.

The program unit must explicitly commit or roll back the autonomous transaction before yielding control to the parent transaction. |
| BEGIN | BEGIN

The BEGIN statement marks the start of a block of program control statements. It could be the first statement in a PL/SQL block—if there are no variable declarations—but it will more commonly follow variable declarations that follow a DECLARE statement, or FUNCTION, PROCEDURE, or PACKAGE declaration. |

PL/SQL Language Elements *(Continued)*

BULK COLLECT 8i	RETURNING *column_spec* **BULK COLLECT** 　　　　　　INTO {*collection_name*|*host_array*} SELECT ... **BULK COLLECT** INTO {*collection_name*|*host_array*} BULK COLLECT instructs Oracle to use array processing when returning rows from an UPDATE, INSERT, or DELETE operation, or when using SELECT INTO (see RETURNING). Since multiple rows are returned in a single operation, the destination must either be one or more collections of the appropriate record structure—for instance, a nested table of a specific %ROWTYPE—or one or more host arrays.
CALL	**CALL** *routine_specification* INTO *bind_variable* Calls a routine from SQL. This is an SQL command, not a PL/SQL command. *Routine_specification* is the name of a procedure or function, possibly qualified by a package name. *Bind_variable* specifies the name of the bind variable that will receive the return value from a function.
CLOSE	**CLOSE** *cursor_name* The CLOSE statement closes an open cursor. The cursor must, of course, be open. Cursors should be closed when no further rows are to be retrieved. *Cursor_name* may refer to an explicit cursor or to a PL/SQL cursor variable.
COMMENTS	/* *comment_text* */ -- *comment_text* PL/SQL comments follow the conventions of SQL comments.

PL/SQL Language

PL/SQL Language Elements *(Continued)*

COMMENTS (CONT.)	Multi-line comments start with "/*" and conclude with "*/". Single-line comments start with "- -" and take effect until the end of the line.
COMMIT	COMMIT [WORK] [COMMENT *comment*] The COMMIT statement commits the current transaction, making all changes made by DML statements executed within the transaction permanent. It is equivalent to the SQL COMMIT statement. The WORK clause has no effect and is provided for compatibility purposes. *Comment* is a string literal that is useful for identifying in-doubt distributed transactions. Note that the FORCE clause, available in SQL, is not available in PL/SQL. See Chapter 3, "Data Manipulation and Transaction Control," for details of the COMMIT statement.
CONSTANT	*constant_name* CONSTANT *datatype* := *value* CONSTANT specifies that the variable declared may not be altered within the executable part of the PL/SQL program. The CONSTANT variable must be initialized when declared.
COUNT **8.0+**	*collection_name.* COUNT The COUNT method returns the number of elements in the specified collection.
CREATE FUNCTION	See FUNCTION.
CREATE PACKAGE (SPECIFICATION)	CREATE [OR REPLACE] PACKAGE *package_name* [AUTHID {CURRENT_USER	DEFINER}] {IS|AS} declaration_section END [*package_name*];

PL/SQL Language Elements *(Continued)*

CREATE PACKAGE (SPECIFICATION) (CONT.)	The CREATE PACKAGE statement creates a package specification. The package specification defines the public interface to the package. It defines the variables, cursors, procedures, and functions that can be accessed by calling programs.

The *declaration_section* can include the following types of declarations:

- User-defined types.
- Variables.
- Cursors.
- Functions.
- Procedures.
- PRAGMA declarations.

8i   AUTHID controls the execution privileges of the package. See the AUTHID entry in this table for more details.

CREATE PACKAGE BODY

```
CREATE [OR REPLACE] PACKAGE BODY package_name
       {IS|AS}
       declaration_section
    [BEGIN
       initialization_section]
    END];
```

The CREATE PACKAGE BODY statement creates a package body. A package body contains the implementations of the module specifications contained in the package specification, together with the implementations of internal subroutines, variables, types, procedures, and functions.

The *declaration_section* typically contains private variable definitions, cursor bodies, functions bodies, and procedure bodies—these declarations have scope only within the package body itself. The optional *executable_section* contains program statements that will be executed whenever the package is first accessed by a session.

PL/SQL Language

PL/SQL Language Elements *(Continued)*

CREATE PROCEDURE	See PROCEDURE.

CREATE TRIGGER (DATABASE EVENT)
 	
 8i
	CREATE [OR REPLACE] TRIGGER *trigger_name*
	   {AFTER|BEFORE}
	   {SERVERERROR|LOGON|LOGOFF|STARTUP|SHUTDOWN}
	     [OR {SERVERERROR| …}] …
	   ON {DATABASE | SCHEMA}
	   {*plsql_block*| CALL *module_name*}
	
	 In this context, CREATE TRIGGER defines statements to be executed when specified database events occur.
	
	 The AFTER and BEFORE keywords determine whether the trigger will fire before or after the specified event occurs.
	
	 The keywords SERVERERROR, LOGON, LOGOFF, STARTUP, and SHUTDOWN determine the event that will initiate the trigger.
	
	 ON DATABASE indicates that the trigger applies to the entire database. ON SCHEMA indicates that it applies to the current schema only.
	
	 CALL allows a stored PL/SQL program to be invoked when the trigger fires. If CALL is not specified, a pl/sql block must be declared.

CREATE TRIGGER (DDL)
 	
 8i
	CREATE [OR REPLACE] TRIGGER *trigger_name*
	   {BEFORE|AFTER }
	   {CREATE|ALTER|DROP}
	   ON {DATABASE | SCHEMA}
	   {*plsql_block*| CALL *module_name*}
	
	 In this context, CREATE TRIGGER defines statements to execute whenever an object is CREATEd, ALTERed, or DROPped.

PL/SQL Language Elements *(Continued)*

CREATE TRIGGER (DDL) (CONT.)	ON DATABASE indicates that the trigger applies to the entire database. ON SCHEMA indicates that it applies to the current schema only. CALL allows an external procedure to be invoked. Otherwise, a PL/SQL block must be declared.

CREATE TRIGGER (DML)	CREATE [OR REPLACE] TRIGGER *trigger_name*
	    {AFTER|BEFORE|INSTEAD OF}
	    {INSERT|UPDATE|DELETE [OR INSERT|UPDATE|DELETE ...] }
	    ON {*table*|*nested_table*|*view*}
	    [REFERENCING [OLD AS *old*] [NEW AS *new*]
	        [PARENT AS *parent*]]
	    [FOR EACH ROW]
	    [WHEN *condition*]
	    {*plsql_block*| CALL *module_name*}
	
	DML triggers fire when DML statements—INSERT, UPDATE, and DELETE—are executed on the specified table or view. The trigger may execute BEFORE the DML statement takes effect, AFTER the statement takes effect, or—in the case of views—may execute INSTEAD OF the DML statement.
	
	Triggers may be defined against a table, a nested table type, or a view. However, in the case of nested tables or views, only INSTEAD OF triggers are permitted.
	
	A trigger may fire once for all modified rows, or may be executed once FOR EACH ROW affected. In a FOR EACH ROW trigger, the old and new column values may be referenced, qualifying the column names with the prefixes specified by the OLD and NEW clauses. By default, these prefixes are "NEW" and "OLD".

8.0+   The REFERENCING PARENT clause is applicable to triggers on nested tables only. It allows the trigger to reference the columns in the parent row—the row that includes the nested table row being modified.

PL/SQL Language

PL/SQL Language Elements *(Continued)*

CREATE TRIGGER (DML) (CONT.)	The optional WHEN clause provides any additional conditions to satisfy before the trigger will fire. This prevents unnecessary processing of trigger code that is applicable to only a subset of the rows being modified. CALL allows an external procedure to be invoked. Otherwise, a PL/SQL block must be declared.

CREATE TYPE (SPECIFICATION)
 	
8.0+
	CREATE [OR REPLACE] TYPE *type_name*
	[IS|AS
	          OBJECT (*attributes*) |
	          TABLE OF *datatype* |
	          VARRAY(*limit*) OF [FIXED] *datatype*
	          [MAP|ORDER MEMBER *function_specification*]
	          [MEMBER *procedure_specification*|
	                    function_specification
	                    [MEMBER ....]]
	          [PRAGMA RESTRICT_REFERENCES
	          (*module_name, restrictions*) ...]]
	
	CREATE TYPE creates a *type specification*. The type specification specifies the type attributes and specifications for type methods. The implementation of the type methods are contained in the *type body*.
	
	Four categories of type specifications are defined:
	
	• An *incomplete type* contains no definition of the type other than its name. An incomplete type can serve as a forward declaration to allow the creation of interdependent types. The full type definition must be made before any objects that include the type are made valid.
	
	• The IS OBJECT clause denotes an *object type*, which is a user-defined combination of attributes.
	
	• The IS TABLE OF clause denotes a *nested table*, which is an unbounded, unordered collection of object types or scalar datatypes.

PL/SQL Language Elements *(Continued)*

CREATE TYPE (SPECIFICATION) (CONT.)	• The IS VARRAY clause denotes a fixed-sized, ordered collection of *scalar datatypes*. Object type *attributes* consist of any number of attribute names and datatypes. This specification is similar to that of the CREATE TABLE statement, except that check constraints, not null constraints or default clauses, are not permitted. Some datatypes, most notably long, rowid, and PL/SQL-specific datatypes, may not be used.
8i	For a VARRAY, *limit* defines the number of elements to be created. FIXED instructs Oracle to store numeric varrays as fixed-width numbers. The MAP function returns a scalar datatype, which can then be used for ordering object types. The MAP function takes no arguments (other than the implicit SELF parameter), and returns a NUMBER, DATE, or VARCHAR2 datatype. MEMBER procedures and functions define methods to be applied to the type. Normal procedure and function syntax applies. The ORDER clause defines a function that provides a way to compare the relative magnitude of two objects. The *order method* accepts a single parameter, which must be of the same object type as the object concerned. The body of the *order function* should implement the rules by which this object can be compared to the built-in object SELF. The order method must return –1, 0, or 1, indicating whether SELF should be regarded as less than, equal to, or greater than the other object.

CREATE TYPE BODY
 	
8.0+
	CREATE [OR REPLACE] TYPE BODY *type_name* IS|AS
	   [MAP|ORDER MEMBER *function_body*]
	   [MEMBER [LANGUAGE JAVA]
	   procedure_body|*function_body*
	     [MEMBER ....]]

PL/SQL Language Elements *(Continued)*

CREATE TYPE BODY (CONT.)	CREATE TYPE BODY creates a type body. A type body implements the member functions declared in the type header. The MAP function returns a scalar datatype, which can then be used for ordering object types. The MAP function takes no arguments (other than the implicit SELF parameter), and returns a NUMBER, DATE, or VARCHAR2 datatype.
8i	LANGUAGE JAVA allows a member body to be written in Java.

CURSOR	CURSOR *cursor_name* [*(cursor_parameters)*]
	        [RETURN *rowtype*]
	        [IS *select_statement*]
	
	The CURSOR statement creates a PL/SQL cursor, which defines a SQL query to be processed within the executable part of a PL/SQL program.
	
	The *cursor_parameters* clause defines query parameters for which the values must be provided when the cursor is OPENed. These parameters may be included within the query—typically as selection criteria within the WHERE clause. Cursor parameter syntax is similar to that for stored procedures, except that the parameters must be IN parameters only.
	
	The RETURN clause defines the structure of the rows returned by the query. This section is optional, but must be specified if no SELECT statement is included. A cursor without a select statement is referred to as a *cursor specification*. Each cursor specification will normally have a corresponding *cursor body*, which will typically be defined in the package body.
	
	The *select_statement* defines the SQL statement that is executed within the cursor.

PL/SQL Language Elements *(Continued)*

DECLARE	DECLARE
	    declarative_section
	BEGIN
	    executable_section
	END;
	
	DECLARE marks the start of the declarative section of an anonymous block. If used, it is the first statement in the anonymous block, although anonymous blocks may also be started by the BEGIN statement.

DELETE (COLLECTION METHOD) **8.0+**	*collection_name*.DELETE [({*element_number* | *start_element, end_element*})] The DELETE method is used to delete elements in a collection. If no elements are specified, all are deleted. Otherwise, a single element or a range of element numbers may be specified.
DELETE (SQL STATEMENT)	DELETE *delete_options* The DELETE statement has the same functionality and syntax in PL/SQL as in standard SQL. See Chapter 3, "Data Manipulation and Transaction Control," for further details.
END	END [{LOOP|IF}] END—without qualifiers—marks the end of a PL/SQL block such as an anonymous block, procedure, function, or package. When used with the LOOP or IF keywords, it marks the end of a LOOP or IF block.
EXCEPTION (DECLARATION)	*exception_name* EXCEPTION In a declarative block, the EXCEPTION keyword declares a user-defined *exception_name*. This exception can be raised either by use of the RAISE command within a PL/SQL program or by associating it with an Oracle error code with the EXCEPTION_INIT pragma.

PL/SQL Language Elements *(Continued)*

EXCEPTION (HANDLER)	BEGIN
	
	…
	
	EXCEPTION
	
	    WHEN *exception_name* THEN *statement_or_block;*
	    [WHEN …]
	
	END;
	
	The EXCEPTION statement indicates the start of an exception-handling block. This block contains clauses for dealing with error conditions.
	
	The WHEN clause defines the actions to be taken when the specified exception is encountered. A list of standard exception names can be found in Table 5-2. Additional exceptions may be defined by use of the EXCEPTION declaration keyword.
	
	Exception_name defines the exception to be matched. The special exception name OTHERS will match any exception that has not been matched in preceding WHEN statements.
	
	The WHEN clause may stipulate any legal PL/SQL statement, a PL/SQL block, or it may specify the NULL statement to indicate that the exception should be ignored.

EXCEPTION_INIT	PRAGMA EXCEPTION_INIT *(exception_name, error_number)* The EXCEPTION_INIT pragma associates an Oracle error code with a user-defined exception name. This exception name can then be used in the same way as predefined exceptions.

EXECUTE IMMEDIATE
 	
8i
	EXECUTE IMMEDIATE *sql_statement*
	    [INTO *variablelist_or_record*]
	    [USING *bind_varaible_values*]
	
	EXECUTE IMMEDIATE executes *sql_statement* dynamically. The *sql_statement* can be any SQL or PL/SQL block, but it may not be a multi-row query.

PL/SQL Language Elements *(Continued)*

EXECUTE IMMEDIATE (CONT.)	The *sql_statement* can contain bind variables—prefixed by ":"—values for which must then be provided in the USING clause. For single-row queries, the INTO clause must contain a compatible variable list or record.
EXISTS 8.0+	*collection_name*.EXISTS(*ItemNumber*) EXISTS returns true if the specified item in the collection exists and false otherwise.
EXIT	EXIT [*label_name*] [WHEN *condition*] EXIT is used to exit a loop. If no *label_name* is specified, then the current, innermost loop is terminated. If a *label_name* is specified, then the loop identified (immediately preceded by) by *label_name* is terminated. The WHEN clause can be used to specify the condition under which the loop will be terminated. *Condition* must evaluate to true or false.
EXTEND 8.0+	*collection_name*.EXTEND({*number_to_add* | *number_to_copy, element_to_copy*}) The EXTEND method adds elements to a collection. Either *number_to_add* null elements may be added, or *number_to_copy* copies of the *element_to_copy* element may be added.
FETCH 8i	FETCH *cursor_name* [BULK COLLECT] INTO *variables* FETCH retrieves one or more rows from an open cursor into PL/SQL variables or host bind variables. The BULK COLLECT clause allows batches of results to be returned to a host array or PL/SQL collection. In this case, a single FETCH statement retrieves all rows in the result set.

PL/SQL Language

PL/SQL Language Elements *(Continued)*

FETCH (CONT.)	*Variables* may be a list of PL/SQL scalar variables, a PL/SQL record, or (Oracle8i and above) a collection or host array (if BULK COLLECT is specified).
FIRST **8.0+**	*collection_name*.FIRST The FIRST method returns the subscript of the first element in a collection. For nested tables, FIRST might not return 1 if the DELETE method was used to delete elements.

FOR (CURSOR LOOP)	[*<<label_name>>*]
	FOR *record_name* IN
	    { *cursor_name*[(*cursor_parameter_values*)] |
	    (*select_statement*) } LOOP
	        statements
	END LOOP [*<<label_name>>*];
	
	The "cursor for loop" loops through each record in a cursor or SQL SELECT statement. The loop is terminated automatically and the cursor closed after the last row is retrieved.
	
	If the cursor was declared with cursor parameters, these must be specified in *cursor_parameter_values*.
	
	Record_name will be implicitly declared to the %ROWTYPE of the cursor or SQL statement. This implicit record cannot be referenced outside the loop.

FOR (ITERATIVE)	[*<<label_name>>*] FOR *index_variable* IN [REVERSE] *low_value..high_value* LOOP *statements* END LOOP [*<<label_name>>*]; The "iterative for loop" iterates through an integer range from *low_value* to *high_value*. The *index_variable* assumes the value of the current iteration. The iteration may proceed in reverse order, but the increment will always be either one or negative one (e.g., it is not possible to increment by a fraction or by numbers greater than one).

PL/SQL Language Elements *(Continued)*

FORALL

8i

FORALL *index_variable* IN *start_value* .. *end_value*
    sql_statement

FORALL specifies a range of elements in a collection that are to be used in a bulk bind. All elements that match the range specified by FORALL will be applied to the statement in question in a single operation. This is most useful when optimizing the performance of multi-row inserts.

Index_variable will be used in the SQL statement to refer to the collection elements to be bulk-processed.

The *sql_statement* can be an UPDATE, INSERT, or DELETE statement. In the case of an INSERT statement, the FORALL statement will typically be used to identify elements of a collection to be inserted. In the case of UPDATE and DELETE, FORALL will typically identify collection elements to be referenced in a WHERE clause.

FUNCTION

[CREATE [OR REPLACE]] FUNCTION *function_name*
    [*(parameter_list)*]
    RETURN *datatype*
    [DETERMINISTIC] [PARALLEL_ENABLE]
    [AUTHID {CURRENT_USER | DEFINER}]
    [IS
        [*declaration_section*]
    BEGIN
        executable_section
    [EXCEPTION
        exception_handlers]
    END]

PL/SQL functions can be created as stand-alone stored programs, or they can be included within PL/SQL packages. As stand-alone programs, stored functions are created by a CREATE FUNCTION statement. Within packages, the CREATE statement is not required.

PL/SQL Language

PL/SQL Language Elements *(Continued)*

FUNCTION (CONT.)	Functions may take any legal combination of parameters and may return any legal PL/SQL datatype.
	The function body—those sections including and following the IS keyword—may be omitted to create a *function specification*. A function specification can be used in a package header to define a public interface, or in a package body as a forward reference.
8i	DETERMINISTIC indicates that the function will always return the same result given the same inputs. Using DETERMINISTIC may improve performance of functions called within SQL, and also allows functions within materialized views that are enabled for query rewrite.
8i	PARALLEL_ENABLE indicates that a function can be executed in parallel when included in parallelized SQL statements.
8i	AUTHID controls the execution privileges of the package. See the AUTHID entry in this table for more details.
GOTO	GOTO *label*
	GOTO causes execution to branch immediately to the statement following the nominated *label*. The statement following *label* must be executable, must not be within an IF block or loop, and must be within the current block or an enclosing block.
IF	IF *condition* THEN *statements* [ELSEIF *condition* THEN *statements*...] [ELSE *statements*] END IF
	The IF statement allows conditional execution of program statements.
	Condition must be a boolean expression, resolvable only to true, false, or null.

PL/SQL Language Elements *(Continued)*

INSERT	INSERT *insert_clauses*

The INSERT statement in PL/SQL has the same syntax as in standard SQL. See Chapter 3 for detailed syntax.

INTO	See SELECT INTO.

LABEL	*<<label_name>>*

PL/SQL labels are names enclosed by "<<" and ">>". They may be placed directly before a PL/SQL block, LOOP statement, or executable statement.

When a loop is labelled, the label may be the target of an EXIT or GOTO statement. When preceding an executable statement, a label may be the target of GOTO statements.

LANGUAGE
 	
8.0+
	{FUNCTION|PROCEDURE} *module_name*
	     [(*parameters*)] [RETURN *datatype*] IS|AS
	       [EXTERNAL]
	         LANGUAGE {JAVA NAME *java_definition* |C
	           LIBRARY *library_name*
	           [NAME *c_language_name*]
	           [CALLING STANDARD C|PASCAL]
	           [WITH CONTEXT]
	           [PARAMETERS(*parameter_list*)] }

The LANGUAGE clause is used to indicate that the stored procedure is a wrapper for an external program. The program must exist within the shared library identified by the CREATE LIBRARY command.

The LANGUAGE clause identifies the language in which the external routine was written. Prior to Oracle8i, only LANGUAGE C was permitted. In Oracle8i, LANGUAGE JAVA is also permitted.

PL/SQL Language Elements *(Continued)*

LANGUAGE (CONT.) 8i	The JAVA NAME clause is used to define the Java implementation of an existing stored Java program. See Chapter 7, "Oracle Java," for examples of publishing Java stored procedures in this way.
8i	In Oracle8i, the EXTERNAL clause is optional. The LANGUAGE C statement is sufficient.

The LIBRARY clause identifies a shared library identifier defined by the CREATE LIBRARY command.

The NAME clause identifies the name of the C routine within the shared library. The default is the name of the stored program being created.

CALLING STANDARD is required only for Oracle 8.0 on Windows NT. It specifies the argument-calling standard under which the external program was compiled.

The WITH CONTEXT clause causes a context pointer to be passed to the calling program. This pointer gives the internal OCI routines in the external program access to information about the PL/SQL execution environment.

PARAMETERS map the external program's parameters to PL/SQL variables. Each parameter specification may be defined as follows:

```
{CONTEXT | SELF [{TDO | parameter_property}]
        | {parameter_name | RETURN}
    [parameter_property]
    [BY {VALUE|REFERENCE}] [external_datatype]
```

CONTEXT is a special parameter that contains context information required by the WITH CONTEXT clause.

The SELF parameter passes the implicit self argument of object methods.

PL/SQL Language Elements *(Continued)*

LANGUAGE (CONT.)	The RETURN parameter receives the return value for an external function.

Parameter_property defines the type of variable being defined. Valid types are:

{INDICATOR [{STRUCT|TDO}] |

LENGTH | MAXLEN|CHARSETID|

CHARSETFORM}

When no *parameter_property* is specified, then the parameter will contain the actual data being passed. INDICATOR parameters are used to identify null values. LENGTH and MAXLEN parameters store the maximum and minimum lengths of the parameter. CHARSETID and CHARSETFORM identify the character set of the parameter.

BY VALUE requires a copy of the parameter to be passed. BY REFERENCE passes the actual memory location of the parameter variable.

The *external_datatype* defines the datatype of the parameter in the terms of the program being called. For C programs, valid values include INT, FLOAT, DOUBLE, STRING, RAW, OCILOBLOCATOR, OCINUMBER, OCINUMBER, and OCIDATE.

LAST	*collection_name*.LAST
8.0+	The LAST method returns the index number of the last element in a collection.

LIMIT	*collection_name*.LIMIT
8.0+	The LIMIT method returns the maximum number of elements allowed in a collection. Because nested tables and by-index tables have no upper limit, this method is only appropriate for varray collections.

PL/SQL Language Elements *(Continued)*

LOCK TABLE	LOCK TABLE *table_name* IN *lock_mode* MODE [NOWAIT]
	The LOCK TABLE statement in PL/SQL has the same syntax as in standard SQL. See Chapter 3 for detailed syntax of the LOCK command.
LOOP (SIMPLE)	[*<<label_name>>*] LOOP 　　*statements* END LOOP [*<<label_name>>*];
	The simplest construction of the LOOP statement implements an infinite loop, which will only be terminated if an EXIT or GOTO statement is activated within the loop or if an exception is encountered.
	The loop may be preceded and followed by labels that could be the targets of EXIT or GOTO statements.
	The LOOP command is more commonly used in conjunction with the FOR or WHILE keywords, which define the conditions under which the loop will continue.
MAP	See CREATE TYPE.
MEMBER	See CREATE TYPE.
NEXT	*collection_name*.NEXT(*element_number*)
8.0+	The NEXT method returns the index of the element number that succeeds the specified element or null if there is no succeeding element.
NULL	NULL
	The NULL statement does nothing. It is useful in circumstances where a statement is required—for instance, within an IF block—but where there is no appropriate action.

PL/SQL Language Elements *(Continued)*

OPEN	OPEN *cursor_name*[(*cursor_parameter_values*)]

The OPEN statement activates the nominated cursor. Opening a cursor based on a query readies the cursor to return rows when the FETCH statement is executed.

If the *cursor_parameters* were defined when the cursor was defined (see CURSOR), then these must be specified in the OPEN statement.

OPEN FOR	OPEN *cursor_variable* FOR *select_statement* [USING *bind_variable_values*]

The OPEN FOR statement associates a *cursor variable* with a SELECT statement and opens the associated cursor.

The *select_statement* is a literal or variable containing the text of any valid SQL statement. However, the *select_statement* may not include the FOR UPDATE clause.

If the SQL statement contains bind variable placeholders (replacement variables prefixed by ":"), then values for these must be supplied in the USING clause.

ORDER	See CREATE TYPE.

PRAGMA	PRAGMA *pragma_definition*

PRAGMA is a compiler directive that influences the behavior of the compiled PL/SQL object. Four pragmas are currently available. Each has its own entry in this section:

RESTRICT_REFERENCES   Restrict module access to the database and/or package variables.

EXCEPTION_INIT   Associate an Oracle error code with a user-defined exception name.

PL/SQL Language

PL/SQL Language Elements *(Continued)*

PRAGMA 8i	AUTONOMOUS_TRANSACTION Run module within the scope of an autonomous transaction.
8.0+	SERIALLY_REUSABLE Make procedure memory global and reusable.

PRIOR

*Collection_name.*PRIOR(*element_number*)

8.0+

PRIOR returns the subscript of the collection element that precedes the specified element or null if there is no preceding element.

PROCEDURE

[CREATE [OR REPLACE]] PROCEDURE *procedure_name*
   [(*parameter_list*)]
   [AUTHID {CURRENT_USER | DEFINER}]
    [IS
     [*declaration_section*]
    BEGIN
     executable_section
    [EXCEPTION
     exception_handlers]
    END]

PL/SQL procedures can be created as stand-alone stored programs, or they can be included within PL/SQL packages. As stand-alone programs, stored procedures are created by a CREATE PROCEDURE statement. Within packages, the CREATE statement is not required.

Procedures may take any legal combination of parameters and may return any legal PL/SQL datatype.

The procedure body—those sections including and following the IS keyword—may be omitted to create a *procedure specification*. A procedure specification can be used in a package header to define a public interface or in a package body as a forward reference.

8i

The AUTHID clause determines the execution privileges for the procedure. See the AUTHID entry in this table.

PL/SQL Language Elements *(Continued)*

RAISE	RAISE *exception_name*

The RAISE statement causes the named exception to be immediately invoked. Program control then passes to the appropriate exception handler or, if no such handler has been defined, the unhandled exception error occurs and program execution ceases.

RAISE_ APPLICATION_ ERROR	RAISE_APPLICATION_ERROR(*error_no, error_text* [, *replace_tack*])

RAISE_APPLICATION_ERROR raises a user-defined error condition—one which is not associated with an Oracle error code.

Error_no is a user-defined number in the range –20000 to –20999.

Error_text is a user-defined text string.

Replace_stack is a Boolean value that indicates if the error should clear all other errors on the error stack (true) or if the stack should be preserved (false).

RECORD	See TYPE.

RESTRICT_ REFERENCES 8i	PRAGMA RESTRICT_REFERENCES ({DEFAULT | *module_name*}, {RNDS | WNDS | RNPS | WNPS} [,{RNDS | WNDS | RNPS | WNPS} ...] [TRUST])

The RESTRICT_REFERENCES pragma is used to notify Oracle of restrictions on a module's access to the database or to package variables. These restrictions are required to ensure that modules can be used safely in circumstances where database or package variable access would be illegal. In particular, functions that are to be used with SQL statements must not write to the database and cannot reference package variables from clauses such as GROUP BY.

PL/SQL Language Elements *(Continued)*

RESTRICT_ **REFERENCES** **(CONT.)** 8i	In Oracle8i, the RESTRICT_REFERENCES pragma is not required to allow a function to be called from PL/SQL. *Module_name* identifies the module to which the restriction applies. A specification for this module will have already been declared—usually within the same package or type header as the pragma. The restrictions that may be applied are: RNDS The module will not attempt to read from the database. WNDS The module will not attempt to update, insert, or delete rows. RNPS The module will not attempt to read package variables. WNPS The module will not attempt to update any package variables.
8i	The TRUST keyword indicates that the restrictions will not be enforced, but that other PL/SQL packages will "trust" the module not to violate the listed restrictions.
RETURN	RETURN [(*return_value*)] The RETURN statement terminates execution of a subprogram and returns control to the calling program. In procedures, the RETURN statement may not include a *return_value*. Within functions, the RETURN statement must include a *return_value*, and the datatype of the *return_value* must be compatible with the datatype specified in the RETURN clause within the FUNCTION declaration.

PL/SQL Language Elements *(Continued)*

ROLLBACK	ROLLBACK [WORK] [TO [SAVEPOINT] *savepoint_name]*

The ROLLBACK statement undoes all changes made in the current transaction. The usage of ROLLBACK in PL/SQL programs is equivalent to its usage in standard SQL.

SAVEPOINT	SAVEPOINT *savepoint_name*

SAVEPOINT identifies a rollback point within a transaction. Rollback statements can roll back to this savepoint as an alternative to rolling back the entire transaction. The usage of SAVEPOINT in PL/SQL programs is equivalent to its usage in standard SQL.

SELECT	SELECT *column_list* [BULK COLLECT] INTO *variable_list* *rest_of_sql_statement*

The SELECT statement in PL/SQL follows standard SQL syntax, but has two additional facilities:

The INTO clause specifies a list of variables to receive the results of the query. If the BULK COLLECT clause is not specified (Oracle8i+ only), then the SELECT statement must return no more than a single row.

8i

If BULK COLLECT is specified, then the variable list must consist of PL/SQL collections or host arrays which can receive all the rows retrieved from the query.

SELF	SELF

SELF is an implied parameter that is available in member functions (methods) to object types. It refers to the current object.

PL/SQL Language Elements *(Continued)*

SERIALLY_ REUSABLE **8.0+**	PRAGMA SERIALLY_REUSABLE The SERIALLY_REUSABLE pragma reduces package memory consumption by allowing package memory to be deallocated or reused after the package ceases execution. Package variables cannot persist across calls in a reusable package.

SET TRANSACTION	SET TRANSACTION
	    [{READ ONLY |READ WRITE}]
	    [ISOLATION LEVEL {SERIALIZABLE | READ COMMITTED}]
	    [USE ROLLBACK SEGMENT *rollback_segment_name*]
	
	The SET TRANSACTION statement controls various transaction options. Its usage in PL/SQL is equivalent to its usage in normal SQL. See Chapter 4, "Data Definition Language (DDL)," for details on SET TRANSACTION options.

SQL (DEFAULT CURSOR NAME)	When SQL statements are executed without an explicit cursor, they are assigned the default cursor name SQL. The SQL cursor implements all the standard cursor attributes such as %FOUND, %ISOPEN, %NOTFOUND, and %ROWCOUNT.
SQLCODE	SQLCODE Accessible only from within exception handlers, the SQLCODE function contains the Oracle error code number that triggered the exception. If the exception that fired was a user-defined exception *not* created by the EXCEPTION_INIT pragma and therefore not associated with an Oracle error code, then SQLCODE returns +1. If the NO_DATA_FOUND exception is raised, then SQLCODE equals +100 (not +1403, as might be expected by PRO*C programmers).

PL/SQL Language Elements *(Continued)*

SQLERRM	SQLERRM[(*sqlcode*)]
	If no argument is passed to SQLERRM, then it returns the error message string associated with the most recent Oracle error. If a *sqlcode* argument is provided, then SQLERRM returns the error text associated with the specified Oracle error code.
SUBTYPE	SUBTYPE *subtype_name basetype* [RANGE *low..high*]
	SUBTYPES are user-defined types that implement an existing datatype or user type, but which may have a more restricted range of values.
TABLE	See TYPE.
TRIM	*collection_name*.TRIM[(*number_of_elements*)]
	The TRIM method removes elements from the end of a collection. If *number_of_elements* is not specified, then a single item is removed. Otherwise, *number_of_elements* elements are removed.
TYPE	TYPE *type_name* IS

```
         {datatype                              |
          REF CURSOR [RETURN rowtype]           |
          VARRAY (limit) OF datatype [NOT NULL] |
          RECORD (field_definitions...)         |
          TABLE OF datatype [NOT NULL]          |
          TABLE OF datatype
             INDEX BY BINARY_INTEGER}
```

The TYPE statement is used to create a PL/SQL user-defined type. It is similar in some respects to the CREATE TYPE statement, except that the type definition does not persist beyond program execution, the types may not be used to create persistent objects, and object types may not be created.

PL/SQL Language

PL/SQL Language Elements *(Continued)*

TYPE **(CONT.)**	In its simplest form, TYPE creates a user-defined type based on a single datatype. This can improve readability by associating relatively unwieldy terms—for instance, %ROWTYPE declarations—with a simple type name. REF CURSOR creates a cursor parameter type. *Rowtype* specifies an optional record %TYPE or %ROWTYPE declaration, which specifies the return format for the cursor.
8.0+	VARRAY creates a varying array type. *Limit* specifies the number of elements in the varray and *datatype* may specify any datatype other than PL/SQL-specific datatypes or the long datatype. RECORD creates a PL/SQL record type. *Field_definitions* specify one or more PL/SQL datatypes that comprise the record. The ref cursor datatype is not permitted. Field definitions may include NOT NULL and DEFAULT clauses.
8.0+	TABLE OF, without the INDEX BY clause, defines a nested table type. *Datatype,* in this context, consists of an object type defined with the CREATE TYPE command or a single scalar datatype. TABLE OF .... INDEX BY BINARY INTEGER creates an *index-by table*. For index-by tables, the table *datatype* may be any valid PL/SQL datatype.
UPDATE	UPDATE *update_statement_options* The UPDATE statement in PL/SQL has the same functionality and syntax in PL/SQL as in standard SQL. See Chapter 3 for further details.

PL/SQL Language Elements *(Continued)*

VARIABLE DECLARATION	*variable_name datatype* [NOT NULL] [{:=|DEFAULT} *expression*] Variable declarations must be included within a declarative section in a PL/SQL block or module definition. *Datatype* must conform to a legal PL/SQL datatype. See the section titled "PL/SQL Variables and Datatypes" in this chapter for details. The assignment operator (":=") or DEFAULT clause can be used to provide an initial value for the variable.
WHEN (EXCEPTION)	See EXCEPTION.
WHEN (EXIT)	See EXIT.
WHERE CURRENT OF	{UPDATE|DELETE} ... WHERE CURRENT OF *cursor_name* The WHERE CURRENT OF clause allows an UPDATE or DELETE statement to process the row most recently fetched by the cursor identified by *cursor_name*. This avoids having to re-access the row via an index lookup or table scan. The cursor concerned must have locked the rows in question using the FOR UPDATE clause (see Chapter 1, "The SELECT Statement").
WHILE LOOP	[*<<label_name>>*] WHILE *condition* LOOP *statements* END LOOP [*<<label_name>>*]; The WHILE loop iterates as long as *condition* evaluates to true. *Condition* must return a Boolean value.

Oracle-Supplied PL/SQL Packages

Introduction

Oracle provides a number of PL/SQL packages that extend the PL/SQL language or implement Oracle-specific functionality. For instance, packages exist to provide file and console output capabilities in PL/SQL programs. Other packages implement new Oracle features such as advanced queuing and the log miner facility.

This chapter provides procedure and function references for some of the more commonly used packages. It is not possible to provide full descriptions of all packages—such an undertaking would require a substantial reference book in its own right. Only packages that are widely and frequently used are fully described here.

Table 6-1 lists some of the packages found in a standard installation of Oracle8i. Note that not all these packages are described in this chapter.

References

In Oracle8i, supplied packages are described in *Oracle8i Application Developer's Reference—Packages*.

In other versions of Oracle, supplied packages are documented in *Oracle Server Application Developer's Guide*.

Packages relating to snapshots and replication are documented in *Oracle Server Replication*.

Table 6–1 Oracle-Supplied PL/SQL Packages

Package Name	Script Name	Description
DBMS_ALERT	*dbmsalrt.sql*	Implements database alerts.
DBMS_APPLICATION_INFO	*dbmsapin.sql*	Registers application information with Oracle.
DBMS_AQ	*dbmsaq.sql*	Advanced queuing interface.
DBMS_AQADM	*dbmsaqad.sql*	Advanced queuing administration.
DBMS_BACKUP_RESTORE	*dbmsbkrs.sql*	Backup and restore utilities.
DBMS_DDL	*dbmsutil.sql*	Executes DDL statements in PL/SQL.
DBMS_DEBUG	*pbload.sql*	Defines the probe API, which provides PL/SQL debugging services.
DBMS_DEFER	*dbmsdfrd.sql*	Submits deferred transactions.
DBMS_DEFER_SYS	*dbmsdfrd.sql*	Administers deferred transaction queues.
DBMS_DESCRIBE	*dbmsdesc.sql*	Describes PL/SQL program headers.
DBMS_HS	*dbmshs.sql*	Manages heterogeneous services.
DBMS_JAVA	*initdbj.sql*	Utilities for Java programs.
DBMS_JOB	*dbmsjob.sql*	Manages job queues.
DBMS_LOB	*dbmslob.sql*	Utilities for working with LOB datatypes.
DBMS_LOCK	*dbmslock.sql*	Utilities for working with user-defined locks.
DBMS_LOGMNR	*dbmslogmnr.sql*	Starts and stops the log miner utility.

Table 6–1 Oracle-Supplied PL/SQL Packages *(Continued)*

Package Name	Script Name	Description
DBMS_LOGMNR_D	*dbmslogmnrd.sql*	Generates the text file containing data dictionary information for the log miner utility.
DBMS_MVIEW	*dbmssnap.sql*	Materialized view management.
DBMS_OFFLINE_OG	*dbmsofln.sql*	Initializes new master replication data.
DBMS_OFFLINE_SNAPSHOT	*dbmsofsn.sql*	Creates a new snapshot from a master table.
DBMS_ORACLE_TRACE_AGENT	*dbmsotrc.sql*	Starts Oracle trace in another session.
DBMS_ORACLE_TRACE_USER	*dbmsotrc.sql*	Starts Oracle trace in the current session.
DBMS_OUTPUT	*dbmsotpt.sql*	Generates output from PL/SQL programs.
DBMS_PIPE	*dbmspipe.sql*	Creates and uses database pipes.
DBMS_RANDOM	*dbmsrand.sql*	Random number generator.
DBMS_REFRESH	*dbmssnap.sql*	Refreshes snapshots.
DBMS_REPAIR	*dbmsrpr.sql*	Repairs corrupt database blocks.
DBMS_REPCAT	*catreps.sql*	Administers the replication catalog.
DBMS_REPCAT_ADMIN	*catreps.sql*	Administers replication users.
DBMS_REPCAT_AUTH	*catreps.sql*	Administers surrogate replication users.
DBMS_REPUTIL	*catreps.sql*	Replication utilities.
DBMS_RESOURCE_MANAGER	*dbmsrmad.sql*	Manages resource groups.

Table 6–1 Oracle-Supplied PL/SQL Packages *(Continued)*

Package Name	Script Name	Description
DBMS_RESOURCE_MANAGER_PRIVS	*dbmsrmpriv.sql*	Manages resource manager permissions.
DBMS_RLS	*dbmsrl.sql*	Row-level security interface.
DBMS_ROWID	*dbmsutil.sql*	Queries and converts ROWIDs.
DBMS_RULE	*dbmsread.sql*	Evaluates database rules.
DBMS_RULE_ADM	*dbmsread.sql*	Maintains database rule sets.
DBMS_RULE_EXIMP	*dbmsread.sql*	Exports and imports rule sets.
DBMS_SESSION	*dbmsutil.sql*	Manages database sessions.
DBMS_SHARED_POOL	*dbmspool.sql*	Manages objects in the shared pool.
DBMS_SNAPSHOT	*dbmssnap.sql*	Manages snapshots and materialized views.
DBMS_SPACE	*dbmsutil.sql*	Analyzes segment space utilization.
DBMS_SPACE_ADMIN	*dbmsspace.sql*	Utilities for managing space in locally managed tablespaces.
DBMS_SQL	*dbms.sql*	Executes dynamic SQL.
DBMS_STANDARD	*dbmsstdx.sql*	Standard PL/SQL language elements.
DBMS_STATS	*dbmsstat.sql*	Manages optimizer statistics.
DBMS_SUMMARY	*dbmssum.sql*	Manages database summaries.
DBMS_SYSTEM	*dbmsutil.sql*	Performs system administration.
DBMS_TRACE	*dbmspbt.sql*	Manages PL/SQL tracing.

Table 6–1 Oracle-Supplied PL/SQL Packages *(Continued)*

Package Name	Script Name	Description
DBMS_TRANSACTION	*dbmsutil.sql*	Transaction control and monitoring.
DBMS_UTILITY	*dbmsutil.sql*	Utility functions.
OUTLN_PKG	*dbmsot.sql*	Utilities for managing outlines (stored execution plans).
UTL_COLL	*utlcoll.sql*	Uses collection locators.
UTL_FILE	*utlfile.sql*	Operating system file interface.
UTL_HTTP	*utlhttp.sql*	HTTP callouts.
UTL_PG	*utlpg.sql*	Converts COBOL numeric data to or from Oracle numbers.
UTL_RAW	*utlraw.sql*	Manages RAW datatypes.
UTL_REF	*utlref.sql*	Uses REF datatypes.

Calling Supplied Packages

The reference section below summarizes the procedures and functions that make up each package. Most packages are owned by the SYS user, so a fully-qualified call could be represented as:

```
[ Function_return_value:= ]
SYS.package_name.function_or_procedure_name(parameters)
```

Parameters may be provided in positional or named notation (see Chapter 5, "PL/SQL Language"). If provided in named notation, then the parameter names shown in the syntax summaries below should be used.

Installing Supplied Packages

Many supplied packages are installed during a normal Oracle installation. If a package is not installed in the initial installation, then it is usually necessary to run a SQL*PLUS installation script while connected to the SYS account. The installation scripts can be found in the *rdbms/admin* directory of the Oracle installation. For Oracle versions 7 and 8 under NT, the directory may be *rdbms73\admin* and *rdbms80\admin,* respectively.

Table 6-1 lists the primary installation script for each package. Many of the packages are associated with a "*PRVT*.PLB*" script, which contains the private "wrapped" package bodies. So, for an instance to install the packages in the *dbmsutil.sql* script, it is also necessary to run the *prvtutil.sql* script.

Package DBMS_ALERT

The DBMS_ALERT package implementing blocking database alerts. Database alerts provide a form of inter-session communication. A session registers an interest in one or more alerts and then waits until another session issues the alert.

DBMS_ALERT Functions and Procedures

REGISTER	REGISTER(*name*)
	REGISTER registers interest in the alert specified by *name*.

REMOVE	REMOVE(*name*)
	REMOVE removes or cancels interest in the named alert.

REMOVEALL	REMOVEALL()
	REMOVEALL removes interest in all registered alerts.

SET_DEFAULTS	SET_DEFAULTS(*sensitivity*)
	SET_DEFAULTS sets the default time to sleep between polls, in seconds.

SIGNAL	SIGNAL(*name, message*)
	SIGNAL signals an alert with the given *name*. A *message* can be associated with the alert that will be passed to sessions having registered interest in the alert.

WAITANY	WAITANY(*name, message, status, timeout*)
	WAITANY allows a session to wait for any of the registered alerts to occur.

DBMS_ALERT Functions and Procedures *(Continued)*

Name, message, and *status* are OUT parameters that will be populated with the name of the alert and alert message if WAITANY terminates because of an alert.

Status is an OUT variable that is set to 1 if WAITANY terminated due to a timeout and 0 if WAITANY terminated due to an alert firing.

Timeout specifies the maximum wait time permitted.

WAITONE	WAITONE(*name, message, status, timeout*)

WAITONE allows a session to wait for a specific alert to occur. *Name* identifies the name of the alert.

Message is an OUT parameter that will be populated with the alert message if WAITONE terminates because of an alert.

Status is an OUT variable that is set to 1 if WAITANY terminated due to a timeout and 0 if WAITANY terminated due to an alert firing.

Timeout specifies the maximum wait time permitted.

Package DBMS_APPLICATION_INFO

The DBMS_APPLICATION_INFO package allows an application to register its module name, activity, and client information. This information is available in the V$SESSION and V$SQLAREA dynamic performance views, as well as in Oracle trace output.

DBMS_APPLICATION_INFO Functions and Procedures

READ_CLIENT_INFO	READ_CLIENT_INFO(*client_info*)

READ_CLIENT_INFO reads the current client information as set by SET_CLIENT_INFO into the OUT parameter *client_info*.

DBMS_APPLICATION_INFO Functions and Procedures *(Continued)*

READ_MODULE	READ_MODULE(*module_name, action_name*)
	READ_MODULE reads the current module and action names as set by SET_MODULE and SET_ACTION.
SET_ACTION	SET_ACTION(*action_name*)
	SET_ACTION sets the name of the current action within a module.
SET_CLIENT_INFO	SET_CLIENT_INFO(*client_info*)
	SET_CLIENT_INFO sets a string defining client information.
SET_MODULE	SET_MODULE(*module_name, action_name*)
	SET_MODULE sets strings identifying the current module name and an action identifier within the module.
SET_SESSION_ LONGOPS 8.0+	SET_SESSION_LONGOPS(*rindex, slno, op_name, target, context, sofar, totalwork, target_desc, units*)
	SET_SESSION_LONGOPS populates data in the V@SESSION_LONGOP table. This table records the progress of long-running operations.
	Rindex is an IN OUT parameter that denotes the row in V$SESSION_LONGOP being updated. Set it to DBMS_APPLICATION_INFO.SET_SESSION_LONGOPS_NOHINT to create a new row. Use the value returned from this initial call in subsequent calls.
	Op_name, target, context, sofar, totalwork, target_desc, and *units* all correspond to columns of the same name in the V$SESSION_LONGOPS table.
	Slno is for internal use only.

Package DBMS_DDL

The DBMS_DDL package allows certain DDL statements and administrative commands to be executed within PL/SQL.

DBMS_DDL Functions and Procedures

ALTER_COMPILE	ALTER_COMPILE(*type, schema, name*)
	ALTER_COMPILE compiles a PL/SQL program. *Type* defines the type of object: PROCEDURE, FUNCTION, PACKAGE, PACKAGE BODY, or TRIGGER. *Schema* and *name* define the schema (account) and name of the object to be compiled.
ALTER_TABLE_ NOT_ REFERENCEABLE	ALTER_TABLE_NOT_REFERENCEABLE(*table_name, table_schema, affected_schema*)
	ALTER_TABLE_NOT_REFERENCEABLE undoes the actions of ALTER_TABLE_REFERENCEABLE.
ALTER_TABLE_ REFERENCEABLE	ALTER_TABLE_REFERENCEABLE(*table_name, table_schema, affected_schema*)
	ALTER_TABLE_REFERENCEABLE makes the object table specified the default for references from other tables within the specified schema.
ANALYZE_OBJECT	ANALYZE_OBJECT(*type, schema, name, method, estimate_rows, estimate_percent, method_opt, partname*)
	ANALYZE_OBJECT performs the actions of the ANALYZE command (see Chapter 4, "Data Definition Language (DDL)") on the specified object.
	Type is one of {TABLE|CLUSTER|INDEX}.
	Schema and *name* define the object to be analyzed.
	Method is one of {ESTIMATE|COMPUTE|DELETE}.

DBMS_DDL Functions and Procedures *(Continued)*

ANALYZE_OBJECT (CONT.)	*Estimate_rows* specifies an absolute number of rows to be used when the method is ESTIMATE. *Estimate_percent* specifies a percentage of total rows to be used. *Method_opt* is a string of the form: {FOR TABLE | FOR ALL [INDEXED] COLUMNS] [SIZE *histogram_size*] | FOR ALL INDEXES } *Partname* specifies a specific partition of a partitioned table that is to be analyzed. See the entry on the ANALYZE command in Chapter 4 for more details.

Package DBMS_JOB

The DBMS_JOB package implements Oracle server job queues. These queues allow PL/SQL programs to be scheduled for non-interactive execution on a regular or ad-hoc basis. Job queue servers must have been implemented by setting a non-zero value for the initialization parameter JOB_QUEUE_PROCESSES.

Definitions of all jobs can be found in the DBA_JOBS and DBA_JOBS_RUNNING data dictionary views. Jobs defined by the current user can be found in USER_JOBS.

DBMS_JOB Functions and Procedures

BROKEN	BROKEN(*job, broken, next_date*) BROKEN deactivates a *job* in the job queue, or reactivates a "broken" *job*. *Job* is the job identifier obtained from the SUBMIT procedure. *Broken* is a Boolean indicating whether the *job* is considered broken. If *broken* is false, *next_date* specifies the next execution time for the *job*.

DBMS_JOB Functions and Procedures *(Continued)*

CHANGE	CHANGE(*job, what, next_date, interval, instance, force*)

CHANGE modifies the characteristics of *job*.

Job is the job identifier obtained from the SUBMIT procedure.

What indicates the PL/SQL code to be run.

Next_date indicates the date (and time) of the next execution.

Interval indicates the interval between executions. *Interval* is expressed as an offset from SYSDATE. For instance, "SYSDATE+1/24" specifies hourly execution.

8i   *Instance* optionally specifies an Oracle parallel server instance number against which the *job* will run. *Force* allows an instance number for an inactive or non-existent instance to be specified.

INSTANCE	INSTANCE(*job, instance, force*)

8i   INSTANCE changes the Oracle parallel server instance that will run *job*. *Force* allows the *instance* identifier specified to be unavailable or non-existent.

INTERVAL	INTERVAL(*job, interval*)

INTERVAL changes the frequency of job execution.

Job is the job identifier obtained from the SUBMIT procedure.

Interval indicates the interval between executions. Interval is expressed as an offset from SYSDATE. For instance, "SYSDATE+1/24" specifies hourly execution.

DBMS_JOB Functions and Procedures *(Continued)*

ISUBMIT	ISUBMIT(*job, what, next_date, interval, no_parse*)
	ISUBMIT is the same as SUBMIT, except that a specific job number may be specified. In SUBMIT, *job* is an OUT parameter; in ISUBMIT, *job* is an IN parameter.
NEXT_DATE	NEXT_DATE(*job, next_date*)
	NEXT_DATE specifies the next date and time on which the specified *job* will run.
	Job is the job identifier obtained from the SUBMIT procedure.
	Next_date indicates the date (and time) of the next execution.
REMOVE	REMOVE(*job*)
	REMOVE permanently removes *job* from a job queue.
RUN	RUN(*job, force*)
	RUN causes the specified *job* to be run immediately.
	Job is the job identifier obtained from the SUBMIT procedure.
	Force is a Boolean which, if true, causes the *job* to run even if broken.
SUBMIT	SUBMIT(*job, what, next_date, interval, no_parse, instance, force*)
	SUBMIT submits *job* for execution.
	Job is an OUT parameter that accepts the job number assigned to *job*.
	What indicates the PL/SQL code to be run.

DBMS_JOB Functions and Procedures *(Continued)*

SUBMIT (CONT.)   *Next_date* indicates the date (and time) of the next execution.

Interval indicates the interval between executions. Interval is expressed as an offset from SYSDATE. For instance, "SYSDATE+1/24" specifies hourly execution.

No_parse is a Boolean parameter which, if true, suppresses a parse check on the PL/SQL specified in the *what* parameter.

8i   *Instance* optionally specifies an Oracle parallel server instance number against which *job* will run. *Force* allows an instance number for an inactive or non-existent instance to be specified.

USER_EXPORT   USER_EXPORT(*job, mycall*)

USER_EXPORT generates a string that can be used to recreate *job*. The string is stored in the OUT parameter *mycall*.

WHAT   WHAT(*job, what*)

WHAT changes the PL/SQL program associated with *job*.

Package DBMS_LOB

The DBMS_LOB package contains utilities for working with Oracle8 LOB   **8.0+**
datatypes (BLOB, CLOB, BFILE, etc.). These large datatypes can only be manipulated through use of the DBMS_LOB package.

Most DBMS_LOB procedures and functions work with "*LOB locators*," which are pointers to lob storage. LOB locators can be obtained by fetching the specific lob into a PL/SQL variable of the corresponding datatype. When DBMS_LOB operations are performed on the LOB locators, the underlying lob is modified accordingly.

Parameters that refer to amounts of data or offsets within LOBS are measured in bytes for BLOBs and BFILEs and in characters for CLOBs.

DBMS_LOB Functions and Procedures

APPEND	APPEND(dest_lob, src_lob) APPEND appends the contents of *src_lob* to *dest_lob*.
CLOSE	CLOSE(*lob_loc*) CLOSE disassociates the LOB locator from its underlying LOB.
COMPARE	*Compare_result*:=COMPARE(*lob_1, lob_2, amount, offset_1, offset_2*) COMPARE compares the contents of the LOBs located by *lob_1* and *lob_2*. *Amount* specifies the number of characters or bytes to be compared. *Offset_1* and *offset_2* specify the starting points in each LOB for the comparison to be performed. The *compare_result* is 0 if the two lob portions are identical, and non-zero otherwise.
COPY	COPY(*dest_lob, src_lob, amount, dest_offset, src_offset*) COPY copies characters or bytes from *src_lob* to *dest_lob*. *Amount* specifies the number of characters or bytes to be copied. *Dest_offset* specifies the point within the destination LOB to which the data will be copied. *Src_offset* specifies the point in the source LOB from which the data will be taken.
CREATE TEMPORARY 8i	CREATETEMPORARY(*lob_loc, cache, dur*) CREATETEMPORARY creates a temporary LOB. *Lob_loc* receives the LOB locator, which can be used for further operations on the LOB. *Cache* is a Boolean that determines whether or not LOB data should be stored in the buffer cache. *Dur* specifies the duration of the LOB's existence. It is SESSION, TRANSACTION, or CALL.

DBMS_LOB Functions and Procedures *(Continued)*

ERASE	ERASE(*lob_loc, amount, offset*)
	ERASE erases data from *lob_loc*. *Amount* specifies the amount of characters or bytes to be erased. *Offset* specifies the starting point in the LOB for the erasure.
FILECLOSE	FILECLOSE(*file_loc*)
	FILECLOSE closes a BFILE referenced through *file_loc*.
FILECLOSEALL	FILECLOSEALL()
	FILECLOSEALL closes all open BFILES.
FILEEXISTS	*Exists:*=FILEEXISTS(*file_loc*)
	FILEEXISTS returns 1 if the BFILE pointed to by *file_loc* exists, and 0 if it does not.
FILEGETNAME	FILEGETNAME(*file_loc, dir_alias, filename*)
	FILEGETNAME gets the directory and *filename* for the BFILE locator *file_loc*.
	Dir_alias and *filename* are OUT parameters that receive the directory alias (as specified by CREATE DIRECTORY) and filename.
FILEISOPEN	*isopen:*=FILEISOPEN(*file_loc*)
	FILEISOPEN returns 1 if the specified BFILE is open, and 0 otherwise.
FILEOPEN	FILEOPEN(*file_loc, open_mode*)
	FILEOPEN opens the BFILE located by *file_loc*. *Open_mode* must currently be unspecified or set to DBMS_LOB.FILE_READONLY.

DBMS_LOB Functions and Procedures *(Continued)*

FREETEMPORARY	FREETEMPORARY(*lob_loc*)
	FREETEMPORARY frees storage allocated to a temporary LOB created by the CREATETEMPORARY procedure.
GETCHUNKSIZE	*Chunksize*:=GETCHUNKSIZE(*lob_loc*)
	GETCHUNKSIZE returns the chunk size for the specified LOB.
GETLENGTH	*length*:=GETLENGTH(*lob_loc*)
	GETLENGTH returns the number of characters or bytes in the specified LOB.
INSTR	*Location*:=INSTR(*lob_loc, pattern, offset, nth*)
	INSTR searches *lob_loc* for the *nth* occurrence of *pattern,* starting at *offset.* If not found, 0 is returned; otherwise, the location of the *pattern* within the LOB is returned.
ISOPEN	*open*:=ISOPEN(*lob_loc*)
	ISOPEN returns 1 if the LOB locator *lob_loc* is associated with a LOB, and 0 otherwise.
ISTEMPORARY	*Istemporary*:=ISTEMPORARY(*lob_loc*)
	ISTEMPORARY returns 1 if the LOB locator points to a temporary LOB, and 0 otherwise.
LOADFROMFILE	LOADFROMFILE(*dest_lob, src_lob, amount, dest_offset, src_offset*)
	LOADFROMFILE loads data from a BFILE (*src_lob*) into an internal LOB (*dest_lob*). *Amount* specifies the number of characters or bytes to be copied. *Dest_offset* specifies the point within the destination LOB to which the data will be copied. *Src_offset* specifies the point in the source LOB from which the data will be taken.

DBMS_LOB Functions and Procedures *(Continued)*

OPEN	OPEN(*lob_loc, open_mode*)
	OPEN opens the LOB located by *lob_loc. Open_mode* must be unspecified or set to DBMS_LOB.FILE_READONLY.
READ	READ(*lob_loc, amount, offset, buffer*)
	READ transfers the *amount* of bytes or characters from *lob_loc*, starting at the position specified by *offset*, into the RAW or VARCHAR2 OUT parameter *buffer*.
SUBSTR	*Raw_data*:=SUBSTR(*lob_loc, amount, offset*)
	SUBSTRING returns the *amount* of bytes or characters, starting at *offset* from the LOB referred to by *lob_loc*.
TRIM	TRIM(*lob_loc, newlen*)
	TRIM reduces the LOB referred to by *lob_loc* to *newlen* characters or bytes. Any data beyond *newlen* is lost.
WRITE	WRITE(*lob_loc, amount, offset, buffer*)
	WRITE writes the *amount* of bytes or characters from *buffer* into the LOB identified by *lob_loc*, starting at *offset* bytes or characters from the start of the LOB.
WRITEAPPEND	WRITEAPPEND(*lob_loc, amount, buffer*)
	WRITEAPPEND adds the *amount* of bytes or characters from *buffer* to the end of the LOB identified by *lob_loc*.

Package DBMS_LOCK

The DBMS_LOCK package allows sessions to create user-defined locks that behave in similar ways to locks on tables or rows. These locks can be used to coordinate the activities of multiple sessions. All Oracle lock services (such as deadlock detection) are available to user locks.

DBMS_LOCK Functions and Procedures

ALLOCATE_ UNIQUE	ALLOCATE_UNIQUE(*lockname, lockhandle, expiration_secs*) ALLOCATE UNIQUE generates a *lockhandle* ID for a user-defined lock called *lockname*. *Expiration_secs* specifies the number of seconds that must pass since the last ALLOCATE_UNIQUE operation on a specific *lockname* before the *lockname* will be removed from system tables.
CONVERT	*return_value*:=CONVERT({*lockhandle*|*id*}, *lockmode, timeout*) CONVERT changes the mode of a lock currently held by the session. *Lockhandle* is the handle allocated to the named lock generated by ALLOCATE_UNIQUE. Alternately, *id* is a user-defined number representing a user lock. *Lockmode* is a number from 1 to 6, each number representing a higher locking level. The lock levels correspond to: 　　1 : Null. 　　2 : Row share. 　　3 : Row exclusive. 　　4 : Share. 　　5 : Share row exclusive. 　　6 : Exclusive. *Timeout* defines the number of seconds after which the function will fail if the lock cannot be converted. The *return_value* indicates the status of the request. Values returned are:

DBMS_LOCK Functions and Procedures *(Continued)*

*Oracle-Supplied PL/
SQL Packages*

CONVERT **(CONT.)**	0 : Lock converted. 1 : Failed to acquire lock before timeout expired. 2 : Deadlock detected. 3 : Invalid parameters. 4 : Lock not held. 5 : Invalid *lockhandle*.

RELEASE

return_value:=**RELEASE**({*lockhandle*|*id*})

RELEASE releases a lock is currently held by the session.

Lockhandle is the handle allocated to the named lock generated by ALLOCATE_UNIQUE. Alternately, *id* is a user-defined number representing a user lock.

The *return_value* indicates the status of the request. Values returned are:

   0 : Lock released.
   3 : Invalid parameters.
   4 : Lock not held.
   5 : Invalid *lockhandle*.

REQUEST

return_value:=**REQUEST**({*lockhandle*|*id*}, *lockmode,
timeout, release_on_commit*)

REQUEST allows a session to take out the specified lock in the specified mode.

Lockhandle is the handle allocated to the named lock generated by ALLOCATE_UNIQUE. Alternately, *id* is a user-defined number representing a user lock.

Lockmode is a number from 1 to 6, each number representing a higher locking level. The lock levels correspond to:

DBMS_LOCK Functions and Procedures *(Continued)*

REQUEST **(CONT.)**	1 : Null. 2 : Row share. 3 : Row exclusive. 4 : Share. 5 : Share row exclusive. 6 : Exclusive.

Timeout defines the number of seconds after which the function will fail if the lock cannot be acquired.

Release_on_commit is a Boolean which, if true, indicates that the lock should be released on a COMMIT or ROLLBACK.

The *return_value* indicates the status of the request. Values returned are:

0 : Lock acquired.
1 : Failed to acquire lock before timeout expired.
2 : Deadlock detected.
3 : Invalid parameters.
4 : Lock already held.
5 : Invalid *lockhandle.*

SLEEP	SLEEP(*seconds*) SLEEP pauses execution for the specified number of *seconds.*

Package DBMS_LOGMNR

8i The DBMS_LOGMNR utility controls execution of the log miner utility. When the log miner utility is active, contents of specified redo log files will be available in the dynamic performance table V$LOGMNR_CONTENTS for specified time periods.

DBMS_LOGMNR Functions and Procedures

ADD_LOGFILE	ADD_LOGFILE(*logfilename, options*)

ADD_LOGFILE adds the log,file *logfilename* to the log miner log list.

Options should be one of the following constants: DBMS_LOGMNR.NEW, for a new list; DBMS_LOGMNR.REMOVEFILE, to remove a file from the list; or DBMS_LOGMNR.ADDFILE, to add a file to the list.

END_LOGMNR	END_LOGMNR()

END_LOGMNR ends a log miner session and clears the relevant dynamic performance tables.

START_LOGMNR	START_LOGMNR(*startscn, endscn, starttime, endtime, dictfilename, options*)

START_LOGMNR starts a log miner session.

Startscn and *endscn* specify a start and end *System Change Number* (SCN) of interest. Likewise, *starttime* and *endtime* identify a start and end time of interest. Only redo log entries made between the specified times and SCNs will be visible.

Package DBMS_LOGMNR_D

The DBMS_LOGMNR_D package creates a data dictionary file, which is required by the log miner utility. The DBMS_LOGMNR_D.BUILD procedure should be called before the log miner utility is initialized by the DBMS_LOGMNR package.

8i

DBMS_LOGMNR_D Functions and Procedures

BUILD	BUILD(*dictionary_filename, dictionary_location*)

BUILD builds a log miner data dictionary file named *dictionary_filename* in the directory *dictionary_location*.

Package DBMS_OUTPUT

The DBMS_OUTPUT package allows PL/SQL programs to generate output that can be displayed in the calling program's environment. Calls to PUT or PUT_LINE add text to a buffer that can be retrieved after program execution by making calls to GET_LINE or GET_LINES. In SQL°PLUS, DBMS_OUTPUT output can be viewed by setting "SET SERVEROUTPUT ON" (see Chapter 9, "SQL°PLUS").

DBMS_OUTPUT Functions and Procedures

DISABLE	DISABLE()
	DISABLE suppresses buffering of data passed through PUT and PUT_LINE and purges the buffer of any existing data.
ENABLE	ENABLE(*buffer_size*)
	ENABLE enables calls to DBMS_OUTPUT procedures and creates a buffer of *buffer_size* bytes.
GET_LINE	GET_LINE(*line, status*)
	GET_LINE retrieves a single line of output from the buffer into the OUT parameter *line*. The *status* variable will be set to 0 if the call succeeds, and 1 if there are no lines in the buffer.
GET_LINES	GET_LINES(*lines, numlines*)
	GET_LINES retrieves multiple lines—the number is defined by *numlines*—into the OUT parameter *lines*, which is defined as an index-by table of VARCHAR2 datatype.
NEW_LINE	NEW_LINE()
	NEW_LINE puts an end-of-line marker into the buffer. This is useful in conjunction with the PUT procedure to mark a new line of data.

DBMS_OUTPUT Functions and Procedures *(Continued)*

PUT	PUT(*a*)
	PUT places data into the buffer, but does not append an end-of-line marker. The data will typically be a string, but may also consist of numeric or date data.

PUT_LINE	PUT_LINE(*a*)
	PUT_LINE places data into the buffer and appends an end-of-line marker. The data will typically be a string, but may also consist of numeric or date data.

Package DBMS_PIPE

The DBMS_PIPE package allows the creation and maintenance of database pipes. Database pipes provide a mechanism for inter-session communication. Messages may be placed in named pipes and retrieved by other sessions on a first-in, first-out manner.

DBMS_PIPE Functions and Procedures

CREATE_PIPE	*return_value*:=CREATE_PIPE(*pipename, maxpipesize, private*)
	CREATE_PIPE creates a pipe named *pipename*. CREATE_PIPE always returns 0. An exception is raised if a pipe cannot be created.
	Maxpipesize specifies the maximum amount of data that may be buffered in the pipe.
	Private is a Boolean which, if true, indicates that the pipe may only be used by sessions with the same username as the user who created the pipe.
	Note that pipes can also be implicitly created by the SEND_MESSAGE function.

DBMS_PIPE Functions and Procedures *(Continued)*

NEXT_ITEM_TYPE	*Item_type*:=NEXT_ITEM_TYPE()

NEXT_ITEM_TYPE reveals the datatype of the next item in the pipe buffer. NEXT_ITEM_TYPE should be called after RECEIVE_MESSAGE and before UNPACK_MESSAGE. The *item_type* returned is a code, which is interpreted as follows:

> 0 : Buffer is empty.
> 6 : Numeric data.
> 9 : VARCHAR2 data.
> 11 : ROWID data.
> 12 : Date data.
> 23 : RAW data.

PACK_MESSAGE	PACK_MESSAGE(*item*)

PACK_MESSAGE prepares a message for transmission through a pipe. *Item* may be character, numeric, or date data. Multiple calls to PACK_MESSAGE may be made before calling SEND_MESSAGE.

PACK_MESSAGE _RAW	PACK_MESSAGE_RAW(*item*)

PACK_MESSAGE_RAW is the same as PACK_MESSAGE, except that *item* must be a RAW datatype.

PACK_MESSAGE _ROWID	PACK_MESSAGE_ROWID(*item*)

PACK_MESSAGE_ROWID is the same as PACK_MESSAGE, except that *item* must be a ROWID datatype.

PURGE	PURGE(*pipename*)

PURGE empties the contents of the specified pipe.

RECEIVE_ MESSAGE	*Return_value*:=RECEIVE_MESSAGE(*pipename, timeout*)

RECEIVE_MESSAGE extracts a message from the named pipe into a local buffer. UNPACK_MESSAGE is called after RECEIVE_MESSAGE to place the message into local variables.

DBMS_PIPE Functions and Procedures *(Continued)*

RECEIVE_ MESSAGE (CONT.)	*Timeout* specifies the number of seconds to wait for a message before terminating the call.

Return_value may be one of the following:

0 : Message received.
1 : Timeout period expired before message received.
2 : Message too large for buffer.
3 : Interrupt occurred.

REMOVE_PIPE

Return_code:=REMOVE_PIPE(*pipename*)

REMOVE_PIPE removes a pipe created by CREATE_PIPE.

RESET_BUFFER

RESET_BUFFER()

RESET_BUFFER empties the local message buffer, removing any data that may have been left by a PACK_MESSAGE or RECEIVE_MESSAGE call that was not followed by SEND_MESSAGE or UNPACK_MESSAGE.

SEND_MESSAGE

Return_value:=SEND_MESSAGE(*pipename, timeout, maxpipesize*)

SEND_MESSAGE sends a message prepared by PACK_MESSAGE into the specified pipe.

Timeout specifies the number of seconds to continue to attempt to send the message while the pipe is full or otherwise unable to accept the message.

Maxpipesize specifies the maximum pipe size for an implicit pipe (one not created by CREATE_PIPE), or overrides the pipe size for an explicit pipe.

Return_value can be one of the following codes:

0 : Message sent.
1 : Timeout occurred.
3 : Interrupt occurred.

DBMS_PIPE Functions and Procedures *(Continued)*

UNIQUE_SESSION _NAME	*name*:=UNIQUE_SESSION_NAME ()
	UNIQUE_SESSION_NAME returns a unique string that can be used to create a pipe name that will not conflict with pipes created in other sessions.
UNPACK_ MESSAGE	UNPACK_MESSAGE(*item*)
	UNPACK_MESSAGE extracts a message from the message buffer into the OUT parameter *item. Item* may be a character, numeric, or date datatype. UNPACK_MESSAGE should be called after RECEIVE_MESSAGE.
UNPACK_ MESSAGE_RAW	UNPACK_MESSAGE_RAW(*item*)
	UNPACK_MESSAGE_RAW is the same as UNPACK_MESSAGE, except that *item* must be a RAW variable.
UNPACK_ MESSAGE_ROWID	UNPACK_MESSAGE_ROWID(*item*)
	UNPACK_MESSAGE_ROWID is the same as UNPACK_MESSAGE, except that *item* must be a ROWID variable.

Package DBMS_RANDOM

8.0+   The DBMS_RANDOM package generates random numbers. The numbers generated are random, 32-bit, signed integers. A seed value is required to initialize random number generation. A good candidate for the seed value is the HSEC column in the V$TIMER view. The following example generates a random number between 0 and 1:

```
DECLARE
  l_seed binary_integer;
BEGIN
  SELECT hsecs INTO l_seed FROM v$timer;
  sys.dbms_random.initialize(l_seed);
  dbms_output.put_line
      (ABS(sys.dbms_random.random/POWER(2,31)));
END;
```

Note: Before using DBMS_RANDOM, you may need to install the DBMS_CRYPTO_TOOLKIT and UTL_RAW packages.

DBMS_RANDOM Functions and Procedures

INITIALIZE	INITIALIZE(*seed*)
	INITIALIZE starts the random number generator. The seed value should be set to an unpredictable integer value.
RANDOM	*Random_number*:=RANDOM()
	RANDOM returns a random eight-digit integer.
SEED	SEED(*seed*)
	SEED changes the seed value.
TERMINATE	TERMINATE()
	TERMINATE uninitializes the random number generator.

Package DBMS_ROWID

The DBMS_ROWID package contains utilities for interpreting and converting Oracle8 ROWIDs.

8.0+

Each row in a table is associated with a ROWID that represents the physical location of the row, and is always the fastest way to retrieve the row's data. The format of the ROWID changed between versions Oracle7 to Oracle8. The DBMS_ROWID package allows applications to extract information from opaque Oracle8 ROWIDs that was available transparently in Oracle7 ROWIDs.

ROWIDs in Oracle7 format are referred to as *restricted ROWIDs*. The Oracle8 format is known as the *extended ROWID*.

DBMS_ROWID Functions and Procedures

ROWID_BLOCK_ NUMBER	*Block_no*:=ROWID_BLOCK_NUMBER(*row_id*)
	ROWID_BLOCK_NUMBER returns the block number of the specified *row_id* within a database file.

DBMS_ROWID Functions and Procedures *(Continued)*

ROWID_CREATE	*rowid:=*ROWID_CREATE(*rowid_type, object_number, relative_fno, block_number, row_number*)

ROWID_CREATE generates a ROWID based on the properties provided.

Rowid_type may be 0 for a *restricted* ROWID, or 1 for an *extended* ROWID.

Object_number is the segment object identifier as shown in the DBA_OBJECTS view. For restricted ROWIDs, this should be set to DBMS_ROWID.ROWID_OBJECT_UNDEFINED.

Relative_fno is the relative file number of the file in which the row resides.

Block_number denotes the block number within the relative file number.

Row_number is the row number within the block.

ROWID_INFO	ROWID_INFO(*rowid_in, rowid_type, object_number, relative_fno, block_number, row_number*)

ROWID_INFO returns information about a ROWID. *Rowid_in* is the ROWID for which information is to be returned and is the only IN parameter.

Rowid_type returns 0 for a restricted ROWID, or 1 for an extended ROWID.

Object_number returns the segment object identifier as shown in the DBA_OBJECTS view.

Relative_fno returns the relative file number of the file in which the row resides.

Block_number returns the block number within the relative file number.

Row_number returns the row number within the block.

DBMS_ROWID Functions and Procedures *(Continued)*

ROWID_OBJECT	*Object_number*:=ROWID_OBJECT(*row_id*) ROWID_OBJECT returns the segment object identifier as shown in the DBA_OBJECTS view for the provided *row_id*.
ROWID_RELATIVE _FNO	*Relative_file_number*:=ROWID_RELATIVE_FNO(*row_id*) ROWID_RELATIVE_FNO returns the relative file number for the provided *row_id*.
ROWID_ROW_ NUMBER	*Row_number*:=ROWID_ROW_NUMBER(*row_id*) ROWID_ROW_NUMBER returns the row number within the block for the provided *row_id*.
ROWID_TO_ ABSOLUTE_FNO	*number*:=ROWID_TO_ABSOLUTE_FNO(*row_id*, *schema_name*, *object_name*) ROWID_TO_ABSOLUTE_FNO returns the *absolute file number* for the ROWID, which must exist within the specified schema and object.
ROWID_TO_ EXTENDED	*Extended_rowid*:=ROWID_TO_EXTENDED(*old_rowid*, *schema_name*,*object_name*, *conversion_type*) ROWID_TO_EXTENDED converts the restricted ROWID *old_rowid* into an *extended* ROWID. The *old_rowid* must exist within the specified *schema_name* and *object_name*. *Conversion_type* should be set to the constant ROWID_CONVERT_INTERNAL if the *old_rowid* is stored in a ROWID variable, or EXTERNAL_CONVERT_EXTERNAL if the *old_rowid* is stored as a character string.
ROWID_TO_ RESTRICTED	*Restricted_rowid*:=ROWID_TO_RESTRICTED(*old_rowid*, *conversion_type*) ROWID_TO_RESTRICTED converts the extended *old_rowid* into a *restricted* ROWID.

Oracle-Supplied PL/ SQL Packages

DBMS_ROWID Functions and Procedures *(Continued)*

ROWID_TO_ RESTRICTED (CONT.)	*Conversion_type* should be set to the constant ROWID_CONVERT_INTERNAL if the *old_rowid* is stored in a ROWID variable, or EXTERNAL_CONVERT_EXTERNAL if the *old_rowid* is stored as a character string.
ROWID_TYPE	*type*:=ROWID_TYPE(*row_id*) ROWID_TYPE returns 0 if *row_id* is restricted, and 1 if *row_id* is extended.
ROWID_VERIFY	*Return_value*:=ROWID_VERIFY(*rowid_in, schema_name, object_name, conversion_type*) ROWID_VERIFY returns 0 if the restricted *rowid_in*, which must exist within the specified *schema_name* and *object_name*, can be converted to extended format, and 1 otherwise. *Conversion_type* should be set to the constant ROWID_CONVERT_INTERNAL if the *old_rowid* is stored in a ROWID variable, or EXTERNAL_CONVERT_EXTERNAL if the *old_rowid* is stored as a character string.

Package DBMS_SESSION

The DBMS_SESSION package provides a number of utilities for managing the current session.

DBMS_SESSION Functions and Procedures

CLOSE_DATABASE _LINK	CLOSE_DATABASE_LINK(*dblink*) CLOSE_DATABASE_LINK closes the specified database link.
FREE_UNUSED_ USER_MEMORY	FREE_UNUSED_USER_MEMORY() FREE_UNUSED_USER_MEMORY releases memory from the session that is not currently in use.

DBMS_SESSION Functions and Procedures *(Continued)*

IS_ROLE_ ENABLED	*enabled*:=IS_ROLE_ENABLED(*rolename*) IS_ROLE_ENABLED returns true if the *rolename* is currently enabled, and false otherwise.
IS_SESSION_ ALIVE	*alive*:=IS_SESSION_ALIVE(*uniqueid*) IS_SESSION_ALIVE returns true if the session identified by *uniqueid* is alive. *Uniqueid* is the same value returned by DBMS_SESSION.UNIQUE_SESSION_ID.
LIST_CONTEXT 8i	LIST_CONTEXT(*list, lsize*) LIST_CONTEXT returns the active context namespaces for the current session (see CREATE CONTEXT in Chapter 4, "Data Definition Language (DDL)"). *List* is a table of records defined by the type APPCTXTABTYP. *Lsize* returns the number of elements in the list.
RESET_PACKAGE	RESET_PACKAGE() RESET_PACKAGES resets all package variables and de-initializes all packages in the session.
SET_CLOSE_ CACHED_OPEN_ CURSORS	SET_CLOSE_CACHED_OPEN_CURSORS(*close_cursors*) SET_CLOSE_CACHED_OPEN_CURSORS controls the behavior of open cursors when a COMMIT or ROLLBACK occurs. If *close_cursors* is set to true, then all cursors are closed on a COMMIT or ROLLBACK. If false, cursors remain open.
SET_CONTEXT	SET_CONTEXT(*namespace, attribute, value*) SET_CONTEXT sets the *value* of a context's *namespace* and *attribute*.

DBMS_SESSION Functions and Procedures *(Continued)*

SET_NLS	SET_NLS(*param, value*)
	SET_NLS sets the National Language Support parameter to a new *value*.
SET_ROLE	SET_ROLE(*role_cmd*)
	SET_ROLE emulates the SQL statement SET ROLE (see Chapter 4). *Role_cmd* is a string with the following format:
	{*role_name* [IDENTIFIED BY *password*] [, *role_name*...] | ALL EXCEPT *role_list*| NONE }
SET_SQL_TRACE	SET_SQL_TRACE(*sql_trace*)
	SET_SQL_TRACE initiates or suppresses SQL tracing. If *sql_trace* is true, then tracing will commence; if false, tracing will cease.
SWITCH_ CURRENT_ CONSUMER_ GROUP 8i	SWITCH_CURRENT_CONSUMER_GROUP(*new_consumer_group, old_consumer_group*) SWITCH_CURRENT_CONSUMER_GROUP allows a session to change its current *resource consumer group* to *new_consumer_group*. *Old_consumer_group* is an OUT parameter that contains the old consumer group identifier.
UNIQUE_ SESSION_ID	*Unique_id*:=UNIQUE_SESSION_ID() UNIQUE_SESSION_ID returns a unique session identifier for the current session.

Package DBMS_SHARED_POOL

The DBMS_SHARED_POOL package displays objects in the shared pool and allows them to be "pinned" in the shared pool so that they are never flushed out. This can improve performance for procedures and reduce memory fragmentation.

DBMS_SHARED_POOL Functions and Procedures

ABORTED_ REQUEST_ THRESHOLD	ABORTED_REQUEST_THRESHOLD(*threshold_size*) ABORTED_REQUEST_THRESHOLD limits certain memory reclamation procedures to shared memory allocations greater than *threshold_size*. If a memory allocation is greater than *threshold_size*, then objects may be flushed from the shared pool to make way for the new allocation.
KEEP	KEEP(*name, flag*) KEEP specifies that the nominated object should not be flushed from the shared pool. *Flag* determines the type of the object. Options are: P : Procedure, which is the default. T : Type. R : Trigger. Q : Sequence.
KEEP	UNKEEP(*name, flag*) UNKEEP specifies that the nominated object may be flushed from the shared pool. It revokes the effect of the KEEP procedure.
SIZES	SIZES(*minsize*) SIZES prints the names and sizes of objects in the shared pool greater than *minsize*. Since SIZES uses DBMS_OUTPUT to generate the report, the SQL*PLUS SET SERVEROUTOUTPUT option, or some other means of retrieving the output, should be employed.

Oracle-Supplied PL/ SQL Packages

Package DBMS_SNAPSHOT

The DBMS_SNAPSHOT package provides utilities for managing snapshots.

DBMS_SNAPSHOT Functions and Procedures

BEGIN_TABLE_REORGANIZATION	BEGIN_TABLE_REORGANIZATION(*tabowner, tabname*) BEGIN_TABLE_REORGANIZATION is called before the reorganization of a master table and ensures validity of snapshot log data. *Tabowner* and *tabname* identifiy the table to be reorganized.
DROP_SNAPSHOT 7.3	DROP_SNAPSHOT(*mowner, master, snapshot*) DROP_SNAPSHOT drops snapshots based on the master table specified by *mowner* and *master*. Obsolete from Oracle8 onwards.
END_TABLE_REORGANIZATION	END_TABLE_REORGANIZATION(*tabowner, tabname*) END_TABLE_REORGANIZATION is called after the reorganization of a master table and ensures validity of snapshot log data. *Tabowner* and *tabname* identifiy the table that was reorganized.
PURGE_LOG	PURGE_LOG(*master, num, flag*) PURGE_LOG removes rows from the snapshot log. *Master* defines the master table that owns the log. *Num* indicates the maximum number of snapshots that will be prevented from refreshing as a result of the purge. *Flag*, if set to the string 'DELETE', indicates that at least one of the snapshot's log entries will be deleted. This overrides the *Num* parameter.

DBMS_SNAPSHOT Functions and Procedures *(Continued)*

REFRESH	REFRESH(*list, method, rollback_seg, push_deferred_rpc, refresh_after_errors, purge_option, parallelism, heap_size, atomic_refresh*)

REFRESH causes one or more snapshots to be refreshed.

List is either a comma-separated list of snapshots to be refreshed or a PL/SQL table of type DBMS_UTILITY.UNCL_ARRAY, where each element is a snapshot to be refreshed.

Method is "F" for fast refresh, "C" for complete refresh, or "?" for default refresh.

Rollback_seg specifies a rollback segment to be used for the refresh.

Push_deferred_rpc, if true, indicates that any changes made to an *updateable snapshot* should be propagated before the refresh occurs.

Refresh_after_errors, if true, indicates that an updateable snapshot should be refreshed even if outstanding replication conflicts exit.

8.0+   The *purge_option* determines how the remote procedure transaction queue will be purged if *push_deferred_rpc* is true. If 0, the queue will not be purged; if 1, the queue will be subject to a quick but possibly imprecise purge; and if 2, the purge may be slower, but more precise.

8.0+   *Parallelism* determines the number of parallel streams of execution for the snapshot process (0=serial refresh).

8.0+   *Heap_size* determines the number of parallel transactions to be employed for a parallel refresh.

8i   *Atomic_refresh*, if true, requires that all snapshots or materialized views in *list* be refreshed in a single transaction.

DBMS_SNAPSHOT Functions and Procedures *(Continued)*

REFRESH_ALL	REFRESH_ALL()
	REFRESH_ALL causes all snapshots due for automatic refresh to be refreshed.
REFRESH_ALL_ MVIEWS	REFRESH_ALL_MVIEWS(*number_of_failures, method, rollback_seg, refresh_after_errors, atomic_refresh*)
	REFRESH_ALL_MVIEWS causes all snapshots based on local master tables to be refreshed, if necessary.
	Number_of_failures is an OUT parameter that returns the number of snapshots that could not be refreshed.
	Method is "F" for fast refresh, "C" for complete refresh, or "?" for default refresh.
	Rollback_seg specifies a rollback segment to be used for the refresh.
	Refresh_after_errors, if true, indicates that an updateable snapshot should be refreshed even if outstanding replication conflicts exit.
	Atomic_refresh, if true, requires that all snapshots or materialized views in the list be refreshed in a single transaction.
REFRESH_ DEPENDENT	REFRESH_DEPENDENT(*number_of_failures, list, method, rollback_seg, refresh_after_errors, atomic_refresh*)
	This command refreshes all snapshots dependent on the specified local master tables.
	Number_of_failures is an OUT parameter that returns the number of snapshots that could not be refreshed.
	List is either a string in comma-separated list format or a PL/SQL table containing a list of master tables.

DBMS_SNAPSHOT Functions and Procedures *(Continued)*

REFRESH_ DEPENDENT (CONT.)	*Method* is a string containing one character for each table in the list. *Method* characters may be "F" for fast refresh, "C" for complete refresh, or "?" for default refresh.

Rollback_seg specifies a rollback segment to be used for the refresh.

Refresh_after_errors, if true, indicates that an updateable snapshot should be refreshed even if outstanding replication conflicts exit.

Atomic_refresh, if true, requires that all snapshots or materialized views in *list* be refreshed in a single transaction.

REGISTER_ SNAPSHOT	REGISTER_SNAPSHOT(*snapowner, snapname, snapsite, snapshot_id, flag, qry_txt, rep_type*)

REGISTER_SNAPSHOT is run at a master site to register a snapshot at a remote site.

Snapowner is the owner of the snapshot.

Snapname is the name of the snapshot.

Snapsite is the name of the snapshot site.

Snapshot_id is the snapshot identifier.

Qry_txt is the query that defines the snapshot.

Rep_type is the version of the snapshot. This can be one of the following: DBMS_SNAPSHOT.REG_UKNOWN(the default), DBMS_SNAPSHOT.REG_V7_GROUP, DBMS_SNAPSHOT.REG_V8_GROUP, or DBMS_SNAPSHOT.REG_REPAPI_GROUP.

DBMS_SNAPSHOT Functions and Procedures *(Continued)*

SET_I_AM_A_ REFRESH	SET_I_AM_A_REFRESH() SET_I_AM_A_REFRESH returns true if the local site is executing a snapshot refresh.
UNREGISTER_ SNAPSHOT	UNREGISTER_SNAPSHOT(*snapowner, snapname, snapsite*) UNREGISTER_SNAPSHOT is run at a master site to deregister a snapshot at a remote site. *Snapowner* is the owner of the snapshot. *Snapname* is the name of the snapshot. *Snapsite* is the name of the snapshot site.

Package DBMS_SPACE

DBMS_SPACE contains utilities to examine space utilization within segments.

DBMS_SPACE Functions and Procedures

FREE_BLOCKS	FREE_BLOCKS(*segment_owner, segment_name, segment_type, freelist_group_id, free_blks, scan_limit, partition_name*) FREE_BLOCKS returns the number of free blocks within the segment defined by *segment_owner* and *segment_name*. The number of free blocks is returned in the OUT parameter *free_blks*. *Segment_type* is one of the following: "TABLE," "INDEX," "CLUSTER," or "LOBSEGMENT." *Freelist_group_id* restricts the free block scan to blocks that appear in the specified free list. *Scan_limit*, if present, restricts the search to the specified number of blocks. *Partition_name*, if specified, restricts the analysis to the specified partition.

DBMS_SPACE Functions and Procedures *(Continued)*

UNUSED_SPACE	UNUSED_SPACE(*segment_owner, segment_name, segment_type,* total_blocks, total_bytes, unused_blocks, unused_bytes, last_used_extent_file_id, last_used_extent_block_id, last_used_block, partition_name)

UNUSED_SPACE returns information about unused space within the segment defined by *segment_owner* and *segment_name.*

Total_blocks, total_bytes, unused_blocks, unused_bytes, last_used_extent_file_id, last_used_extent_block_id, and *last_used_block* are OUT parameters that return information about total space allocations, unused space, and the segment high-water mark.

Partition_name, if specified, restricts the analysis to the specified partition.

Package DBMS_SQL

The DBMS_SQL package provides a generic interface for executing dynamic SQL within PL/SQL procedures. This interface closely resembles the Oracle7 OCI interface. Figure 6–1 illustrates DBMS_SQL program flow.

DBMS_SQL Functions and Procedures

BIND_ARRAY	BIND_ARRAY(*c, name, n_table*)

BIND_ARRAY binds an array of values into an open cursor, for instance, to insert multiple rows in a single call.

C represents the cursor, which must have been OPENed and PARSEd. *Name* represents the name of the bind variable within the cursor. *N_table* is a PL/SQL table of the appropriate datatype that contains the array to be bound.

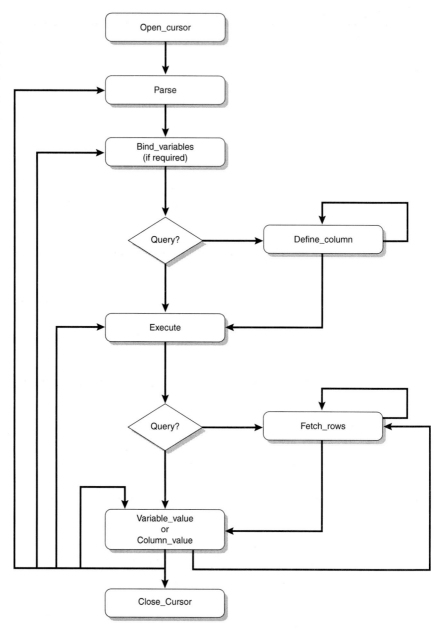

Figure 6-1   DBMS_SQL Program Flow

DBMS_SQL Functions and Procedures *(Continued)*

BIND_VARIABLE	BIND_VARIABLE(*c, name, value*)

BIND_VARIABLE binds a scalar variable to an open cursor.

C represents the cursor, which must have been OPENed and PARSEd.

Name represents the name of the bind variable within the cursor.

Value represents the variable to be bound. The value may be of the following datatypes: NUMBER, DATE, VARCHAR2, BLOB, CLOB, or BFILE.

BIND_VARIABLE _CHAR	BIND_VARIABLE_CHAR(*c, name, value*)

BIND_VARIABLE_CHAR is the same as BIND_VARIABLE, except that it may accept a datatype of CHAR.

BIND_VARIABLE _RAW	BIND_VARIABLE_RAW(*c, name, value*)

BIND_VARIABLE_RAW is the same as BIND_VARIABLE, except that it may accept a datatype of RAW.

BIND_VARIABLE _ROWID	BIND_VARIABLE_ROWID(*c, name, value*)

BIND_VARIABLE_ROWID is the same as BIND_VARIABLE, except that it may accept a datatype of ROWID.

CLOSE_CURSOR	CLOSE_CURSOR(*c*)

CLOSE_CURSOR closes the specified cursor. This has a somewhat different function than the CLOSE_CURSOR command in PL/SQL: CLOSE_CURSOR completely removes the cursor. In PL/SQL, CLOSE_CURSOR merely "logically" closes the cursor.

Oracle-Supplied PL/ SQL Packages

DBMS_SQL Functions and Procedures *(Continued)*

COLUMN_VALUE	COLUMN_VALUE(*c, position, value,column_error, actual_length*) COLUMN_VALUE returns one or more values for a specific column retrieved by FETCH_ROWS. *C* defines the cursor, which must have been fetched from. *Position* denotes the position of the column within the result set. *Value* is the PL/SQL variable that receives the results. This may be of datatype NUMBER, VARCHAR2, DATE, BLOB, CLOB, or BFILE, or it may be an index-by table of one of those datatypes (for bulk fetches). *Column_error* (OUT parameter) may optionally contain any error or warning code for the column. *Actual_length* will contain the actual length of the variable before any truncation.
COLUMN_VALUE _CHAR	COLUMN_VALUE_CHAR(*c, position, value*) COLUMN_VALUE_CHAR is the same as COLUMN_VALUE, except that *value* must be defined as a CHAR datatype.
COLUMN_VALUE _LONG	COLUMN_VALUE_LONG(*c, position, length, offset, value, value_length*) COLUMN_VALUE_LONG is the same as COLUMN_VALUE, except that *value* must be defined as a LONG datatype. *Length* and *offset* retrieve only part of the long column—*length* bytes long, starting at *offset*.
COLUMN_VALUE _RAW	COLUMN_VALUE_RAW(*c, position, value*) COLUMN_VALUE_RAW is the same as COLUMN_VALUE, except that *value* must be defined as a RAW datatype.

DBMS_SQL Functions and Procedures *(Continued)*

COLUMN_VALUE _ROWID	COLUMN_VALUE_ROWID(*c, position, value*)

COLUMN_VALUE_ROWID is the same as COLUMN_VALUE, except that *value* must be defined as a ROWID datatype.

DEFINE_ARRAY	DEFINE_ARRAY(*c, position, table, cnt, lower_bound*)

DEFINE_ARRAY defines the index-by table to be used to retrieve values from the FETCH_ROWS call.

C is the cursor from which the rows will be fetched.

Table is an index-by table of an appropriate datatype (NUMBER, VARCHAR2, DATE, BLOB, CLOB, or BFILE).

Cnt defines the number of rows to be added with each fetch. *Lower_bound* defines the index in the table of the first row fetched.

DEFINE_COLUMN	DEFINE_COLUMN(*c, position, column, column_size*)

DEFINE_COLUMN defines a column in a SELECT cursor with a PL/SQL variable that will receive the column's value.

C is the cursor from which the column will be fetched. *Position* denotes the column position within the result set with which the variable is associated.

Column is a PL/SQL variable of an appropriate datatype (NUMBER, VARCHAR2, DATE, BLOB, CLOB, or BFILE).

Column_size optionally indicates the maximum expected size of the column.

DEFINE_COLUMN _CHAR	DEFINE_COLUMN_CHAR(*c, position, column, column_size*)

DEFINE_COLUMN_CHAR is the same as DEFINE_COLUMN, except that COLUMN must be of a CHAR datatype.

DBMS_SQL Functions and Procedures *(Continued)*

DEFINE_COLUMN _LONG	DEFINE_COLUMN_LONG(*c, position, column*) DEFINE_COLUMN_LONG is the same as DEFINE_COLUMN, except that *column* must be of a LONG datatype.
DEFINE_COLUMN _RAW	DEFINE_COLUMN_RAW(*c, position, column, column_size*) DEFINE_COLUMN_RAW is the same as DEFINE_COLUMN, except that *column* must be of a RAW datatype.
DEFINE_COLUMN _ROWID	DEFINE_COLUMN_ROWID(*c, position, column*) DEFINE_COLUMN_ROWID is the same as DEFINE_COLUMN, except that *column* must be of a ROWID datatype.
DESCRIBE_ COLUMNS	DESCRIBE_COLUMNS(*c, col_cnt, desc_t*) DESCRIBE_COLUMNS returns the descriptions of a result set associated with a SELECT cursor. *C* is the cursor. *Col_cnt* is an OUT parameter that returns the number of columns in the result set. *Desc_t* is a table of the DBMS_SQL.DESC_TAB type which, in turn, is based on the DBMS_SQL.DESC_REC record type. This structure contains fields that contain descriptions of the result set such as column name, column datatype, etc.
EXECUTE	*Return_value*:=EXECUTE(*c*) EXECUTE executes the cursor. For a non-SELECT cursor, the EXECUTE call executes the statement in its entirety. For a SELECT cursor, the EXECUTE call prepares the cursor for fetching. For INSERT, UPDATE, and DELETE statements, the *return_value* indicates the number of rows processed.

DBMS_SQL Functions and Procedures *(Continued)*

EXECUTE_AND_ FETCH	*Return_value*:=EXECUTE_AND_FETCH(*c, exact*) EXECUTE_AND_FETCH combines an EXECUTE call and a FETCH_ROWS call for a SELECT cursor. *C* is the cursor. If *exact* is set to true, then an exception is raised if the cursor returns more than one row. *Return_value* is set to the number of rows fetched.
FETCH_ROWS	*Return_value*:=FETCH_ROWS(*c*) FETCH_ROWS retrieves one or more rows from the specified cursor. The number actually retrieved depends on the smallest number of elements in all variables associated with columns by DEFINE_ARRAY and DEFINE_COLUMN calls. The *return_value* indicates the number of rows that were actually fetched.
IS_OPEN	*Return_value*:=IS_OPEN(*c*) IS_OPEN returns true if the cursor is open, and false otherwise.
LAST_ERROR_ POSITION	*Parse_error_offset*:=LAST_ERROR_POSITION() LAST_ERROR_POSITION returns the parse error offset, which is the location within a SQL statement associated with a parse error. This statement must appear after a PARSE call.
LAST_ROW_ COUNT	*rowcount*:=LAST_ROW_COUNT() LAST_ROW_COUNT should be called after a FETCH_ROWS or EXECUTE_AND_FETCH call. It returns the cumulative number of rows returned from the query.

DBMS_SQL Functions and Procedures *(Continued)*

LAST_ROW_ID	*rowid*:=LAST_ROW_ID()
	LAST_ROW_ID should be called after a FETCH_ROWS or EXECUTE_AND_FETCH call. It returns the last ROWID retrieved by the fetch.
LAST_SQL_FUNCTION_CODE	*sqlcode*:=LAST_SQL_FUNCTION_CODE()
	This call returns the SQL function code returned by the previous call.
OPEN_CURSOR	*C*:=OPEN_CURSOR()
	OPEN_CURSOR allocates memory for a cursor and returns the cursor identifier, which is used in all subsequent operations on the cursor.
	OPEN_CURSOR is very different from OPEN CURSOR in PL/SQL: It creates a cursor that is not yet associated with an SQL statement and which is not yet ready for execution.
PARSE	PARSE(*c, statement, language_flag*)
	PARSE(*c, statement, lb, ub, lfflg, language_flag*)
	PARSE checks the syntactic validity of the SQL *statement*, determines its execution plan, and associates the *statement* and execution plan with the cursor, *c*.
	If the SQL statement is too large to be stored in a single VARCHAR2 datatype, then *statement* may be defined as a table of type VARCHAR2, each element of which contains a portion of the SQL statement. *Lb* and *ub* define the lower and upper bounds for the table elements to be concatenated. *Lfflg*, if set to true, indicates that a line feed should be appended to each element in the table as it is concatenated.
	Language_flag may be set to v7, v8, or NATIVE to determine if the program will comply with Oracle7, Oracle8, or default behavior.

DBMS_SQL Functions and Procedures *(Continued)*

VARIABLE_VALUE	VARIABLE_VALUE(*c, name, value*)
	VARIABLE_VALUE returns the value of the bind variable *name* into the PL/SQL variable or table *value*. The named bind variables may be found within a PL/SQL block or within a returning clause (see Chapter 5, "PL/SQL Language").
	Value should be a PL/SQL variable or table of an appropriate datatype (NUMBER, VARCHAR2, DATE, BLOB, CLOB, or BFILE).
VARIABLE_ VALUE_CHAR	VARIABLE_VALUE_CHAR(*c, name, value*)
	VARIABLE_VALUE_CHAR is the same as VARIABLE_VALUE, except that *value* must be of a CHAR datatype.
VARIABLE_ VALUE_RAW	VARIABLE_VALUE_RAW(*c, name, value*)
	VARIABLE_VALUE_RAW is the same as VARIABLE_VALUE, except that *value* must be of a RAW datatype.
VARIABLE_ VALUE_ROWID	VARIABLE_VALUE_ROWID(*c, name, value*)
	VARIABLE_VALUE_ROWID is the same as VARIABLE_VALUE, except that *value* must be of a ROWID datatype.

Package DBMS_STATS

The DBMS_STATS package provides utilities for managing optimizer statistics. **8i**
Optimizer statistics are used by the cost-based optimizer to determine the execution plan for SQL statements. This package provides the functionality of the ANALYZE command, together with the ability to export and import optimizer statistics and collect statistics in parallel.

Optimizer statistics may be held in local tables identified by the *stattab* parameter in many DBMS_STATS procedures. If this parameter is null, then the procedures work against the live data dictionary statistics tables. *Statid* allows multiple sets of statistics to be stored in a single *stattab*.

DBMS_STATS Functions and Procedures

CONVERT_RAW_ VALUE	CONVERT_RAW_VALUE(*rawval, resval*) CONVERT_RAW_VALUE converts a raw maximum or minimum endpoint value for a histogram bucket into an "actual" value of the same datatype as the column to which the histogram belongs. *Rawval* is the raw representation of the endpoint. *Resval* is the actual value, which should be of the datatype NUMBER, VARCHAR2, DATE, BLOB, CLOB, or BFILE.
CONVERT_RAW_ VALUE_ NVARCHAR	CONVERT_RAW_VALUE_NVARCHAR(*rawval, resval*) CONVERT_RAW_VALUE_NVARCHAR is the same as CONVERT_RAW_VALUE, except that *rawval* must be taken from an NVARCHAR column and *resval* must be of type NVARCHAR.
CONVERT_RAW_ VALUE_ROWID	CONVERT_RAW_VALUE_ROWID(*rawval, resval*) CONVERT_RAW_VALUE_ROWID is the same as CONVERT_RAW_VALUE, except that *rawval* must be taken from a ROWID column and *resval* must be of type ROWID.
CREATE_STAT_ TABLE	CREATE_STAT_TABLE(*ownname, stattab, tblspace*) CREATE_STAT_TABLE creates a table that can be passed as a *stattab* argument to other procedures in this package. *Ownername* defines the account that owns the table. *Stattab* is the name of the table. *Tblspace* defines the tablespace in which *stattab* will be created.
DELETE_ COLUMN_STATS	DELETE_COLUMN_STATS(*ownname, tabname, colname, partname, stattab, statid, cascade_parts*) DELETE_COLUMN_STATS removes column statistics from a local statistics table or from the data dictionary. *Ownername, tabname,* and *colname* define the column from which statistics will be deleted.

DBMS_STATS Functions and Procedures *(Continued)*

DELETE_COLUMN _STATS (CONT)	*Partname* defines the partition from which statistics will be deleted. If null, then all partitions will be processed. *Stattab* defines a local statistics table, created by CREATE_STAT_TABLE, from which statistics will be deleted. If null, then statistics are deleted from the data dictionary. If *stattab* is not null, then *statid* may be specified to identify a specific set of statistics within *stattab*. *Cascade_parts*, if true, requires that statistics for all partitions or sub-partitions also be deleted.
DELETE_INDEX_ STATS	DELETE_INDEX_STATS(*ownname, indname, partname, stattab, statid, cascade_parts*) DELETE_INDEX_STATS removes index statistics from a local statistics table or from the data dictionary. *Ownername* and *indname* define the index from which statistics will be deleted. *Partname* defines the partition from which statistics will be deleted. If null, then all partitions will be processed. *Stattab* defines a local statistics table, created by CREATE_STAT_TABLE, from which statistics will be deleted. If null, then statistics are deleted from the data dictionary. If *stattab* is not null, then *statid* may be specified to identify a specific set of statistics within *stattab*. *Cascade_parts*, if true, requires that statistics for all partitions or sub-partitions also be deleted.
DELETE_ SCHEMA_STATS	DELETE_SCHEMA_STATS(*ownname, stattab, statid*) DELETE_SCHEMA_STATS deletes all statistics for the current schema. *Ownname* defines the schema from which statistics will be deleted.

DBMS_STATS Functions and Procedures *(Continued)*

DELETE_SCHEMA _STATS (CONT.)	*Stattab* defines a local statistics table, created by CREATE_STAT_TABLE, from which statistics will be deleted. If null, then statistics are deleted from the data dictionary. If *stattab* is not null, then *statid* may be specified to identify a specific set of statistics within *stattab*.
DELETE_TABLE_ STATS	DELETE_TABLE_STATS(*ownname, tabname, partname, stattab, statid, cascade_parts, cascade_columns, cascade_indexes*) DELETE_COLUMN_STATS removes table-related statistics from a local statistics table or from the data dictionary. *Ownername* and *tabname* define the table from which statistics will be deleted. *Partname* defines the partition from which statistics will be deleted. If null, then all partitions will be processed. *Stattab* defines a local statistics table, created by CREATE_STAT_TABLE, from which statistics will be deleted. If null, then statistics are deleted from the data dictionary. If *stattab* is not null, then *statid* may be specified to identify a specific set of statistics within *stattab*. *Cascade_parts*, if true, requires that statistics for all partitions or sub-partitions also be deleted. *Cascade_columns*, if true, requires that statistics for all columns of the table also be deleted. *Cascade_indexes*, if true, requires that statistics for all indexes belonging to the table be deleted.
DROP_STAT_ TABLE	DROP_STAT_TABLE(*ownname, stattab*) DROP_STAT_TABLE drops a statistics table created by CREATE_STAT_TABLE. *Ownname* and *stattab* define the table to be dropped.

DBMS_STATS Functions and Procedures *(Continued)*

EXPORT_COLUMN _STATS	EXPORT_COLUMN_STATS(*ownname, tabname, colname, partname, stattab, statid*)
	EXPORT_COLUMN_STATS copies data dictionary statistics for the column defined by *ownname, tabname,* and *colname* into the local statistics table *stattab. Statid* optionally identifies the identifier within the *stattab.*
	If *partname* is specified, then only statistics from the specified partition will be exported.
EXPORT_INDEX_ STATS	EXPORT_INDEX_STATS(*ownname, indname, partname, stattab, statid*)
	EXPORT_INDEX_STATS copies data dictionary statistics for the index defined by *ownname* and *indname* into the local statistics table *stattab. Statid* optionally identifies the identifier within the *stattab.*
	If *partname* is specified, then only statistics from the specified partition will be exported.
EXPORT_ SCHEMA_STATS	EXPORT_SCHEMA_STATS(*ownname, stattab, statid*)
	EXPORT_SCHEMA_STATS copies data dictionary statistics for the schema defined by *ownname* into the local statistics table *stattab. Statid* optionally identifies the identifier within the *stattab.*
EXPORT_TABLE_ STATS	EXPORT_TABLE_STATS(*ownname, tabname, partname, stattab, statid, cascade*)
	EXPORT_TABLE_STATS copies data dictionary statistics for the table defined by *ownname* and *tabname* into the local statistics table *stattab. Statid* optionally identifies the identifier within the *stattab.*
	If *partname* is specified, then only statistics from the specified partition will be exported.
	Cascade, if true, requires that column and index statistics for the table also be exported.

DBMS_STATS Functions and Procedures *(Continued)*

GATHER_ DATABASE_STATS	GATHER_DATABASE_STATS(*estimate_percent, block_sample, method_opt, degree, granularity, cascade, stattab, statid, options, objlist*)

GATHER_DATABASE_STATS collects optimizer statistics for all schemas in the database.

Estimate_percent specifies the percentage of rows to sample. If null, then statistics are computed on all rows.

If *block_sample* is true, then a random selection of blocks—rather than a random selection of rows—is sampled.

Method_opt is a string of the form:

```
FOR ALL [{INDEXED | HIDDEN}]
    COLUMNS [SIZE histogram_size]
```

See the ANALYZE command (Chapter 4) for details of the *method_opt* clause.

Degree indicates the degree of parallel execution for statistics-gathering. If null, the default for the table is used.

Granularity determines the level of statistics-gathering for partitioned tables. It must be one of the following: DEFAULT, PARTITION, SUBPARTITION, GLOBAL, or ALL.

Cascade, if true, indicates that statistics for indexes should be collected for each table processed.

Stattab defines a local statistics table, created by CREATE_STAT_TABLE, in which statistics will be stored. If null, then statistics are deleted from the data dictionary. If *stattab* is not null, then *statid* may be specified to identify a specific set of statistics within *stattab*.

DBMS_STATS Functions and Procedures *(Continued)*

GATHER_ DATABASE_STATS (CONT.)	*Options* define the criteria for statistics collection. It is one of the following: GATHER STALE, GATHER EMPTY, LIST STALE, or LIST EMPTY, or it may be omitted. *Objlist* is a table of type DBMS_STAT.OBJECTTAB, which itself is a record of type DBMS_STAT.OBJECTELEM. Objects that satisfy the "LIST STALE" or "LIST EMPTY" options are stored in this structure.
GATHER_INDEX_ STATS	GATHER_INDEX_STATS(*ownname, indname, partname, estimate_percent, stattab, statid*) GATHER_INDEX_STATS collects optimizer statistics for a specific index, as defined by *owname* and *indname*. If *partname* is specified, then only statistics for the specified partition will be collected. *Estimate_percent* specifies the percentage of rows to sample. If null, then statistics are computed on all rows. *Stattab* defines a local statistics table, created by CREATE_STAT_TABLE, in which statistics will be stored. If null, then statistics are deleted from the data dictionary. If *stattab* is not null, then *statid* may be specified to identify a specific set of statistics within *stattab*.
GATHER_ SCHEMA_STATS	GATHER_SCHEMA_STATS(*ownname, estimate_percent, block_sample, method_opt, degree, granularity, cascade, options, objlist*) GATHER_SCHEMA_STATS collects optimizer statistics for the schemas identified by *ownname*. *Estimate_percent* specifies the percentage of rows to sample. If null, then statistics are computed on all rows. If *block_sample* is true, then a random selection of blocks—rather than a random selection of rows—is sampled.

Oracle-Supplied PL/
SQL Packages

DBMS_STATS Functions and Procedures *(Continued)*

GATHER_SCHEMA _STATS (CONT.)	*Method_opt* is a string of the form: FOR ALL [{INDEXED | HIDDEN}] COLUMNS [SIZE *histogram_size*]

See the ANALYZE command (Chapter 4) for details of the *method_opt* clause.

Degree indicates the degree of parallel execution for statistics-gathering. If null, the default for the table is used.

Granularity determines the level of statistics-gathering for partitioned tables. It must be one of the following: DEFAULT, PARTITION, SUBPARTITION, GLOBAL, or ALL.

Cascade, if true, indicates that statistics for indexes should be collected for each table processed.

Stattab defines a local statistics table, created by CREATE_STAT_TABLE, in which statistics will be stored. If null, then statistics are deleted from the data dictionary. If *stattab* is not null, then *statid* may be specified to identify a specific set of statistics within *stattab*.

Options define the criteria for statistics collection. It is one of the following: GATHER STALE, GATHER EMPTY, LIST STALE, or LIST EMPTY, or it may be omitted.

Objlist is a table of type DBMS_STAT.OBJECTTAB, which is itself a record of type DBMS_STAT.OBJECTELEM. Objects that satisfy the LIST STALE or LIST EMPTY options are stored in this structure.

GATHER_TABLE_ STATS	GATHER_TABLE_STATS(*ownname, tabname, partname, estimate_percent, block_sample, method_opt, degree, granularity, cascade, stattab, statid*)

GATHER_TABLE_STATS collects statistics for a single table.

DBMS_STATS Functions and Procedures *(Continued)*

GATHER_TABLE_
STATS (CONT.)

Ownname and *tabname* identify the table for which statistics are to be collected, and *partname* optionally identifies a partition within the table.

Estimate_percent specifies the percentage of rows to sample. If NULL, then statistics are computed on all rows.

If *block_sample* is true, then a random selection of blocks—rather than a random selection of rows—is sampled.

Method_opt is a string of the form:

> FOR ALL [{INDEXED | HIDDEN}]
> > COLUMNS [SIZE *histogram_size*] [*column_list*]

See the ANALYZE command (Chapter 4) for details of the *method_opt* clause.

Degree indicates the degree of parallel execution for statistics gathering. If null, the default for the table is used. Collection of statistics for indexes is not parallelized.

Granularity determines the level of statistics-gathering for partitioned tables. It must be one of the following: DEFAULT, PARTITION, SUBPARTITION, GLOBAL, or ALL.

Cascade, if true, indicates that statistics for indexes should be collected for each table processed.

Stattab defines a local statistics table, created by CREATE_STAT_TABLE, in which statistics will be stored. If null, then statistics are deleted from the data dictionary. If *stattab* is not null, then *statid* may be specified to identify a specific set of statistics within *stattab*.

DBMS_STATS Functions and Procedures *(Continued)*

GENERATE_ STATS	GENERATE_STATS(*ownname, objname, organized*) GENERATE_STATS generates statistics for indexes (including bitmap indexes) using table statistics already collected as the data source. *Ownname* and *objname* identify the object that contains the source statistics. *Organized* is a number from 0–10, indicating the degree to which consecutive entries in the index tend to reside in the same data block. Zero (0) indicates high organization.
GET_COLUMN_ STATS	GET_COLUMN_STATS(*ownname, tabname, colname, partname, stattab, statid, distcnt, density, nullcnt, srec, avgclen*) GET_COLUMN_STATS retrieves column-level statistics. *Ownname, tabname, colname,* and *partname* identify the column and (optionally) the partition from which statistics will be extracted. *Stattab* defines a local statistics table, created by CREATE_STAT_TABLE, from which statistics will be extracted. If null, then statistics are extracted from the data dictionary. If *stattab* is not null, then *statid* may be specified to identify a specific set of statistics within *stattab*. The OUT parameters *distcnt, density, nullcnt,* and *avgclen* receive the number of distinct values, column density, number of nulls, and average length of the column. *Srec* is a variable of type DBMS_STATS.STATREC, which is a record holding minimum, maximum, and histogram values for the column.

DBMS_STATS Functions and Procedures *(Continued)*

| GET_INDEX_ STATS | GET_INDEX_STATS(*ownname, indname, partname, stattab, statid, numrows, numlblks, numdist, avglblk, avgdblk, clstfct, indlevel*) |

GET_INDEX_STATS retrieves index statistics.

Ownname, indname, and *partname* identify the index and (optionally) the partition from which statistics will be extracted.

Stattab defines a local statistics table, created by CREATE_STAT_TABLE, from which statistics will be extracted. If null, then statistics are extracted from the data dictionary. If *stattab* is not null, then *statid* may be specified to identify a specific set of statistics within *stattab*.

The OUT parameters *numrows, numlblks, numdist, avglblk, avgdblk, clstfct,* and *indlevel* receive the number of rows, number of leaf blocks, number of distinct keys, average number of leaf blocks for each distinct key, average number of table blocks for each distinct key, clustering factor, and the height of the index or partition.

| GET_TABLE_ STATS | GET_TABLE_STATS(*ownname, tabname, partname, stattab, statid, numrows, numblks, avgrlen*) |

GET_TABLE_STATS retrieves table statistics.

Ownname, tabname, and *partname* identify the table and (optionally) the partition from which statistics will be extracted.

Stattab defines a local statistics table, created by CREATE_STAT_TABLE, from which statistics will be extracted. If null, then statistics are extracted from the data dictionary. If *stattab* is not null, then *statid* may be specified to identify a specific set of statistics within *stattab*.

DBMS_STATS Functions and Procedures *(Continued)*

GET_TABLE_ STATS (CONT.)	The OUT parameters *numrows, numblks,* and *avgrlen* retrieve the number of rows, number of blocks, and average row length for the table or partition.
IMPORT_COLUMN _STATS	IMPORT_COLUMN_STATS(*ownname, tabname, colname, partname, stattab, statid*) IMPORT_COLUMN_STATS transfers column statistics for the column identified by *ownname, tabname, colname,* and, optionally, *partname* (partition) from the local statistics table *stattab,* and, optionally, from the statistics set identified by *statid,* into the data dictionary.
IMPORT_INDEX_ STATS	IMPORT_INDEX_STATS(*ownname, indname, partname, stattab, statid*) IMPORT_INDEX_STATS transfers index statistics for the index identified by *ownname, indname,* and, optionally, *partname* (partition) from the local statistics table *stattab,* and, optionally, from the statistics set identified by *statid,* into the data dictionary.
IMPORT_ SCHEMA_STATS	IMPORT_SCHEMA_STATS(*ownname, stattab, statid*) IMPORT_SCHEMA_STATS transfers all statistics for the schema identified by *ownname* from the local statistics table *stattab,* and, optionally, from the statistics set identified by *statid,* into the data dictionary.
IMPORT_TABLE_ STATS	IMPORT_TABLE_STATS(*ownname, tabname, partname, stattab, statid, cascade*) IMPORT_TABLE_STATS transfers table statistics for the table identified by *ownname, tabname,* and, optionally, *partname* (partition) from the local statistics table *stattab,* and, optionally, from the statistics set identified by *statid,* into the data dictionary. *Cascade,* if true, indicates that statistics for the table's indexes and columns should also be imported.

DBMS_STATS Functions and Procedures *(Continued)*

PREPARE_ COLUMN_ VALUES	PREPARE_COLUMN_VALUES(*srec, histogram_array*)
	PREPARE_COLUMN_VALUES prepares column statistics that can be loaded by SET_COLUMN_STATS.
	Srec is a record of type DBMS_STATS.STATREC. *Srec.epc* should be set to the number of elements in the input array. Other fields in *srec* contain the internal representation that can be fed to SET_COLUMN_STATS.
	Histogram_array contains the start and end values of a height-balanced histogram (or simply, minimum and maximum values if there are only two entries).
PREPARE_ COLUMN_ VALUES_ NVARCHAR	PREPARE_COLUMN_VALUES_NVARCHAR(*srec, nvmin, nvmax*)
	PREPARE_COLUMN_VALUES_NVARCHAR is the same as PREPARE_COLUMN_VALUES, but it works on NVARCHAR columns. Because such columns do not support histograms, *nvmin* and *nvmax* specify minimum and maximum values for the column instead of the *histogram_array* used in PREPARE_COLUMN_VALUES.
PREPARE_ COLUMN_ VALUES_ROWID	PREPARE_COLUMN_VALUES_ROWID(*srec, rvmin, rvmax*)
	PREPARE_COLUMN_VALUES_ROWID is the same as PREPARE_COLUMN_VALUES, but it works on rowid columns. Because such columns do not support histograms, *rvmin* and *rvmax* specify minimum and maximum values for the column instead of the *histogram_array* used in PREPARE_COLUMN_VALUES.
SET_COLUMN_ STATS	SET_COLUMN_STATS(*ownname, tabname, colname, partname, stattab, statid, distcnt, density, nullcnt, srec, avgclen, flags*)
	SET_COLUMN_STATS stores column-level statistics.
	Ownname, tabname, colname, and *partname* identify the column and (optionally) the partition for which statistics will be stored.

DBMS_STATS Functions and Procedures *(Continued)*

SET_COLUMN_STATS (CONT.)	*Stattab* defines a local statistics table, created by CREATE_STAT_TABLE, in which statistics will be stored. If null, then statistics are stored in the data dictionary. If *stattab* is not null, then *statid* may be specified to identify a specific set of statistics within *stattab*. The parameters *distcnt, density, nullcnt,* and *avgclen* set the number of distinct values, column density, number of nulls, and average length of the column. *Srec* is a variable of type DBMS_STATS.STATREC, which is a record holding minimum, maximum, and histogram values for the column. *Flags* are currently unused and should be left null.
SET_INDEX_STATS	SET_INDEX_STATS(*ownname, indname, partname, stattab, statid, numrows, numlblks, numdist, avglblk, avgdblk, clstfct, indlevel, flags*) SET_INDEX_STATS stores index statistics. *Ownname, indname,* and *partname* identify the index and (optionally) the partition for which statistics will be stored. *Stattab* defines a local statistics table, created by CREATE_STAT_TABLE, into which statistics will be stored. If null, then statistics are stored in the data dictionary. If *stattab* is not null, then *statid* may be specified to identify a specific set of statistics within *stattab*. The parameters *numrows, numlblks, numdist, avglblk, avgdblk, clstfct,* and *indlevel* set the number of rows, number of leaf blocks, number of distinct keys, average number of leaf blocks for each distinct key, average number of table blocks for each distinct key, clustering factor, and the height for the index or partition. *Flags* are currently unused and should be left null.

*Oracle-Supplied PL/
SQL Packages*

DBMS_STATS Functions and Procedures *(Continued)*

SET_TABLE_ STATS	SET_TABLE_STATS(*ownname, tabname, partname, stattab,* *statid, numrows, numblks, avgrlen, flags*)

SET_TABLE_STATS sets table statistics.

Ownname, tabname, and *partname* identify the table
and (optionally) the partition for which statistics will be
stored.

Stattab defines a local statistics table, created by
CREATE_STAT_TABLE, into which statistics will be stored. If
null, then statistics are stored in the data dictionary. If
stattab is not null, then *statid* may be specified to
identify a specific set of statistics within *stattab*.

The parameters *numrows, numblks,* and *avgrlen* set the
number of rows, number of blocks, and average row
length for the table or partition.

Package DBMS_SYSTEM

DBMS_SYSTEM contains mainly undocumented internal procedures. Only
SET_SQL_TRACE_IN_SESSION is suitable for general use.

DBMS_SYSTEM Functions and Procedures

SET_SQL_TRACE _IN_SESSION	SET_SQL_TRACE_IN_SESSION(*sid, serial#, sql_trace*)

Set SQL_TRACE_IN_SESSION initiates SQL_TRACE tracing
for the session identified by *sid* and *serial#*, which
correspond to the columns of the same name in
V$SESSION.

Sql_trace, if true, initiates tracing, and if false,
terminates tracing.

Package DBMS_TRANSACTION

DBMS_TRANSACTION provides access to various transaction control options from within PL/SQL.

DBMS_TRANSACTION Functions and Procedures

ADVISE_COMMIT	ADVISE_COMMIT()
	ADVISE_COMMIT is equivalent to the SQL statement ALTER SESSION ADVISE COMMIT (see Chapter 4).
ADVISE_NOTHING	ADVISE_NOTHING()
	ADVISE_NOTHING is equivalent to the SQL statement ALTER SESSION ADVISE NOTHING (see Chapter 4).
ADVISE_ ROLLBACK	ADVISE_ROLLBACK()
	ADVISE_ROLLBACK is equivalent to the SQL statement ALTER SESSION ADVISE ROLLBACK (see chapter 4).
BEGIN_DISCRETE _TRANSACTION	BEGIN_DISCRETE_TRANSACTION()
	BEGIN_DISCRETE_TRANSACTION marks the start of a *discrete transaction*.
COMMIT	COMMIT()
	Equivalent to the SQL statement COMMIT (see Chapter 3).
COMMIT_ COMMENT	COMMIT_COMMENT($cmnt$)
	COMMIT_COMMENT is equivalent to the SQL statement COMMIT COMMENT (see Chapter 3).
COMMIT_FORCE	COMMIT_FORCE(xid, scn)
	COMMIT_FORCE is equivalent to the SQL statement COMMIT FORCE (see Chapter 3).

DBMS_TRANSACTION Functions and Procedures *(Continued)*

LOCAL_ TRANSACTION_ID	*Transaction_id*:=LOCAL_TRANSACTION_ID(*create_transaction*) LOCAL_TRANSACTION_ID returns the transaction ID for the current transaction. If no transaction is current, then it returns null, unless *create_transaction* is true, in which case, a transaction will be created.
PURGE_LOST_DB _ENTRY	PURGE_LOST_DB_ENTRY(*xid*) PURGE_LOST_DB_ENTRY removes an entry for an in-doubt transaction that applies to a database that no longer exists. *Xid* is the transaction identifier from DBA_2PC_PENDING.LOCAL_TRAN_ID.
PURGE_MIXED	PURGE_MIXED(*xid*) PURGE_MIXED removes an entry for an in-doubt transaction that applies to a transaction that has been COMMITTed at some sites and ROLLBACKed at others. *Xid* is the transaction identifier from DBA_2PC_PENDING.LOCAL_TRAN_ID.
READ_ONLY	READ_ONLY() READ_ONLY is equivalent to the SQL statement SET TRANSACTION READ ONLY (see Chapter 3).
READ_WRITE	READ_WRITE() READ_WRITE is equivalent to the SQL statement SET TRANSACTION READ WRITE (see Chapter 3).
ROLLBACK	ROLLBACK() Equivalent to the SQL statement ROLLBACK.
ROLLBACK_ ORCE	ROLLBACK_FORCE(*xid*) ROLLBACK_FORCE is equivalent to the SQL statement ROLLBACK FORCE. *Xid* is the transaction identifier (see Chapter 3).

DBMS_TRANSACTION Functions and Procedures *(Continued)*

ROLLBACK_ SAVEPOINT	ROLLBACK_SAVEPOINT(*savept*) ROLLBACK_SAVEPOINT is equivalent to the SQL statement ROLLBACK TO (see Chapter 3).
SAVEPOINT	SAVEPOINT(*savept*) Equivalent to the SQL statement SAVEPOINT (see Chapter 3).
STEP_ID	*step*:=STEP_ID STEP_ID returns the sequence of the most recent DML statement within the transaction.
USE_ROLLBACK_ SEGMENT	USE_ROLLBACK_SEGMENT(*rb_name*) USE_ROLLBACK_SEGMENT is equivalent to the SQL statement SET TRANSACTION USE ROLLBACK SEGMENT.

Package DBMS_UTILITY

DBMS_UTILITY implements assorted utility routines.

DBMS_UTILITY Functions and Procedures

ACTIVE_ INSTANCES	ACTIVE_INSTANCES(*instance_table, instance_count*) ACTIVE_INSTANCES is an Oracle parallel server utility that returns a PL/SQL table of active instance numbers in *instance_table*, and the number of active instances in *instance_count*.
ANALYZE_ DATABASE	ANALYZE_DATABASE(*method, estimate_rows, estimate_percent, method_opt*) ANALYZE_DATABASE analyzes all objects in the database. *Method* is one of {ESTIMATE|COMPUTE|DELETE}.

DBMS_UTILITY Functions and Procedures *(Continued)*

ACTIVE_ INSTANCES (CONT.)	*Estimate_rows* specifies an absolute number of rows to be used when *method* is ESTIMATE. *Estimate_percent* specifies a percentage of total rows to be used. *Method_opt* is a string of the form: FOR ALL [{INDEXED | HIDDEN}] COLUMNS [SIZE *histogram_size*] [*column_list*] See the ANALYZE command in Chapter 4 for more details.

ANALYZE_PART_ OBJECT	ANALYZE_PART_OBJECT(*schema, object_name, object_type, command_type, command_opt, sample_clause*)
	
	ANALYZE_PART_OBJECT generates multiple tasks to analyze each partition in the object defined by *schema* and *object_name*.
	
	Object type is T for table and I for index.
	
	Command_type is one of the following:
	
	  C : Compute statistics.
	  E : Estimate statistics.
	  D : Delete statistics.
	  V : Validate structure.
	
	Command_opt is a string of the form:
	
	FOR ALL [{INDEXED | HIDDEN}]
	  COLUMNS [SIZE *histogram_size*] [*column_list*]
	
	Sample_clause is a string of the form:
	
	SAMPLE *sample_size* [ROWS|PERCENT]
	
	See the description of the ANALYZE command in Chapter 4 for more details.

DBMS_UTILITY Functions and Procedures *(Continued)*

ANALYZE_SCHEMA	ANALYZE_SCHEMA *(schema, method, estimate_rows, estimate_percent, method_opt)*

ANALYZE_SCHEMA analyzes all objects in the *schema* specified.

Method is one of {ESTIMATE|COMPUTE|DELETE}.

Estimate_rows specifies an absolute number of rows to be used when *method* is ESTIMATE. *Estimate_percent* specifies a percentage of total rows to be used.

Method_opt is a string of the form:

FOR ALL [{INDEXED | HIDDEN}]
    COLUMNS [SIZE *histogram_size*] [*column_list*]

See the description of the ANALYZE command in Chapter 4 for more details.

COMMA_TO_TABLE	COMMA_TO_TABLE(*list, tablen, tab*)

COMMA_TO_TABLE converts the string *list*, which is a comma-separated list of elements, into the PL/SQL table *tab*, which contains one row for each of the elements in *list*. *Tablen* returns the number of elements in the table.

COMPILE_SCHEMA	COMPILE_SCHEMA(*schema*)

COMPILE_SCHEMA compiles all PL/SQL programs in the specified *schema*.

CURRENT_INSTANCE	*instance_number*:=CURRENT_INSTANCE

In an Oracle parallel server environment, CURRENT_INSTANCE returns the current instance identifier.

DATA_BLOCK_ADDRESS_BLOCK	*block_number*:=DATA_BLOCK_ADDRESS_BLOCK(*dba*)

DATA_BLOCK_ADDRESS_BLOCK returns the block number within a data block address (DBA).

DBMS_UTILITY Functions and Procedures *(Continued)*

DATA_BLOCK_ ADDRESS_FILE	*file_number*:=DATA_BLOCK_ADDRESS_FILE(*dba*) DATA_BLOCK_ADDRESS_FILE returns the file number within a data block address (DBA).
DB_VERSION	DB_VERSION(*version, compatibility*) DB_VERSION returns the Oracle server version in the OUT parameter *version*, and the value of the configuration parameter COMPATIBILITY in the OUT parameter *compatible*.
EXEC_DDL_ STATEMENT	EXEC_DDL_STATEMENT(*parse_string*) EXEC_DDL_STATEMENT executes a DDL statement provided by *parse_string*.
FORMAT_CALL_ STACK	*varchar2*:=FORMAT_CALL_STACK FORMAT_CALL_STACK returns a string containing the current call stack.
FORMAT_ERROR _STACK	*varchar2*:=FORMAT_ERROR_STACK FORMAT_ERROR_STACK returns a string containing the current error stack. This may contain more information than is contained in the SQLERRM variable.
GET_HASH_ VALUE	*hash_value*:=GET_HASH_VALUE(*name, base, hash_size*) GET_HASH_VALUE returns a hash value for the string provided by *name*. A hash value is a numerical representation of the string, which can be used as an index in PL/SQL tables to provide rapid access to specific table values. *Base* indicates the lowest hash value to be generated. *Hash_size* indicates the number of unique hash values that should be returned.

DBMS_UTILITY Functions and Procedures *(Continued)*

GET_PARAMETER _VALUE	*parameter_type*:=GET_PARAMETER_VALUE(*parnam, intval, strval*)
	GET_PARAMETER_VALUE retrieves the value of a server configuration parameter. *Parnam* is the name of the parameter to be retrieved.
	Parameter_type is 0 if the parameter has a Boolean or numeric value, and 1 if it has a string value. If the parameter is numeric, then the result is stored in *intval*. If the parameter has a character value, then the result is stored in *strval*.
GET_TIME	*number*:=GET_TIME
	GET_TIME returns the elapsed time in hundredths of a second since an arbitrary point in time.
IS_PARALLEL_ SERVER	*Parallel_server*:=IS_PARALLEL_SERVER
	IS_PARALLEL_SERVER returns true if the instance is part of an *Oracle parallel server,* and false otherwise.
MAKE_DATA_ BLOCK_ADDRESS	*dba*:=MAKE_DATA_BLOCK_ADDRESS(*file, block*)
	MAKE_DATA_BLOCK_ADDRESS constructs a data block address (DBA) from the *file* and *block* numbers provided.
NAME_RESOLVE	NAME_RESOLVE(*name, context, schema, part1, part2, dblink, part1_type, object_number*)
	NAME_RESOLVE resolves full details of the object provided by *name*.
	Name can be a qualified or unqualified object name. NAME_RESOLVE returns additional qualifications that reveal if the name resolves to an object in the current schema or an object in some other schema, is accessed through a database link, and so on.

DBMS_UTILITY Functions and Procedures *(Continued)*

NAME_RESOLVE (CONT.)	*Context* is currently unused.
	Schema returns the schema in which the object exists.
	Part1 indicates the first part of the name, which will normally be the object name itself.
	For packages, *part2* indicates a procedure name within the package.
	Dblink specifies the database link, if any, through which the object is resolved.
	Object_number maps to the OBJECT_ID in DBA_OBJECTS.
NAME_TOKENIZE	NAME_TOKENIZE(*name, a, b, c, dblink, nextpos*)
	NAME_TOKENIZE breaks up a database object name of the form "A [. B [. C]][@ DBLINK]". *Name* is the object's name. *A,b,c*, and *dblink* indicate starting positions in the string for each component of the object name.
PORT_STRING	*port*:=PORT_STRING
	PORT_STRING identifies the operating system port for the Oracle server.
TABLE_TO_ COMMA	TABLE_TO_COMMA(*tab, tablen, list*)
	TABLE_TO_COMMA converts the PL/SQL table *tab* into the string *list*, which is a comma-separated list of names corresponding to each element in the table. *Tablen* specifies the number of elements in the table.

Package UTL_FILE

UTL_FILE allows PL/SQL programs to perform I/O on operating system files.

For security reasons, file access is limited to directories identified by the UTL_FILE_DIR configuration parameter.

UTL_FILE Functions and Procedures

FCLOSE	FCLOSE(*file*)
	FCLOSE closes the specified file.
	File is the file handle returned by FOPEN.
FCLOSE_ALL	FCLOSE_ALL()
	FCLOSE_ALL closes all open files.
FFLUSH	FFLUSH(*file*)
	FFLUSH flushes any buffered changes to the file.
FOPEN	*file*:=FOPEN(*location, filename, open_mode*)
	FOPEN opens the specified file for processing.
	Location specifies the directory in which the file exists. *Filename* is the name of the file.
	Open_mode is one of "r", "w", or "a" for read access, read-write, or read-append.
GET_LINE	GET_LINE(*file, buffer*)
	GET_LINE reads a line from *file* into the local variable *buffer*.
IS_OPEN	*open*:=IS_OPEN(*file*)
	IS_OPEN returns true if the specified *file* handle refers to an open file, and false otherwise.
NEW_LINE	NEW_LINE(*file, lines*)
	NEW_LINE writes *lines* end-of-line characters to *file*.
PUT	PUT(*file, buffer*)
	PUT writes the contents of the local variable *buffer* to *file* without an end-of-line marker.

UTL_FILE Functions and Procedures *(Continued)*

PUT_LINE	PUT_LINE(*file, buffer*)
	PUT_LINE writes the contents of the local variable *buffer* to *file* and appends an end-of-line marker.
PUTF	PUTF(*file, format, arguments*)
	PUTF writes formatted output to *file*. It resembles a simplified version of the C *fprintf* function. *Format* may contain literals, the newline character '\n', and the %s symbol, which substitutes for the string literals provided by *arguments*.

Package UTL_RAW

UTL_RAW provides utility procedures for processing and converting raw datatypes.

UTL_RAW Functions and Procedures

BIT_AND	*raw*:=BIT_AND(*r1, r2*)
	BIT_AND returns a bitwise and of two RAW values.
BIT_COMPLEMENT	*raw*:=BIT_COMPLEMENT(*r*)
	BIT_COMPLEMENT returns the logical complement of a RAW value.
BIT_OR	*raw*:=BIT_OR(*r1, r2*)
	BIT_OR returns a bitwise or of two RAW values.
BIT_XOR	*raw*:=BIT_XOR(*r1, r2*)
	BIT_XOR returns a bitwise exclusive or of two RAW values.
CAST_TO_RAW	*raw*:=CAST_TO_RAW(*c*)
	CAST_TO_RAW converts a VARCHAR2 value into a RAW value.

UTL_RAW Functions and Procedures *(Continued)*

CAST_TO_ VARCHAR2	*varchar2*:=CAST_TO_VARCHAR2(*r*) CAST_TO_VARCHAR2 converts a RAW value into a VARCHAR2 value.
COMPARE	*number*:=COMPARE(*r1, r2, pad*) COMPARE compares two RAW values. It returns 0 if the two RAWS are identical, otherwise, it returns the position of the first non-matching byte. *Pad* defines a character that is used to "pad out" the shorter of the two RAW values, if necessary.
CONCAT	*raw*:=CONCAT(*r1, r2, r3, r4, r5, r6, r7, r8, r9, r10, r11, r12*) CONCAT returns a concatenation of up to 12 RAW values.
CONVERT	*raw*:=CONVERT(*r, to_charset, from_charset*) CONVERT changes a RAW value from one NLS character set to another.
COPIES	*raw*:=COPIES(*r, n*) COPIES returns a RAW composed of *n* copies of the specified RAW value *r*.
LENGTH	*number*:=LENGTH(*r*) LENGTH returns the length of the RAW value.
OVERLAY	*raw*:=OVERLAY(*overlay_str, target, pos, len, pad*) Overlays the RAW *overlay_str* on the RAW *target*, starting at *pos* and proceeding for *len* bytes. If *overlay_str* is less than *len* bytes long, pads out with the *pad* value.
REVERSE	*raw*:=REVERSE(*r*) REVERSE returns the RAW value in reverse byte order.

UTL_RAW Functions and Procedures *(Continued)*

SUBSTR	*raw*:=SUBSTR(*r, pos, len*)
	SUBSTR returns a substring of the RAW value *r*, starting at *pos* and proceeding for *len* bytes.
TRANSLATE	*raw*:=TRANSLATE(*r, from_set, to_set*)
	TRANSLATE translates bytes in *r*, which appear in *from_set*, to the corresponding byte in *to_set*. If *to_set* is shorter than *from_set*, then matching bytes may be deleted.
TRANSLITERATE	*raw*:=TRANSLITERATE(*r, to_set, from_set, pad*)
	TRANSLITERATE translates bytes in *r*, which appear in *from_set*, to the corresponding bytes in *to_set*. If there are no matching bytes in *from_set*, then the *pad* byte will be substituted.

Oracle Java

Introduction

The Oracle8i RDBMS includes a Java Virtual Machine (JVM)—the Aurora JVM—and integrated Java database connectivity APIs that allow Java programs to be stored and executed within the database environment. These Java stored programs may be executed as stored procedures, through a built-in CORBA Object Request Broker, or as Enterprise Java Beans. Oracle refers to this Java environment as the Oracle JServer.

Oracle provides two interfaces to allow Java programs to access Oracle data. These interfaces may be used by stand-alone Java programs accessing Oracle7 or Oracle8 databases, or within the Oracle8i JServer environment:

- JDBC is an industry-standard, low-level API, implemented as Java classes, which allows access to any compliant relational database, including Oracle.
- SQLJ provides a higher-level programming paradigm and allows SQL statements to be directly embedded in Java code. A SQLJ translator program converts these embedded SQL statements into JDBC calls.

Reference

The following Oracle manuals describe JDBC, SQLJ, and Java-stored procedures:

- *Oracle8i SQLJ Developer's Guide and Reference*
- *Oracle8i JDBC Developer's Guide and Reference*
- *Oracle8i Java Stored Procedures Developer's Guide*
- *Oracle8i Java Developer's Guide*

JDBC and Java documentation can be downloaded from http://www.javasoft.com.

Overview of JDBC

JDBC is an API that allows Java programs to communicate with relational databases and other data sources. It is based on the X/Open CLI specification for portable database access and consequently resembles ODBC, which is based on the same specification.

Oracle's implementation of JDBC contains Java classes which allow a Java program to interface with an Oracle database. The fundamental interfaces and classes of JDBC are:

- **DriverManager**, which loads and initializes the Oracle JDBC driver and which establishes a `Connection` object.
- **Connection**, which represents an individual session within the Oracle database. Methods of **Connection** allow **statements** to be created, transactions to be committed or rolled back, and session disconnection.
- **DatabaseMetaData**, which contains information relating to the database that established the **Connection**.
- **Statement**, which represents an individual SQL statement. Methods of **Statement** allow for SQL statements to be executed and for queries to generate a result set. A **PreparedStatement** object allows SQL statements to be re-executed, and a **CallableStatement** object provides access to stored procedures.
- **ResultSet**, which represents the output of an SQL query. Methods of **ResultSet** allow for navigation through the result set and retrieval of data from the result set.
- **ResultSetMetaData**, which describes the structure of a result set.

1. JDBC classes such as `Connection` and `Statement` are often referred to as interfaces in JDBC documentation. Although the JDBC specification defines them as interfaces, they are delivered as fully implemented classes within the Oracle JDBC driver.

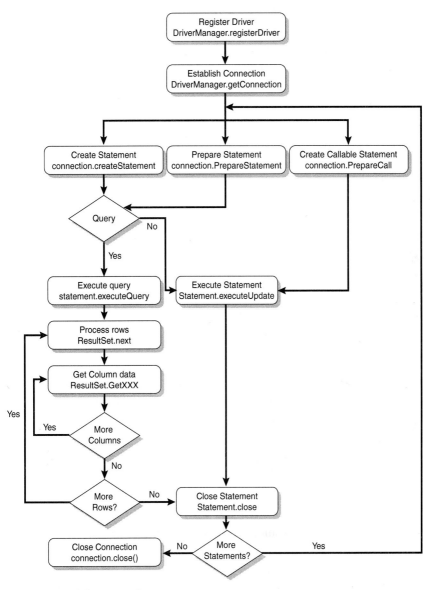

Oracle Java

Figure 7-1   JDBC program flow.

Required Classes

You will normally include the following classes when writing a JDBC program:

```
import java.sql.*;
import java.math.*;
```

To use the Oracle JDBC extensions, you will need to include at least some of the following classes:

```
import oracle.jdbc.driver.*;
import oracle.sql.*
import oracle.jdbc2.*
```

Establishing a Connection

Oracle provides three categories of JDBC driver:

- The JDBC OCI driver, which connects through the standard SQL*NET layer. This driver requires that SQL*NET be installed. This driver is initiated through the `DriverManager.getConnection` method.
- The JDBC thin driver, which establishes a SQL*NET TCP/IP connection to an Oracle database through a simplified version of the SQL*NET protocol implemented entirely in Java. This driver is also initiated through the `DriverManager.getConnection` method. SQL*NET need not be installed on the client computer when using the thin driver.
- The KPRB server driver, which is available only to JDBC programs running within the Oracle server JVM. The server driver effectively passes a handle to the current connection through the `OracleDriver.defaultConnection` method.

Here is an example of connecting through the thin driver to a database BIGDB, which resides on the computer "product07". The Oracle SQL*NET listener program is attached to port 1521, and the username and password are "scott" and "tiger":

```
Connection OraConnect1=DriverManager.getConnection(
    "jdbc:oracle:thin:@product07:1521:BIGDB",
        "scott", "tiger");
```

In this example, an Oracle8 JDBC OCI driver is used. The client computer must support a TNS alias, BIGDB, which could be defined in the TNSNAMES.ORA file, or known to an Oracle names server:

```
Connection OraConnect1=DriverManager.getConnection(
    "jdbc:oracle:oci8:@BIGDB.world,
            "scott", "tiger");
```

In the next code fragment, the JDBC server driver is invoked. This method works only for JDBC programs executing within the JServer JVM.

There is no need to specify connection details, since the program is already running within a connected session.

```
Connection conn = new OracleDriver().defaultConnection();
```

Error Handling in JDBC

Oracle or JDBC errors that occur within JDBC methods will cause the SQLException exception to be thrown. This SQLException class contains methods to return JDBC-specific error properties, such as getSQLstate and getErrorCode, together with the methods of the java.lang.Throwable class, which include getMessage and printStackTrace.

Methods that include JDBC calls should use either the throws clause in the method declaration or use a try-catch block which catches the SQLException. For instance, the following code fragment declares a method, initalize_sql, which might throw a SQLException. If a SQLException occurs, it is caught in the catch block of the main method.

```
static public void initialize_sql(Connection con)
          throws SQLException
    {
//initialize_sql implementation
    }

public static void main(String[] args)
{
    try {
            EsOracle.initialize_sql(OraConnect1); }

    catch (SQLException ex)
          {
        sqlcode=ex.getErrorCode();
        System.out.println
            ("\n*** SQLException caught ***\n");
        while (ex != null) {
          System.out.println ("SQLState: " +
                              ex.getSQLState ());
          System.out.println ("Message: " +
                              ex.getMessage ());
          System.out.println ("Error code: " +
                              ex.getErrorCode ());
          ex = ex.getNextException ();}
      }
}
```

Creating SQL Statements

The createStatement method of the Connection object creates a Statement object.

```
Statement CustQry1=connection.createStatement();
```

Another method of the Connection object, called prepareStatement, associates a SQL statement with the object on creation. This form allows the statement to contain parameters, which are indicated by question marks ("?").

The prepareStatement method creates an object that is permanently associated with a specific SQL statement. This form allows the statement to contain parameters—indicated by question marks ("?")—and allows for the SQL statement to be re-executed with minimal overhead. The following example shows a prepared statement that retrieves a customer_id for a specific customer_name:

```
PreparedStatement CustQry=connection.prepareStatement(
                    "SELECT customer_id " +
                    " FROM customers " +
                    " WHERE customer_name=?");
```

Using prepareStatement is generally more efficient than createStatement for any statement that might be executed more than once or which is executed by multiple users with variable parameters.

The prepareCall method creates a CallableStatement object, which is associated with a stored procedure call. See "Stored Procedures" below.

Executing SQL Statements

The execute and executeUpdate methods of Statement and preparedStatement objects allow SQL statements that are not queries to be executed. The execute method differs from executeUpdate in that it can be used to prepare queries which will return multiple result sets. Because Oracle queries never return multiple result sets, this usage of execute does not apply in Oracle.

For a preparedStatement, executeUpdate and execute take no arguments. For an unprepared Statement, executeUpdate and execute accept the SQL string to be executed. The following example shows prepared and unprepared statements issuing an equivalent DELETE statement:

```
PreparedStatement pstatement=connection.prepareStatement
```

```
                   ("DELETE FROM sales WHERE customer_id=1");
    rows=pstatement.executeUpdate();

    Statement upstatement=connection.createStatement();
    rows=upstatement.executeUpdate("DELETE FROM sales
                                   WHERE customer_id=1");
```

Processing Queries

The executeQuery method of a Statement object returns a ResultSet object, which allows access to the result set returned by a query. The next method allows the program to step through the result set. The next method must be called before any data can be retrieved.

Query results are retrieved through a set of ResultSet methods, which are of the form getDtype, where Dtype represents the datatype of the column whose value is being retrieved, for instance, getString, get-Int, getFloat, etc.

The following code fragment executes a query to retrieve all customer names and print them to standard output:

```
    Statement CustQry1=connection.createStatement();

    ResultSet CustResult=CustQry1.executeQuery(
                     "select customer_name " +
                     "from customers " );

    while   (CustResult.next ())
    {
        CustName=CustResult.getString("customer_name");
            System.out.println(CustName+"\n");
    }
```

Bind and Substitution Variables

Prepared statements may contain parameters that allow a single statement to be reused with different input or selection criteria. The parameters correspond to bind variables in Oracle SQL.

Parameter values are set using Statement methods of the form setDtype method, where Dtype represents the datatype of the column whose value is being retrieved, for instance, setString, setInt, set-Float, etc. The parameters are identified by their position in the statement.

The following code fragment prepares an INSERT statement, which accepts four parameters, sets those parameters, and executes the insert:

```
PreparedStatement SalesInsert=connection.prepareStatement
            ("insert into sales(customer_id,product_id, " +
                " sale_date,quantity,sale_value)  " +
                " values(?,?,SYSDATE,?,?)");

        SalesInsert.setInt(1,CustNum);
        SalesInsert.setInt(2,ProdNum);
        SalesInsert.setInt(3,qty);
        SalesInsert.setInt(4,SaleVal);

        rows=SalesInsert.executeUpdate();
```

Dynamic Queries

When queries are generated dynamically at run-time, the JDBC programmer may be unaware of the nature of the result set that will be returned. To allow the programmer to deal with these sorts of dynamic queries, the get-MetaData method of the ResultSet object creates a ResultMetaData object, which can be used to determine the number, names, types, and other properties of columns that will be returned.

For instance, the following example uses the ResultSetMetaData interface to return the names of the columns that would be returned by the query SELECT * from CUSTOMERS:

```
Statement statement1=connection.createStatement();
ResultSet ResultSet1=statement1.executeQuery
            ("SELECT * from CUSTOMERS");
ResultSetMetaData meta1=ResultSet1.getMetaData();

for   (i=1 ; i <=meta1.getColumnCount(); i++)
        {
                System.out.println("Column " + i + " is " +
                    meta1.getColumnLabel(i));
        }
```

Stored Procedures

The prepareCall method of the Connection object creates a CallableStatement object and associates it with a stored procedure, stored function, or PL/SQL block. As with PreparedStatements, input parameters are specified by "?". However, CallableStatements may also support

OUT parameters (see Chapter 5, "PL/SQL Language," for a discussion of OUT parameters).

OUT parameters must be defined by the registerOutParameter method of the CallableStatement object. Once the CallableStatement has been executed (by executeUpdate), then OUT parameters can be retrieved by get*Dtype* methods, where *Dtype* represents the datatype of the column whose value is being retrieved, for instance, getString, get-Int, or getFloat. These methods differ from their implementation in the Statement class in that they specify the parameter position rather than the column name.

The next example calls a pfactorial stored function that accepts the Java variable input_number as input. The getInt method is used to retrieve the output from the function.

```
int input_number=10;

CallableStatement pfactorial = connection.prepareCall
               ("BEGIN ? := pfactorial(?); END;");

pfactorial.registerOutParameter(1,Types.INTEGER);
pfactorial.setInt(2, input_number);
pfactorial.executeUpdate();
System.out.println("The factorial of 10 is
   " +pfactorial.getInt(1));
```

Transaction Control

The commit and rollback methods of the Connection class allow transactions to be committed or rolled back. In addition, the autocommit property of a connection can be used to issue an implicit commit after every statement. The autocommit property is controlled by the setAutoCommit method of the Connection class.

Autocommit is not enabled within Java stored procedures and functions—it is available only in stand-alone programs.

Oracle JDBC Extensions

The examples shown so far all conform to JDBC 1.0 syntax and—with the exception of connection strings—are valid for all relational database systems. However, not all Oracle functionality can be implemented in JDBC 1.0, and some facilities that are implemented are not implemented effi-

Oracle Java

ciently. Consequently, Oracle provides extensions to their JDBC implementation.

Oracle JDBC extensions fall into the following broad categories:

- Native support for Oracle specific datatypes such as ROWIDS, refs, and
  lobs.
- Native support for Oracle8 object types.
- Facilities that conform to JDBC 2.0, but not to JDBC 1.0.
- Facilities that improve performance such as array insert and array
  fetch.

Many of these facilities require that you use Oracle-supplied descendents of the standard JDBC interfaces and classes such as OracleStatement and OracleResultSet.

It is often sufficient to cast a standard JDBC object into the corresponding Oracle implementation to use an Oracle-specific feature. For
instance, a standard JDBC connection can be cast to OracleConnection
to exploit the row pre-fetch capability of the Oracle driver:

```
Connection connection =
        DriverManager.getConnection(
          "jdbc:oracle:thin:@192.168.2.143:1521:ORCL0",
                    "sqltune", "sqltune");

((OracleConnection)connection).setDefaultRowPrefetch(20);
```

Table 7–1 Oracle Extensions to Core JDBC Classes

Oracle Class	Implements...
oracle.jdbc.driver. OracleCallableStatement	java.sql.CallableStatement
oracle.jdbc.driver. OracleConnection	java.sql.Connection
oracle.jdbc.driver. OracleDatabaseMetaData	java.sql.DatabaseMetaData
oracle.jdbc.driver. OracleDriver	java.sql.Driver
oracle.jdbc.driver. OraclePreparedStatement	java.sql.PreparedStatement

Table 7-1 Oracle Extensions to Core JDBC Classes *(Continued)*

Oracle Class	Implements...
`oracle.jdbc.driver.` `OraclePreparedStatement`	`java.sql.PreparedStatement`
`oracle.jdbc.driver.` `OracleResultSetMetaData`	`java.sql.ResultSetMetaData`
`oracle.jdbc.driver.` `OracleServerDriver`	`java.sql.Driver`
`oracle.jdbc.driver.` `OracleStatement`	`java.sql.Statement`

The Oracle extension classes are described in the "JDBC Language Reference" section later in this chapter.

Overview of SQLJ

SQLJ offers an alternative model for Java programs that need to access Oracle. SQLJ provides simpler methods for executing SQL statements and for retrieving result sets. SQLJ statements are converted by the *SQLJ translator* into JDBC statements and to other SQLJ-specific Java statements before execution.

A JDBC program may require many lines of code to prepare, set parameters, execute, iterate through the result set, and retrieve column values. An equivalent SQLJ program can implement the same functionality in only a few lines of code.

Importing Classes

You will generally import the following packages if you want to be able to use all SQLJ features:

```
import sqlj.runtime.*;
import java.sql.*;
import oracle.jdbc.*;
```

Oracle Java

SQLJ Statements

All SQLJ statements start with the `#sqlj` directive. This directive lets the SQLJ translator know that what follows is a SQLJ command that must be translated into corresponding JDBC commands or SQLJ run-time calls.

SQLJ statements come in three main varieties:

• Context declarations.
• Iterator declarations.
• Executable statements.

Context Declarations

A SQLJ context is roughly equivalent to a JDBC connection.

There is always a default connection context in an SQLJ program. In a SQLJ program running within the Oracle8i JVM, this context is automatically attached to the current sessions connection. In stand-alone programs, the default context needs to be associated with a JDBC connection.

Explicit `context` declarations are required when a SQLJ program establishes multiple Oracle sessions. A `context` declaration takes the form:

#sql [*class_modifiers*] context *context_name*;

`Class_modifiers` are general Java modifiers such as `public`, `private`, etc. `Context_name` can be any user-defined name. This name is used to construct a class definition that is used later when establishing a connection.

Iterator Declarations

An iterator declaration creates a class definition that can be used to manipulate the results from a query. An iterator declaration has the general form:

```
#sql [class_modifiers] iterator iterator_name
(type_declarations);
```

`Class_modifiers` are general Java modifiers such as `public`, `private`, etc. `Iterator_name` can be any user-defined name. This name is used to construct a class definition that is used later when retrieving columns from a query.

`Type_declarations` can either be:

- A list of Java types corresponding to the datatypes to be returned by the query, for instance, (String, String, int). This form defines a positional iterator.
- A list of Java parameter declarations corresponding to the datatypes to be returned by the query, for instance, (String Surname, String Firstname, int age). This defines a named iterator.

Executable Statement Declarations

An executable SQLJ declaration includes a SQL statement within braces. The general form is:

```
#sql [context_declaration] [{return_value|iterator}=]
     { SQL_Statement };
```

Context_declaration is a context identifier as described above. The context_declaration is optional, but if present, it is enclosed in square brackets, "[ ]".

If the SQL_Statement is a stored function, then return_value retrieves the return value from the function. If SQL_Statement is a query, then an iterator class—created using the iterator syntax defined above—can be declared to receive the results of the query.

The SQL_Statement may be any SQL statement or a PL/SQL block.

Setting Up a Connection

SQLJ programs in stored procedures do not need to establish a connection. All SQLJ statements in such a stored procedure will use the default connection.

Outside of stored procedures, a SQLJ context must be associated with a database connection before any statements may be executed.

First, the Oracle JDBC driver must be loaded and registered:

```
Driver SQLJdriver = (Driver)
     (Class.forName
        "oracle.jdbc.driver.OracleDriver").newInstance());

DriverManager.registerDriver(SQLJdriver);
```

Then the DriverManager.getConnection method is used to establish a Connection object and the setDefaultContext method is used to associate this connection with the default SQLJ context. This example uses the Oracle thin JDBC driver:

Oracle Java

```
DefaultContext.setDefaultContext(
        new DefaultContext(DriverManager.getConnection(
            "jdbc:oracle:thin:@host_name:port:sid",
            "username", "password")));
```

Creating additional contexts—if multiple connections are required—requires a context declaration (see "Context Declarations" above). This statement creates a context class Ctx:

```
#sql context Ctx ;
```

An instance of the Ctx class is then created:

```
static Ctx Ctxt2;
```

This context is then initialized to a connection using the JDBC thin driver:

```
Ctxt2 = new Ctx(DriverManager.getConnection(
            "jdbc:oracle:thin:@host_name:port:sid",
            "username", "password"));
```

You can also "piggyback" a connection onto an existing JDBC connection by simply specifying the connection when creating the context:

```
// Create the JCBC connection
Connection JDBCconnection=DriverManager.getConnection(
            " jdbc:oracle:thin:@host_name:port:sid",
            "username", "password");

// Associate the SQLJ context Ctxt3
// with the JDBC connection
Ctx Ctxt3 = new Ctx(JDBCconnection);
```

Simple SQL Statements

SQL statements that are not queries are simply enclosed in braces following the #sql directive. For instance, the following update statement is legal:

```
#sql {INSERT INTO sales
            (customer_id,product_id, sale_date,
            quantity,sale_value)
        VALUES(43,23,SYSDATE,10,2200) } ;
```

Query Processing

To process result sets from a query object, an iterator class is declared. The iterator class is created using the #sql iterator directive. The following example creates a named iterator class called `CustIter`, which can be used to manage a result set with `VARCHAR2` columns `customer_id` and `customer_name`:

```
#sql iterator CustIter (String customer_id, String
customer_name) ;
```

An instance of the iterator is declared and referenced in the query execution statement:

```
CustIter custiter1;
#sql custiter1 = {  SELECT customer_name,customer_id
                    FROM customers};
```

The iterator class `custiter1` contains the attributes of the result set and can be used to navigate the result set:

```
while (custiter1.next())
  { System.out.println(custiter1.customer_id() + " " +
                  custiter1.customer_name()); }
```

Error Handling

Because SQLJ statements are translated into standard JDBC, they may cause the `SQLException` exception to be thrown. Error handling therefore follows normal JDBC conventions. Methods and classes containing SQLJ statements should either contain a `throws SQLException` clause or `try` ... `catch(SQLException)` blocks.

Bind Variables

Any Java variable of an appropriate type may serve as a SQL bind variable. Bind variables are prefixed by ":" within SQL statements and allow SQL statements to be efficiently re-executed when query parameters change.

```
int customer_id=2;
int product_id=3;
int quantity=10;
int sale_value=1000;
#sql {INSERT INTO sales
           (customer_id,product_id, sale_date,
           quantity,sale_value)
       VALUES(:customer_id,:product_id,SYSDATE,
             :quantity,:sale_value) } ;
```

Bind variables may be arrays, such as in the following example, which inserts an array called `sales`:

```
for ( i =0; i < 9; i++) {
    #sql {INSERT INTO sales
                (customer_id,product_id, sale_date,
                quantity,sale_value)
            VALUES(:(cust_array[i]),
                    :(prod_array[i]), SYSDATE,
                    :(quant_array[i]),
                    :(value_array[i])) }; }
```

You can select into a bind variable without an iterator using the INTO clause, providing that the query returns only one row.

```
#sql { SELECT count(*) INTO :sale_count FROM sales };
System.out.println("There are " + sale_count + " sales");
```

Transaction Control

The COMMIT and ROLLBACK statements may be included with SQLJ statements to provide manual control over transaction processing. Additionally, the autocommit property of a JDBC connection causes a COMMIT to be silently issued after every statement. You can specify the autocommit flag in SQLJ using the following syntax (Ctxt is the SQLJ context):

```
Ctxt.getConnection().setAutoCommit({true|false});
```

The autocommit facility is not available within stored procedures.

Translating SQLJ Programs

SQLJ programs must be translated into Java programs before they can be executed. The SQJ program, described in Chapter 8, "Command Line Utilities," performs this translation. It is not necessary to translate SQLJ programs before loading them into the database.

Some tools can perform SQLJ translation for you automatically. For instance, loadjava will translate .sqlj programs as they are loaded, and Oracle JDeveloper performs the necessary translations automatically.

Creating Java Stored Procedures and Functions

Before a Java program can be called as a stored procedure or function in Oracle8i, two things need to happen:

• The Java classes concerned must be loaded into the database.

• The Java classes must be "published" by defining a PL/SQL interface that maps a PL/SQL call specification to a Java call specification.

In the following discussion, we load and publish an interface to a simple JDBC program. The class EsOracleW, described below, defines the interface to the program.

```
import java.sql.*;
import oracle.jdbc.driver.*;
import java.math.*;

public class EsOracleW {

    static public void initialize_sql()
        throws SQLException
    {
      Connection conn =
      new OracleDriver().defaultConnection();
      EsOracle.initialize_sql(conn);
    }

    static public int
    jdbc_transaction(java.lang.String Custname,
                     java.lang.String ProdName,
                     int qty)
        throws SQLException
    {
      Connection conn =
      new OracleDriver().defaultConnection();
    return(EsOracle.jdbc_transaction(conn,Custname,
                                     ProdName, qty));

    }

}
```

The method initialize_sql establishes a default connection, which it passes to EsOracle.initialize_sql to prepare SQL statements. The method jdbc_transaction passes a default connection to EsOracle.jdbc_transaction, which implements a simple transaction.

We can see that it is the EsOracle class that does most of the work. The purpose of the EsOracleW class is to insulate the EsOracle class from its Oracle connection. In that way, EsOracle may be used in a stand-alone Java run-time environment or from within a stored procedure.

Oracle Java

Loading Java into the Database

The `loadjava` utility can be used to load a Java class into a database. Chapter 8 documents the full syntax of `loadjava`, but for our examples, we can load the `EsOracle` and `EsOracleW` classes by issuing the following commands:

```
loadjava -v -r -f -u username/password@host:port:sid
EsOracle.java
loadjava -v -r -f -u username/password@host:port:sid
EsOracleW.java
```

Alternately, Java classes can be created using the CREATE JAVA command (see Chapter 4, "Data Definition Language (DDL)"):

```
CREATE OR REPLACE AND RESOLVE JAVA SOURCE NAMED
"EsOracleW"
    AS
    import java.sql.*;
    import oracle.jdbc.driver.*;
    import java.math.*;

    public class EsOracleW {

        static public void initialize_sql()
            throws SQLException
        {
          Connection conn =
          new OracleDriver().defaultConnection();
          EsOracle.initialize_sql(conn);
        }

        static public int jdbc_transaction
                    (java.lang.String Custname,
                     java.lang.String ProdName, int qty)
            throws SQLException
        {
          Connection conn =
          new OracleDriver().defaultConnection();
          return(EsOracle.jdbc_transaction(conn,
              Custname,ProdName, qty));
        }
    }
```

Resolver Specifications

Resolver specifications—determined by the setting of the loadjava option `resolver` or by the RESOLVER clause of the CREATE JAVA statement—act in a similar way to the CLASSPATH environment variable. Resolver specifications associate name wildcards with Oracle schemas which are to be searched for a matching reference. If multiple identical wildcards are specified, then the schemas are searched in order. For instance, the following resolver specification requires that SYSTEM be searched first, followed by SCOTT, followed by SYS:

```
"((* system) (* scott) (* sys))"
```

Stored Procedure Privileges

Java stored procedures have a much greater potential for interaction with the external operating system than stored procedures written in PL/SQL. Java stored procedures may potentially open TCP/IP sockets, execute operating system commands, and perform file I/O. When a Java stored procedure interacts with the operating system, it inherits the operating system security privileges of the Aurora JVM, which may have more privileges than the user executing the procedure.

Database roles limit the types of activities that a Java procedure may perform. If the user has the JAVASYSPRIV role enabled, then all operating system interaction is enabled. If the user has JAVAUSERPRIV, then external I/O is allowed, subject to the same restrictions as the UTL_FILE packaged procedure (that is, the directory must be listed in the configuration parameter UTL_FILE_DIR) and sockets can be opened only on the host running the JServer. If neither JAVASYSPRIV nor JAVAUSERPRIV privileges are granted, then no external interaction is allowed.

Publishing Java Stored Procedures

"Publishing" a Java stored program means defining a PL/SQL procedure or function with compatible parameters and return values which uses the AS LANGUAGE JAVA clause to associate the PL/SQL program with the Java program:

```
CREATE OR REPLACE FUNCTION JDBC_TRANSACTION
    (custname VARCHAR2,
            prodname VARCHAR2, qty NUMBER)
        RETURN number
    AS LANGUAGE JAVA
```

Oracle Java

```
NAME 'EsOracleW.jdbc_transaction(java.lang.String,
        java.lang.String,int)
    return int';
```

Once the Java program has been published, it may accessed by calling the published PL/SQL program.

```
DECLARE
    result NUMBER;
BEGIN
    initialize_sql;
    result:=jdbc_transaction
    ('MARSH and Sons','Product 1', 10);
END;
```

JDBC Language Reference

Datatypes

Table 7-2 displays the JDBC datatypes that are defined in the `java.sql.Types` and `oracle.jdbc.driver.OracleTypes` classes. For each of these types, a set*Type* and get*Type* method is defined in either the core JDBC classes or in an Oracle extension.

Table 7–2 JDBC Datatypes

Type	Source
ARRAY	oracle.jdbc.driver.OracleTypes
BFILE	oracle.jdbc.driver.OracleTypes
BIGINT	java.sql.Types
BINARY	java.sql.Types
BIT	java.sql.Types
BLOB	oracle.jdbc.driver.OracleTypes
CHAR	java.sql.Types
CLOB	oracle.jdbc.driver.OracleTypes
CURSOR	oracle.jdbc.driver.OracleTypes

Table 7–2 JDBC Datatypes *(Continued)*

Type	Source
DATE	java.sql.Types
DECIMAL	java.sql.Types
DOUBLE	java.sql.Types
FLOAT	java.sql.Types
INTEGER	java.sql.Types
LONGVARBINARY	java.sql.Types
LONGVARCHAR	java.sql.Types
NULL	java.sql.Types
NUMBER	oracle.jdbc.driver.OracleTypes
NUMERIC	java.sql.Types
OTHER	java.sql.Types
RAW	oracle.jdbc.driver.OracleTypes
REAL	java.sql.Types
REF	oracle.jdbc.driver.OracleTypes
ROWID	oracle.jdbc.driver.OracleTypes
SMALLINT	java.sql.Types
STRUCT	oracle.jdbc.driver.OracleTypes
TIME	java.sql.Types
TIMESTAMP	java.sql.Types
TINYINT	java.sql.Types
VARBINARY	java.sql.Types
VARCHAR	java.sql.Types

DriverManager Class

DriverManager loads and initializes JDBC drivers and creates Connection objects for specific drivers.

DriverManager Methods Description

GETCONNECTION   public static synchronized Connection
                    getConnection(String *URL*, String *user*,
                        String *password*) throws SQLException

The getConnection method establishes a connection to the Oracle instance and returns a Connection object that is used to conduct operations against the database.

The format of the URL depends on the type of Oracle driver being used to establish the connection. For the Oracle thin JDBC driver, the format is:

```
jdbc:oracle:thin:@hostname:port_number:si
d
```

where *hostname* is the name of the computer on which the instance resides, *port_number* is the port address of the listener (usually 1521 or 1526), and *sid* is the Oracle instance identifier.

For the OCI driver, the URL is of the form:

```
jdbc:oracle:oci8:@TnsAlias
```

where *TnsAlias* is the TNS alias for the instance as defined in the TNSNAMES.ORA file or as known to an Oracle names server.

GETDRIVER   public static Driver **getDriver**(String url)
                    throws SQLException

getDriver attempts to locate a driver that understands the given URL. The DriverManager attempts to select an appropriate driver from the set of registered JDBC drivers.

DriverManager Methods Description *(Continued)*

GETDRIVERS	```public static java.util.Enumeration getDrivers()``` getDrivers returns an enumerated list of currently registered JDBC drivers.
GETLOGIN TIMEOUT	```public static int getLoginTimeout()``` getLoginTimeout returns the number of seconds for which a login attempt can wait before failing.
GETLOGSTREAM	```public static java.io.PrintStream getLogStream()``` getLogStream returns the logging/tracing PrintStream that is used by the DriverManager and all drivers.
PRINTLN	```public static void println(String message)``` println prints a message to the JDBC log stream.

REGISTERDRIVER	```public static synchronized void registerDriver(java.sql.Driver driver) throws SQLException```
	
	Each JDBC driver must register itself with the DriverManager before being called. In an Oracle context, you would register the Oracle driver as follows:
	
	```DriverManager.registerDriver(new oracle.jdbc.driver.OracleDriver());```

SETLOGIN TIMEOUT	```public static void setLoginTimeout(int seconds)``` setLoginTimeout sets the number of seconds for which a login attempt can wait before failing.
SETLOGSTREAM	```public static void setLogStream(java.io.PrintStream out)``` setLogStream sets the logging/tracing PrintStream that is used by the DriverManager and all drivers.

Oracle Java

Connection Interface

The Connection interface defines a class that represents a connection to an Oracle database. The DriverManager.getConnection method returns an object that conforms to the Connection interface.

Connection Methods

CLEARWARNINGS	void **clearWarnings**()
	clearWarnings() clears any existing warnings.
CLOSE	void **close**()
	The close method terminates the current session.
COMMIT	void **commit**()
	commit commits the current transaction.
CREATE STATEMENT	Statement **createStatement**()
	createStatement creates a Statement object which can then be used by executeUpdate or executeQuery to execute a SQL statement.
GETAUTOCOMMIT	boolean **getAutoCommit**()
	getAutoCommit returns true if the database is in autocommit mode.
GETMETADATA	DatabaseMetaData **getMetaData**()
	getMetaData returns a DatabaseMetaData object which describes the properties of the current connection.
GETTRANSACTION ISOLATION	int **getTransactionIsolation**()
	getTransactionIsolation returns the current transaction isolation level as set by setTransactionIsolation.

Connection Methods *(Continued)*

GETWARNINGS	SQLWarning **getWarnings**()
	getWarnings returns any warnings issued for this connection.
ISCLOSED	boolean **isClosed**()
	isClosed returns true if the connection is closed.
ISREADONLY	boolean **isReadOnly**()
	isReadOnly returns true if the connection is in read-only mode.
NATIVESQL	String **nativeSQL**(String *sql*)
	Some drivers may convert the JDBC SQL grammar into their system's native SQL grammar prior to sending it; nativeSQL returns the native form of the statement that the driver would have sent.
PREPARECALL	CallableStatement **prepareCall**(String *sql*)
	prepareCall creates a CallableStatement object which can be associated with a PL/SQL block or stored procedure call.
	The SQL statement is either an anonymous PL/SQL block, e.g.:
	"BEGIN *statements* END"
	or SQL92-style stored procedure call, e.g.:
	"{ [? =] CALL *procedure_or_function_name* ([?] [,?...]) }"
	When using PL/SQL syntax, bind variables/parameters may be specified either as bind variables, e.g., ":1", ":2", or as standard JDBC notation in which each parameter is specified by a "?".

Oracle Java

Connection Methods *(Continued)*

PREPARE STATEMENT	PreparedStatement **prepareStatement**(String *sql*)

prepareStatement creates a PreparedStatement object which is associated with the SQL statement specified. The SQL statement may include parameters denoted by "?".

ROLLBACK	void **rollback**()

rollback issues a rollback on the current transaction.

SETAUTOCOMMIT	void **setAutoCommit**(boolean *autoCommit*)

If setAutoCommit is true, then a commit is issued after each statement is executed. This method has no effect within stored procedures.

SETREADONLY	void **setReadOnly**(boolean *readOnly*)

setReadOnly indicates to the driver that no database updates will be performed.

SETTRANSACTION ISOLATION	void **setTransactionIsolation**(int *level*)

setTransactionIsolation sets the transaction isolation level. JDBC allows the following constants to be specified, but TRANSACTION_READ_UNCOMMITTED and TRANSACTION_REPEATABLE_READ are not available in Oracle:

TRANSACTION_READ_UNCOMMITTED = 1
TRANSACTION_READ_COMMITTED = 2
TRANSACTION_REPEATABLE_READ = 4
TRANSACTION_SERIALIZABLE = 8

OracleConnection Extensions

The `OracleConnection` class implements the JDBC `Connection` interface, together with the following Oracle-specific methods:

OracleConnection Methods

GETREMARKS REPORTING	public boolean **getRemarksReporting**() getRemarksReporting returns true if TABLE_REMARKS reporting is enabled. See setRemarksReporting.
GETTYPEMAP	public java.util.Dictionary **getTypeMap**() getTypeMap retrieves the type map for this connection. This is usually the first step in mapping Oracle8 object types to custom Java classes.
SETDEFAULT EXECUTEBATCH	public synchronized void **setDefaultExecuteBatch** (int *batch_size*) setDefaultExecuteBatch sets the default update-batching value for this connection. Update-batching allows the JDBC driver to transparently accumulate database modifications (typically inserts). When the *batch_size* is reached, all the modifications are sent to the database in one call.
SETDEFAULT ROWPREFETCH	public synchronized void **setDefaultRowPrefetch** (int *prefetch_size*) setDefaultRowPrefetch sets the default row pre-fetch value for this connection. The row pre-fetch facility allows multiple rows to be returned in a single call to the Oracle database, which can substantially improve query performance.

Oracle Java

OracleConnection Methods *(Continued)*

SETREMARKS REPORTING	`public void `**`setRemarksReporting`**`(boolean remarks)` `setRemarksReporting` enables or disables TABLE_REMARKS reporting. By default, the Oracle JDBC driver does not report table or column comments when returning data from the `DatabaseMetaData` object. Setting `setRemarksReporting` to true causes comments to be returned, but at a substantial performance cost.
SETTYPEMAP	`public void `**`setTypeMap`**`(java.util.Dictionary type_map)` `setTypeMap` initializes or updates the type map for this connection. The `typeMap` is an object of type `java.util.Dictionary`, which may be created by `getTypeMap`. This structure contains mappings between custom Java classes and Oracle8 object types.

Statement Class

The `Statement` class provides methods for processing SQL statements. SQL statements executed by the `Statement` class do not include parameters and are not stored procedures (or at least, do not have OUT parameters).

Statement Methods

CANCEL	`void `**`cancel`**`()` `cancel` cancels a SQL statement being executed in another thread.
CLEARWARNINGS	`void `**`clearWarnings`**`()` `clearWarnings()` clears any existing warnings.
CLOSE	`void `**`close`**`()` `close` closes the specified statement. This releases resources and closes the result set.

Statement Methods *(Continued)*

EXECUTE	boolean **execute**(String sql)
	execute executes the sql statement, which may return multiple results. Since Oracle SQL statements never return multiple result sets, this method is not applicable in an Oracle JDBC program.
EXECUTEQUERY	ResultSet **executeQuery**(String *sql*)
	executeQuery executes the sql statement specified— which is a query—and returns a result set.
EXECUTEUPDATE	int **executeUpdate**(String *sql*)
	executeUpdate executes the sql statement—which is not a query—and returns the number of rows processed.
GETMAXFIELDSIZE	int **getMaxFieldSize**()
	getMaxFieldSize gets the maximum length in bytes for any column in a result set returned by the query. It is set by setMaxFieldSize.
GETMAXROWS	int **getMaxRows**()
	getMaxRows returns the maximum number of rows that a result set will contain. It is set by setMaxRows.
GETMORE RESULTS	boolean **getMoreResults**()
	getMoreResults moves to the next result set if the statement returns more than one result set. Because Oracle SQL statements never return multiple result sets, this method is not applicable in an Oracle JDBC program.
GETQUERYTIME OUT	int **getQueryTimeout**()
	getQueryTimeout returns the number of seconds that will elapse before a statement will time out. It is set by setQueryTimeout.

Oracle Java

Statement Methods *(Continued)*

GETRESULTSET	`ResultSet` **`getResultSet`**`()`
	GetResultSet returns a result set from an SQL statement that returns multiple result sets. Because Oracle SQL statements never return multiple result sets, this method is not applicable in an Oracle JDBC program.

GETUPDATE COUNT	`int` **`getUpdateCount`**`()`
	getUpdateCount returns the number of rows processed by the statement.

GETWARNINGS	`SQLWarning` **`getWarnings`**`()`
	getWarnings returns any warnings issued for this statement.

SETCURSORNAME	`void` **`setCursorName`**`(String name)`
	setCursorName associates the current statement with a cursor name, which can be used in WHERE CURRENT OF clauses of UPDATE and DELETE statements.

SETESCAPE PROCESSING	`void` **`setEscapeProcessing`**`(boolean enable)`
	If false, then substitution parameters will not be processed. The default is true.

SETMAXFIELD SIZE	`void` **`setMaxFieldSize`**`(int max)`
	setMaxFieldSize sets the maximum length, in bytes, which will be returned by any column in a query.

SETMAXROWS	`void` **`setMaxRows`**`(int max)`
	setMaxRows sets the maximum number of rows that a result set may contain.

SETQUERYTIME OUT	`void` **`setQueryTimeout`**`(int seconds)`
	setQueryTimeout sets the number of seconds that will elapse before a statement will time out.

OracleStatement Extensions

The OracleStatement class implements the Statement interface and adds the following Oracle-specific methods:

OracleStatement Methods

DEFINECOLUMN TYPE	public synchronized void **defineColumnType(**
	    int *columnindex*, int *datatype* [, int
	    length])
	
	defineColumnType allows you to set the datatype of a particular column in a query, avoiding the database accesses which would otherwise be required to determine this.
	
	Columnindex is the position of the column in the result set. Datatype is a Java type from java.sql.Types or oracle.jdbc.driver.OracleTypes. Length optionally defines the column length.

GETROW PREFETCH	public int **getRowPrefetch()** getRowPrefetch returns the row pre-fetch value for the statement.
SETROW PREFETCH	public synchronized void **setRowPrefetch(**int *prefetch*) setRowPrefetch sets the row pre-fetch value for this statement The row pre-fetch facility allows multiple rows to be returned in a single call to the Oracle database, which can substantially improve query performance.

Oracle Java

PreparedStatement Class

PreparedStatement is a subclass of Statement, which allows SQL statements to be prepared and then executed multiple times. Using Prepared-Statements is more efficient than simply re-executing Statements because it reduces SQL *parse* overhead.

PreparedStatements are created by the prepareStatement method of a Connection object. The SQL associated with a PreparedStatement is defined when the PreparedStatement is created. PreparedStatements inherit the methods and properties of the `Statement` class, but add methods for setting parameters—equivalent to Oracle bind variables—which are represented within the SQL statement by "?". The *parameterIndex* argument to the `PreparedStatement` method specifies the relative position of the parameter within the statement.

PreparedStatement Methods

CLEAR PARAMETERS	void **clearParameters**() `clearParameters` clears (unsets) all values for all parameters.
EXECUTE	boolean **execute**() `execute` executes an SQL statement that may return multiple results. Because Oracle SQL statements never return multiple result sets, this method is not applicable in an Oracle JDBC program.
EXECUTEQUERY	ResultSet **executeQuery**() `executeQuery` executes a prepared statement that is a query and returns a result set.
EXECUTEUPDATE	int **executeUpdate**() `executeUpdate` executes a prepared statement that is not a query and returns the number of rows processed.
SETASCIISTREAM	void **setAsciiStream**(int *parameterIndex*, java.io.InputStream x, int *length*) `setAsciiStream` associates the parameter identified by *parameterIndex* with a Java `Inputstream`. The value of the parameter will then be obtained from the `InputStream`. Length specifies the maximum number of bytes to be read—if not specified, then the `InputStream` will be read until an end-of-file is encountered.

PreparedStatement Methods *(Continued)*

SETBIGDECIMAL	void **setBigDecimal**(int *parameterIndex*, BigDecimal *x*) setBigDecimal associates the parameter identified by *parameterIndex* with the BigDecimal variable *x*.
SETBINARY STREAM	void **setBinaryStream**(int *parameterIndex*, java.io.InputStream *x*, int *length*) setBinaryStream is the same as setAsciiStream, except that binary data will be read from the InputStream.
SETBOOLEAN	void **setBoolean** (int *parameterIndex*, boolean *x*) setBoolean associates the parameter identified by *parameterIndex* with the boolean variable *x*.
SETBYTE	void **setByte** (int *parameterIndex*, byte *x*) setByte associates the parameter identified by *parameterIndex* with the byte variable *x*.
SETBYTES	void **setBytes**(int *parameterIndex*, byte *x*[]) setBytes associates the parameter identified by *parameterIndex* with the byte array *x*.
SETDATE	void **setDate** (int *parameterIndex*, java.sql.Date *x*) setDate associates the parameter identified by *parameterIndex* with the java.sql.Date variable *x*.
SETDOUBLE	void **setDouble**(int *parameterIndex*, double *x*) setDouble associates the parameter identified by *parameterIndex* with the double variable *x*.
SETFLOAT	void **setFloat** (int *parameterIndex*, float *x*) setFloat associates the parameter identified by *parameterIndex* with the float variable *x*.

Oracle Java

PreparedStatement Methods *(Continued)*

SETINT	void **setInt**(int *parameterIndex*, int *x*) setInt associates the parameter identified by *parameterIndex* with the int variable *x*.
SETLONG	void **setLong**(int *parameterIndex*, long *x*) setLong associates the parameter identified by *parameterIndex* with the long variable *x*.
SETNULL	void **setNull**(int *parameterIndex*, int *sqlType*) setNull sets the parameter identified by *parameterIndex* to null.
SETOBJECT	void **setObject**(int *parameterIndex*, Object *x*, int *targetSqlType*, int *scale*) setObject sets the value of the parameter identified by *parameterIndex* to the Object x. Object x is converted to targetSqlType, which is one of the types defined in java.sql.Types.
SETSHORT	void **setShort**(int *parameterIndex*, *x*) setShort associates the parameter identified by *parameterIndex* with the short variable *x*.
SETSTRING	void **setString**(int *parameterIndex*, String *x*) setString associates the parameter identified by *parameterIndex* with the String variable *x*.
SETTIME	void **setTime**(int *parameterIndex*, java.sql.Time x) setTime associates the parameter identified by *parameterIndex* with the java.sql.Time variable *x*.

PreparedStatement Methods *(Continued)*

SETTIMESTAMP	void **setTimestamp**(int *parameterIndex*, java.sql.Timestamp *x*)

setTimestamp associates the parameter identified by *parameterIndex* with the java.sql.Timestamp variable *x*.

SETUNICODE STREAM	void **setUnicodeStream**(int *parameterIndex*, java.io.InputStream *x*, int *length*)

setUnicodeStream is the same as setAsciiStream, except that Unicode data will be read from the InputStream.

OraclePreparedStatement Extensions

The OraclePreparedStatement class extends the OracleStatement class, implements the PreparedStatement interface, and also defines the following Oracle-specific methods:

OraclePreparedStatement Methods

GETEXECUTE BATCH	public int **getExecuteBatch**()

getExecuteBatch retrieves the update-batching value for this statement. See setExecuteBatch.

SENDBATCH	public synchronized int **sendBatch**()

sendBatch causes the current batch of database modifications to be submitted immediately, even if the update-batch value has not yet been reached. It returns the number of rows affected.

SETARRAY	public synchronized void **setArray** (int *parameterIndex*, oracle.jdbc2.Array *x*)

setArray binds an array of data to the parameter identified by *parameterIndex*.

OraclePreparedStatement Methods *(Continued)*

SETBFILE	`public synchronized void` **`setBFILE`**`( int`
	`        parameterIndex, oracle.sql.BFILE x)`
	
	`setBFILE` associates the parameter identified by `parameterIndex` with the BFILE variable *x*.

SETBLOB	`public synchronized void` **`setBLOB`**`( int`
	`        parameterIndex, oracle.sql.BLOB x)`
	
	`setBLOB` associates the parameter identified by `parameterIndex` with the BLOB variable *x*.

SETCLOB	`public synchronized void` **`setCLOB`**`( int`
	`        parameterIndex, oracle.sql.CLOB x)`
	
	`setCLOB` associates the parameter identified by `parameterIndex` with the CLOB variable *x*.

SETCURSOR	`Public synchronized void` **`setCursor`**`(Int`
	`        parameterIndex , java.sql.ResultSet x)`
	
	`SetCursor` binds the `java.sql.ResultSet` to the parameter identified by `parameterIndex` . This is used to emulate a PL/SQL cursor variable parameter.

SETCUSTOM DATUM	`Public synchronized void` **`setCustomDatum`**`(Int`
	`        parameterIndex, oracle.sql.CustomDatum x)`
	
	`SetCustomDatum` binds a `CustomDatum` object (used for mapping Oracle object types to Java) to the parameter identified by `parameterIndex`.

SETEXECUTE BATCH	`public synchronized void` **`setExecuteBatch`**`(int`
	`        batch_size)`
	
	`setExecuteBatch` sets the update-batching value for this statement. Update-batching allows the JDBC driver to transparently accumulate database modifications (typically inserts). When the `batch_size` is reached, all the modifications are sent to the database in one call.

OraclePreparedStatement Methods *(Continued)*

SETNUMBER	`public synchronized void` **`setNUMBER`**`(int` *`parameterIndex`* `, oracle.sql.NUMBER` *`x`*`)`
	setNUMBER associates the parameter identified by *parameterIndex* with the NUMBER variable *x*.
SETORACLE OBJECT	`public synchronized void` **`setOracleObject`**`(int` *`parameterIndex`* `, oracle.sql.Datum` *`x`*`)`
	setOracleObject associates the parameter identified by *parameterIndex* with the oracle.sql.Datum object variable *x*.
	oracle.sql.Datum is the superclass of all Oracle datatype classes and can represent any Oracle datatype in native form. Typically, the oracle.sql.Datum object will have been retrieved by the getOracleObject method of OracleResultSet and OracleCallableStatement.
SETRAW	`public synchronized void` **`setRAW`**`(int` *`parameterIndex`* `, oracle.sql.RAW` *`x`*`)`
	setRAW associates the parameter identified by *parameterIndex* with the RAW variable *x*.
SETREFTYPE	`public void` **`setRefType`**`(int` *`parameterIndex`* `,` `oracle.sql.REF` *`x`*`)`
	setRefType associates the parameter identified by *parameterIndex* with the oracle.jdbc2.Ref variable *x*, which corresponds to an Oracle8 ref type.
SETROWID	`public synchronized void` **`setROWID`**`(int` *`parameterIndex`* `, oracle.sql.ROWID` *`x`*`)`
	setROWID associates the parameter identified by *parameterIndex* with the ROWID variable *x*.

Oracle Java

OraclePreparedStatement Methods *(Continued)*

SETSTRUCT	public synchronized void **setSTRUCT**(int *parameterIndex* , oracle.sql.STRUCT *x*)

setSTRUCT associates the parameter identified by *parameterIndex* with the oracle.sql.STRUCT datatype *x*. The oracle.sql.STRUCT datatype stores Oracle's internal representation of column data together with the column's datatype.

CallableStatement Interface

The CallableStatement class extends the PreparedStatement class and provides mechanisms that are suitable when executing stored procedures or PL/SQL blocks. Specifically, the CallableStatement interface permits PL/SQL OUT parameters and function return values to be defined and accessed.

CallableStatement objects are created by the prepareCall method of a Connection object. The CallableStatement inherits the methods and properties of the PreparedStatement class, but also defines routines for defining and accessing OUT parameters.

As in the PreparedStatement class, parameters are denoted by "?" and referenced by their relative position within the call statement. The parameterIndex argument to methods of PreparedStatement defines the position of the parameter within the stored procedure call or PL/SQL block.

CallableStatement Methods

GETBIGDECIMAL	BigDecimal **getBigDecimal**(int *parameterIndex*, int *scale*)

getBigDecimal retrieves the value of the BigDecimal OUT parameter identified by *parameterIndex*.

GETBOOLEAN	boolean **getBoolean**(int *parameterIndex*)

getBoolean retrieves the value of the boolean OUT parameter identified by *parameterIndex*.

CallableStatement Methods *(Continued)*

GETBYTE	byte **getByte**(int *parameterIndex*)
	getByte retrieves the value of the byte OUT parameter identified by *parameterIndex*.
GETBYTES	byte[] **getBytes**(int *parameterIndex*)
	getBytes retrieves the value of the byte[] OUT parameter identified by *parameterIndex*.
GETDATE	java.sql.Date **getDate**(int *parameterIndex*)
	getDate retrieves the value of the java.sql.Date OUT parameter identified by *parameterIndex*.
GETDOUBLE	double **getDouble**(int *parameterIndex*)
	getDouble retrieves the value of the double OUT parameter identified by *parameterIndex*.
GETFLOAT	float **getFloat**(int *parameterIndex*)
	getFloat retrieves the value of the float OUT parameter identified by *parameterIndex*.
GETINT	int **getInt**(int *parameterIndex*)
	getInt retrieves the value of the int OUT parameter identified by *parameterIndex*.
GETLONG	long **getLong**(int *parameterIndex*)
	getLong retrieves the value of the long OUT parameter identified by *parameterIndex*.
GETOBJECT	Object **getObject**(int *parameterIndex*)
	GetObject returns a Java object for the parameter value. The object type corresponds to the SQL type used in registerOutParameter.

CallableStatement Methods *(Continued)*

GETSHORT	short **getShort**(int *parameterIndex*)
	getShort retrieves the value of the short OUT parameter identified by *parameterIndex*.
GETSTRING	String **getString**(int *parameterIndex*)
	getString retrieves the value of the String OUT parameter identified by *parameterIndex*.
GETTIME	java.sql.Time **getTime**(int *parameterIndex*)
	getTime retrieves the value of the java.sql.Time OUT parameter identified by *parameterIndex*.
GETTIMESTAMP	java.sql.Timestamp **getTimestamp**(int *parameterIndex*)
	getTimestamp retrieves the value of the java.sql.Timestamp OUT parameter identified by *parameterIndex*.
REGISTEROUT PARAMETER	void **registerOutParameter**(int *parameterIndex*, int sqlType [,int *scale*])
	registerOutParameter registers the parameter specified by parameterIndex as an OUT parameter of the specified type. *SqlType* is one of the datatypes defined in java.sql.types. For decimal and numeric types, the *scale* argument may optionally define the number of digits supported to the right of the decimal point.
WASNULL	boolean **wasNull**()
	wasNull returns true if the last OUT parameter retrieved was null.

OracleCallableStatement

OracleCallableStatement extends OraclePreparedStatement and implements CallableStatement. It also implements the following Oracle-specific methods:

OracleCallableStatement Methods

GETARRAY	public oracle.sql.ARRAY **getARRAY**(int *parameterindex*)
	getARRAY retrieves an PL/SQL table OUT parameter into an array.
GETBFILE	public oracle.sql.BFILE **getBFILE**(int *parameterindex*)
	Returns a BFILE locator from the parameter identified by *parameterindex*..
GETBLOB	public oracle.sql.BLOB **getBLOB**(int *parameterindex*)
	Returns a BLOB locator from the parameter identified by *parameterindex*.
GETCLOB	public oracle.jdbc2.Clob **getCLOB**(int *parameterindex*)
	Returns a CLOB locator from the parameter identified by *parameterindex*.
GETCURSOR	public java.sql.ResultSet **getCursor**(int *parameterindex*)
	Returns a ResultSet from the parameter identified by *parameterindex*. This parameter will be a PL/SQL cursor variable.

Oracle Java

OracleCallableStatement Methods *(Continued)*

GETCUSTOM DATUM	```public java.lang.Object getCustomDatum(int```
	     parameterindex,
	     ```oracle.sql.CustomDatumFactory```
	     CustMethod)
	
	 getCustomDatum returns an Oracle8 object type as a custom Java class. *CustMethod* defines a constructor method for the class.

GETNUMBER	```public oracle.sql.NUMBER getNUMBER(int``` *parameterindex)* Returns a NUMBER from the parameter identified by *parameterindex.*
GETORACLE OBJECT	```public oracle.sql.Datum getOracleObject(int``` *parameterindex)* Returns an oracle.sql.Datum object from the parameter identified by *parameterindex.* The oracle.sql.Datum class is the superclass for all Oracle datatype objects and can hold data of any datatype.
GETRAW	```public oracle.sql.RAW getRAW(int``` *parameterindex)* Returns a RAW datatype value from the parameter identified by *parameterindex.*
GETREF	```public oracle.sql.REF getREF(int``` *parameterindex)* Returns a REF datatype value from the parameter identified by *parameterindex.*
GETROWID	```public oracle.sql.ROWID getROWID(int``` *parameterindex)* Returns a ROWID datatype value from the parameter identified by *parameterindex.*

OracleCallableStatement Methods *(Continued)*

GETSTRUCT
```
public oracle.sql.STRUCT getSTRUCT(int
    parameterindex)
```

Returns an `oracle.sql.STRUCT` datatype value from the parameter identified by *parameterindex*. The `oracle.sql.STRUCT` datatype stores Oracle's internal representation of column data together with the column's datatype.

Oracle Java

ResultSet interface

A `ResultSet` object is created by the `executeQuery` method of the `Statement` class and its descendents. A `ResultSet` represents the results from an SQL query.

ResultSet Methods

CLEARWARNINGS
```
void clearWarnings()
```

`clearWarnings` clears all warnings for this result set.

CLOSE
```
void close()
```

`close` releases the result set object.

FINDCOLUMN
```
int findColumn(String columnName)
```

`findColumn` returns the position of the column named *columnName* within the result set.

GETASCIISTREAM
```
java.io.InputStream getAsciiStream(int
    columnIndex)
```
```
java.io.InputStream getAsciiStream(String
    columnName)
```

`getAsciiStream` associates a column value (typically a LONG column) with an `InputStream`.

The column can either be specified by position (*columnIndex*) or name (*columnName*).

ResultSet Methods *(Continued)*

GETBIGDECIMAL	BigDecimal **getBigDecimal**(int *columnIndex*, int *scale*)

BigDecimal **getBigDecimal**(String *columnName*, int *scale*)

getBigDecimal returns the value of the specified column as a BigDecimal.

The column can either be specified by position (*columnIndex*) or name (*columnName*).

GETBINARY STREAM	java.io.InputStream **getBinaryStream**(int columnIndex)

java.io.InputStream **getBinaryStream**(String columnName)

getBinaryStream is the same as getAsciiStream, except that binary (RAW) data is retrieved.

GETBOOLEAN	boolean **getBoolean**(int *columnIndex*)

boolean **getBoolean**(String *columnName*)

getBoolean returns the value of the specified column as a boolean.

The column can either be specified by position (*columnIndex*) or name (*columnName*).

GETBYTE	byte **getByte**(int *columnIndex*)

byte **getByte**(String *columnName*)

getByte returns the value of the specified column as a byte.

The column can either be specified by position (*columnIndex*) or name (*columnName*).

ResultSet Methods *(Continued)*

GETBYTES	`byte[] getBytes(int columnIndex)`
	`byte[] getBytes(String columnName)`
	`getBytes` returns the value of the specified column as a `byte[]`.
	The column can either be specified by position (*columnIndex*) or name (*columnName*).
GETCURSORNAME	`String getCursorName()`
	`GetCursorName` returns the cursor name associated with the result set. The cursor name can be specified using the `setCursorName` method of the `Statement` class.
GETDATE	`java.sql.Date getDate(int columnIndex)`
	`java.sql.Date getDate(String columnName)`
	`getDate` returns the value of the specified column as a `java.sql.Date`.
	The column can either be specified by position (*columnIndex*) or name (*columnName*).
GETDOUBLE	`double getDouble(int columnIndex)`
	`double getDouble(String columnName)`
	`getDouble` returns the value of the specified column as a `double`.
	The column can either be specified by position (*columnIndex*) or name (*columnName*).
GETFLOAT	`float getFloat(int columnIndex)`
	`float getFloat(String columnName)`

ResultSet Methods *(Continued)*

GETFLOAT (CONT.)	getFloat returns the value of the specified column as a float.
	The column can either be specified by position (*columnIndex*) or name (*columnName*).

GETINT	int **getInt** (int *columnIndex*)
	int **getInt** (String *columnName*)
	getInt returns the value of the specified column as an int.
	The column can either be specified by position (*columnIndex*) or name (*columnName*).

GETLONG	long **getLong** (int *columnIndex*)
	long **getLong** (String *columnName*)
	getLong returns the value of the specified column as a long.
	The column can either be specified by position (*columnIndex*) or name (*columnName*).

GETMETADATA	ResultSetMetaData **getMetaData** ()
	GetMetaData creates a ResultSetMetaData object, which can be used to describe the result set.

GETOBJECT	Object **getObject** (int *columnIndex*)
	Object **getObject** (String *columnName*)
	getObject returns the value of the specified column as an Object.
	The column can either be specified by position (*columnIndex*) or name (*columnName*).

ResultSet Methods *(Continued)*

GETSHORT	`short` **`getShort`**`(int `*`columnIndex`*`)`

`short` **`getShort`**`(String `*`columnName`*`)`

`getShort` returns the value of the specified column as a short.

The column can either be specified by position (*`columnIndex`*) or name (*`columnName`*).

GETSTRING	`String` **`getString`**`(int `*`columnIndex`*`)`

`String` **`getString`**`(String `*`columnName`*`)`

`getString` returns the value of the specified column as a String.

The column can either be specified by position (*`columnIndex`*) or name (*`columnName`*).

GETTIME	`java.sql.Time` **`getTime`**`(int `*`columnIndex`*`)`

`java.sql.Time` **`getTime`**`(String `*`columnName`*`)`

`getTime` returns the value of the specified column as a java.sql.Time.

The column can either be specified by position (*`columnIndex`*) or name (*`columnName`*).

GETTIMESTAMP	`java.sql.Timestamp` **`getTimestamp`**`(int `*`columnIndex`*`)`

`java.sql.Timestamp` **`getTimestamp`**`(String `*`columnName`*`)`

`getTimestamp` returns the value of the specified column as a java.sql.Timestamp.

The column can either be specified by position (*`columnIndex`*) or name (*`columnName`*).

ResultSet Methods *(Continued)*

GETUNICODE STREAM	`java.io.InputStream` **`getUnicodeStream`**`(int columnIndex)`
	`java.io.InputStream` **`getUnicodeStream`**`(String columnName)`
	`getUnicodeStream` is the same as `getAsciiStream`, except that binary (RAW) data is retrieved.
GETWARNINGS	`SQLWarning` **`getWarnings`**`()`
	`GetWarnings` returns any warning issued for the result set.
NEXT	`boolean` **`next`**`()`
	`next` moves the focus to the next row in the result set. After a result set is first created, `next` must be called to move the focus to the first row.
WASNULL	`boolean` **`wasNull`**`()`
	`wasNull` returns true if the last column accessed was null.

OracleResultSet Extensions

The `OracleResultSet` class implements the `ResultSet` interface and adds Oracle-specific methods, mainly for retrieving Oracle-specific datatypes.

OracleResultSet Methods

GETARRAY	`public oracle.sql.ARRAY` **`getARRAY`**`(int columnIndex)`
	`public oracle.sql.ARRAY` **`getARRAY`**`(java.lang.String columnName)`
	`getARRAY` retrieves an array of data from the specified column.

OracleResultSet Methods *(Continued)*

GETARRAY (CONT.)	The column can either be specified by position (*columnIndex*) or name (*columnName*).

GETBFILE	`public oracle.sql.BFILE` **`getBFILE`**`(int`
	    `columnIndex)`
	
	`public oracle.sql.BFILE`
	    `getBFILE``(java.lang.String columnName)`
	
	`getBFILE` retrieves a BFILE locator from the specified column.
	
	The column can either be specified by position (*columnIndex*) or name (*columnName*).

GETBLOB	`public oracle.sql.BLOB` **`getBLOB`**`(int`
	    `columnIndex)`
	
	`public oracle.sql.BLOB`
	    `getBLOB``(java.lang.String columnName)`
	
	`getBLOB` retrieves a BLOB locator from the specified column.
	
	The column can either be specified by position (*columnIndex*) or name (*columnName*).

GETCLOB	`public oracle.sql.CLOB` **`getCLOB`**`(int`
	    `columnIndex)`
	
	`public oracle.sql.CLOB`
	    `getCLOB``(java.lang.String columnName)`
	
	`getCLOB` retrieves a CLOB locator from the specified column.
	
	The column can either be specified by position (*columnIndex*) or name (*columnName*).

OracleResultSet Methods *(Continued)*

GETNUMBER	`public oracle.sql.NUMBER `**`getNUMBER`**`(int` `    columnIndex)`
	`public oracle.sql.NUMBER` `    `**`getNUMBER`**`(java.lang.String columnName)`
	getNUMBER retrieves a NUMBER datatype from the specified column.
	The column can either be specified by position (*columnIndex*) or name (*columnName*).
GETORACLE OBJECT	`public oracle.sql.Datum `**`getOracleObject`**`(int` `    columnIndex)`

	`public oracle.sql.Datum`
	`    `**`getOracleObject`**`(java.lang.String`
	`    columnName)`

	getOracleObject returns the specified column as an oracle.sql.Datum object. Oracle.sql.Datum is the superclass of all Oracle Java datatypes and can hold values of any datatype.
	The column can either be specified by position (*columnIndex*) or name (*columnName*).
GETRAW	`public oracle.sql.RAW `**`getRAW`**`(int` `    columnIndex)`
	`public oracle.sql.RAW` `    `**`getRAW`**`(java.lang.String columnName)`
	getRAW retrieves a RAW datatype from the specified column.
	The column can either be specified by position (*columnIndex*) or name (*columnName*).
GETREF	`public oracle.sql.REF `**`getREF`**`(int` `    columnIndex)`
	`public oracle.sql.REF` `    `**`getREF`**`(java.lang.String columnName)`

OracleResultSet Methods *(Continued)*

GETREF (CONT.)	`getREF` retrieves a REF datatype from the specified column. The column can either be specified by position (`columnIndex`) or name (`columnName`).

GETROWID	`public oracle.sql.ROWID` **`getROWID`**`(int`
	    `columnIndex)`
	
	`public oracle.sql.ROWID`
	    `getROWID``(java.lang.String columnName)`
	
	`getROWID` retrieves a ROWID datatype from the specified column.
	
	The column can either be specified by position (`columnIndex`) or name (`columnName`).

GETSTRUCT	`public oracle.sql.STRUCT` **`getSTRUCT`**`(int`
	    `columnIndex)`
	
	`public oracle.sql.STRUCT`
	    `getSTRUCT``(java.lang.String columnName)`
	
	`getSTRUCT` retrieves an `oracle.sql.STRUCT` datatype from the specified column. The `oracle.sql.STRUCT` datatype stores Oracle's internal representation of column data together with the column's datatype.
	
	The column can either be specified by position (`columnIndex`) or name (`columnName`).

Oracle Java

ResultSetMetaData Interface

A `ResultSetMetaData` object provides a mechanism for determining the structure of a result set.

`ResultSetMetaData` objects are created by the `getMetaData` method of `ResultSet` objects.

Many methods of `ResultSetMetaData` take a *column* argument. This argument corresponds to the position of the column within the result set (starting with 1).

ResultSetMetaData Methods

GETCATALOG NAME	String **getCatalogName**(int *column*) This returns the catalog name for the column. This method does not appear to be implemented in Oracle. *column* is the numerical position of the column in the result set.
GETCOLUMN COUNT	int **getColumnCount**() getColumnCount returns the number of columns in the result set.
GETCOLUMN DISPLAYSIZE	int **getColumnDisplaySize**(int *column*) getColumnDisplaySize returns the maximum width of the column. *column* is the numerical position of the column in the result set.
GETCOLUMN LABEL	String **getColumnLabel**(int *column*) GetColumnLabel returns a label for the column. This will usually be the same as the column name. *column* is the numerical position of the column in the result set.
GETCOLUMN NAME	String **getColumnName**(int *column*) GetColumnName returns the name of the column. *column* is the numerical position of the column in the result set.
GETCOLUMNTYPE	int **getColumnType**(int *column*) getColumnType returns the datatype of the column. The return value corresponds to one of the constants defined in java.sql.Types. *column* is the numerical position of the column in the result set.

ResultSetMetaData Methods *(Continued)*

GETCOLUMN TYPENAME	`String getColumnTypeName(int column)` GetColumnTypeName returns the datatype of the column as a string. The datatype returned is the Oracle datatype, not the Java datatype. *column* is the numerical position of the column in the result set.
GETPRECISION	`int getPrecision(int column)` getPrecision returns the numerical precision (number of decimal digits) of the column. *column* is the numerical position of the column in the result set.
GETSCALE	`int getScale(int column)` getScale returns the number of digits to the right of the decimal point that are permitted in the column's definition. *column* is the numerical position of the column in the result set.
GETSCHEMA NAME	`String getSchemaName(int column)` GetSchemaName returns the schema of the specified column. *column* is the numerical position of the column in the result set.
GETTABLENAME	`String getTableName(int column)` GetTableName returns the table corresponding to the specified column. This method does not seem to be implemented in Oracle. *column* is the numerical position of the column in the result set.

Oracle Java

ResultSetMetaData **Methods** *(Continued)*

ISAUTO INCREMENT	`boolean ` **`isAutoIncrement`** `(int column)`

isAutoIncrement returns true if the column is an automatically-generated sequence number. It will always return false in an Oracle database.

column is the numerical position of the column in the result set.

ISCASESENSITIVE	`boolean ` **`isCaseSensitive`** `(int column)`

isCaseSensitive returns true if the column is case-sensitive. This will return true for Oracle character datatypes.

column is the numerical position of the column in the result set.

ISCURRENCY	`boolean ` **`isCurrency`** `(int column)`

isCurrency returns true if the column is a currency datatype. Because Oracle does not support a currency type, this will return false.

column is the numerical position of the column in the result set.

ISDEFINITELY WRITABLE	`boolean ` **`isDefinitelyWritable`** `(int column)`

isDefinitelyWritable returns true if the column is definitely updateable by the user.

column is the numerical position of the column in the result set.

ISNULLABLE	`int ` **`isNullable`** `(int column)`

isNullable returns true if the column is allowed to be null.

column is the numerical position of the column in the result set.

ResultSetMetaData Methods *(Continued)*

ISREADONLY	boolean **isReadOnly**(int *column*)

isReadOnly returns true if the column is read-only.

column is the numerical position of the column in the result set.

ISSEARCHABLE	boolean **isSearchable**(int *column*)

isSearchable returns true if the column may be used in a WHERE clause.

column is the numerical position of the column in the result set.

ISSIGNED	boolean **isSigned**(int *column*)

isSigned returns true if the column can contain signed numeric data.

column is the numerical position of the column in the result set.

ISWRITABLE	boolean **isWritable**(int *column*)

isWriteable returns true if the column is writeable by the user.

column is the numerical position of the column in the result set.

DatabaseMetaData Interface

The DatabaseMetaData class contains methods for retrieving information about the current database. DatabaseMetaData objects are created by the getMetaData method of the Connection object.

DatabaseMetaData is most useful when writing generic programs that must operate efficiently against a variety of back-end databases. Since our scope in this chapter is limited to Oracle only, full descriptions of each method are not provided, although basic method declarations are shown below. You can find full details regarding the DatabaseMetaData API from http://www.javasoft.com/products/jdk/1.2/docs/api/java/sql/DatabaseMetaData.html.

Table 7–3 DatabaseMetaData

DatabaseMetaData Method	Definition
allProceduresAreCallable	`boolean allProceduresAreCallable()`
allTablesAreSelectable	`boolean allTablesAreSelectable()`
DataDefinitionCauses- TransactionCommit	`boolean dataDefinitionCausesTrans-` `actionCommit()`
dataDefinitionIgnoredIn- Transactions	`boolean dataDefinitionIgnoredIn-` `Transactions()`
doesMaxRowSizeIncludeBlobs	`boolean doesMaxRowSizeInclude-` `Blobs()`

getBestRowIdentifier	`ResultSet getBestRowIdentifier(`
	`    String catalog,`
	`    String schema,`
	`    String table,`
	`    int scope,`
	`    boolean nullable)`

getCatalogs	`ResultSet getCatalogs()`
getCatalogSeparator	`String getCatalogSeparator()`
getCatalogTerm	`String getCatalogTerm()`

getColumnPrivileges	`ResultSet getColumnPrivileges(`
	`    String catalog,`
	`    String schema,String table,`
	`    String columnNamePattern)`

getColumns	`ResultSet getColumns(String cata-`
	`log,`
	`    String schemaPattern,`
	`    String tableNamePattern,`
	`    String columnNamePattern)`

Table 7–3 DatabaseMetaData *(Continued)*

DatabaseMetaData Method	Definition

getCrossReference	ResultSet getCrossReference(
	    String primaryCatalog,
	    String primarySchema,
	    String primaryTable,
	    String foreignCatalog,
	    String foreignSchema,
	    String foreignTable)

getDatabaseProductName	String getDatabaseProductName()
getDatabaseProductVersion	String getDatabaseProductVersion()
getDefaultTransactionIsolation	int getDefaultTransactionIsola- tion()
getDriverMajorVersion	int getDriverMajorVersion()
getDriverMinorVersion	int getDriverMinorVersion()
getDriverName	String getDriverName()
getDriverVersion	String getDriverVersion()

getExportedKeys	ResultSet getExportedKeys(
	    String catalog,
	    String schema,
	    String table)

getExtraNameCharacters	String getExtraNameCharacters()
getIdentifierQuoteString	String getIdentifierQuoteString()

getImportedKeys	ResultSet getImportedKeys(
	    String catalog,
	    String schema,
	    String table)

Oracle Java

Table 7–3 DatabaseMetaData *(Continued)*

DatabaseMetaData Method	Definition

getIndexInfo	`ResultSet getIndexInfo(`
	`    String catalog,`
	`    String schema,`
	`    String table,`
	`    boolean unique,`
	`    boolean approximate)`

getMaxBinaryLiteralLength	`int getMaxBinaryLiteralLength()`
getMaxCatalogNameLength	`int getMaxCatalogNameLength()`
getMaxCharLiteralLength	`int getMaxCharLiteralLength()`
getMaxColumnNameLength	`int getMaxColumnNameLength()`
getMaxColumnsInGroupBy	`int getMaxColumnsInGroupBy()`
getMaxColumnsInIndex	`int getMaxColumnsInIndex()`
getMaxColumnsInOrderBy	`int getMaxColumnsInOrderBy()`
getMaxColumnsInSelect	`int getMaxColumnsInSelect()`
getMaxColumnsInTable	`int getMaxColumnsInTable()`
getMaxConnections	`int getMaxConnections()`
getMaxCursorNameLength	`int getMaxCursorNameLength()`
getMaxIndexLength	`int getMaxIndexLength()`
getMaxProcedureNameLength	`int getMaxProcedureNameLength()`
getMaxRowSize	`int getMaxRowSize()`
getMaxSchemaNameLength	`int getMaxSchemaNameLength()`
getMaxStatementLength	`int getMaxStatementLength()`
getMaxStatements	`int getMaxStatements()`

Table 7–3 DatabaseMetaData *(Continued)*

DatabaseMetaData Method	Definition
getMaxTableNameLength	`int getMaxTableNameLength()`
getMaxTablesInSelect	`int getMaxTablesInSelect()`
getMaxUserNameLength	`int getMaxUserNameLength()`
getNumericFunctions	`String getNumericFunctions()`

getPrimaryKeys	`ResultSet getPrimaryKeys(`
	`    String catalog,`
	`    String schema,`
	`    String table)`

getProcedureColumns	`ResultSet getProcedureColumns(`
	`    String catalog,`
	`    String schemaPattern,`
	`    String procedureNamePattern,`
	`    String columnNamePattern)`

getProcedures	`ResultSet getProcedures(`
	`    String catalog,`
	`    String schemaPattern,`
	`    String procedureNamePattern)`

getProcedureTerm	`String getProcedureTerm()`
getSchemas	`ResultSet getSchemas()`
getSchemaTerm	`String getSchemaTerm()`
getSearchStringEscape	`String getSearchStringEscape()`
getSQLKeywords	`String getSQLKeywords()`
getStringFunctions	`String getStringFunctions()`
getSystemFunctions	`String getSystemFunctions()`

Oracle Java

Table 7–3 DatabaseMetaData *(Continued)*

DatabaseMetaData Method	Definition

getTablePrivileges	`ResultSet getTablePrivileges(`
	`    String catalog,`
	`    String schemaPattern,`
	`    String tableNamePattern)`

getTables	`ResultSet getTables(`
	`    String catalog,`
	`    String schemaPattern)`

getTableTypes	`ResultSet getTableTypes()`
getTimeDateFunctions	`String getTimeDateFunctions()`
getTypeInfo	`ResultSet getTypeInfo()`
getURL	`String getURL()`
getUserName	`String getUserName()`

getVersionColumns	`ResultSet getVersionColumns(`
	`    String catalog,`
	`    String schema,`
	`    String table)`

isCatalogAtStart	`boolean isCatalogAtStart()`
isReadOnly	`boolean isReadOnly()`
nullPlusNonNullIsNull	`boolean nullPlusNonNullIsNull()`
nullsAreSortedAtEnd	`boolean nullsAreSortedAtEnd()`
nullsAreSortedAtStart	`boolean nullsAreSortedAtStart()`
nullsAreSortedHigh	`boolean nullsAreSortedHigh()`
nullsAreSortedLow	`boolean nullsAreSortedLow()`
storesLowerCaseIdentifiers	`boolean storesLowerCaseIdentifi-` `ers()`

Table 7–3 DatabaseMetaData *(Continued)*

DatabaseMetaData Method	Definition
storesLowerCaseQuoted-Identifiers	`boolean storesLowerCaseQuotedIden-tifiers()`
storesMixedCaseIdentifiers	`boolean storesMixedCaseIdentifi-ers()`
storesMixedCaseQuoted-Identifiers	`boolean storesMixedCaseQuotedIden-tifiers()`
storesUpperCaseIdentifiers	`boolean storesUpperCaseIdentifi-ers()`
storesUpperCaseQuoted-Identifiers	`boolean storesUpperCaseQuotedIden-tifiers()`
supportsAlterTableWith-AddColumn	`boolean supportsAlterTableWithAd-dColumn()`
supportsAlterTableWithDrop-Column	`boolean supportsAlterTableWithDrop-Column()`
supportsANSI92EntryLevel-SQL	`boolean supportsANSI92EntryLevelSQL()`
supportsANSI92FullSQL	`boolean supportsANSI92FullSQL()`
supportsANSI92Intermediate SQL	`boolean supportsANSI92IntermediateSQL()`
supportsCatalogsInData-Manipulation	`boolean supportsCatalogsInDataMa-nipulation()`
supportsCatalogsInIndex-Definitions	`boolean supportsCatalogsInIndex-Definitions()`
supportsCatalogsInPrivilege-Definitions	`boolean supportsCatalogsInPrivi-legeDefinitions()`
supportsCatalogsInProcedure-Calls	`boolean supportsCatalogsInProce-dureCalls()`

Table 7–3 DatabaseMetaData *(Continued)*

DatabaseMetaData Method	Definition
supportsCatalogsInTable-Definitions	`boolean supportsCatalogsInTable-Definitions()`
supportsColumnAliasing	`boolean supportsColumnAliasing()`
supportsConvert	`boolean supportsConvert()`

supportsConvert	`boolean supportsConvert(`
	`    int fromType,`
	`    int toType)`

supportsCoreSQLGrammar	`boolean supportsCoreSQLGrammar()`
supportsCorrelatedSubqueries	`boolean supportsCorrelatedSubqueries()`
supportsDataDefinitionAnd-DataManipulationTransactions	`boolean supportsDataDefinitionAnd-DataManipulationTransactions()`
supportsDataManipulation-TransactionsOnly	`boolean supportsDataManipulation-TransactionsOnly()`
supportsDifferentTableCorre-lationNames	`boolean supportsDifferentTableCor-relationNames()`
supportsExpressionsInOrderBy	`boolean supportsExpressionsInOr-derBy()`
supportsExtendedSQL-Grammar	`boolean supportsExtendedSQLGram-mar()`
supportsFullOuterJoins	`boolean supportsFullOuterJoins()`
supportsGroupBy	`boolean supportsGroupBy()`
supportsGroupByBeyondSelect	`boolean supportsGroupByBeyondSe-lect()`
supportsGroupByUnrelated	`boolean supportsGroupByUnrelated()`

Table 7–3 DatabaseMetaData *(Continued)*

DatabaseMetaData Method	Definition
supportsIntegrityEnhancement-Facility	`boolean supportsIntegrityEnhance-mentFacility()`
supportsLikeEscapeClause	`boolean supportsLikeEscapeClause()`
supportsLimitedOuterJoins	`boolean supportsLimitedOuterJoins()`
supportsMinimumSQL-Grammar	`boolean supportsMinimumSQLGrammar()`
supportsMixedCaseIdentifiers	`boolean supportsMixedCaseIdentifi-ers()`
supportsMixedCaseQuoted-Identifiers	`boolean supportsMixedCaseQuotedI-dentifiers()`
supportsMultipleResultSets	`boolean supportsMultipleResult-Sets()`
supportsMultipleTransactions	`boolean supportsMultipleTransac-tions()`
supportsNonNullableColumns	`boolean supportsNonNullableCol-umns()`
supportsOpenCursorsAcross-Commit	`boolean supportsOpenCursorsAcross-Commit()`
supportsOpenCursorsAcross-Rollback	`boolean supportsOpenCursorsAcross-Rollback()`
SupportsOpenStatements-Across Commit	`boolean supportsOpenStatement-sAcrossCommit()`
SupportsOpenStatements-Across Rollback	`boolean supportsOpenStatement-sAcrossRollback()`
supportsOrderByUnrelated	`boolean supportsOrderByUnrelated()`
supportsOuterJoins	`boolean supportsOuterJoins()`

Oracle Java

Table 7–3 DatabaseMetaData *(Continued)*

DatabaseMetaData Method	Definition
supportsPositionedDelete	`boolean supportsPositionedDelete()`
supportsPositionedUpdate	`boolean supportsPositionedUpdate()`
supportsSchemasInData-Manipulation	`boolean supportsSchemasInDataManip-ulation()`
supportsSchemasInIndex-Definitions	`boolean supportsSchemasInIndexDefi-nitions()`
supportsSchemasInPrivilege-Definitions	`boolean supportsSchemasInPrivilege-Definitions()`
supportsSchemasInProcedure-Calls	`boolean supportsSchemasInProcedure-Calls()`
supportsSchemasInTable-Definitions	`boolean supportsSchemasInTableDefi-nitions()`
supportsSelectForUpdate	`boolean supportsSelectForUpdate()`
supportsStoredProcedures	`boolean supportsStoredProcedures()`
supportsSubqueriesIn-Comparisons	`boolean supportsSubqueriesInCompar-isons()`
supportsSubqueriesInExists	`boolean supportsSubqueriesInEx-ists()`
supportsSubqueriesInIns	`boolean supportsSubqueriesInIns()`
supportsSubqueriesIn-Quantifieds	`boolean supportsSubqueriesInQuanti-fieds()`
supportsTableCorrelation-Names	`boolean supportsTableCorrelation-Names()`
supportsTransactionIsolation-Level	`boolean supportsTransactionIsola-tionLevel(int level)`
supportsTransactions	`boolean supportsTransactions()`

Table 7–3 DatabaseMetaData *(Continued)*

DatabaseMetaData Method	Definition
supportsUnion	`boolean supportsUnion()`
supportsUnionAll	`boolean supportsUnionAll()`
tableNamePattern	`String tableNamePattern, String types[]`
usesLocalFilePerTable	`boolean usesLocalFilePerTable()`
usesLocalFiles	`boolean usesLocalFiles()`

SQLJ Language Reference

This section briefly outlines SQLJ syntax, including methods of the major run-time classes and formats for SQLJ #sql directives.

The #sql Directives

#SQL	**#sql** [*connection_context* [, *execution_context*]] [*result_variable*|*iterator_object* =] { *SQL_operation* };

This default #sql directive allows a SQL statement to be executed.

A *connection_context* may be declared if it is required that the statement be run in a non-default context. In additional, an *execution_context* may be declared if the statement will be executed in a multi-threaded environment (each thread must use a separate *execution_context*).

If the *SQL_operation* is a call to a stored function, then a *result_variable* (in conjunction with a VALUES clause) may be declared to receive the result of the function. If the *SQL_operation* is a query, then an *iterator_object* may be declared to process the results.

SQL_operation can be any valid SQL statement.

The #sql Directives *(Continued)*

#SQL … CONTEXT	**#sql** *[class properties]* **context** *context_classname;*

A `context` declaration defines a connection context class. You do not need to declare a context class for the default connection.

Class properties can include any valid Java class modifiers such as `private`, `static`, `public`, etc.

The context declaration creates a context class definition. Specific instances of this class must be created before the context class can be used.

#SQL … ITERATOR	**#sql** *[class properties]* **iterator** *iterator_classname* *(datatype [column_name] [, datatype [column_name] …]);*

The `iterator` declaration creates an iterator class, which is used to process result sets from a query.

Class properties can include any valid Java class modifiers such as `private`, `static`, `public`, etc.

`Iterator` declarations may be named or positional. For positional iterators, only the *datatypes* need to be specified after the *iterator_name*. For named iterators, a *column_name* declaration that matches each *column_name* in the result set should also be declared.

The `iterator` declaration creates an iterator class only. You must create an iterator object of this class before the iterator can be used.

CALL	**#sql** { **call** *procedure_name(arguments)* };

CALL can be used to call a PL/SQL procedure without the need to enclose it in a PL/SQL BEGIN … END block.

SET	**#sql** { **set** *:host_variable* = expression }

The SET directive sets the value of *host_variable*. This also changes the value of the associated Java variable. The SET command implicitly wraps the assignment statement in a PL/SQL BEGIN … END block, so any PL/SQL operators can be used in the block.

The #sql Directives *(Continued)*

VALUES	**#sql** *java_variable* = { **VALUES**(*function_name*()) };
	The VALUES clause retrieves the result from a PL/SQL stored function and places it in *java_variable*.

Connection Context Methods

The default context class and context classes created by a #sql context declaration have a number of methods that can be used in SQLJ programs.

Connection Context Instance Methods

CLOSE	`public abstract void close();`
	This closes the connection.

GETCONNECTION	`public abstract java.sql.Connection` `     getConnection();`
	This returns the JDBC connection used by the context.

GETEXECUTIONC
ONTEXT
	`public abstract`
	`     sqlj.runtime.ExecutionContext`
	`     getExecutionContext()`

	This gets the execution context associated with the context. Methods of the execution context (see below) allow control over SQL statement execution.

ISCLOSED	`public abstract boolean isClosed();`
	This returns true if the connection is closed, and false otherwise

In addition to the above instance methods, these class methods return information about the context class itself (as opposed to any objects that have been instantiated from the class):

Connection Context Class Methods

| **GETDEFAULT CONTEXT** | ```
public static
    sqlj.runtime.ref.DefaultContext
getDefaultContext();
``` |
| | This method returns the default context for this class. This is not the same as the DefaultContext object, which is created automatically by SQLJ. |
| **SETDEFAULT CONTEXT** | ```
public static void
    setDefaultContext
    (sqlj.runtime.ref.DefaultContext);
``` |
| | This method sets (changes) the default context for the context class. It does not set the global SQLJ default context, but allows the getDefaultContext method to return a specific context from all the contexts instantiated from a user-defined context class. |

Execution Context Methods

Even if an execution context has not been declared in a #sql executable statement, a *connection context* is always associated with an implicit *execution context*, which can be retrieved by the getExecutionContext method of a context class.

Methods of the execution context provide some options for fine control over SQL statement execution. These generally correspond to methods in the JDBC Statement class.

Execution Context Methods

CANCEL	`public void cancel()`
	This cancels an executing statement, either from another thread or before all rows have been retrieved.
GETMAXFIELD SIZE	`public int getMaxFieldSize()`
	getMaxFieldSize gets the maximum length in bytes for any column in a result set returned by the query. It is set by setMaxFieldSize.

Execution Context Methods *(Continued)*

GETMAXROWS	`public int getMaxRows()` `getMaxRows` returns the maximum number of rows that a result set will contain. It is set by `setMaxRows`.
GETQUERY TIMEOUT	`public int getQueryTimeout()` `getQueryTimeout` returns the number of seconds that will elapse before a statement will time out. It is set by `setQueryTimeout`.
GETUPDATE COUNT	`public int getUpdateCount()` `getUpdateCount` returns the number of rows processed by the most recent statement.
GETWARNINGS	`public java.sql.SQLWarning getWarnings()` This returns any warning issued against the context.
SETMAXFIELD SIZE	`public void setMaxFieldSize(int max)` `setMaxFieldSize` sets the maximum length in bytes that will be returned by any column in a query.
SETMAXROWS	`public void setMaxRows(int max)` `setMaxRows` sets the maximum number of rows that a result set may contain.
SETQUERY TIMEOUT	`public void setQueryTimeout(int seconds)` `setQueryTimeout` sets the number of seconds that will elapse before a statement will time out.

Iterator Class Methods

Iterator classes provide access to result sets generated by SQL queries. Iterator classes are created by the `#sql iterator` statement. All iterator classes support the following methods, most of which are derived from the JDBC `ResultSet` interface.

Oracle Java

Iterator Class Methods

CLEARWARNINGS | `public void clearWarnings()`

This clears any warnings.

CLOSE | `public void close()`

This closes the result set.

ENDFETCH | `public boolean endFetch()`

This returns true if the last row has been fetched.

GETCURSORNAME | `public java.lang.String getCursorName()`

This gets the cursor name associated with the result set. You can use this name in subsequent WHERE CURRENT OF clauses of UPDATE or DELETE statements.

GETRESULTSET | `public java.sql.ResultSet getResultSet()`

This returns the JDBC result set associated with the SQLJ iterator.

GETWARNINGS | `public abstract java.sql.SQLWarning`
        `getWarnings()`

GetWarnings returns any warning issued for the result set.

ISCLOSED | `public boolean isClosed()`

This returns true if the result set is closed, and false otherwise.

NEXT | `public boolean next()`

next moves the focus to the next row in the result set. When a result set is first created, next must be called to move the focus to the first row.

Command Line Utilities

Introduction

Oracle provides command line utilities to perform administrative and utility functions. Oracle Enterprise Manager allows many of these functions to be performed within a GUI environment, but there are many circumstances in which the command line equivalent is indicated, for instance, within batch scripts or when Oracle Enterprise Manager is not available.

Naming Conventions

In a UNIX environment, the names of command line utilities stay constant from release to release, with different versions of a particular command being located in separate "ORACLE_HOME" directories. However, in NT environments prior to Oracle8i, different versions of a command would usually reside in the same directory, and therefore could not have the same name. This conflict was resolved by suffixing the command with a two-digit version number. For example, in a UNIX environment, the export utility is known as "exp"; under NT Oracle 7.3, the command is known as "exp73"; and under NT Oracle 8.0, it is "exp80". Most tools are prefixed by the Oracle version number, while some use the version number of some other component. For instance, the wrap command is suffixed by the PL/SQL version.

From Oracle8i onwards, the NT architecture more closely follows the UNIX architecture by maintaining multiple ORACLE_HOME directories for each version and using unqualified program names.

In the command summaries that follow, each possible command name is listed.

Command Summaries

Command Summaries

ADAPTERS	**adapters** [*program file*]
UNIX	adapters lists installed SQL*NET or NET8 protocol drivers. If a *program_file* is specified, then this file will be searched for drivers. Otherwise, ADAPTERS will search standard Oracle libraries.

CMCTL CMCTL80	**cmctl** *command process_type*
8.0+	cmctl controls the *Connection Manager* service, which provides advanced SQL*NET facilities such as connection concentrating, network access control, and multiple protocol support.
	If no arguments are provided, cmctl provides a command prompt from which multiple commands may be entered. Otherwise, a single command and process type may be specified as arguments.
	process_type may be one of the following:

CMAN　Applies command to both main process (cmgw) and the administration process (cmadm).

ADM　Applies the command to only the administration process.

CM　Applies the command to the main process only.

Command Summaries *(Continued)*

CMCTL **CMCTL80** **(CONT.)**	*commands* may be any of the following: START Starts the nominated process(es). STOP Stops the nominated process(es). STATS Shows statistics for the nominated process. STATUS Shows the status of the nominated process. **Example** Start both Connection Manager processes: `cmctl start cman` Reference *Oracle NET8 Administrator's Guide.*

CORAENV
 	
UNIX
	source **coraenv**
	
	The coraenv script is used to set up a UNIX C-shell (csh) environment for a specific Oracle instance. If the environment variable ORAENV_ASK is not set to "FALSE", then coraenv will prompt for an Oracle instance identifier ("SID"); otherwise, the existing ORACLE_SID is used to define the environment.
	
	Because coraenv manipulates the environment of the current shell, it must be "sourced" using the source command. coraenv adjusts the values of the environment variables ORACLE_SID, ORACLE_HOME, and PATH.
	
	Examples
	
	Allow coraenv to prompt for a database instance and set the environment for the instance to DEV:
	
	`% source coraenv`
	`ORACLE_SID = [W732] ? DEV`
	
	Reference *Oracle Administrator's Guide for UNIX.*

Command Line Utilities

Command Summaries *(Continued)*

DB_VERIFY **DBV** **DBVERF73** **DBVERF80**	**db_verify** file_name [keyword=value …] db_verify performs consistency and integrity checks on Oracle data files. The following arguments may be specified: FILE Name of the file to be checked (compulsory). START Starts checking at this block number. END Stops checking at this block number. BLOCKSIZE Block size (if not 2K). LOGFILE Reports all messages to this file. FEEDBACK Displays a feedback message every *n* rows. PARFILE Parameter containing command line arguments. HELP If "Y", displays a help message. ***Example*** `dbverf80 file=tmp1orcl.ora blocksize=4096` Reference *Oracle Utilities Manual.*
DBSHUT **UNIX**	**dbshut** dbshut causes all nominated databases on a UNIX instance to be shut down. Instances are eligible for shut down if the third field in the *oratab* file is set to "Y".

Command Summaries *(Continued)*

DBSTART	**dbstart**
UNIX	dbshut causes all nominated databases on a UNIX instance to be started. Instances are eligible for startup if the third field in the *oratab* file is set to "Y".

DROPJAVA

8i

dropjava `[{-v | -verbose}] [{-t | -thin} |`
`{-o | -oci81}]`
`[{-u| -user} username/password@database]`
`{filename.java | filename.class |`
`filename.jar} ...`

Dropjava drops nominated Java classes, sources, and archives from the database.

-user specifies the account and database from which the Java programs are to be dropped. The syntax of the database connection depends on whether the oci8 or thin JDBC driver is specified, as noted by the -oci8 or -thin option. See Chapter 7, "Oracle Java," for details of specifying thin and OCI connection strings.

-verbose prints progress messages during the drop.

Command Line Utilities

EXP
EXP73
EXP80

exp `[keywords=values...]`

The *exp* command invokes the export utility, which extracts database definitions and data to an operating system file. Exp can be used to perform a backup, to "reorg" fragmented or sparsely populated segments, or to migrate data between databases.

If no arguments are specified, exp will prompt for parameters. Otherwise, the following parameters may be specified on the command line:

USERID   Connect string for Oracle connection.

FULL   If "Y," exports entire database.

BUFFER   Size of array fetch in bytes.

Command Summaries *(Continued)*

EXP **EXP73** **EXP80** **(CONT.)**	OWNER	List of accounts to be exported.
	FILE	Name of export dump file.
	TABLES	List of tables to be exported.
	COMPRESS	If "Y", segment storage definitions will be sized to store all data in a single extent.
	RECORDLENGTH	Length of I/O record.
	GRANTS	If "Y", grant definitions will be exported.
	INCTYPE	Incremental export type:
	COMPLETE:	Export all data.
	CUMULATIVE:	Export all tables changed since last cumulative or complete export.
	INCREMENTAL:	Export only tables changed since the last incremental, cumulative, or complete export.
	INDEXES	If "Y", index definitions are exported.
	RECORD	Stores incremental export information in system tables.
	ROWS	If "N", table rows are not exported.
	PARFILE	Specifies a parameter file containing export keywords and arguments.
	CONSTRAINTS	If "N", does not export constraints.

Command Summaries *(Continued)*

EXP **EXP73** **EXP80** **(CONT.)**	CONSISTENT	If "Y," maintains cross-table consistency during the export. This may fail if rollback segments are too small or transaction rate too high.
	LOG	Records log messages to this file (and the screen).
	STATISTICS	Inserts *analyze* statements into the export so that statistics are calculated during import. Valid options are ESTIMATE, COMPUTE, or none.
	DIRECT	If "Y", performs a direct path export (bypassing the *buffer cache*).
	FEEDBACK	Displays a progress marker every *n* rows.
8.0+	POINT_IN_TIME_RECOVER	If "Y", selected tablespaces will be exported compatible with point-in-time recovery during import.
8.0+	RECOVERY_TABLESPACES	Lists tablespaces subject to point-in-time recovery.

Examples

Execute a full database export:

exp full=y buffer=1048576 file=full_exp.dmp
    userid=system/manager

Export all files for the user `katie`:

NT

exp owners=(katie)
    file=katie.dmp userid=system/manager

UNIX

exp owners='(katie)'
    file=katie.dmp userid=system/manager

Reference *Oracle Server Utilities Manual.*

Command Line Utilities

Command Summaries *(Continued)*

IMP **IMP73** **IMP80**	**imp** [*keywords=values...*] The imp command invokes the import utility, which loads database definitions and data from a file created by exp into a database. If no arguments are specified, imp will prompt for parameters. Otherwise, the following parameters may be specified on the command line:

USERID	Username/password.
FULL	Imports entire file (N).
BUFFER	Size of data buffer.
FROMUSER	Lists owner usernames.
FILE	Input file (EXPDAT.DMP).
TOUSER	Lists usernames.
SHOW	Just lists file contents (N).
TABLES	Lists table names.
IGNORE	Ignores create errors (N).
RECORDLENGTH	Length of I/O record.
GRANTS	Imports grants (Y).
INCTYPE	Incremental import type.
INDEXES	Imports indexes (Y).
COMMIT	Commits array insert (N).
ROWS	Imports data rows (Y).
PARFILE	Parameter filename.

Command Summaries *(Continued)*

IMP **IMP73** **IMP80** **(CONT.)**	LOG	Log file of screen output.
	DESTROY	Overwrites tablespace data file (N).
	INDEXFILE	Writes table/index information to specified file.
	CHARSET	Character set of export file (NLS_LANG).
	POINT_IN_TIME_RECOVER	Tablespace point-in-time recovery (N).
	SKIP_UNUSABLE_INDEXES	Skips maintenance of unusable indexes (N).
	ANALYZE	Executes ANALYZE statements in dump file (Y).
	FEEDBACK	Displays progress every *n* rows(0).

Reference *Oracle Server Utilities Manual.*

JPUB **8i**	**jpub** -user=*username/password* [-input=input_file] [-sql=*object_name*[:java_class [:*mapping_class*]] [,*object_name...*]] [-case={mixed|same|lower|upper}] [-dir=*output_directory*] [-driver=*jdbc_driver*] [-mapping={objectjdbc|oracle|<u>jdbc</u>}] [-omit_schema_names] [-package=*package_name*] [-props=*property_file*] [-url=database_url]

Jpub generates JDBC and SQLJ source code which can represent Oracle8 object types, collections, and PL/SQL packages[a].

Command Summaries *(Continued)*

JPUB **(CONT.)**	–user specifies the connection username and password. The database to connect to is defined by –url, which identifies the database using JDBC conventions (see Chapter 7). The –sql flag specifies the Oracle objects to be converted and their converted names. The specification lists the oracle object name, an optional alternative Java class name, and an optional mapping class. Classes to convert may also be listed in the *input_file* identified by the –input parameter. Entries in the *input_file* have the following syntax: SQL *oracle_type* [GENERATE *JavaClass*] [AS *MapClass*] –case determines any case conversions that may occur. Upper and lower specify that the Java names will be entirely in upper- or lower-case. Mixed specifies that the first letter of each name will be in upper-case, the rest lower. Same indicates no conversion. –dir specifies a directory into which the .java or .sqlj files will be written. –driver specifies the JDBC driver to use. The default is the Oracle JDBC driver. –mapping determines how Java datatypes will be mapped. jdbc mapping uses standard Java primitives such as int and float. objectjdbc uses the equivalent datatypes in the java.lang package. Oracle mapping uses the equivalent datatypes from the oracle.sql package. If –omit_schema_names is not specified, each class generated by Jpub will be qualified by the schema name. –package specifies the name of the package to which generated Java classes should belong.

Command Summaries *(Continued)*

JPUB (CONT.)	The –props flag specifies a *property_file*, which can contain any jpub command line arguments.

LOADJAVA 8i	```loadjava [-user user/password@database]
	        [{-oci8|-thin}]
	        [-help] [-verbose]
	        [{-resolve|-andresolve}]
	        [-force] [-synonym]
	        [{-resolver resolver|-oracleresolver}]
	        [-grant user, user...] [-debug] input_files```

loadjava loads one or more Java programs into an Oracle8i database.

–user specifies the account and database into which the Java programs are to be loaded. The syntax of the database connection depends on whether the oci8 or thin JDBC driver is specified, as noted by the –oci8 or –thin option. See Chapter 7 for details of specifying thin and OCI connection strings.

–help prints a help message.

–verbose prints progress messages during the load.

–andresolve compiles source files as each file is loaded. –resolve compiles and resolves references only when all files are loaded. If neither option is specified, the files are loaded without compilation.

–force causes previously loaded Java class files to be reloaded.

–debug invokes the Java compiler with the compilation (–g) option.

–definer causes methods to execute with definer's privileges rather than invoker's privileges. See the entry on CREATE JAVA in Chapter 4, "Data Definition Language (DDL)," for more details.

Command Summaries *(Continued)*

LOADJAVA **(CONT.)**	-resolver provides a user-defined resolver specification. -oracleresolver uses the pre-defined resolver specification "((* *definers_schema*) (* public))"

-grant confers execute permissions on the classes being loaded to the specified users.

-schema specifies the schema in which the objects are to be created.

-synonym creates public synonyms for all classes.

Input_files consist of Java source, class, and resource files, SQLJ files, and JAR or ZIP archives.

LSNRCTL
LSNRCTL80

lsnrctl [*arguments*]

Use lsnrctl to configure and control the *TNS listener* process.

If no arguments are provided to the command, lsnrctl will enter an interactive mode in which multiple commands may be specified. Otherwise, a single command may be specified as command line parameters. Most commands will accept an argument specifying the name of the listener. Otherwise, the default listener is assumed.

The following commands may be specified:

START	Starts the TNS listener process.
STOP	Stops the listener.
STATUS	Shows the status of the listener process.
SERVICES	Lists the services available from the listener. These will include known database instances and *MTS* services.

Command Summaries *(Continued)*

LSNRCTL LSNRCTL80 (CONT.)	VERSION	Displays the version of the listener.
	RELOAD	Reprocesses the contents of the LISTENER.ORA file.
	SAVE_CONFIG	Saves any configuration changes to the LISTENER.ORA file.
	TRACE	Sets the trace level. Valid arguments are OFF, USER, ADMIN, and SUPPORT.
	DBSNMP_START	Starts the *SNMP* agent.
	DBSNMP_STOP	Stops the *SNMP* agent.
	DBSNMP_STATUS	Displays the status of the *SNMP* agent.
	CHANGE_PASSWORD	Changes the listener password.
	EXIT	Exits lsnrctl.
	SET	Sets the value of a configuration variable.
	SHOW	Shows the value of a configuration variable.

Command Line Utilities

Configuration Parameters

The following parameters can be provided as arguments to the SET and SHOW commands:

CURRENT_LISTENER	Specifies the listener to be used in subsequent commands.
CONNECT_TIMEOUT	Specifies the maximum amount of time allowed to establish a session with the listener.
LOG_FILE	Changes the name of the listener log file.

Command Summaries *(Continued)*

LSNRCTL LSNRCTL80 (CONT.)	LOG_DIRECTORY	Changes the directory where logs will be written.
	LOG_STATUS	Enables or disables logging.
	PASSWORD	Specifies the password used to authenticate the user to the listener process.
	SAVE_CONFIG_ON_STOP	If on, configuration changes are saved to the LISTENER.ORA file immediately upon exiting lsnrctl.
	SPAWN	Instructs the listener to run the specified command. The command must be defined in the LISTENER.ORA file.
	STARTUP_WAITTIME	Sets a delay (in seconds) before responding to the START command.
	TRC_FILE	Changes the name of the trace file.
	TRC_DIRECTORY	Changes the directory of the trace file.
	TRC_LEVEL	Sets the trace level. Valid values are OFF, USER, ADMIN, and SUPPORT.
	USE_PLUGANDPLAY	If on, requests that the listener continually attempt to register with a well-known names server until successful.

Reference *Oracle Net Administrator's Guide.*

Command Summaries *(Continued)*

NAMESCTL **NAMESCTL80**	`namesctl {command	@batch_file}`

Use `namesctl` to control and configure an Oracle names service, which provides a directory service for resolving SQL°NET names or aliases.

If no arguments are provided to the command, `namesctl` will enter an interactive mode in which multiple commands may be specified. Otherwise, a single command may be specified as command line parameters, or a file containing multiple commands may be processed via the "@" operator.

The following commands may be specified:

DELEGATE_DOMAIN
domain_name names_server server_address

The specified *domain_name* is delegated to the specified *names_server* at the *server_address*. *domain_name* is a subregion of the current region.

DOMAIN_HINT
domain_name names_server server_address

Notifies names servers in the current region of *names_server*, which can be found at *server_address* and which has responsibility for the *domain_name*. *domain_name* is not in the current region.

FLUSH   [*names_server...*]

Drops all cached data pertaining to *names_server* or, if no *names_server* is specified, for all foreign regions.

FLUSH_NAME   *name*

Removes a cached name from the names server. The name must not reside in the current region.

HELP   Provides a summary of commands.

Command Line Utilities

Command Summaries *(Continued)*

NAMESCTL
NAMESCTL80
(CONT.)

LOG_STATS   [*names_server*...]

Dumps statistics for the specified server to the log or, if no *names_servers* are specified, for the current server.

PASSWORD   Sets the password for privileged operations.

PING   [*server_name*...]

Tests the connection with the specified *server_name* and displays round-trip time. If no *server_name* is specified, test the current server.

QUERY   *name* [*type*] [*modifiers*]

Gets the definition of the specified *name*. Valid types are:

A.SMD   Service (usually database) definition.

CNAME.SMD   Alias name.

NS.SMD   Names server name.

Modifiers are:

AUTHORITY   Resolves the name in a remote region, even if the data is from a remote region and cached locally.

NOFORWARD   Doesn't look for names in remote regions.

TRACE   Shows the network path traversed.

REGISTER
name [-T *type*] [-D *address*] [-H *host*] [-L *listener*]

Command Summaries *(Continued)*

NAMESCTL **NAMESCTL80** **(CONT.)**	Defines a new names definition.

      -T   Type of definition; typically "database", "host", or "listener".

      -D   Address associated with the name; usually a TNS address.

      -H   Name of host (if -T = "host").

      -L   Name of listener.

RELOAD   [*names_server...*]

Reloads all database names and other data for the specified *names_server* or for the current server if no *names_server* is specified.

REORDER_NS   [*address*]

Generates a names definition file, which lists servers in order of response time. A TNS address may be given to define the initial server. This option is used for dynamic discovery of names servers.

REPEAT   *number* QUERY *name type*

Repeats the specified QUERY *number* times and computes the average response times.

RESET_STATS   [*names_server...*]

Resets statistic counters for the nominated servers or, if no *names_server* is specified, for the current server only.

RESTART   [*names_server...*]

Restarts the nominated names server or, if no *names_server* is specified, the current server.

Command Line Utilities

Command Summaries *(Continued)*

NAMESCTL **NAMESCTL80** **(CONT.)**	SET Sets names server options. Valid options are: CACHE_CHECKPOINT_INTERVAL, DEFAULT_DOMAIN, FORWARDING_AVAILABLE, LOG_FILE_NAME, LOG_STATS_INTERVAL, NAMESCTL_TRACE_LEVEL, PASSWORD, REQUESTS_ENABLED, RESET_STATS_INTERVAL, SERVER, TRACE_FILE_NAME, TRACE_LEVEL, and CACHE_CHECKPOINT_INTERVAL.

SHOW
Shows the value of server options. Options are the same as for SET.

SHUTDOWN   [*names_server...*]
Shuts down the specified servers or, if no *names_server* is specified, the current server.

START
Starts up the current server.

START_CLIENT_CACHE
Starts a client cache process, which caches names information retrieved from names servers on the client side.

STATUS
Shows status and statistics for the nominated servers or, if no server is specified, the current server.

STOP
Stops the nominated servers or, if no server is specified, the current server.

TIMED_QUERY   [*time*]
Returns the definitions of all names registered since the given *time*.

Command Summaries *(Continued)*

NAMESCTL **NAMESCTL80** **(CONT.)**	UNREGISTER *name* [-D *address*] [-H *host*] [-L *listener*] Deletes a name's definition. Arguments are the same as for the REGISTER operation.

VERSION
Shows server version information.

Reference *Oracle Net Administrator's Guide.*

OCOPY **OCOPY73** **OCOPY80** **NT**	**ocopy** [/b] `source_file destination_filecopy` ocopy is used to copy an Oracle data file to an operating system file. ocopy can copy Oracle data files even when they are in use by Oracle, and can copy data files that are located on raw partitions. It is typically used to copy files during an on-line backup.

/B   Copies to multiple diskettes.

Example

Copy a data file on a raw partition, located on drive I:
to d:\backup\datafile_i.bak:

```
ocopy80 \\.\I: d:\backup\datafile_i.bak
```

OERR **UNIX**	**oerr** `facility errorcode` oerr displays the error text associated with a particular error message. Both arguments must be provided:

facility	The three-letter prefix to the error code. This will most frequently be "ORA".

errorcode The error number reported.

Example

Show the error message for error `ORA-00942`:

Command Summaries *(Continued)*

OERR
(CONT.)
	`$ oerr ora 960`
	
	`00960, 00000, "ambiguous column naming in`
	`select list"`
	`// *Cause: A column name in the order-by list`
	`// matches more than one select list columns.`
	`// *Action: Remove duplicate column naming in`
	`// select list.`

ORADIM **ORADIM73** **ORADIM80** **NT**	`oradim {-NEW arguments	-EDIT arguments |` ` -DELETE arguments	-SHUTDOWN arguments` `	-help }`  oradim is used to configure and control the Windows NT services that support Oracle database instances.  If no argument is specified, `oradim` loads a GUI utility that allows creation, deletion, and modification of database service configurations. Otherwise, the following arguments may be specified: ***Arguments*** -NEW Creates a new database service. -EDIT Changes the properties of a database service. -DELETE Deletes a database service. -STARTUP Starts a database service. -SHUTDOWN Shuts down a database service. -HELP Shows a help message. ***Qualifiers*** The following qualifiers can be provided for the arguments outlined above:

Command Summaries *(Continued)*

ORADIM **ORADIM73** **ORADIM80** **(CONT.)**	-SID	Instance to be processed.
	-SRVC	Service to be processed.
	-INITPWD	Specifies the password to be used for internal access.
	-MAXUSERS	Specifies the maximum number of users that can be stored in the password file.
	-STARTMODE	Specifies whether the database should be started automatically (AUTO) or manually (MANUAL) at boot time.
	-PFILE	Name of the password file.
	-NEWSID	For −EDIT, changes the instance name.
	-USRPWD	Internal account password (for verification).
	-SHUTTYPE	For −SHUTDOWN, specifies one or more of SRVC and INST to specify shutdown of service or instance or both.
	-SHUTMODE	For −SHUTDOWN, specifies mode A (abort), I (immediate), or N (normal).

Reference *Oracle Getting Started for Windows NT.*

ORAENV **UNIX**	`. oraenv` The `oraenv` script is used to set up a UNIX *korn* or *bourne* shell environment for a specific Oracle instance. If the environment variable ORAENV_ASK is not set to "FALSE", then `oraenv` will prompt for an Oracle instance identifier ("ORACLE_SID"); otherwise, the existing ORACLE_SID is used to define the environment.

Command Summaries *(Continued)*

**ORAENV
(CONT.)**

Because `oraenv` manipulates the environment of the current shell, it must be "sourced" using the "." operator. `oraenv` adjusts the values of the environment variables ORACLE_SID, ORACLE_HOME, and PATH.

Examples

Allow `oraenv` to prompt for a database instance and set the environment for instance to DEV:

```
$ . oraenv
ORACLE_SID = [PROD] ? DEV
```

Set up the environment for database DEV without interaction:

```
$ ORAENV_ASK=NO
$ ORACLE_SID=W732
$ . oraenv
```

Reference *Oracle Administrator's Guide for UNIX.*

ORAKILL

NT

Orakill *sid thread*

ORAKILL terminates a selected database session. *Sid* identifies the thread to be terminated. *Thread* indicates the thread ID to terminate. The thread ID matches the spid column in the *v$process* file. The following query shows the thread IDs for all sessions:

```
SELECT spid, osuser, s.program
  FROM v$process p, v$session s
  WHERE p.addr=s.paddr
```

**ORAPWD
ORAPWD80**

orapwd FILE=*file_name* PASSWORD=*password*
    ENTRIES=*max_users*

orapwd creates an Oracle password file that allows access to the SYS and INTERNAL accounts.

Command Summaries *(Continued)*

ORAPWD **ORAPWD80** **(CONT.)**	FILE	Name of the password file to be created. Under NT, the default location is *ORACLE_HOME*/DATABASE/PWD*SID*.ORA. Under UNIX, the default location is $ORACLE_HOME/dbs/orapw{$ORACLE_SID}.
	PASSWORD	Password for INTERNAL or SYS access.
	ENTRIES	Maximum number of users who will be granted SYSDBA or SYSOPER privilege.

Notes

The Oracle password file is activated only if the server configuration parameter REMOTE_LOGIN_ PASSWORDFILE is set to "EXCLUSIVE" or "SHARED".

Reference *Oracle Administrator's Guide.*

ORASTACK

NT

orastack *program_file stack_size*

orastack is used to alter the amount of stack space allocated to each thread run by Oracle server or listener processes. This may be useful where the NT limit on process virtual memory (2GB by default in NT 4.0) constrains the Oracle server. If invoked with no arguments, an informational message will be displayed.

> *program_file*   Program file to be patched with an adjusted stack size. Usually, this will be files such as *oracle73.exe, oracle80.exe, tnslsnr80.exe*, etc.

> *stack_size*   Maximum stack size per thread in bytes.

Reference *Oracle Bulletin #1234455.*

Command Summaries *(Continued)*

OSSLOGIN	`osslogin` [-d] [*X_509_name*]

osslogin is used to attach to an Oracle Security Server to download a *wallet*, which contains an X.509 certificate and private/public encryption keys.

> *X_509_name*   X.509 identification for the user as specified in the IDENTIFIED GLOBALLY clause of the CREATE USER statement.

Reference *Oracle Security Server Guide.*

OTRCCOL	`otrccol` {START	STOP	FORMAT	DCF	DFD} [*options...*]

The otrccol command provides a command line interface for managing Oracle trace collections. It takes the following forms:

START   *job_id parameter_file*

> Starts an Oracle trace collection file identified as *job_id*.

STOP   *job_id parameter_file*

> Stops the Oracle trace collection identified by *job_id*.

DCF   *collection_name cdf_file*

> Deletes data for the specified collection from the specified collection file.

DFD   *collection_name username password tns_service*

> Deletes data for the specified collection from formatted database tables owned by the specified user.

Reference *Oracle Tuning Guide.*

Command Summaries *(Continued)*

OTRCCREF

`otrccref`

`otrccref` creates the Oracle trace configuration files *regid.dat, facility.dat*, and *collect.dat*.

Reference *Oracle Tuning Guide.*

OTRCFMT

`otrcfmt` `[-f ]` `[-c` `commit_freq]` `cdf_file`
`username/password@database`

`otrcfmt` loads data from Oracle trace collection files into Oracle database tables. The database tables must have already been created using the OTRCFMTC.SQL script.

-F   Reloads the entire collection file. Otherwise, only the previously unformatted data is loaded.

-C   Issues a COMMIT after loading this many rows.

cdf_file   Oracle trace collection file.

username/password@database   Connection details for user who owns the database files.

Reference *Oracle Tuning Guide.*

OTT
OTT80

8.0+

`ott` USERID=*connect_string* [KEYWORD=*value...*]

`ott` invokes the oracle object type translator, which generates host language structure definitions for Oracle8 object types. These definitions may be included in OCI programs that need to access the object types. The following options may be specified:

CASE   Specifies case translation for object type definitions. Values are LOWER, UPPER, and SAME.

CODE   C language type. Options are C, KR_C, and ANSI_C

Command Line Utilities

Command Summaries *(Continued)*

OTT **OTT80** **(CONT.)**	CONFIG	Configuration file containing standard options.
	ERRTYPE	File to which error messages will be written.
	HFILE	Source file to which object definitions will be written.
	INITFILE	Source file containing an initialization function.
	INITFUNC	Name of the initialization function.
	INTYPE	File containing definitions of object types to be translated and the output structure names.
	OUTTYPE	Output listing file. This file can be used as an in-type file in future invocations of `ott`.
	SCHEMA_NAMES	Controls qualification of types with schemas in the out-type file. Values are ALWAYS, IF_NEEDED, and FROM_INTYPE.
	USERID	The username/password [@dbname] connect string.

Reference *Oracle Call Interface Programmer's Guide.*

SQLJ **8i**	`Sqlj` [keyword=*option* ...] *input_file* The `sqlj` command invokes the `sqlj` translator which translates SQLJ program constructs into JDBC code. See Chapter 7 for a more detailed description of SQLJ. The following keywords are accepted:

	`-encoding`	Specifies the character set representation of input and output files.

Command Summaries *(Continued)*

SQLJ (CONT.)	`-log`	Logs file name.
	`-compile`	Controls whether output Java files are passed to `javac` for compilation.
	`-props`	Property file that contains SQLJ options.
	`-compiler-output-file`	Name of a file that receives output from the `javac` compiler.
	`-version`	Prints SQLJ version.
	`-profile`	Enables or disables processing of `.ser` files by the SQLJ profile customizer.
	`-compiler-executable`	Name of the Java compiler. `Javac` is the default.
	`-v`	Turns verbose line mapping on or off.
	`-ser2class`	If true, `.ser` files are converted to `.class` files.
	`-linemap`	If true, line numbers from the `.sqlj` source file are embedded in the `.class` file.
	`-default-customizer`	Sets a non-default profile customizer.
	`-compiler-encoding-flag`	Controls whether the value of the `-encoding` flag is passed to the `javac` compiler.
	`-status`	Enables or disables the SQLJ processing display.
	`-help`	Shows a command line option summary.
	`-d`	Sets directory where `.ser` files are placed.

Command Line Utilities

Command Summaries *(Continued)*

SQLJ **(CONT.)**	`-offline`	Specifies the name of a Java class that will perform syntactical checks on SQL when there is no connection to the database.
	`-warn`	Sets the level of warning messages. It can be set to a combination of: `all`, `none`, `verbose`, `noverbose`, `null`, `nonull`, `precision`, `noprecision`, `portable`, `noportable`, `strict`, `nostrict`.
	`-online`	Specifies the name of a Java class that will perform syntactical checking when a connection to the database exists.
	`-cache`	If true, SQL check results will be cached in the hope of avoiding database accesses.
	`-url`	Database identification string. This follows conventions for the thin or `oci` JDBC drivers as described in Chapter 7.
	`-driver`	JDBC driver to use.
	`-password`	Password for database user.
	`-user`	Username for database user.
	`-dir`	Directory location for Java files.
	`-d`	Directory location for `.ser` files.
SQLLDR **SQLLDR73** **SQLLDR80**	`sqlldr` [KEYWORD=*value* …]	

The `sqlldr` command invokes the SQL°LOADER program, which loads data from flat files into Oracle tables.

Options may be any of the following:

USERID	Oracle connect string.

Command Summaries *(Continued)*

SQLLDR **SQLLDR73** **SQLLDR80** **(CONT.)**	CONTROL	Name of the control file that contains SQL*LOADER commands.
	LOG	Log filename.
	BAD	File to contain rejected rows.
	DATA	File containing input data.
	DISCARD	File containing discarded data.
	DISCARDMAX	Number of discards to allow.
	SKIP	Number of records to skip before loading.
	LOAD	Number of records to load.
	ERRORS	Number of errors permitted.
	ROWS	Number of rows in each insert batch.
	BINDSIZE	Number of bytes in each insert batch.
	SILENT	If true, suppresses messages during load.
	DIRECT	If true, uses direct path load.
	PARFILE	File containing command line parameter settings.
	PARALLEL	If true, load is concurrent with other loads on the same table.
	FILE	Data file in which to allocate extents.
	SKIP_UNUSABLE_INDEXES	If true, unusable indexes will be ignored during the load.

Command Line Utilities

Command Summaries *(Continued)*

SQLLDR **SQLLDR73** **SQLLDR80** **(CONT.)**	SKIP_INDEX_MAINTENANCE Disregards indexes during the load and marks those indexes as unusable. COMMIT_DISCONTINUED Commits rows already loaded if the load is discontinued. READIZE Size of input read buffer in bytes. MAX_RECORD_SIZE Maximum allowable record size in bytes. Reference *Oracle Utilities Guide.*
SQLPLUS **PLUS80** **PLUS33**	**sqlplus** [*options*] [*connect_string*] sqlplus provides an interactive, command line driven interface for processing SQL statements. SQL*PLUS is fully described in Chapter 9, "SQL°PLUS."
SVRMGRL **SVRMGR23** **SVRMGR30**	**svrmgrl** [COMMAND=@*scriptname*] svrmgrl invokes the Oracle Server Manager in command line mode. Server Manager can be used to start, stop, and perform administrative functions on Oracle databases. The COMMAND= argument may be used to specify a file containing Server Manager commands to be executed. Otherwise, svrmgrl will display a prompt from which commands may be entered. Any SQL statement may be entered at the svrmgr prompt. In addition, the STARTUP, SHUTDOWN, ARCHIVE LOG, and RECOVER commands are also understood. These commands are documented in Chapter 9.
TKPROF **TKPROF73** **TKPROF80**	**tkprof** *trace_file output_file* [*keyword=value* ...] tkprof formats trace files generated by the SQL TRACE facility. These trace files are generated as a result of an ALTER SESSION SET SQL_TRACE=TRUE statement, the DBMS_SYSTEM.SET_SQL_TRACE_IN_SESSION procedure, or Oracle *event* 10046.

Command Summaries *(Continued)*

TKPROF **TKPROF73** **TKPROF80** **(CONT.)**	*trace_file* Name of the trace file to be processed. The file will normally be located in the directory specified by the server parameter USER_DUMP_DEST. *output_file* Name of the output file to be generated.

Keywords

EXPLAIN   Specifies the connection that will be used to generate SQL execution plans. If you don't specify the EXPLAIN keyword, no execution plans will be generated.

SORT   Displays the SQL statements in descending values of the sort keys. The sort keys "(PRSELA, EXEELA, FCHELA)" sort the SQL statements in descending order of elapsed time and are a common choice. Other sort keys are outlined below.

PRINT   Restricts the number of SQL statements printed.

AGGREGATE   If set to "yes" (the default), SQL statements in the trace file that are identical will be reported only once and execution statistics will be summed. If set to "no", each time a SQL statement is parsed, a separate entry will be written to the tkprof output, even if the statement is identical to one encountered previously.

SYS   If set to "no", statements executed as the SYS user will not be included in the trace output. These statements are often recursive SQL, which, in some cases, might not be of interest.

RECORD   Specifies a file to which all the SQL statements (aside from recursive SQL) in the trace file will be stored.

Command Line Utilities

Command Summaries *(Continued)*

TKPROF **TKPROF73** **TKPROF80** **(CONT.)**	INSERT Specifies a file that can be run under SQL°PLUS to keep a record of the SQL statements in the trace file and their execution statistics. This facility was introduced to allow you to set and compare SQL statement execution over time, perhaps to establish the effect of increasing data volumes or user load.

Sort Option

The sort option can take one or more arguments. If more than one argument is specified, then the SQL statements will be sorted by the sum of the specified measurements.

PRSCNT   Number of parse calls.

PRSCPU   CPU time parsing.

PRSELA   Elapsed time parsing.

PRSDSK   Disk reads during parse.

PRSQRY   Consistent reads during parse.

PRSCU   Current reads during parse.

PRSMIS   Misses in library cache during parse.

EXECNT   Number of execute calls.

EXECPU   CPU time spent executing.

EXEELA   Elapsed time executing.

EXEDSK   Disk reads during execute.

EXEQRY   Consistent reads during execute.

EXECU   Current reads during execute.

Command Summaries *(Continued)*

TKPROF **TKPROF73** **TKPROF80** **(CONT.)**	EXEROW	Rows processed during execute.
	EXEMIS	Library cache misses during execute.
	FCHCNT	Fetch calls.
	FCHCPU	CPU time spent fetching.
	FCHELA	Elapsed time fetching.
	FCHDSK	Disk reads during fetch.
	FCHQRY	Consistent reads during fetch.
	FCHCU	Current reads during fetch.
	FCHROW	Rows fetched.
	USERID	Parsing user ID.

Example

Process trace file `ora_00123.trc`, outputting to `mytrace.sql`, generating `explain` plans with `scott/tiger`, and sorting by the sum of elapsed times:

```
tkprof ora_0123.trc mytrace.sql
explain=scott/tiger
    sort=(prsela,exeela,fchela)
```

Reference *Oracle Server Tuning Guide*.

TNSPING **TNSPING80**	**tnsping** *service_name* [*count*]

`tnsping` attempts to connect to the listener responsible for the given service name. It is used to validate SQL°NET or NET8 configuration and network availability.

Command Line Utilities

Command Summaries *(Continued)*

TNSPING **TNSPING80** **(CONT.)**	*service_name* Service name to connect to. This will normally be an alias stored in the TNSNAMES.ORA file or known to an Oracle names server. *count* Number of connect attempts to be made. Reference *Oracle Net Administrator's Guide.*

TRCASST

8.0+

```
trcasst [-O {C|D} {U|T} Q] [-P] [-S] [-E
   {0|1|2}] file_name
```

trcasst invokes the Oracle trace assistant, which extracts and refines information contained in Net8 trace files.

-O   Shows SQL*Net and TTC (two-task common) information:

    C   Shows summary SQL*NET information.

    D   Shows detailed SQL*NET information.

    U   Shows summary TTC information.

    T   Shows detailed TTC information.

    Q   Shows SQL commands.

-P   Shows application performance measurements.

-S   Displays statistical information.

-E   Display error information:

    0   Translates NS errors.

    1   Translates NS error translation, plus all other errors.

    2   Displays error number without translation.

Reference *Oracle Net Administrator's Guide.*

Command Summaries *(Continued)*

TRCEVAL	`trceval` `[-C]` `[-D]` `[-F]` `[-S]` `[-T]` `[-U]` `[-Q]` `file_name`

7.3

`trceval` extracts and refines information contained in SQL°NET 2.x trace files.

-C   Summary connectivity information.

-D   Detailed connectivity information.

-F   Forms application trace statistics generated.

-S   Overall trace statistics generated.

-T   Detailed two-task packet information.

-U   Summary two-task packet information.

-Q   SQL commands completed for the -U option.

TRCROUTE   `trcroute` *service_name*

`trcroute` displays details of each listener involved in a connection to the specified service.

service_name   Target SQL°NET service name.

Reference *Oracle Network Products Troubleshooting Guide.*

TSTSHM   `tstshm`

UNIX

`tstshm` analyzes shared memory configuration on a UNIX system. It shows the number and size of available shared memory segments and ensures that segments can be attached.

Command Line Utilities

Command Summaries *(Continued)*

UNIXENV	`unixenv`
UNIX	unixenv prints useful information about the UNIX environment. This includes machine and operating system versions, CPU, memory and disk resources, resource limits, and environment variables.

| WRAP WRAP23 WRAP80 | **wrap** INAME=*input_file* [ONAME=*output_file*]

 wrap converts source code for stored program units into portable object files. These object files cannot be read or modified.

 Reference *PL/SQL User's Guide and Reference.* |

a. Jpub was beta in Oracle 8.1.5, which was the current Oracle version when this book was written. Usage might change in subsequent versions of Oracle.

SQL*PLUS

Introduction

SQL*PLUS is a command line program that provides a standard interface for executing SQL statements, performing database administration, retrieving result sets, and writing simple reports.

Although SQL*PLUS presents a simplistic interface, it has the advantage of being present in virtually all Oracle installations and—from Oracle8i onwards—supports administrative commands such as STARTUP, SHUTDOWN, and ARCHIVE LOG.

Reference

SQL*PLUS is documented in the *SQL*PLUS User's Guide and Reference*.

Command-Line Arguments

SQL*PLUS can be invoked from the command line with one of the following commands:

sqlplus	On UNIX or NT, invokes the default version of SQL*PLUS.
sqlplusw	On NT, invokes the graphical version of SQL*PLUS.
plus80	On NT, invokes the Oracle 8.0 version of SQL*PLUS.
plus33	On NT, invokes the Oracle7.3 version of SQL*PLUS.

Command line options for SQL°PLUS are shown below:

```
sqlplus {-? | -s } [username[/password] [@db_alias]]
        [/nologon] [@filename [arguments]]
```

-?   Generates a help message.

-s   Runs SQL°PLUS in "silent" mode—suppressing all banners and
              prompts.

/nologin   Bypasses the logon dialogue and starts SQL°PLUS without a database
              connection.

@filename   Specifies a command file to run. Arguments consist of space-separated
              parameters which may be referenced within the command file as *&1*,
              &2, and so on.

SQL*PLUS Features

SQL°PLUS is available as a command line-driven program under UNIX
and NT, and in a minimally graphical incarnation under Microsoft Windows environments. In any case, the user either types commands in at a (by
default) SQL> prompt, or places files in command scripts for subsequent
execution.

Parameter Substitution

SQL°PLUS variables can be defined using the ACCEPT and DEFINE commands. By default, these variables can be embedded in SQL statements
prefixed with "&" and optionally terminated by ".".

In addition, arguments to command files are available within the command file as "&1", "&2", etc.

For example, this command file uses ACCEPT to query the user for a
customer_id:

```
accept customer_id prompt "Enter customer ID: "
select * from customers where customer_id=&customer_id.;
```

This command file should be executed with the customer_id as the
first argument:

```
select * from customers where customer_id=&1;
```

SQL*PLUS Edit Buffer

When SQL*PLUS statements are entered interactively, they are maintained in an edit buffer. Basic line editing commands are available to manipulate, display, or run the edit buffer, and the edit buffer can also be edited in an operating system editor using the EDIT command. Other commands allow the edit buffer to be saved to, or loaded from, a file.

Bind Variables

The VAR command creates a SQL*PLUS bind variable. This bind variable may be assigned values within PL/SQL blocks, used in SQL statements, and printed by the PRINT command. The following example uses a bind variable to store a total sales figure. This figure is then used to calculate a percent of total sales amount for each customer.

```
var tot_sales number

BEGIN
    SELECT sum(sale_value)
    INTO :tot_sales
    FROM sales;
END;
./

SELECT customer_id,sum(sale_value)*100/
        :tot_sales pct_of_total
    FROM sales
    GROUP BY customer_id
    ORDER BY pct_of_total desc
/
```

Formatting Options

Various commands—most notably the COLUMN command—allow you to specify format masks for columns output from the SELECT statement.

For alphanumeric data, you change the length of a column with the format mask An, where "A" indicates an alphanumeric format and n denotes the display length of the field. You can use the SET WRAP command (see "Options of the SET Command" below) to choose between truncation or word wrap when the column data exceeds the format width.

Date columns are treated as character strings by SQL*PLUS. To adjust the date display format, you should use the TO_CHAR function.

SQL*PLUS

For numeric columns, SQL°PLUS supports a subset of the SQL number format masks. The supported format elements are shown in Table 9-1.

Table 9–1 SQL*PLUS Numeric Format Elements

Numeric Format Mask	Description
$	Prefixes the number with a dollar sign.
,	Prints a comma at the specified location.
.	Prints a decimal point at the specified location.
0	Denotes a numeric placeholder. If the location is unused—for instance, the number is of a magnitude less than that allowed for—a 0 will be printed.
9	Denotes a numeric placeholder. If the location is unused—for instance, the number is of a magnitude less than that allowed for—a blank will be printed.
9.99EEEE	Returns the number in scientific notation. The number of digits after the decimal point specifies the precision of the number returned.
B	Returns blanks instead of zeroes in the integral portion of a number if the number is less than 1. This overrides any "0" format masks that may have been set.
C	Returns the ISO currency symbol as defined by NLS_ISO_CURRENCY.
D	Displays a decimal point.
G	Returns the character defined by NLS_NUMERIC_CHARACTER in the specified position. This character—often ","—is used to mark magnitudes of one thousand (1,000), one million (1,000,000), etc.
L	Returns the local currency symbol defined by NLS_CURRENCY.
MI	Returns a trailing negative sign for negative numbers.
PR	Causes negative values to be enclosed in "<>".
RM	Returns the number in Roman numerals.

Table 9–1 SQL*PLUS Numeric Format Elements *(Continued)*

Numeric Format Mask	Description
S	Prints a plus or minus sign, depending on the value supplied.
DATE	Displays a number that represents a Julian date in DD/MM/YY format.
X	Returns the integer part of an input number, formatted in hexadecimal.

SQL*PLUS Commands

The following commands can be executed at the SQL*PLUS command line or included within SQL*PLUS command scripts.

SQL*PLUS Commands

/

/

The slash character executes the SQL or PL/SQL command in the SQL buffer.

@

@*file_name* [*parameter1* [*paramter2* ...]]

The @ symbol runs the SQL*PLUS commands in *file_name*. *Parameter1, parameter2*, and subsequent parameters are substituted for the symbols &1, &2, etc.

@@

@@ *file_name* [*parameter1* [*parameter2* ...]]

The @@ symbol runs the SQL*PLUS commands in *file_name*. It differs from the @ symbol in that it may be included in SQL*PLUS command scripts and will return control to the calling script when the script completes. @@ searches the directory from which its calling script was initiated, rather than searching the current directory.

SQL*PLUS Commands *(Continued)*

ACCEPT	ACC[EPT] *variable_name* [{NUMBER|CHAR|DATE}]
	    [FORMAT *format_mask*] [DEFAULT *default_value*]
	    [PROMPT {*prompt_text*|NOPROMPT}] [HIDE]
	
	ACCEPT prompts the user for a value to assign to *variable_name*.
	
	The variable may be defined as being of the type NUMBER, CHAR, or DATE. If the type is not defined, then CHAR is assumed. FORMAT can be used to assign a format mask. These format masks are defined in the entry for the COLUMN command.
	
	DEFAULT specifies the value to be assigned to the value if the user specifies no value.
	
	PROMPT prompts the user with the specified text. If NOPROMPT is specified, then no prompt text is displayed. If the PROMPT clause is omitted, a system-generated prompt is provided.
	
	HIDE suppresses the display of the variable value as it is typed, for instance, when providing a password value.

APPEND	A[PPEND] *append_text* APPEND adds the specified text to the current line in the edit buffer. A space is appended before the text.
ARCHIVE LOG 8i	ARCHIVE LOG {LIST|STOP}|{START|NEXT|ALL|*log_sequence*} [TO *destination*] The ARCHIVE LOG command provides convenient access to the clauses contained within the ALTER SYSTEM ARCHIVE LOG command. START commences automatic archiving of redo logs. STOP ceases automatic archiving.

SQL*PLUS Commands *(Continued)*

ARCHIVE LOG (CONT.)	NEXT, ALL, and *log_sequence* request archiving of the next log due for archiving, all logs due for archiving, or the specified archive log sequence.

The TO clause changes the archive log destination.

Prior to Oracle8i, the ARCHIVE LOG command was available through the Server Manager program (svrmgrl). |
| **ATTRIBUTE**

8.0+ | ATTRIBUTE [*type_name.attribute_name*] [ALIAS *alias_name*] [CLEAR] [FORMAT *format_name*] LIKE {*type_name.attribute_name*|*alias*}[{ON|OFF}]

ATTRIBUTE sets characteristics for attributes of Oracle8 object types. It is similar in some respects to the COLUMN command.

type_name.attribute_name defines the object attribute involved. ALIAS specifies an alias for the attribute, which can be used in the LIKE clause of other attribute commands.

CLEAR clears all format settings for the attribute.

FORMAT specifies a display format for the attribute. It takes the same arguments as the FORMAT clause in the COLUMN command.

LIKE indicates that the attribute should inherit display attributes from the named attribute.

ON and OFF enable and suppress attribute settings. |
| **BREAK** | BREAK [ON {*column_name* | *expression* | ROW | REPORT} [ON ...]] [{SKIP *number_of_lines*|SKIP PAGE}] [{NODUPLICATES|DUPLICATES}] |

*SQL*PLUS*

SQL*PLUS Commands *(Continued)*

BREAK (CONT.)	BREAK controls grouping of data within SQL°PLUS result sets. BREAK defines what happens when the specified column or expression changes value. By default, BREAK suppresses printing of duplicate values of the specified column or expression.

SKIP allows multiple lines to be skipped or a page break issued when the column or expression changes.

NODUPLICATES (the default) suppresses printing of BREAK columns if the columns have not changed; DUPLICATES causes these duplicate columns to be printed.

BREAK ON ROW and BREAK ON REPORT allow for breaks to occur after each line or after the entire result set. BREAK ON REPORT is most commonly used when it is required to print column summaries after all rows are printed.

BTITLE	BTITLE [*printoption* {*text*	*variable*} [*printoption*...]]	[OFF|ON]

BTITLE prints text at the bottom of each page of output.

Printoption controls the positioning and format of the text. The following print options are supported:

COL *col_no*	Move to the specified column.
SKIP [*skip_count*]	Skip the specified number of rows.
TAB *tab_count*	Skip forward the specified number of tab characters.
LEFT	Left-align the following text.
CENTER	Center the following text.
RIGHT	Right-align the following text.
BOLDFORMAT	Print in bold.

SQL*PLUS Commands *(Continued)*

BTITLE (CONT.)	OFF suppresses the printing of the BTITLE; ON reinstates the BTITLE.

Variables in the title may include any user variables and also the following system variables:

SQL.LNO	Current line number.
SQL.PNO	Current page number.
SQL.RELEASE	Oracle version number.
SQL.SQLCODE	Current error code.
SQL.USER	Current username.

CHANGE	C[HANGE] *separator old_text* [*separator*] [*new_text* [*separator*]]

CHANGE substitutes the first occurrence of *old_text* with *new_text* in the current line of the input buffer.

Any non-alphabetic character may be used as the separator. Typical separators are 'and /.

CLEAR	CLEAR [BREAKS] [BUFFER] [COMPUTES] [COLUMNS] [SQL] [TIMING]

CLEAR clears settings of the BREAK, COMPUTE, TIMING, or COLUMN commands. BUFFER and SQL clauses both cause the edit buffer to be cleared.

COLUMN	COL[UMN] [{*column_name* I *expression*} [ALIAS alias] [CLEAR] [FOLD_A[FTER]] [FOLD_B[EFORE]] [FORMAT *format_mask*] [HEADING *heading_text*] [{ON|OFF}] [NEW_VALUE *variable*] [JUSTIFY {L[EFT] I C[ENTER] I R[IGHT]} [LIKE {*expression* I *alias*}] [NEWLINE] [{NOPRINT| PRINT}] [NULL text] [OLD_VALUE *variable*] [{WRA[PPED] I WOR[D_WRAPPED] I TRU[NCATED] }]

•

SQL*PLUS Commands *(Continued)*

COLUMN (CONT.)	COLUMN controls the display characteristics of columns from SQL SELECT commands. Issued with no arguments, COLUMN displays all current column settings. If any arguments are specified, the first argument should be the name of a column from the SELECT list of a query, or a column alias defined by the ALIAS option of a previous COLUMN command.
	ALIAS assigns an alias to the column which can be used in BREAK, COMPUTE, and other COLUMN commands.
	CLEAR clears all settings for the column.
	FOLD_AFTER generates a carriage return after the column heading and values. FOLD_BEFORE generates a carriage return before the column. NEWLINE has the same effect as FOLD_BEFORE.
	FORMAT specifies the display format for the column. See "Formatting Options" above for details of valid *format_masks*.
	HEADING specifies a column heading.
	OFF temporarily removes column attributes; ON reinstates previously assigned attributes.
	NEW_VALUE causes the specified variable to be assigned the value of the column whenever a BREAK occurs. OLD_VALUE causes the variable to be assigned the value that the column held prior to the break.
	JUSTIFY LEFT, RIGHT, or CENTER justifies a column.
	LIKE causes the column to acquire the characteristics of the column identified by name or alias.
	NOPRINT suppresses printing of the column. PRINT reinstates printing.
	NULL sets the character which is printed if the column value is null.

SQL*PLUS Commands *(Continued)*

COLUMN **(CONT.)**	WRAP causes the column to wrap to the next line if the data is too long to fit within the column definition. WORD_WRAPPED causes the wrapping to occur on a word boundary. TRUNCATE causes the column to be truncated.

COMPUTE	COMP[UTE] [*function* [LABEL text]]
	    OF {*expression*|*column_name*|*column_alias*}
	    ON {*expression*|*column_name*|*column_alias*|
	    REPORT|ROW}...]
	
	COMPUTE calculates and prints summary values when a BREAK condition occurs.
	
	Function defines the type of summary information to print. Valid values are AVG, COUNT, SUM, MAX, MIN, STD, and VARIANCE. See Chapter 2, "SQL Expressions and Functions," for descriptions of these functions.
	
	LABEL defines the text to be printed with the summary value.
	
	OF defines the columns or expressions in the SELECT list for which summaries are to be printed.
	
	ON specifies when the computed values are to be displayed. There must be a corresponding break condition current for the column or expression specified.

CONNECT	CONN[ECT] [*username*[/*password*]][@*database_specification*]|/] [AS [SYSOPER|SYSDBA]]|[INTERNAL] CONNECT establishes a new connection to the database. The AS clause enables the connection with SYSOPER or SYSDBA privileges, if they are available. INTERNAL establishes an "internal" SYS connection. The CONNECT INTERNAL form is depreciated in Oracle8i and might not be included in a future release of Oracle.

SQL*PLUS

SQL*PLUS Commands *(Continued)*

CONNECT **(CONT.)**	"/" indicates that the connection should be "identified externally". This most commonly connects the user to an account "OPS$userid", where userid is the operating system username.

COPY

COPY [FROM *username*[*/password*]*@database_specification*]
   [TO username[/password]@database_specification]
   {APPEND|CREATE|INSERT|REPLACE}
   destination_table   [*(column_list)*]
   USING query

COPY copies data to and from remote tables.

FROM specifies a connection from which data will be retrieved; TO specifies the connection to which data will be copied. If either are omitted, then the current connection will be used.

APPEND adds rows to an existing table or creates a new table, if necessary. CREATE creates a new table and inserts rows. INSERT adds rows to an existing table only. REPLACE truncates an existing table before copying rows.

Destination_table and *column_list* define the table and columns into which data will be inserted.

USING specifies the query that will be used to retrieve data.

DEFINE

DEF[INE] [*variable* [= *value*]]

DEFINE sets or shows the values of SQL°PLUS variables.

DEL

DEL [*start_line* [*end_line*] }

DEL deletes one or more lines from the edit buffer. If no line number is specified, then the current line is deleted. If a single line number is listed, then that line is deleted. If two line numbers are listed, then all lines between and including those line numbers will be deleted.

SQL*PLUS Commands *(Continued)*

DEL **(CONT.)**	The terms "*" and "LAST" may be used to denote the current and last lines, respectively.
DESCRIBE	DESC[RIBE] *object_specification* DESCRIBE prints the definition of the specified object, which may be a table, view, synonym, stored program, or type.
DISCONNECT	DISCONNECT DISCONNECT terminates the current database connection. Any incomplete connections are committed.
EDIT	ED[IT] [*file_name*] EDIT invokes an operating system editor to edit the contents of the edit buffer or the specified file. The editor invoked is either the system default editor or the editor defined by the variable _EDITOR (for instance, *define _editor=vi*).
EXECUTE	EXEC[UTE] *stored_procedure* This EXECUTEs a stored procedure.

EXIT	EXIT [{SUCCESS|FAILURE|WARNING|*return_code*|
	                variable|:*BindVariable*}]
	   [COMMIT|ROLLBACK]
	
	This exits SQL*PLUS. The SUCCESS, FAILURE, or WARNING keywords cause SQL*PLUS to terminate with an appropriate operating system return code. Alternately, a specific error code can be specified directly or through a SQL*PLUS or bind variable.
	
	An implicit COMMIT is issued upon exit, unless the ROLLBACK keyword is specified.

*SQL*PLUS*

SQL*PLUS Commands *(Continued)*

GET	GET *file_name* [{LIST|NOLIST}]
	GET loads the specified file into the SQL°PLUS buffer. The LIST option causes the file to be listed once it is loaded.
HELP	HELP [*help_topic*]
	HELP displays help for the specified topic or, if no topic is specified, displays a help menu.
HOST	HO[ST] [*operating_system_command*]
	HOST executes the specified operating system command.
INPUT	I[NPUT] [*text*]
	INPUT adds the specified text into a new line, following the current line in the SQL°PLUS edit buffer.
LIST	LIST [*start_line* [*end_line*]]
	LIST lists one or more lines from the edit buffer. If no line number is specified, then the current line is displayed. If a single line number is listed, then that line will be displayed. If two line numbers are listed, then all lines between and including those line numbers will be displayed.
	The terms "°" and LAST may be used to denote the current and last lines, respectively.
PASSWORD	PASSW[ORD] [*username*]
8i	PASSWORD prompts for a new password and changes the password. If no user is specified, the password for the current user is changed.

SQL*PLUS Commands *(Continued)*

PAUSE	PAU[SE] [*text*]
	PAUSE prints the specified text (if any) and waits for the user to press Return (Enter) before continuing.
PRINT	PRI[NT] [*bind_variable* [*bind_variable*...]]
	PRINT displays the values of the specified bind variables.
PROMPT	PRO[MPT] [*text*]
	PROMPT displays the specified text to the screen.
QUIT	QUIT [{SUCCESS|FAILURE|WARNING|*return_code*|
	variable|:*BindVariable*}]
	[COMMIT|ROLLBACK]
	QUIT is a synonym for EXIT.
RECOVER	RECOVER [[AUTOMATIC [FROM *location*]]
	[UNTIL {CANCEL|TIME *time_spec*|CHANGE *scn_number*}]
8i	[USING BACKUP CONTROLFILE]
	[[STANDBY] TABLESPACE *tablespace_list*
	[UNTIL CONTROLFILE]]
	[LOGFILE *logfile_name*]
	[CONTINUE [DEFAULT]]
	[CANCEL [IMMEDIATE]]
	[TIMEOUT *timeout_minutes*]
	RECOVER provides interactive access to the RECOVER clauses of the ALTER DATABASE command. See Chapter 4, "Data Definition Language (DDL)," for details of the ALTER DATABASE RECOVER clause.
	Prior to Oracle8i, this command was available from within the Server Manager (svrmgrl) program.
REMARK	REM[ARK]
	REMARK indicates that the current line is a comment.

*SQL*PLUS*

SQL*PLUS Commands *(Continued)*

REPFOOTER	REPF[OOTER] [PAGE] [*printoption* {*text* I *variable*} [*printoption*...]] [OFFION]

REPFOOTER prints a line at the end of a report or result set. *Printoptions* are the same as those for BTITLE and TTITLE.

REPHEADER	REPH[EADER] [PAGE] [*printoption* {*text* I *variable*} [*printoption*...]] [OFFION]

REPFOOTER prints a line at the beginning of a report or result set. *Printoptions* are the same as those for BTITLE and TTITLE.

RUN	R[UN]

RUN executes the command in the current input buffer.

SAVE	SAV[E] *file_name* {[CRE[ATE] I REP[LACE] I APP[END]}

SAVE writes the contents of the edit buffer into the specified operating system file. By default, the file must not exist. REPLACE and APPEND options allow an existing file to be overwritten or appended to.

SET	SET *system_variable value*

SET sets the value for a SQL°PLUS system variable or option. System variables and options are described in the section titled "Options of the SET Command."

SHOW	SHO[W] *system_variable* [ALL] [BTI[TLE]] [ERR[ORS]][*object_type*] *object_name*] [LNO] [PNO] [PARAMETERS [*parameter_name*]] [REL[EASE]] [REPF[OOTER]] [REPH[EADER]] [SGA] [SPOO[L]] [SQLCODE] [TT[ITLE]] [USER]

SQL*PLUS Commands *(Continued)*

SHOW (CONT.)	SHOW shows the value of a SQL*PLUS environment variable or one of the following properties:
	ALL shows the values of all variables and properties.
	BTITLE shows the current BTITLE setting.
	ERRORS displays any compilation errors for the specified PL/SQL stored program or, if no program is specified, for the last program compiled. *Object_type* may be one of the following: FUNCTION, PROCEDURE, PACKAGE, PACKAGE BODY, TRIGGER, VIEW, TYPE, or TYPE BODY. *Object_name* is an object of the specified type for which compilation errors are to be displayed.
	LNO shows the current line number within the page; PNO shows the current page number.
	RELEASE displays a string indicating the Oracle server release.
	REPFOOTER, REPFOOTER, TTITLE, and BTITLE show the current definitions for the corresponding SQL*PLUS commands.
8i	PARAMETERS displays server configuration parameters that include the string *parameter_mask*.
8i	SGA shows a breakdown of memory allocated to the Oracle *SGA*.
	SPOOL shows the current spool destination.
	USER shows the current Oracle username.

SQL*PLUS

SQL*PLUS Commands *(Continued)*

SHUTDOWN	SHUTDOWN [{ABORT|IMMEDIATE|<u>NORMAL</u>}]
8i	SHUTDOWN shuts the Oracle instance down. With no arguments or with the NORMAL option, SHUTDOWN waits until all users disconnect before closing the instance. IMMEDIATE logs all users off and then performs an orderly shutdown. ABORT immediately terminates Oracle processes. After a SHUTDOWN ABORT, Oracle must perform instance recovery before the database can be restarted. Prior to Oracle8i, the SHUTDOWN command was available through the Server Manager program (svrmgrl).
SPOOL	SPO[OL] [{*file_name*|OFF|OUT}] SPOOL sends output from SQL°PLUS commands to the nominated file. OFF terminates writing to the file. OUT spools output to the system default printer.
START	STA[RT] *file_name* [*arguments...*] START executes the nominated command file. It is equivalent to "@". *Arguments* will be available within the command file as the variables &P1, &P2, and so on.
STARTUP 8i	STARTUP [FORCE] [RESTRICT] [PFILE=*filename*] [{NOMOUNT|MOUNT|OPEN}] [RECOVER] [*database_name*] [{EXCLUSIVE|{PARALLEL|SHARED}}] [RETRY] STARTUP starts an Oracle instance. FORCE causes any exiting database processes and resources to be terminated before the startup is commenced. RESTRICT starts the database for those with RESTRICTED_SESSION privilege only.

SQL*PLUS Commands *(Continued)*

STARTUP **(CONT.)**	PFILE specifies a parameter *init.ora* file, which contains instance configuration items. NOMOUNT starts Oracle processes, but does not open the control file. MOUNT opens the control files and acquires an instance lock. OPEN initializes the database for normal operations. RECOVER initiates media recovery during the startup process. *Database_name* specifies the name of the database to start. EXCLUSIVE indicates that the database is not available in a parallel server configuration. SHARED or PARALLEL indicates that the database may be opened in a parallel server mode. RETRY indicates that in a parallel server environment, the startup will be periodically retried while the database is being recovered by another instance. Prior to Oracle8i, the STARTUP command was available through the Server Manager program (svrmgrl).
STORE	STORE SET *file_name* {CRE[ATE]|REP[LACE]|APP[END]} STORE SET generates a command file that contains SET commands which would reinstate the current SQL°PLUS environment. REPLACE should be specified if a file is to be overwritten. APPEND will add the set commands to an existing file.

*SQL*PLUS*

SQL*PLUS Commands (Continued)

TIMING	TIMI[NG] [START *timer_name*|SHOW|STOP]

TIMING reports on elapsed times.

START initiates a timer. SHOW shows the time elapsed in the current time. STOP stops the timer and displays timer values.

TTITLE	TTITLE [*printoption* {*text*|*variable*} [*printoption*...]]|[OFF|ON]

TTITLE prints text at the top of each page of output.

Printoption controls the positioning and format of the text. The following print options are supported:

COL *col_no*   Move to the specified column.

SKIP [*skip_count*]   Skip the specified number of rows.

TAB *tab_count*   Skip forward the specified number of tab characters.

LEFT   Left-align the following text.

CENTER   Center the following text.

RIGHT   Right-align the following text.

BOLDFORMAT   Print in bold.

OFF suppresses the printing of the TTITLE; ON reinstates the TTITLE.

Variables in the title may include any user variables and also the following system variables:

SQL.LNO   Current line number.

SQL.PNO   Current page number.

SQL.RELEASE   Oracle version number.

SQL.SQLCODE   Current error code.

SQL.USER   Current Oracle user.

SQL*PLUS Commands *(Continued)*

UNDEFINE	**UNDEF[INE]** *variable_name* [*variable_name* ...]

This undefines a variable established by the DEFINE or ACCEPT commands.

VARIABLE	**VAR[IABLE]** [*variable_name* {NUMBER I CHAR ICHAR (n)I NCHAR I

NCHAR(n)IVARCHAR2(n)INVARCHAR2(n)ICLOBI NCLOBIREFCURSOR}]

VARIABLE defines a bind variable that can be referenced within PL/SQL and SQL statements.

WHENEVER OSERROR	WHENEVER OSERROR 　{EXIT [SUCCESS IFAILUREI *return_value*I*variable_name* 　　　I:*bind_variable*] 　　　　[COMMITIROLLBACK] I 　　CONTINUE [COMMITIROLLBACKINONE] }

WHENEVER OSERROR defines the actions that will occur when an operating system error (such as a file I/O error) occurs.

EXIT and CONTINUE determine whether or not SQL°PLUS will continue operating following the error.

The operating system return code can be set to *return_value* or the value of a SQL°PLUS *variable_name* or *bind_variable*. Alternately, SUCCESS or FAILURE indicate generic success or failure codes.

The COMMIT and ROLLBACK keywords indicate whether a COMMIT or ROLLBACK statement should be issued before SQL°PLUS exits or continues. NONE indicates that neither a COMMIT nor a ROLLBACK should be issued.

SQL*PLUS Commands *(Continued)*

WHENEVER SQLERROR	**WHENEVER SQLERROR** {EXIT [SUCCESS |FAILURE| *return_value*|*variable_name* |:*bind_variable*] [COMMIT|ROLLBACK] | CONTINUE [COMMIT|ROLLBACK|NONE] }

WHENEVER SQLERROR defines the actions that will occur when an Oracle SQL error occurs.

EXIT and CONTINUE determine whether or not SQL°PLUS will continue operating following the error.

The operating system return code can be set to *return_value* or the value of a SQL°PLUS *variable_name* or *bind_variable*. Alternately, SUCCESS or FAILURE indicate generic success or failure codes.

The COMMIT and ROLLBACK keywords indicate whether a COMMIT or ROLLBACK statement should be issued before SQL°PLUS exits or continues. NONE indicates that neither a COMMIT nor a ROLLBACK should be issued.

Options of the SET Command

This section documents the options that can appear after the SET command. The SHOW command can be used to display the value of each option.

SET Command Options

APPINFO	APPI[NFO]{ON|OFF|*text*}

APPINFO controls logging of application information through the DBMS_APPLICATION_INFO package.

ON sets normal logging; OFF suppresses logging.

Text replaces the default logging messages with the provided text.

SET Command Options *(Continued)*

ARRAYSIZE	ARRAY[SIZE] *array_size*

ARRAYSIZE controls the number of rows fetched from Oracle in a single operation. The default is 15.

AUTOCOMMIT	AUTOCOMMIT {OFF|ON|IMMEDIATE|*no_of_statements*}

AUTOCOMMIT controls automatic generation of COMMIT statements following SQL statements. If ON or IMMEDIATE, COMMIT statements are generated after each SQL statement. If *no_of_statements* is specified, then a COMMIT is generated after the specified number of DML statements.

AUTOPRINT	AUTOP[RINT] {OFF|ON}

AUTOPRINT ON causes bind variable values to be printed after they have been referenced in a PL/SQL block.

AUTORECOVERY	AUTORECOVERY {ON|OFF}
8i	

AUTORECOVERY ON causes redo log names to be automatically generated during a media recovery.

AUTOTRACE	AUTOTRACE {OFF|ON|TRACE[ONLY]} [EXPLAIN] [STATISTICS]

AUTOTRACE causes SQL statement statistics to be generated after each SQL execution.

ON starts tracing; OFF inhibits tracing.

TRACEONLY suppresses query output and displays trace output only.

EXPLAIN causes EXPLAIN PLAN output to be printed for each statement executed.

STATISTICS causes SQL statement execution statistics to be printed for each statement executed.

SET Command Options *(Continued)*

BLOCK TERMINATOR	BLO[CKTERMINATOR] *character*

BLOCKTERMINATOR sets the character that terminates a PL/SQL block. The default is ".".

CMDSEP	CMDS[EP] {*character*|OFF|ON}

CMDSEP defines the character that separates multiple SQL statements on the command line.

The default is ";". OFF prevents multiple statements from being entered on one line.

COLSEP	COLSEP *text*

COLSEP defines the text that separates columns in a result set. The default is a single space.

COMPATIBILITY	COM[PATIBILITY] {V7|V8|NATIVE}

Some SQL°PLUS behavior may have changed between Oracle7 and Oracle8. COMPATIBILITY allows you to define which behaviors will be active. NATIVE means that the compatibility level will be determined by the version of Oracle to which you are connected.

CONCAT	CON[CAT] {*character*|OFF|ON}

CONCAT defines the termination character for a SQL°PLUS variable which is embedded within another string. It defaults to ".".

COPYCOMMIT	COPYC[OMMIT] {*commit_rows*}

COPYCOMMIT determines the frequency at which COMMITS will be issued by the SQL°PLUS COPY command. COPYCOMMIT causes a COMMIT to be generated every *commit_rows* rows. The default of 0 indicates that no COMMIT will be issued.

SET Command Options *(Continued)*

COPYTYPECHECK COPYTYPECHECK {OFF|ON}

If OFF, then the COPY command will not check datatype compatibilities. This is intended for copies to or from foreign databases.

DEFINE DEF[INE] {*character* |OFF|ON}

DEFINE sets the substitution character for SQL*PLUS variables. This character must be prefixed to SQL*PLUS variables before they can be substituted with their assigned values. The default is "&".

ECHO ECHO {OFF|ON}

ECHO indicates that each line of a SQL*PLUS command file should be echoed as it is executed.

EDITFILE EDITF[ILE] *file_name*

EDITFILE sets the name of the temporary file used when the EDIT command is specified without a filename. The default is *afiedt.buf*.

EMBEDDED EMB[EDDED] {OFF|ON}

If EMBEDDED is set to OFF, then each new result set must start on a new page. Otherwise, result sets can start anywhere.

ESCAPE ESC[APE] {*character*|OFF|ON}

ESCAPE sets the escape character that is prefixed to the substitution character set by DEFINE to indicate that the substitution character should be treated literally and not as part of a substitution variable. The default is "\".

FEEDBACK FEED[BACK] {*row_count*|OFF|ON}

FEEDBACK controls whether SQL*PLUS will report the number of rows processed after each SQL statement.

SQL*PLUS

SET Command Options *(Continued)*

FEEDBACK (CONT.)	OFF prevents row count reporting; ON reinstates row count reporting.
	If a number (*row_count*) is specified, then SQL*PLUS will report the row count whenever the number of rows processed exceeds this number. The default is 6.
FLAGGER	FLAGGER {OFF|ENTRY|INTERMED[IATE]|FULL}
	FLAGGER controls the FIPS (Federal Information Processing Standards) flagger that flags SQL statements that don't conform to entry, intermediate, or full levels of SQL92 compliance.
FLUSH	FLU[SH] {OFF|<u>ON</u>}
	FLUSH OFF causes SQL*PLUS to buffer output (e.g., not to flush the output at each carriage return). This will improve performance for large queries being spooled to an output file, but should not be used interactively.
HEADING	HEA[DING] {OFF|<u>ON</u>}
	HEADING OFF suppresses the printing of headings in output.
HEADSEP	HEADS[EP] {*character*|OFF|ON}
	HEADSEP defines the *character* that indicates when a heading should word-wrap. The default is "|", so that "THIS|FIELD" prints THIS on the top line and FIELD on the next line in the heading.
INSTANCE **8i**	INSTANCE [*instance*|LOCAL]
	INSTANCE sets the Oracle instance to which certain commands—most notably STARTUP and SHUTDOWN—will be applied.
LINESIZE	LIN[ESIZE] *characters*
	LINESIZE defines the length of an output line. The default is 80.

SET Command Options *(Continued)*

LOBOFFSET	LOBOF[FSET] *start_position*
8.0+	LOBOFFSET controls the starting position when printing a bind variable that has been populated from a LONG or LOB column.
LOGSOURCE	LOGSOURCE *archive_log_location*
8i	LOGSOURCE identifies the location of archived redo logs for recovery.
LONG	LONG *long_display_characters*
	LONG sets the amount of data that will be displayed from columns of the LONG datatype.
LONGCHUNKSIZE	LONGC[HUNKSIZE] *long_chunk_size*
	LONGCHUNKSIZE defines the amount of data that will be retrieved from long or blob data in a single operation.
NEWPAGE	NEWP[AGE] {*number_of_lines*|NONE}
	NEWPAGE defines the number of blank lines to print between each page of output. The default is 1. A value of 0 causes a form feed to be printed.
NULL	NULL *null_string*
	NULL defines the string to print for null column output. By default, nulls are represented by blanks.
NUMFORMAT	NUMF[ORMAT] *number_format*
	NUMFORMAT specifies the default format for printing numbers. See "Formatting Options" in this chapter for details.
NUMWIDTH	NUM[WIDTH] *length*
	NUMWIDTH sets the default width to be allowed for numeric data. The default is 10.

*SQL*PLUS*

SET Command Options *(Continued)*

PAGESIZE	PAGES[IZE] *lines*

SET PAGESIZE sets the number of lines on a page.

PAUSE	PAU[SE] {OFF|ON|*pause_text*}

PAUSE ON sets a pause at the end of each page of output—the user must press Return (Enter) to proceed to the next page. PAUSE OFF suppresses the pause. *Pause_text* defines a message to be written to the screen when the pause occurs.

RECSEP	RECSEP {WR[APPED]|EA[CH]|OFF}

RECSEP specifies when to print record separators. By default, record separators are printed when output lines wrap from one line to another. EACH requires that record separators are printed after each line. OFF suppresses all record separators.

RECSEPCHAR	RECSEPCHAR *record_separator*

RECSEPCHAR defines the character that comprises record separator lines.

SERVEROUTPUT	SERVEROUT[PUT] {OFF|ON} [SIZE *buffer_size*] [FOR[MAT] {WRA[PPED]|WOR[D_WRAPPED]|TRU[NCATED]}]

SERVEROUTPUT allows the output from DBMS_OUTPUT.PUT_LINE calls (see Chapter 6, "Oracle-Supplied PL/SQL Packages") to be printed in a SQL°PLUS session.

SIZE sets the size of the output buffer.

FORMAT controls the behavior when the output line is greater than the value of SET LINESIZE. If WRAPPED, then output wraps to the next line. If WORD_WRAPPED, then wrapping occurs on a word boundary. If TRUNCATED, then excess text is not displayed.

SET Command Options *(Continued)*

SHIFTINOUT	SHIFT[INOUT] {VIS[IBLE]IINV[ISIBLE]}

SHIFTINOUT determines whether shift characters should be visibly displayed. This option is meaningful only if the character set and terminal support printable shift characters.

SHOWMODE	SHOW[MODE] {OFFION}

If SHOWMODE is set to ON, then SQL*PLUS will display the old and new values of a variable when it is changed with the SET command.

SQLCASE	SQLC[ASE] {MIX[ED]ILO[WER]IUP[PER]}

SET SQLCASE converts all text in the edit buffer to UPPER or LOWER case before execution. MIXED indicates no conversion.

SQLCONTINUE	SQLCO[NTINUE] *continuation_character*

SQLCONTINUE sets the continuation prompt, which is displayed when a line of text wraps onto a new input line. The default is ">".

SQLNUMBER	SQLN[UMBER] {OFFION}

SQLNUMBER controls numbering the SQL buffer.

If ON, then second and subsequent lines in the SQL buffer are identified by number. If OFF, lines are prefixed with the value of SET SQLPROMPT.

SQLPREFIX	SQLPRE[FIX] *prefix character*

SQLPREFIX defines the character that is used to execute a SQL statement from within the edit buffer. Statements following the SQLPREFIX are executed immediately, without affecting the state of the current edit buffer. The default is "#".

*SQL*PLUS*

SET Command Options *(Continued)*

SQLPROMPT	SQLP[ROMPT] *prompt*
	SQLPROMPT sets the SQL°PLUS prompt. The default is "SQL>".
SQLTERMINATOR	SQLT[ERMINATOR] {*character*|OFF|ON}
	SQLTERMINATOR defines the character that terminates SQL statements. The default is ";". OFF means that there is no terminator, in which case, SQL statements are terminated by a blank line.
SUFFIX	SUF[FIX] *command_file_extention*
	SUFFIX defines the default extension for files invoked from START, EDIT, and SAVE commands. The default is "SQL", so command files are assumed to end in ".SQL".
TAB	TAB {OFF|<u>ON</u>}
	If TAB is set to ON, then spaces between columns in results sets will be spaced using tab characters. If set to OFF, then spaces will be used.
TERMOUT	TERM[OUT] {OFF|ON}
	SET TERMOUT OFF suppresses all output to the terminal from commands included within command files.
TIME	TI[ME] {<u>OFF</u>|ON}
	SET TIME ON causes the time to be displayed within the SQL°PLUS command prompt.
TIMING	TIMI[NG] {OFF|ON}
	When TIMING is set to ON, timing statistics from the TIMING command are printed at the completion of every SQL command. Otherwise, timing statistics are printed only when requested through the TIMING command.

SET Command Options *(Continued)*

TRIMOUT	TRIM[OUT] {OFF|ON}
	If TRIMOUT is ON, then trailing blanks are removed from the end of each line of terminal output.
TRIMSPOOL	TRIMS[POOL] {ON|OFF}
	TRIMSPOOL is the same as TRIMOUT, but affects only output being spooled to a file.
UNDERLINE	UND[ERLINE] {*character*|ON|OFF}
	UNDERLINE sets the character used to underline headings in SQL*PLUS, or turns such underlining off. The default is "-".
VERIFY	VER[IFY] {OFF|ON}
	When ON, VERIFY causes each substitution variable replacement to be logged to the screen.
WRAP	WRA[P] {OFF|ON}
	When set to ON, WRAP causes lines of output which are longer than that set by LINESIZE to be wrapped onto the next line. Otherwise, these lines are truncated.

*SQL*PLUS*

Initialization Parameters

Introduction

This chapter documents the Oracle server configuration parameters. These parameters are sometimes referred to as "INIT.ORA" parameters because they traditionally appeared in a configuration file named *init.ora* or *initSID.ora*, where *SID* represented the Oracle instance identifier.

Any of these parameters may be altered by changing the value in the INIT.ORA file and restarting the database. Some of the parameters may be dynamically altered by the ALTER SESSION or ALTER SYSTEM commands (see Chapter 4, "Data Definition Language (DDL)). The parameters that can be dynamically changed are noted as such in the "Parameter Descriptions" section below.

You can determine the current values for these parameters with the following query (see your DBA if you don't have access to the V$PARAMETER view):

```
select name,value,description from v$parameter;
```

Configuration parameters that begin with an underscore ("_") are undocumented parameters. These are not included in Oracle documentation and are not included in the V$PARAMETER view. You can list the names and values of these parameters with the following query (which must be run while connected as SYS or INTERNAL):

```
SELECT  ksppinm name,
        ksppstvl, ksppdesc
  FROM  x$ksppi x, x$ksppcv y
```

```
WHERE  x.indx = y.indx
AND    translate(ksppinm,'_','#') like '#%'
```

Reference

Initialization parameters are described in *Oracle Server Reference.*

Parameter Descriptions

Configuration Parameters

ALWAYS_ANTI_JOIN	ALWAYS_ANTI_JOIN={<u>NESTED_LOOPS</u>|HASH|MERGE}
	ALWAYS_ANTI_JOIN determines the join algorithm employed for anti-joins involving "NOT IN" subqueries. The default is NESTED_LOOPS.
ALWAYS_SEMI_JOIN	ALWAYS_SEMI_JOIN={<u>STANDARD</u>|NESTED_LOOPS|HASH|MERGE}
8.0+	ALWAYS_SEMI_JOIN determines the join algorithm to be used for "semi-joins" which involve "EXISTS" subqueries.
AQ_TM_PROCESSES	AQ_TM_PROCESSES=*number*
8.0+	AQ_TM_PROCESSES specifies the *number* of advanced queuing time managers to start. The default is 0.
	May be modified by ALTER SYSTEM.
ARCH_IO_SLAVES	ARCH_IO_SLAVES=*number*
8.0	ARCH_IO_SLAVES specifies the *number* of archiver I/O slaves to start. The default is 0.
ASYNC_READ	ASYNC_READ={TRUE|FALSE}
7.3	ASYNC_READ determines whether asynchronous I/O will be enabled for reads.
	Available in version 7 only and not for all platforms.

Configuration Parameters *(Continued)*

ASYNC_WRITE	ASYNC_WRITE={TRUE|FALSE}
7.3	ASYNC_WRITE determines whether asynchronous I/O will be enabled for writes. Available in version 7 only and not for all platforms
AUDIT_FILE_DEST	AUDIT_FILE_DEST=*directory_name* AUDIT_FILE_DEST defines the directory to which auditing trace files will be written. A typical default value is *?/rdbms/audit*.
AUDIT_TRAIL	AUDIT_TRAIL={<u>NONE</u>|FALSE|DB|TRUE|OS} AUDIT_TRAIL enables Oracle auditing. The default value is NONE.
B_TREE_BITMAP _PLANS 7.3, 8.0	B_TREE_BITMAP_PLANS={TRUE|<u>FALSE</u>} B_TREE_BITMAP_PLANS enables the conversion of B*-tree indexes into temporary bitmaps to allow for bitmap execution optimization. May be modified by ALTER SESSION.
BACKGROUND_ CORE_DUMP	BACKGROUND_CORE_DUMP={FULL|<u>PARTIAL</u>} If FULL, the contents of the SGA are included in core dumps for background processes.
BACKGROUND_ DUMP_DEST	BACKGROUND_DUMP_DEST=*directory_name* BACKGROUND_DUMP_DEST specifies the directory into which log files for detached processes will be written. May be modified by ALTER SYSTEM.

Initialization Parameters

Configuration Parameters *(Continued)*

BACKUP_DISK_IO_SLAVES

BACKUP_DISK_IO_SLAVES=*number*

This specifies the *number* of slave processes to be used by the recovery manager for parallel backup or recovery from or to disk.

May be modified by ALTER SYSTEM.

BACKUP_TAPE_IO_SLAVES

8.0+

BACKUP_TAPE_IO_SLAVES={FALSE|TRUE}

If true, a dedicated slave process is employed by the recovery manager for tape reads and writes.

May be modified by ALTER SYSTEM.

BITMAP_MERGE_AREA_SIZE

BITMAP_MERGE_AREA_SIZE=*bytes*

The amount of memory to allow for bitmap merge operations.

BLANK_TRIMMING

BLANK_TRIMMING={TRUE|FALSE}

This determines whether a string that contains trailing blanks may be copied into a string of lesser length.

BUFFER_POOL_KEEP

8.0+

BUFFER_POOL_KEEP=
    ("BUFFERS:*no_buffers*, LRU_LATCHES:*no_latches*")

BUFFER_POOL_KEEP defines the number of block buffers and LRU latches in the "keep" buffer pool.

Available in versions 8 and 8.1.

BUFFER_POOL_RECYCLE

8.0+

BUFFER_POOL_RECYCLE=
    ("BUFFERS:*no_buffers*, LRU_LATCHES:*no_latches*")

BUFFER_POOL_RECYLE defines the number of block buffers and LRU latches in the "recycle" buffer pool.

Configuration Parameters *(Continued)*

CACHE_SIZE_ THRESHOLD 7.3, 8.0	CACHE_SIZE_THRESHOLD=*blocks* If a table is less than CACHE_SIZE_THRESHOLD *blocks*, then it will remain cached in the SGA after a full table scan. The default value is 20 blocks.
CCF_IO_SIZE 7.3	CCF_IO_SIZE=*bytes* This specifies the number of *bytes* per write when creating a file. Available in version 7 only. Replaced by DB_FILE_DIRECT_IO_COUNT.
CHECKPOINT_ PROCESS 7.3	CHECKPOINT_PROCESS={TRUE|FALSE} If true, a dedicated process is created to perform data file header updates during checkpoints. Available in version 7 only. The checkpoint process is started automatically in subsequent releases.
CLEANUP_ ROLLBACK_ ENTRIES 7.3, 8.0	CLEANUP_ROLLBACK_ENTRIES=*no_of_entries* CLEANUP_ROLLBACK_ENTRIES controls the number of undo entries processed in a single batch during rollback operations. The default value is 20.
CLOSE_CACHED_ OPEN_CURSORS 7.3, 8.0	CLOSE_CACHED_OPEN_CURSORS={TRUE|FALSE} If true, PL/SQL cursors are closed when a COMMIT occurs. Available in versions 7.3 and 8.0. May be modified by ALTER SESSION.
COMMIT_POINT _STRENGTH	COMMIT_POINT_STRENGTH=*number* Higher values of COMMIT_POINT_STRENGTH increase the probability that this instance will be the commit site in a distributed transaction.

Initialization Parameters

Configuration Parameters *(Continued)*

COMPATIBLE	COMPATIBLE=*oracle_version* This specifies the version of Oracle to which this database will conform.
COMPATIBLE_ NO_RECOVERY **7.3, 8.0**	COMPATIBLE_NO_RECOVERY=*oracle_version* This specifies the version of Oracle to which this database conforms, except if a recovery is needed to the earlier version.
COMPLEX_VIEW _MERGING **8.0**	COMPLEX_VIEW_MERGING={TRUE|FALSE} This enables or disables complex view merging. May be modified by ALTER SESSION.
CONTROL_FILE_ RECORD_KEEP_ TIME **8.0+**	CONTROL_FILE_RECORD_KEEP_TIME=*days* This specifies the number of *days* for which reusable control file records are kept. The default value is 7. May be modified by ALTER SYSTEM.
CONTROL_FILES	CONTROL_FILES=*control_file* [,*control_file* ...] CONTROL_FILES specifies the names of the control files for this instance.
CORE_DUMP_ DEST	CORE_DUMP_DEST=*directory* CORE_DUMP_DEST specifies the location of the *directory* to which core dumps will be written. May be modified by ALTER SYSTEM.
CPU_COUNT	CPU_COUNT=*number_of_cpus* CPU_COUNT specifies the number of CPUs available in this instance.

Configuration Parameters *(Continued)*

CREATE_BITMAP _AREA_SIZE	CREATE_BITMAP_AREA_SIZE=*bytes* This specifies the amount of memory available for bitmap index creation.
CURSOR_SPACE _FOR_TIME	CURSOR_SPACE_FOR_TIME={TRUE|<u>FALSE</u>} If CURSOR_SPACE_FOR_TIME is true, then SQL statements are never aged out of the shared pool, providing that there is at least one open cursor referencing the statement.
DB_BLOCK_ BUFFERS	DB_BLOCK_BUFFERS=*number_of_blocks* This parameter determines the *number_of_blocks* allocated to the buffer cache.
DB_BLOCK_ CHECKING 8i	DB_BLOCK_CHECKING={TRUE|<u>FALSE</u>} If true, data blocks are checked for corruption before being written. Available in version 8.1 only, although database events 10310 and 10211 provided similar functionality in earlier versions. May be modified by either ALTER SESSION or ALTER SYSTEM.
DB_BLOCK_ CHECKPOINT_ BATCH 7.3, 8.0	DB_BLOCK_CHECKPOINT_BATCH=*blocks* DB_BLOCK_CHECKPOINT_BATCH determines the number of *blocks* to be written in one batch by the database writer during checkpoints. May be modified by ALTER SYSTEM.

Initialization Parameters

Configuration Parameters *(Continued)*

DB_BLOCK_ CHECKSUM	DB_BLOCK_CHECKSUM={TRUE|<u>FALSE</u>} If DB_BLOCK_CHECKSUM is true, then a checksum is stored in data blocks and checked upon read to ensure the block has not been corrupted. May be modified by ALTER SYSTEM.
DB_BLOCK_LRU_ EXTENDED_ STATISTICS 7.3, 8.0	DB_BLOCK_LRU_EXTENDED_STATISTICS=*number_of_blocks* If greater than 0, Oracle maintains buffer cache statistics which allow an estimation of the hit rate if the buffer cache was *number_of_blocks* bigger. The default value is 0.
DB_BLOCK_LRU_ LATCHES	DB_BLOCK_LRU_LATCHES=*no_of_latches* DB_BLOCK_LRU_LATCHES controls the number of latches on the buffer cache LRU list. The default value is calculated on the number of CPUs.
DB_BLOCK_LRU_ STATISTICS 7.3, 8.0	DB_BLOCK_LRU_STATISTICS={TRUE|<u>FALSE</u>} If true, Oracle maintains statistics that can be used to estimate the hit rate if the buffer cache was smaller.
DB_BLOCK_MAX _DIRTY_TARGET 8.0+	DB_BLOCK_MAX_DIRTY_TARGET=*no_of_blocks* DB_BLOCK_MAX_DIRTY_TARGET sets an upper limit on the number of modified ("dirty") blocks in the buffer cache. May be modified by ALTER SYSTEM.
DB_BLOCK_SIZE	DB_BLOCK_SIZE=*block_size* This gives the size of the database block in bytes. Can be set only when the instance is created.

Configuration Parameters *(Continued)*

DB_DOMAIN	DB_DOMAIN=*domain_name*

This specifies the domain of the database. The default value is "WORLD". |

DB_FILE_DIRECT _IO_COUNT

8.0+ | DB_FILE_DIRECT_IO_COUNT=*blocks*

DB_FILE_DIRECT_IO_COUNT specifies the number of *blocks* to be read or written in a single operation when using direct mode (unbuffered) I/O.

May be modified by ALTER SYSTEM. |

DB_FILE_ MULTIBLOCK_ READ_COUNT	DB_FILE_MULTIBLOCK_READ_COUNT=*blocks*

This specifies the number of blocks to be read in a single operation when performing multi-block I/O, which is typically used when performing a table or index scan.

May be modified by either ALTER SESSION or ALTER SYSTEM. |

DB_FILE_NAME_ CONVERT

8.0+ | DB_FILE_NAME_CONVERT= (*match_string,convert_string*)

DB_FILE_NAME_CONVERT specifies a pattern that is used to convert a data file name for a standby/clone database. Occurrences of *match_string* are translated to *convert_string* in the data file name. |

DB_FILE_ SIMULTANEOUS_ WRITES

7.3, 8.0 | DB_FILE_SIMULTANEOUS_WRITES=*number*

This gives the *number* of simultaneous writes made by the database writer to a single file. |

Initialization Parameters

Configuration Parameters *(Continued)*

DB_FILE_ STANDBY_NAME _CONVERT 7.3	DB_FILE_STANDBY_NAME_CONVERT= *(match_string,convert_string)* DB_FILE_STANDBY_NAME_CONVERT specifies a pattern that is used to convert a data file name for a standby database. Occurrences of *match_string* are translated to *convert_string* in the data file name convert pattern and string for the standby database. Available in version 7.3 only. Replaced by DB_FILE_NAME_CONVERT in subsequent versions.
DB_FILES	DB_FILES=*max_db_files* DB_FILES specifies the maximum allowable number of database files.
DB_NAME	DB_NAME=*database_name* This specifies the name of the database. Must match that specified during CREATE DATABASE.
DB_WRITER_ PROCESSES 8.0+	DB_WRITER_PROCESSES=*processes* DB_WRITER_PROCESSES specifies the number of database writer *processes*.
DB_WRITERS 7.3	DB_WRITERS=*processes* DB_WRITERS specifies the number of database writer *processes*. Available in version 7 only. Replaced by DB_WRITER_PROCESSES in subsequent versions.
DBLINK_ENCRYPT _LOGIN	DBLINK_ENCRYPT_LOGIN={TRUE|FALSE} If true, distributed connections through database links must always use an encrypted password.

Configuration Parameters *(Continued)*

DBWR_IO_SLAVES   DBWR_IO_SLAVES=*no_of_slaves*

8.0+   This parameter controls the number of I/O slave processes employed by the database writer process. If this value is non-zero, then DB_WRITER_PROCESSES will be set to 1.

DELAYED_ LOGGING_BLOCK _CLEANOUTS

DELAYED_LOGGING_BLOCK_CLEANOUTS={TRUE|FALSE}

If true, BLOCK CLEANOUTS occur at commit time with minimal redo log generation.

7.3, 8.0

DISCRETE_ TRANSACTIONS_ ENABLED

DISCRETE_TRANSACTIONS_ENABLED={true|false}

If true, then DISCRETE TRANSACTIONS may be performed.

7.3, 8.0

DISK_ASYNCH_IO   DISK_ASYNCH_IO={true|false}

8.0+   DISK_ASYNCH_IO enables or disables asynchronous I/O on platforms for which it is available.

DISTRIBUTED_ LOCK_TIMEOUT

DISTRIBUTED_LOCK_TIMEOUT =*seconds*

7.3, 8.0   DISTRIBUTED_LOCK_TIMEOUT specifies the number of *seconds* a distributed transaction will wait for a lock. A typical default value is 60.

DISTRIBUTED_ RECOVERY_ CONNECTION_ HOLD_TIME

DISTRIBUTED_RECOVERY_CONNECTION_HOLD_TIME=*seconds*

This gives the number of *seconds* to hold a distributed transaction connection open after a transaction failure.

7.3, 8.0

DISTRIBUTED_ TRANSACTIONS

DISTRIBUTED_TRANSACTIONS=*transactions*

DISTRIBUTED_TRANSACTIONS sets the maximum number of concurrent distributed *transactions*.

Initialization Parameters

Configuration Parameters *(Continued)*

DML_LOCKS	DML_LOCKS=*locks* DML_LOCKS specifies the maximum number of table locks available
ENQUEUE_ RESOURCES	ENQUEUE_RESOURCES=*enqueues* This gives the maximum number of *enqueues* (lock requests) available.
ENT_DOMAIN_ NAME 8i	ENT_DOMAIN_NAME=*domain_name* This designates the enterprise domain name.
EVENT	EVENT=*event_string* EVENT sets various debug events.
FAST_FULL_ SCAN_ENABLED **7.3, 8.0**	FAST_FULL_SCAN_ENABLED={true|false} This enables or disables the fast full scan query access path. Available in version 7.3 and 8.0 only.
FAST_START_IO _TARGET 8i	FAST_START_IO_TARGET=*io_count* FAST_START_IO_TARGET limits the number of I/Os required during instance recovery. Higher values reduce the number of dirty blocks in the buffer cache. May be modified by either ALTER SESSION or ALTER SYSTEM.
FAST_START_ PARALLEL_ ROLLBACK 8i	FAST_START_PARALLEL_ROLLBACK={low|high|false} FAST_START_PARALLEL_ROLLBACK specifies the number of parallel recovery slaves that may be used. May be modified by ALTER SYSTEM.

Configuration Parameters *(Continued)*

FIXED_DATE	FIXED_DATE= *date_string*
	This freezes SYSDATE at the specified value.
	May be modified by ALTER SYSTEM.
FREEZE_DB_FOR _FAST_INSTANCE _RECOVERY **8.0**	FREEZE_DB_FOR_FAST_INSTANCE_RECOVERY={TRUE│FALSE}
	For parallel server, this freezes the entire database during instance recovery for a single instance.
	May be modified by ALTER SYSTEM.
GLOBAL_NAMES	GLOBAL_NAMES={TRUE│FALSE}
	If true, database links must have the same name as a remote database.
	May be modified by either ALTER SESSION or ALTER SYSTEM.
HASH_AREA_SIZE	HASH_AREA_SIZE=*bytes*
	This specifies the size of work area for hash joins.
	May be modified by ALTER SESSION.
HASH_JOIN_ ENABLED	HASH_JOIN_ENABLED={TRUE│FALSE}
	This enables or disables hash joins.
	May be modified by ALTER SESSION.
HASH_ MULTIBLOCK_IO _COUNT	HASH_MULTIBLOCK_IO_COUNT=*blocks*
	HASH_MULTIBLOCK_IO_COUNT specifies the number of *blocks* a hash join will read or write in a single I/O.
	May be modified by either ALTER SESSION or ALTER SYSTEM.

Initialization Parameters

Configuration Parameters *(Continued)*

HI_SHARED_ MEMORY_ ADDRESS **8.0+**	HI_SHARED_MEMORY_ADDRESS=*memory_address* This specifies the SGA starting memory address. Available in versions 8 and 8.1, but not on all platforms.
HS_ AUTOREGISTER **8i**	HS_AUTOREGISTER={TRUE|FALSE} This enables or disables automatic server data dictionary updates in HS agent self-registration. Available in version 8.1 only. May be modified by ALTER SYSTEM.
IFILE	IFILE=*file_name* This specifies the name of a file that contains parameter settings to be applied.
INSTANCE_ GROUPS **8.0+**	INSTANCE_GROUPS= *instance_group* [,*instance_group* ...] In Oracle parallel server, this parameter specifies a list of instance group names to which this instance belongs.
INSTANCE_NAME **8i**	INSTANCE_NAME=*instance_name* This designates the name of the database instance.
INSTANCE_ NUMBER	INSTANCE_NUMBER=*number* In parallel server, this parameter specifies the instance number that is used to map to specific free list groups.
JAVA_MAX_ SESSIONSPACE_ SIZE **8i**	JAVA_MAX_SESSIONSPACE_SIZE=*bytes* This specifies the maximum memory size of a Java session space.

Configuration Parameters *(Continued)*

JAVA_POOL_SIZE 8i	JAVA_POOL_SIZE=*bytes* This gives the size in *bytes* of the Java pool within the SGA.
JAVA_SOFT_ SESSIONSPACE_ LIMIT 8i	JAVA_SOFT_SESSIONSPACE_LIMIT=*bytes* JAVA_SOFT_SESSIONSPACE_LIMIT sets a warning limit on the size in *bytes* of a Java session space.
JOB_QUEUE_ INTERVAL	JOB_QUEUE_INTERVAL=*seconds* This gives the number of *seconds* for which job queue processes sleep when no work is available.
JOB_QUEUE_KEEP _CONNECTIONS 7.3, 8.0	JOB_QUEUE_KEEP_CONNECTIONS={FALSE|TRUE} If true, then job queue processes keep network connections open between the execution of jobs.
JOB_QUEUE_ PROCESSES	JOB_QUEUE_PROCESSES=*number_of_processes* JOB_QUEUE_PROCESSES specifies the number of job queue processes to start. May be modified by ALTER SYSTEM.
LARGE_POOL_ MIN_ALLOC 8.0	LARGE_POOL_MIN_ALLOC=*number*{k|m} LARGE_POOL_MIN_ALLOC sets the minimum allocation size in bytes from the large pool.
LARGE_POOL_SIZE 8.0+	LARGE_POOL_SIZE=*bytes* LARGE_POOL_SIZE sets the size in *bytes* of the large pool, which is an area of the shared pool that provides dedicated memory for MTS and XA configurations.

Initialization Parameters

Configuration Parameters *(Continued)*

LGWR_IO_SLAVES	LGWR_IO_SLAVES=*processes*
8.0	LGWR_IO_SLAVES sets the number of log writer I/O slave processes.

LICENSE_MAX_ SESSIONS	LICENSE_MAX_SESSIONS=*number_of_sessions*
	LICENSE_MAX_SESSIONS sets the maximum number of non-system user sessions.
	May be modified by ALTER SYSTEM.

LICENSE_MAX_ USERS	LICENSE_MAX_USERS=*number_of_users*
	LICENSE_MAX_USERS sets the maximum number of user accounts that can be created in the database.
	May be modified by ALTER SYSTEM.

LICENSE_ SESSIONS_ WARNING	LICENSE_SESSIONS_WARNING=*number_of_sessions*
	This issues a warning when the number of non-system user sessions specified is reached.
	May be modified by ALTER SYSTEM.

LM_LOCKS	LM_LOCKS=*no_of_locks*
	LM_LOCKS sets the number of number of locks configured for the Oracle parallel server lock manager.
	Available in versions 8.0 and 8.1.

LM_PROCS	LM_PROCS=*no_of_processes*
8.0+	LM_PROCS specifies the number of client processes configured for the Oracle parallel server lock manager.

Configuration Parameters *(Continued)*

LM_RESS	LM_RESS=*no_of_resources*
8.0+	LM_RESS specifies the number of lockable resources configured for the Oracle parallel server lock manager.
LOCAL_LISTENER	LOCAL_LISTENER=*listener_address*
8.0+	LOCAL_LISTENER specifies the TNS address of the "local" SQL*NET listener.
LOCK_NAME_SPACE	LOCK_NAME_SPACE= *string*
8.0+	LOCK_NAME_SPACE specifies the *string* to be used for generating lock names for the distributed lock manager.
LOCK_SGA	LOCK_SGA={TRUE|FALSE}
8.0+	If true, this attempts to lock the entire SGA in physical memory.
LOCK_SGA_AREAS	LOCK_SGA_AREAS=*integer*
8.0	LOCK_SGA_AREAS is a bitmap integer that determines specific areas of the SGA which should be locked in physical memory. The sequence of the section in the V$SGA view corresponds to its bit in LOCK_SGA_AREAS.
LOG_ARCHIVE_BUFFER_SIZE	LOG_ARCHIVE_BUFFER_SIZE=*buffer_size*
7.3, 8.0	LOG_ARCHIVE_BUFFER_SIZE specifies the size of the archiver process buffer in redo log file blocks.
LOG_ARCHIVE_BUFFERS	LOG_ARCHIVE_BUFFERS=*no_of_buffers*
7.3, 8.0	LOG_ARCHIVE_BUFFERS specifies the number of buffers to allocate for archiving.

Initialization Parameters

Configuration Parameters *(Continued)*

LOG_ARCHIVE_ DEST	LOG_ARCHIVE_DEST=*destination_path*

LOG_ARCHIVE_DEST specifies the destination and name format for archived redo logs. The path may include both a directory and a file name prefix.

May be modified by ALTER SYSTEM.

LOG_ARCHIVE_ DEST_N
 	
8i
	LOG_ARCHIVE_DEST_N= ({service=*service_name* |
	    LOCATION=*directory_path*} {MANDATORY | OPTIONAL}
	    [REOPEN=*seconds*])

Five parameters of the form LOG_ARCHIVE_DEST_*N*— where *N* is a number from 1–5—specify multiple destinations for redo log archiving.

SERVICE specifies a TNS database address, which identifies a standby database that will receive the logs.

LOCATION is a directory and file name prefix where the archived logs will be written.

MANDATORY indicates that the operation must succeed before the redo log can be marked for re-use; OPTIONAL indicates that the operation need not succeed.

REOPEN specifies an interval in seconds between attempts to retry a failed transfer.

May be modified by either ALTER SESSION OR ALTER SYSTEM.

LOG_ARCHIVE_ DEST_STATE_N 8I	LOG_ARCHIVE_DEST_STATE_N={enable|defer}

Five parameters of the form LOG_ARCHIVE_DEST_STATE_*N* —where *N* is a number from 1–5—specify the current status of the archive destinations specified by LOG_ARCHIVE_DEST_*N*.

May be modified by either ALTER SESSION or ALTER SYSTEM.

Configuration Parameters *(Continued)*

LOG_ARCHIVE_ DUPLEX_DEST **8.0, 8i**	LOG_ARCHIVE_DUPLEX_DEST= *string* This parameter specifies additional archive log destinations. It is available in versions 8 and 8.1, but is depreciated in favor of LOG_ARCHIVE_DEST_*N* in Oracle 8.1. May be modified by ALTER SYSTEM.
LOG_ARCHIVE_ FORMAT	LOG_ARCHIVE_FORMAT=*pattern* LOG_ARCHIVE_FORMAT specifies the format of archived log file names. *Pattern* can include the special characters %s and %t, which indicate the log sequence number and thread number, respectively. A typical default value is *%t_%s.dbf.*
LOG_ARCHIVE_ MAX_PROCESSES **8i**	LOG_ARCHIVE_MAX_PROCESSES=*processes* LOG_ARCHIVE_MAX_PROCESSES specifies the maximum number of active archiver *processes*. May be modified by ALTER SYSTEM.
LOG_ARCHIVE_ MIN_SUCCEED_ DEST **8.0+**	LOG_ARCHIVE_MIN_SUCCEED_DEST=*minimum_number* LOG_ARCHIVE_MIN_SUCCEED_DEST specifies the minimum number of archive destinations that must succeed. This can be set in conjunction with LOG_ARCHIVE_DEST_*N.* Available in versions 8 and 8.1. May be modified by either ALTER SESSION or ALTER SYSTEM.
LOG_ARCHIVE_ START	LOG_ARCHIVE_START={TRUE|FALSE} LOG_ARCHIVE_START determines whether redo log archiving starts automatically when the instance starts.

Initialization Parameters

Configuration Parameters *(Continued)*

LOG_BLOCK_CHECKSUM	LOG_BLOCK_CHECKSUM={TRUE|<u>FALSE</u>} If true, then redo log blocks include a checksum.
LOG_BUFFER	LOG_BUFFER=*bytes* This indicates the size of the redo log buffer in the SGA.
LOG_CHECKPOINT_INTERVAL	LOG_CHECKPOINT_INTERVAL=*blocks* LOG_CHECKPOINT_INTERVAL specifies the number of redo *blocks* that may be written between checkpoints. May be modified by ALTER SYSTEM.
LOG_CHECKPOINT_TIMEOUT	LOG_CHECKPOINT_TIMEOUT=*seconds* This specifies the maximum time interval between checkpoints in *seconds*. May be modified by ALTER SYSTEM.
LOG_CHECKPOINTS_TO_ALERT	LOG_CHECKPOINTS_TO_ALERT={TRUE|<u>FALSE</u>} If true, checkpoint begins and ends are logged to the alert file.
LOG_FILE_NAME_CONVERT 8.0+	LOG_FILE_NAME_CONVERT=*(match_string,convert_string)* LOG_FILE_NAME_CONVERT specifies a pattern that is used to convert a redo log file name for a standby/clone database. Occurrences of *match_string* are translated to *convert_string* in the standby redo log name.
LOG_FILE_STANDBY_NAME_CONVERT 7.3	LOG_FILE_STANDBY_NAME_CONVERT =*(match_string,convert_string)* LOG_FILE_STANDBY_NAME_CONVERT specifies a pattern that is used to convert a redo log file name for a standby database. Occurrences of *match_string* are translated to *convert_string* in the standby redo log name.

Configuration Parameters *(Continued)*

	Available in version 7 only. Replaced in Oracle8 by LOG_FILE_NAME_CONVERT.
LOG_FILES **7.3, 8.0**	LOG_FILES=*number_of_log_files* LOG_FILES specifies the maximum allowable number of log files.
LOG_ SIMULTANEOUS_ COPIES **7.3, 8.0**	LOG_SIMULTANEOUS_COPIES=*number_of_latches* This designates the number of redo buffer copy latches, which determines the number of simultaneous writes to the log buffer.
LOG_SMALL_ ENTRY_MAX_SIZE **7.3, 8.0**	LOG_SMALL_ENTRY_MAX_SIZE=*bytes* Redo entries smaller than this value will be copied on the redo allocation latch; larger entries will be copied on one of the redo copy latches. May be modified by ALTER SYSTEM.
MAX_COMMIT_ PROPAGATION_ DELAY	MAX_COMMIT_PROPAGATION_DELAY=*hundreths_of_a_second* In parallel server, this determines the frequency with which the SCN is updated.
MAX_DUMP_ FILE_SIZE	MAX_DUMP_FILE_SIZE=*blocks* This gives the maximum size in operating system blocks of a dump file. May be modified by either ALTER SESSION or ALTER SYSTEM.
MAX_ENABLED_ ROLES	MAX_ENABLED_ROLES=*no_of_roles* MAX_ENABLED_ROLES determines the maximum number of roles a user can have enabled.

Initialization Parameters

Configuration Parameters *(Continued)*

MAX_ROLLBACK _SEGMENTS	MAX_ROLLBACK_SEGMENTS=*no_of_rollback_segments* MAX_ROLLBACK_SEGMENTS determines the maximum number of rollback segments.
MAX_ TRANSACTION_ BRANCHES 7.3,8.0	MAX_TRANSACTION_BRANCHES=*no_of_branches* MAX_TRANSACTION_BRANCHES sets the maximum number of branches for a distributed transaction.
MTS_ DISPATCHERS	MTS_DISPATCHERS=(*"protocol,number"* [,*"protocol,number"* ...]) MTS_DISPATCHERS specifies the number of MTS dispatchers to initiate for each protocol. May be modified by ALTER SYSTEM.
MTS_LISTENER_ ADDRESS	MTS_LISTENER_ADDRESS= *listener_address* MTS_LISTENER_ADDRESS specifies the address of listener processes which may mediate shared server sessions with the instance.
MTS_MAX_ DISPATCHERS	MTS_MAX_DISPATCHERS= *dispatchers* MTS_MAX_DISPATCHERS specifies the maximum number of dispatcher processes.
MTS_MAX_ SERVERS	MTS_MAX_SERVERS=*servers* MTS_MAX_SERVERS specifies the maximum number of MTS server processes.
MTS_MULTIPLE_ LISTENERS	MTS_MULTIPLE_LISTENERS={TRUE|FALSE} If true, then multiple listeners may be specified in MTS_LISTENER_ADDRESS.

Configuration Parameters *(Continued)*

MTS_RATE_LOG _SIZE	MTS_RATE_LOG_SIZE= "(*keyword=value*) [(*keyword=value*) ...]"
8.0	MTS_RATE_LOG_SIZE determines the sampling size for dispatcher rate calculations. *Keyword* specifies the event being sampled. It is one of the following: DEFAULTS, EVENT_LOOPS, MESSAGES, SERVER_BUFFERS, CLIENT_BUFFERS, TOTAL_BUFFERS, IN_CONNECTS, OUT_CONNECTS, or RECONNECTS. *Value* indicates the number of events to sample.

Available in version 8.0 only. |

MTS_RATE_ SCALE	MTS_RATE_SCALE="(*keyword=value*) [(*keyword=value*) ...]"
8.0	MTS_RATE_SCALE indicates the frequency with which dispatcher rate statistics are reported in hundredths of a second. *Keyword* specifies the event being sampled. It is one of the following: DEFAULTS, EVENT_LOOPS, MESSAGES, SERVER_BUFFERS, CLIENT_BUFFERS, TOTAL_BUFFERS, IN_CONNECTS, OUT_CONNECTS, or RECONNECTS. *Value* indicates the reporting frequency in centiseconds, so that 6000 indicates once-per-minute reporting.

Available in version 8.0 only. |

MTS_SERVERS	MTS_SERVERS=*servers*

MTS_SERVERS indicates the number of MTS servers to start at system initialization.

May be modified by ALTER SYSTEM. |

MTS_SERVICE	MTS_SERVICE=*service_name*

This gives the name of an MTS service supported by this instance. |

NLS_CALENDAR	NLS_CALENDAR=*calander_name*
8.0+	This designates the NLS calendar system name.

Initialization Parameters

Configuration Parameters *(Continued)*

NLS_CALENDAR (CONT.)	Available in versions 8.0 and 8.1.
	May be modified by ALTER SESSION.
NLS_COMP 8i	NLS_COMP=*string* This sets NLS comparison. Available in version 8.1 only. May be modified by ALTER SESSION.
NLS_CURRENCY	NLS_CURRENCY= *symbol* This sets the NLS local currency *symbol*. May be modified by ALTER SESSION.
NLS_DATE_ FORMAT	NLS_DATE_FORMAT= *date_format* This sets the NLS Oracle date format. May be modified by ALTER SESSION.
NLS_DATE_ LANGUAGE	NLS_DATE_LANGUAGE= *nls_language* This sets the NLS date language name. Available in all versions from 7.3 to 8.1. May be modified by ALTER SESSION.
NLS_DUAL_ CURRENCY 8i	NLS_DUAL_CURRENCY= *symbol* This sets the dual currency *symbol*. Available in version 8.1 only. May be modified by ALTER SESSION.

Configuration Parameters *(Continued)*

NLS_ISO_ CURRENCY	NLS_ISO_CURRENCY = *string*
	This designates the NLS ISO currency territory name.
	May be modified by ALTER SESSION.

NLS_LANGUAGE	NLS_LANGUAGE=*language*
	This designates the NLS *language* name.
	May be modified by ALTER SESSION.

NLS_NUMERIC_ CHARACTERS	NLS_NUMERIC_CHARACTERS= *string*
	This specifies NLS numeric characters used for group separators and decimal points.
	May be modified by ALTER SESSION.

NLS_SORT	NLS_SORT= *string*
	This sets the NLS sort definition name.
	May be modified by ALTER SESSION.

NLS_TERRITORY	NLS_TERRITORY=*string*
	This sets the NLS territory name.
	May be modified by ALTER SESSION.

NLS_TIME_ FORMAT **8i**	NLS_TIME_FORMAT= *time_format*
	This designates the NLS time format.
	May be modified by ALTER SESSION.

NLS_TIME_TZ_ FORMAT **8i**	NLS_TIME_TZ_FORMAT= *time_format*
	This sets the NLS time, with time zone format.
	May be modified by ALTER SESSION.

Initialization Parameters

Configuration Parameters *(Continued)*

NLS_TIMESTAMP _FORMAT 8i	NLS_TIMESTAMP_FORMAT= *time_format* This sets the NLS timestamp format. May be modified by ALTER SESSION.
NLS_TIMESTAMP _TZ_FORMAT 8i	NLS_TIMESTAMP_TZ_FORMAT= *time_format* This sets the NLS timestamp, with time zone format. May be modified by ALTER SESSION.
07_DICTIONARY _ACCESSIBILITY 8.0+	07_DICTIONARY_ACCESSIBILITY={true|false} If true, then objects in the SYS schema may be accessed from other accounts—the Oracle7 behavior. If false, SYS objects—the data dictionary, in particular—cannot be directly accessed from other accounts unless specific privileges are granted.
OBJECT_CACHE_ MAX_SIZE_ PERCENT 8.0+	OBJECT_CACHE_MAX_SIZE_PERCENT=*percentage* OBJECT_CACHE_MAX_SIZE_PERCENT specifies the *percentage* that an object cache may expand beyond the setting of OBJECT_CACHE_OPTIMAL_SIZE. May be modified by either ALTER SESSION or ALTER SYSTEM.
OBJECT_CACHE_ OPTIMAL_SIZE 8.0+	OBJECT_CACHE_OPTIMAL_SIZE=*bytes* OBJECT_CACHE_OPTIMAL_SIZE sets the optimal size of a user's object cache in *bytes*. May be modified by either ALTER SESSION or ALTER SYSTEM.
OPEN_CURSORS	OPEN_CURSORS=*no_of_cursors* This sets the maximum number of open cursors for a session.

Configuration Parameters *(Continued)*

OPEN_LINKS	OPEN_LINKS=*open_database_links* This sets the maximum number of open database links for a session.
OPEN_LINKS_ PER_INSTANCE 8.0+	OPEN_LINKS_PER_INSTANCE= *open_database_links* This sets the maximum number of open database links for the instance.
OPS_ADMIN_ GROUP 8.0	OPS_ADMIN_GROUP= *instance_group* OPS_ADMIN_GROUP identifies an Oracle parallel server instance group that can be used for global V$ queries. May be modified by either ALTER SESSION or ALTER SYSTEM.
OPTIMIZER_ FEATURES_ ENABLE 8.0+	OPTIMIZER_FEATURES_ENABLE=*Oracle_version* This sets the compatibility version for the Oracle query optimizer.
OPTIMIZER_ INDEX_CACHING 8.0+	OPTIMIZER_INDEX_CACHING=*percent* OPTIMIZER_INDEX_CACHING provides the query optimizer with an estimate of the percentage of index blocks that will be cached. High values encourage the use (decrease the cost) of index-based plans. May be modified by ALTER SESSION.
OPTIMIZER_ INDEX_COST_ADJ 8.0+	OPTIMIZER_INDEX_COST_ADJ=*percent* OPTIMIZER_INDEX_COST_ADJ adjusts the cost of index-based plans. The default is 100. Lower values effectively discount the cost of index accesses. May be modified by ALTER SESSION.

Configuration Parameters *(Continued)*

OPTIMIZER_MAX_PERMUTATIONS 8.0+	OPTIMIZER_MAX_PERMUTATIONS=*number_of_permutations* OPTIMIZER_MAX_PERMUTATIONS determines the number of join permutations that the optimizer will consider. The default is 80,000. May be modified by ALTER SESSION.
OPTIMIZER_MODE	OPTIMIZER_MODE={RULE|CHOOSE|FIRST_ROWS|ALL_ROWS} OPTIMIZER_MODE sets the default optimization mode. May be modified by ALTER SESSION.
OPTIMIZER_PERCENT_PARALLEL	OPTIMIZER_PERCENT_PARALLEL=*percent* OPTIMIZER_PERCENT_PARALLEL determines the degree to which parallel query will be considered when calculating execution plans. Zero (0) ignores parallelism; 100 uses maximum parallelism. May be modified by ALTER SESSION.
OPTIMIZER_SEARCH_LIMIT	optimizer_search_limit=*number* OPTIMIZER_SEARCH_LIMIT specifies the number of tables for which cartesian products will be considered during join optimization. May be modified by ALTER SESSION.
ORACLE_TRACE_COLLECTION_NAME	ORACLE_TRACE_COLLECTION_NAME=*collection_name* This specifies the Oracle trace default collection name.
ORACLE_TRACE_COLLECTION_PATH	ORACLE_TRACE_COLLECTION_PATH=*directory* This specifies the *directory* in which Oracle trace collection files are stored.

Configuration Parameters *(Continued)*

ORACLE_TRACE_ COLLECTION_SIZE

ORACLE_TRACE_COLLECTION_SIZE=*bytes*

This sets the maximum size of the Oracle trace collection file.

ORACLE_TRACE_ ENABLE

ORACLE_TRACE_ENABLE={TRUE|FALSE}

This enables or disables Oracle trace.

ORACLE_TRACE_ FACILITY_NAME

ORACLE_TRACE_FACILITY_NAME=*facility_name*

This gives the Oracle trace default facility name.

ORACLE_TRACE_ FACILITY_PATH

ORACLE_TRACE_FACILITY_PATH=*directory*

This specifies the *directory* in which Oracle trace facility files are stored.

OS_AUTHENT_ PREFIX

OS_AUTHENT_PREFIX=*prefix*

This specifies the *prefix* for auto-logon accounts. The default is "OPS$".

Available in all versions from 7.x to 8.1.

OS_ROLES

OS_ROLES={TRUE|FALSE}

If true, then roles may be retrieved from the operating system.

PARALLEL_ ADAPTIVE_MULTI _USER

8.0+

PARALLEL_ADAPTIVE_MULTI_USER={TRUE|FALSE}

If true, Oracle dynamically adjusts query parallelism when multiple parallel queries run concurrently.

May be modified by ALTER SYSTEM.

Initialization Parameters

Configuration Parameters *(Continued)*

PARALLEL_ AUTOMATIC_ TUNING 8i	PARALLEL_AUTOMATIC_TUNING={TRUE|FALSE} If true, then Oracle will choose intelligent defaults for most parallel query tuning parameters.
PARALLEL_ BROADCAST_ ENABLED 8.0+	PARALLEL_BROADCAST_ENABLED={TRUE|FALSE} A setting of true improves parallel joins involving both very small and very large tables. May be modified by ALTER SESSION.
PARALLEL_ DEFAULT_MAX_ INSTANCES	PARALLEL_DEFAULT_MAX_INSTANCES=*degree_of_parallelism* This defines the default degree of parallelism for parallel hints or table clauses that use the DEFAULT clause.
PARALLEL_ EXECUTION_ MESSAGE_SIZE 8.0+	PARALLEL_EXECUTION_MESSAGE_SIZE=*bytes* PARALLEL_EXECUTION_MESSAGE_SIZE specifies the default message buffer size for parallel execution.
PARALLEL_ INSTANCE_GROUP 8.0+	PARALLEL_INSTANCE_GROUP= *parallel_instance_group* For parallel server, PARALLEL_INSTANCE_GROUP specifies an instance group to use for all parallel operations. May be modified by either ALTER SESSION or ALTER SYSTEM.
PARALLEL_MAX _SERVERS	PARALLEL_MAX_SERVERS=*no_of_servers* This sets the maximum number of slave processes for parallel execution.

Configuration Parameters *(Continued)*

PARALLEL_MIN_ MESSAGE_POOL 8.0	PARALLEL_MIN_MESSAGE_POOL=*bytes* PARALLEL_MIN_MESSAGE_POOL specifies the initial amount of memory to allocate within the shared pool for parallel execution messages.
PARALLEL_MIN_ PERCENT	PARALLEL_MIN_PERCENT=*percent* This parameter defines the minimum acceptable percentage of parallel slaves, as a percentage of the requested degree of parallelism, which must be available for a parallel SQL to be executed. May be modified by ALTER SESSION.
PARALLEL_MIN_ SERVERS	PARALLEL_MIN_SERVERS=*no_of_processes* PARALLEL_MIN_SERVERS specifies the minimum number of parallel execution slave processes.
PARALLEL_ SERVER	PARALLEL_SERVER={TRUE|FALSE} This is set to true if in parallel server mode.
PARALLEL_ SERVER_IDLE_ TIME 7.3,8.0	PARALLEL_SERVER_IDLE_TIME=*minutes* PARALLEL_SERVER_IDLE_TIME specifies the idle time in *minutes* after which an excess parallel server process will be terminated.
PARALLEL_ SERVER_ INSTANCES 8i	PARALLEL_SERVER_INSTANCES=*no_of_instances* For Oracle parallel server, this specifies the number of instances to use for sizing SGA structures.

Initialization Parameters

Configuration Parameters *(Continued)*

PARALLEL_ THREADS_PER_ CPU **8i**	PARALLEL_THREADS_PER_CPU=2 PARALLEL_THREADS_PER_CPU sets the default number of parallel slaves that should be initiated per CPU. May be modified by ALTER SYSTEM.
PARALLEL_ TRANSACTION_ RESOURCE_ TIMEOUT **8.0**	PARALLEL_TRANSACTION_RESOURCE_TIMEOUT=*seconds* For parallel server, this specifies the timeout for transactions that are awaiting resources held by another instance. May be modified by ALTER SYSTEM.
PARTITION_ VIEW_ENABLED	PARTITION_VIEW_ENABLED={true|false} This enables or disables partitioned views. May be modified by ALTER SESSION.
PLSQL_LOAD_ WITHOUT_ COMPILE **8i**	PLSQL_LOAD_WITHOUT_COMPILE={TRUE|<u>FALSE</u>} This enables or disables the PL/SQL load without compilation flag. May be modified by ALTER SESSION.
PLSQL_V2_ COMPATIBILITY **8.0+**	PLSQL_V2_COMPATIBILITY={true|false} If true, PL/SQL version 2.x compatibility is enforced. Otherwise, PL/SQL v3 behavior is enforced. May be modified by either ALTER SESSION or ALTER SYSTEM.
PRE_PAGE_SGA	PRE_PAGE_SGA={TRUE|<u>FALSE</u>} If true, all pages of the SGA are brought into memory when the instance is started.

Configuration Parameters *(Continued)*

PROCESSES	PROCESSES=*max_processes* PROCESSES specifies the maximum number of processes or threads attached to the instance.
PUSH_JOIN_ PREDICATE 7.3,8.0	PUSH_JOIN_PREDICATE={TRUE|<u>FALSE</u>} If true, join predicates may be "pushed" into view definitions for queries that involve views. May be modified by ALTER SESSION.
QUERY_REWRITE _ENABLED 8i	QUERY_REWRITE_ENABLED={TRUE|<u>FALSE</u>} If true, queries may be rewritten to take advantage of materialized views. May be modified by either ALTER SESSION or ALTER SYSTEM.
QUERY_REWRITE _INTEGRITY 8i	QUERY_REWRITE_INTEGRITY={<u>ENFORCE</u>|NO_ENFORCE|USE_STALE} This performs rewrites using materialized views with desired integrity. May be modified by either ALTER SESSION or ALTER SYSTEM.
RDBMS_SERVER _DN 8i	RDBMS_SERVER_DN= *distinguished_name* This designates RDBMS's distinguished name.
READ_ONLY_ OPEN_DELAYED 8.0+	READ_ONLY_OPEN_DELAYED={<u>FALSE</u>|TRUE} If true, this delays the opening of read-only database files until the first access.

Initialization Parameters

Configuration Parameters *(Continued)*

RECOVERY_ PARALLELISM	RECOVERY_PARALLELISM=*number_of_processes*
	RECOVERY_PARALLELISM specifies the number of server processes to use for parallel recovery.

REDUCE_ALARM	REDUCE_ALARM={true|false}
7.3,8.0	If true, a WMON process is created, which reduces latency in responding to wakeup signals.

REMOTE_ DEPENDENCIES_ MODE	REMOTE_DEPENDENCIES_MODE={TIMESTAMP|SIGNATURE}
	REMOTE_DEPENDENCIES_MODE determines the mode for determining dependencies for remote stored procedure calls.
	May be modified by either ALTER SESSION OR ALTER SYSTEM.

REMOTE_LOGIN_ PASSWORDFILE	REMOTE_LOGIN_PASSWORDFILE={NONE|SHARED|EXCLUSIVE }
	If NONE, this instance does not perform validation via a password file; if SHARED, validation occurs through a shared password file; and if EXCLUSIVE, validation occurs through an exclusive file.

REMOTE_OS_ AUTHENT	REMOTE_OS_AUTHENT={TRUE|FALSE}
	If true, non-secure remote clients may use auto-logon accounts.

REMOTE_OS_ ROLES	REMOTE_OS_ROLES={TRUE|FALSE}
	If true, non-secure remote clients may use operating system roles.

REPLICATION_ DEPENDENCY_ TRACKING	REPLICATION_DEPENDENCY_TRACKING={TRUE|FALSE}
	If true, Oracle tracks read/write dependency information for replication parallel propagation.
8.0,8i	Available in versions 8.0 and 8.1.

Configuration Parameters *(Continued)*

RESOURCE_LIMIT | RESOURCE_LIMIT={TRUE|FALSE}

If true, then resource limits specified by profiles will be enforced.

May be modified by ALTER SYSTEM.

RESOURCE_ MANAGER_PLAN

8i

RESOURCE_MANAGER_PLAN=*string*

RESOURCE_MANAGER_PLAN specifies the top plan for the resource manager. If no plan is specified, then the resource manager is not enabled.

May be modified by ALTER SYSTEM.

ROLLBACK_ SEGMENTS

ROLLBACK_SEGMENTS=*rollback_segment*
    [,*rollback_segment* ...]

This provides the list of ROLLBACK segments to be active at startup.

ROW_CACHE_ CURSORS

7.3, 8.0

ROW_CACHE_CURSORS=*number_of_cursors*

ROW_CACHE_CURSORS specifies the number of cached cursors for row cache (data dictionary) management. The typical default value is 10.

ROW_LOCKING

ROW_LOCKING={ALWAYS|DEFAULT|INTENT }

This defines the degree of row-level locking. ALWAYS and DEFAULT specify normal row-level locking; INTENT specifies that row-level locking should occur in intent locks created by FOR UPDATE only.

SEQUENCE_ CACHE_ENTRIES

7.3, 8.0

SEQUENCE_CACHE_ENTRIES=*no_of_entries*

SEQUENCE_CACHE_ENTRIES specifies the number of cached sequences in the SGA.

Initialization Parameters

Configuration Parameters *(Continued)*

SEQUENCE_ CACHE_HASH_ BUCKETS 7.3, 8.0	SEQUENCE_CACHE_HASH_BUCKETS=*number_of_buckets* This sets the number of sequence cache hash buckets.
SERIAL_REUSE 8.0+	SERIAL_REUSE={DISABLE|SELECT|DML|PLSQL|ALL|NULL} SERIAL_REUSE specifies the types of SQL statements that will take advantage of serially-reusable memory in the shared pool.
SERIALIZABLE	SERIALIZABLE={TRUE|FALSE} If true, then transactions are executed serially.
SERVICE_NAMES 8i	SERVICE_NAMES=*service_names* SERVICE_NAMES provides a list of service names supported by the instance.
SESSION_CACHED _CURSORS	SESSION_CACHED_CURSORS=*cursors* SESSION_CACHED_CURSORS specifies the number of cursors to be stored in the session cursor cache. May be modified by ALTER SESSION.
SESSION_MAX_ OPEN_FILES 8.0+	SESSION_MAX_OPEN_FILES=*files* SESSION_MAX_OPEN_FILES specifies the maximum number of open BFILE handles allowed per session.
SESSIONS	SESSIONS=*number_of_sessions* This sets the maximum number of database sessions.
SHADOW_CORE_ DUMP	SHADOW_CORE_DUMP={FULL|PARTIAL} If true, shadow process core dumps include a dump of the SGA.

Configuration Parameters *(Continued)*

SHARED_ MEMORY_ ADDRESS 8.0+	SHARED_MEMORY_ADDRESS=*address* This specifies the SGA starting *address* (low-order 32 bits on 64-bit platforms).
SHARED_POOL_ RESERVED_MIN _ALLOC 7.3,8.0	SHARED_POOL_RESERVED_MIN_ALLOC=*size*{m|k} Memory allocations larger than SHARED_POOL_RESERVED_MIN_ALLOC will be made from the reserved area of the shared pool.
SHARED_POOL_ RESERVED_SIZE	SHARED_POOL_RESERVED_SIZE=*bytes* This gives the size in *bytes* of the reserved area of shared pool.
SHARED_POOL_ SIZE	SHARED_POOL_SIZE=*bytes* This gives the size in *bytes* of the shared pool.
SNAPSHOT_ REFRESH_KEEP_ CONNECTIONS 7.3, 8.0	SNAPSHOT_REFRESH_KEEP_CONNECTIONS={TRUE|FALSE} If true, job queue processes will keep network connections open between the execution of jobs. Available in versions 7 and 8.0.
SORT_AREA_ RETAINED_SIZE	SORT_AREA_RETAINED_SIZE=*bytes* SORT_AREA_RETAINED_SIZE is the amount of sort memory retained between sorts. May be modified by either ALTER SESSION or ALTER SYSTEM.
SORT_AREA_SIZE	SORT_AREA_SIZE=*bytes* This sets the maximum amount of sort memory available for the session.

Initialization Parameters

Configuration Parameters *(Continued)*

SORT_AREA_SIZE (CONT.)	May be modified by either ALTER SESSION or ALTER SYSTEM.
SORT_DIRECT_ WRITES 7.3, 8.0	SORT_DIRECT_WRITES={TRUE|FALSE|<u>AUTO</u>} If true, this always bypasses the buffer cache when writing sort blocks to the temporary tablespace; if auto, it bypasses the buffer cache if the sort area size is greater than 10 times the block size; and if false, it never bypasses the buffer cache. May be modified by either ALTER SESSION or ALTER SYSTEM.
SORT_ MULTIBLOCK_ READ_COUNT 8i	SORT_MULTIBLOCK_READ_COUNT=*blocks* SORT_MULTIBLOCK_READ_COUNT specifies the number of *blocks* to read in one operation from a temporary sort segment. May be modified by either ALTER SESSION or ALTER SYSTEM.
SORT_READ_FAC 7.3, 8.0	SORT_READ_FAC=*integer* SORT_READ_FAC provides an estimate of the ratio of disk seek time and rotational latency to transfer time. May be modified by either ALTER SESSION or ALTER SYSTEM.
SORT_SPACEMAP _SIZE 7.3, 8.0	SORT_SPACEMAP_SIZE=*bytes* This gives the size in *bytes* of a sort disk area space map. Available in versions 7 and 8.0.
SORT_WRITE_ BUFFER_SIZE	SORT_WRITE_BUFFER_SIZE=*bytes* SORT_WRITE_BUFFER_SIZE specifies the size of each sort direct write buffer. May be modified by either ALTER SESSION or ALTER SYSTEM.

Configuration Parameters *(Continued)*

SORT_WRITE_ BUFFERS 7.3, 8.0	SORT_WRITE_BUFFERS=*buffers* This specifies the number of sort direct write *buffers*. May be modified by either ALTER SESSION or ALTER SYSTEM.
SPIN_COUNT 7.3, 8.0	SPIN_COUNT=*spins* This specifies the number of retries when acquiring a latch before sleeping. May be modified by ALTER SYSTEM.
SQL_TRACE	SQL_TRACE={TRUE|FALSE} This generates tracing of SQL statements, when set to true. May be modified by ALTER SYSTEM or ALTER SESSION.
SQL92_SECURITY	SQL92_SECURITY={TRUE|FALSE} If true, UPDATES or DELETES that search for specific rows require SELECT privilege on the table concerned.
STANDBY_ ARCHIVE_DEST 8i	STANDBY_ARCHIVE_DEST=*directory* This specifies the archive log destination for the standby database. May be modified by ALTER SYSTEM.
STAR_ TRANSFORMATION _ENABLED 8.0+	STAR_TRANSFORMATION_ENABLED={TRUE|FALSE} STAR_TRANSFORMATION_ENABLED enables or disables the use of the star transformation optimizer plan. May be modified by ALTER SESSION.

Initialization
Parameters

Configuration Parameters *(Continued)*

TAPE_ASYNCH_IO 8.0+	TAPE_ASYNCH_IO={<u>TRUE</u>|FALSE} TAPE_ASYNC_IO determines whether asynchronous I/O will be used to tape devices.
TEMPORARY_ TABLE_LOCKS 7.3, 8.0	TEMPORARY_TABLE_LOCKS=*number_of_locks* TEMPORARY_TABLE_LOCKS determines the number of temporary table locks and hence the maximum allowable number of temporary tables.
TEXT_ENABLE	TEXT_ENABLE={TRUE|<u>FALSE</u>} If true, this enables text searching through the Oracle context cartridge. May be modified by either ALTER SESSION or ALTER SYSTEM.
THREAD	THREAD=*redo_thread* In parallel server, THREAD determines which redo thread to mount.
TIMED_OS_ STATISTICS 8.0+	TIMED_OS_STATISTICS=*interval* TIMED_OS_STATISTICS allows the collection of operating system statistics after each call. *Interval* is measured and determines how often the OS statistic counters will be updated. May be modified by ALTER SYSTEM.
TIMED_ STATISTICS	TIMED_STATISTICS={TRUE|<u>FALSE</u>} If true, Oracle maintains CPU and elapsed timings for OCI calls and for resource waits. May be modified by either ALTER SESSION or ALTER SYSTEM.

Configuration Parameters *(Continued)*

TRANSACTION_ AUDITING 8.0+	TRANSACTION_AUDITING={<u>TRUE</u>|FALSE} If TRUE, audit information is added to the redo log. May be modified by ALTER SYSTEM.
TRANSACTIONS	TRANSACTIONS=*no_of_transactions* This indicates the maximum number of concurrent active transactions.
TRANSACTIONS_ PER_ROLLBACK_ SEGMENT	TRANSACTIONS_PER_ROLLBACK_SEGMENT=*transactions* TRANSACTIONS_PER_ROLLBACK_SEGMENT provides an estimate of the number of active *transactions* per rollback segment.
UNLIMITED_ ROLLBACK_ SEGMENTS 7.3	UNLIMITED_ROLLBACK_SEGMENTS={TRUE|<u>FALSE</u>} If true, this allows unlimited extents for rollback segments. Available in version 7 only.
USE_INDIRECT_ DATA_BUFFERS 8.0+	USE_INDIRECT_DATA_BUFFERS={TRUE|<u>FALSE</u>} This enables indirect data buffers, allowing SGAs of more than 4GB on supported platforms.
USE_ISM 7.3, 8.0	USE_ISM={<u>TRUE</u>|FALSE} If true, this uses intimate shared memory (shared page tables) on supported platforms. Available in versions 7 and 8.0.
USE_READV	USE_READV={TRUE|FALSE} On platforms that support it, this uses the *readv()* system call for multi-block read.

Initialization Parameters

Configuration Parameters *(Continued)*

USER_DUMP_ DEST	USER_DUMP_DEST=*directory* This provides the name of the *directory* to which to write user process trace or dump files. May be modified by ALTER SYSTEM.
UTL_FILE_DIR	UTL_FILE_DIR=*directory* This specifies directories that are accessible to the UTL_FILE package for file I/O. A separate entry is required for each directory.

Terms, Acronyms, and Jargon

Introduction

This chapter lists commonly used Oracle terms and acronyms.

Reference

These terms may be defined in many of the Oracle documentation set manuals, but the best single reference for terminology is the *Oracle Server Concepts Manual*.

Terms

Table 11–1 Terms

Term	Description
ANALYZE	The ANALYZE command collects table and index statistics which help the Oracle *optimizer* choose the best execution plan for a SQL statement.
ANTI-JOIN	An anti-join returns all rows in one table that do not have a matching row in the other table. It is typically implemented using a NOT IN subquery.
ARCH PROCESS	See *Archiver Process*.

Table 11–1 Terms *(Continued)*

Term	Description
ARCHIVED LOG	A *redo log* that has been copied by the *archiver process* to an alternative location, usually as a backup measure or to maintain a *standby database*.
ARCHIVER PROCESS	An Oracle process that is responsible for copying completed *redo logs* to an alternative destination if the database is running in ARCHIVELOG mode.
ARRAY PROCESSING	Array processing allows a single SQL call to process multiple rows. For instance, a single execution of an INSERT statement could add multiple rows, or a single FETCH from a SELECT statement could return multiple rows.
ASYNCHRONOUS I/O	Asynchronous I/O allows a process to submit multiple I/O requests without waiting for each to complete. In practice, this means a single process can utilize the bandwidth of multiple disks.
AURORA	The name of the Java Virtual Machine (JVM) incorporated into Oracle8i.
AUTONOMOUS TRANSACTION	An autonomous transaction runs within—but outside the scope of—another *transaction*. COMMITS and ROLLBACKS issued within the autonomous transaction do not affect the parent transaction.
B*-TREE INDEX	An index structure that takes the form of a hierarchy or inverted "tree." This is the default format for Oracle indexes.
BFILE	A Bfile is an external file that appears within the database as a LOB datatype. Bfiles can be accessed only by the DBMS_LOB package.
BIND VARIABLES	Bind variables allow the variable portions of an SQL statement—such as the data values to be inserted or the search criteria—to be defined as "parameters" to the SQL statement. The use of bind variables allows SQL statements to be re-executed without re-parsing the SQL statement. The alternative approach, where substitution variables are embedded as literals within the SQL statement, requires that the SQL statement be re-parsed when the substitution variables change.

Table 11–1 Terms *(Continued)*

Term	Description
BITMAP INDEXES	A bitmap index contains a bitmap for each unique value of the indexed column. These bitmaps can be efficiently manipulated to process queries that are predicated on multiple columns, each of which has only a few distinct values.
BLOB	Binary Large Object. In Oracle, a BLOB may store up to 4GB of unstructured binary data.
BLOCK	The basic unit of storage in an Oracle instance. Block sizes most commonly range between 2 and 32 KB.
BLOCK CLEANOUT	During modifications to data blocks, the *System Change Number* (SCN) for the change is not yet known because the transaction has not yet been committed. Block cleanout is the process of updating these SCN numbers. For most blocks, this will occur when the transaction is committed; but for some blocks, it will occur when the block is next read.
BRANCH BLOCKS	The middle level of blocks in a B°-tree index. Each branch block contains a range of index key values and pointers to the appropriate leaf blocks.
BUFFER CACHE	The area of the SGA that caches data blocks. If a session requires a data or index block from a database file, it will first check the contents of the buffer cache. Data blocks are cleared from the buffer cache according to a *least recently used* algorithm.
CHECKPOINT	A checkpoint occurs when all database blocks that have been modified prior to a specific moment in time are written to disk. Checkpoints can be configured to occur at regular intervals and always occur when Oracle switches *redo log* files. Redo logs cannot be reused until the checkpoint completes, because only then does Oracle know that the information in the redo log is no longer required in the case of instance failure.
CHECKPOINT PROCESS	The checkpoint process updates data file headers during checkpoints.
CKPT PROCESS	See *Checkpoint Process.*
CLOB	Character Large Object. A CLOB may store up to 4GB character data.

Table 11–1 Terms *(Continued)*

Term	Description
CLONE DATABASE	A copy of a database that is used to perform tablespace point-in-time recovery.
CLUSTER	A form of table storage in which the physical location of a row is dependent on the value of the row.
	An index cluster stores rows from one or more tables in the same segment. Rows with common cluster key values are stored together.
	In a hash cluster, the location of rows in a single table is dependent on the hashed value of the table's key.
COLLECTION	Collections are datatypes made up of more than one element. Two collection types are *nested tables* and *varrays*.
CONCATENATED INDEX	An index that is comprised from more than one column.
CONSISTENT READ	Oracle queries return rows that are consistent with the time at which the query commenced. This consistent read may require access to rows that have changed since the query commenced—these rows are accessed from *rollback segments*.
CONSTRAINT	Constraints provide restrictions on the data values that can be stored in Oracle tables. *Primary key* and *unique* constraints prevent rows with duplicate values for the key columns being stored. *Foreign key* constraints allow only rows that match the primary key of another table to be stored. *Check* constraints provide some logical condition that must be satisfied for all rows.
CORBA	Common Object Request Broker Architecture. CORBA is a standard that allows for distributed execution and management of program objects.
	Oracle8i includes a Java-based CORBA 2.0 Object Request Borker (ORB). The Oracle8i ORB can provide access to Java programs stored in the database.
CORRELATED SUBQUERY	A subquery that references a value from the parent query in its WHERE clause. Correlated subqueries may be executed once for each row returned by the parent query.

Table 11–1 Terms *(Continued)*

Term	Description
CURSOR	A session memory structure that contains details of a SQL statement or PL/SQL block. Otherwise referred to as a context area.
DANGLING	An object *ref* that contains an *object identifier* to a non-existent object.
DATA DICTIONARY	The data dictionary comprises a set of Oracle tables which contain the definitions of all objects within the database. The data dictionary is stored in the SYS account.
DATABASE WRITER PROCESS	The database writer process is responsible for writing modified blocks from the *buffer cache* in the SGA to database files on disk. Depending on the configuration of the Oracle database, there may be more than one active database writer process.
DBWR PROCESS	See *Database Writer Process.*
DDL	Data Definition Language. The Data Definition Language of SQL provides commands for creating and maintaining database objects.
DEDICATED SERVER	A dedicated server process performs database operations on behalf of a single client program. Compare with *shared server.*
DEGREE OF PARALLELISM	The number of parallel threads of execution for parallel SQL. If there are no limits on the number of CPUs and disks available, doubling the degree of parallelism can be expected to double the throughput of the SQL statement.
DENORMALIZATION	The process of re-introducing redundant or derived information into a data model, usually with the aim of improving performance.
DISCRETE TRANSACTION	A special *transaction* mode with fairly severe limitations, but which, when used appropriately, can substantially improve transaction performance.
DISPATCHER PROCESS	The dispatcher process is responsible for mediating *multi-threaded server* connections. When a client program requests a multi-threaded server connection, the listener allocates a dispatcher to the client. When the client submits an SQL request, the dispatcher allocates the SQL to an appropriate *shared server* process. Thus, the client may utilize multiple shared servers, but maintains a connection to only one dispatcher.

Table 11–1 Terms *(Continued)*

Term	Description
DML	Data Manipulation Language. The Data Manipulation Language of SQL provides commands for updating, deleting, or inserting rows into database tables.
DOMAIN INDEX	A user-defined index typically created on complex datatypes whose algorithms and optimizer characteristics are provided by the user. Domain indexes are created using the Oracle data cartridge interface API.
DRIVING TABLE	The table that is accessed first in a table join. Choosing the best driving table is a key decision when optimizing join order.
DYNAMIC PERFORMANCE TABLES	A set of views ("V$" views) that provide access to Oracle performance information. The information in the dynamic performance tables comes not from physical tables, but from externalization of Oracle memory structures.
EJB	See *Enterprise Java Bean.*
ENTERPRISE JAVA BEANS	A Java bean is a reusable component written in Java—typically designed to run in a client or browser environment. The Enterprise Java Beans (EJB) standard defines extensions to the bean architecture to allow Java beans to perform server-based and transactional processing. Oracle8i supports enterprise Java beans within the JServer environment.
EVENT	Oracle events set debugging flags within on Oracle instance. Events may be set by the EVENT initialization parameter or through the ALTER SESSION SET EVENTS statement. Oracle recommends that event codes be set only on advice from Oracle worldwide support.
EXCEPTION	In PL/SQL, exceptions are raised either explicitly by the RAISE statement, or when an Oracle error occurs. Exception handlers that define actions that occur when specific exceptions are raised can be declared.
EXTENT	The fundamental unit of space allocation for a *segment*. Segments are comprised of one or more extents. As data is added to a segment, additional extents are automatically allocated as required, subject to storage allocation parameters specified in the segment's STORAGE definition.

Table 11–1 Terms *(Continued)*

Term	Description
FOREIGN KEY	A column or columns within one table which correspond to the *primary key* of a "master" or "parent" table. These matching foreign and primary key columns can be used to join the two tables.
FRAGMENTATION	Oracle can experience fragmentation in one of the following ways: • Free space in data files may fragment so that even if there is sufficient free space overall, there is insufficient contiguous free space to allocate an *extent*. • Segment storage may fragment when many extents are allocated. This is usually harmless. • Rows may fragment when a row expands beyond the storage available in the block. The row will then migrate, leaving the original ROWID and pointer ROWID only in the original block. • Memory in the shared pool may fragment when many small allocations prevent sufficient contiguous space from being available for large memory allocations.
FREE LIST	A list of blocks that are eligible for insert. Each *segment* contains at least one free list. Multiple free lists can be configured using the FREELISTS clause if the segment is subject to high concurrent insert rates. Multiple *free list groups* can be configured in an Oracle parallel server environment so that each instance inserts rows into specific blocks.
FUNCTIONAL INDEX	An index based on a function or expression rather than on a simple column or columns.
HASH CLUSTER	See *Cluster.*
HASH JOIN	One of the algorithms that Oracle can use to join two tables. In a hash join, a *hash table,* a sort of on-the-fly index, is constructed for the larger of the two tables. The smaller table is then scanned, and the hash table is used to find matching rows in the larger table.

Table 11–1 Terms *(Continued)*

Term	Description
HASHING	In general, hashing refers to the technique of mathematically transforming a key value into a relative address that can be used to rapidly locate a record. Oracle uses hashing as a table access method (hash *clusters*) and to optimize certain join operations (*hash join*). Hashing is also used extensively within internal SGA operations.
HIERARCHICAL QUERY	A special case of a self-join in which each row recursively accesses child rows, revealing a hierarchy of parent-child relationships. This is sometimes referred to as "explosion-of-parts."
HIGH-WATER MARK	Indicates the highest block in a segment that has ever contained data. The high-water mark increases as rows are inserted into the segment. However, deleting rows will not reduce the high-water mark.
	Full table scans access all rows in the segment up to the high-water mark.
HINT	Instructions that you can include in your SQL statement to instruct or "guide" the optimizer
	An optimizer hint appears as a comment following the first word of a SQL statement (e.g., SELECT, INSERT, DELETE, or UPDATE). A hint is differentiated from other comments by the presence of the plus sign ("+") following the opening comment delimiter ("/°").
IIOP	Internet Inter-ORB Protocol. The protocol by which CORBA clients make requests across the Internet for CORBA mediated-services. Oracle8i supports IIOP requests.
INDEX CLUSTER	See *Cluster*.
INDEX-ORGANIZED TABLE	An index-organized table appears to the user as a table, but has the physical organization of a *B°-tree index*. *Leaf nodes* in the B°-tree contain primary key column values and selected columns. Other columns are stored in an overflow segment.
INSTANCE	An Oracle instance consists of an SGA and Oracle system ("detached") processes. An instance differs from a database in that a database may be associated with multiple instances in a parallel server environment.

Table 11-1 Terms *(Continued)*

Term	Description
INTERSECT	INTERSECT is a set operator that returns the rows which are common to two result sets.
ITL	Interested Transaction List. Each block contains an ITL that contains details of transactions which hold or which want row level locks within the block.
JDBC	An API that allows Java programs to communicate with relational databases. Oracle8i includes built-in support for JDBC.
JOB QUEUE PROCESS	The job queue processes are responsible for executing jobs submitted via the DBMS_JOB package. The number of job queue processes is controlled by the JOB_QUEUE_PROCESSES initialization parameter.
JSERVER	The Java server platform provided by Oracle8i. JServer includes the Aurora JVM, native JDBC and SQLJ support, the VisiBroker ORB, and Enterprise Java Beans support.
JVM	Java Virtual Machine. A JVM is a program that simulates a hardware platform which runs Java bytecode. Oracle8i includes a JVM—called Aurora—which allows it to support native Java.
LATCH	Internal Oracle locking mechanisms that generally protect memory structures in the SGA.
LCK0 PROCESS	See *Lock Process*.
LEAF BLOCKS	The lowest level of blocks in a *B°-tree index*. Each leaf block contains a range of index key values and pointers (ROWIDS) to appropriate blocks.
LGWR	See *Log Writer Process*.
LIBRARY CACHE	A section of the *shared pool* which contains shared SQL and PL/SQL structures.
LISTENER PROCESS	The listener process establishes network connections to the Oracle instance. A client program requests a connection from the listener which either spawns a *dedicated server* process or assigns a *dispatcher* process for a *shared server* connection.

Table 11–1 Terms *(Continued)*

Term	Description
LOB	Large Object. In Oracle, LOBs can be external, as in the *BFILE* datatype, or internal, as in *CLOBs* or *BLOBs*.
LOB LOCATOR	The LOB locator is stored within a table which includes a LOB datatype and serves as a pointer to a LOB's location. LOBs are typically not stored within the segment itself, so the LOB locator could reference an external file (*BFILE*) or location of a *CLOB* or *BLOB* within a *LOB* segment. Obtaining a LOB locator is the first step in retrieving or manipulating a LOB.
LOCALLY MANAGED TABLESPACE	Locally managed tablespaces maintain storage allocation information within a structure located within each data file. Dictionary-managed tablespaces store this information within the data dictionary.
LOCK PROCESS	An Oracle parallel server process that mediates inter-instance locking.
LOG WRITER PROCESS	The log writer process (LGWR) is responsible for writing transaction entries from the log buffer in the SGA to the *redo logs*.
LRU	Least Recently Used. The Least Recently Used algorithm is used by Oracle to remove cached data blocks that have least recently been accessed. When a block is read from disk, it is placed on the most recently used end of the LRU list, unless it has been read in from a table scan of a "large" table and the CACHE hint has not been specified. If it is not re-accessed, it moves over time to the least recently used end of the list and eventually is flushed from the cache.
MATERIALIZED VIEW	A table that contains the results of a query. Suitable queries may be transparently "rewritten" to use the materialized view, if permitted, and if the optimizer considers that the materialized view will offer superior performance.
MINUS	A set operation that returns all rows in one result set which do not also appear in a second result set.

Table 11–1 Terms *(Continued)*

Term	Description
MOUNT	An intermediate stage during the startup of an Oracle instance. When the database is mounted, the SGA has been allocated, processes have been started, and control files have been opened, but the data files have not yet been accessed. Certain maintenance operations require that the database be mounted but not open.
MTS	Multi-Threaded Server. MTS refers to the architecture that includes *dispatchers*, *shared servers,* and *listener* processes.
MULTIBLOCK READ	Multi-block reads occur when Oracle reads more than one database block in a single read operation. This most common occurs when Oracle is performing a *full table scan* or an index scan.
MULTI-BYTE CHARACTER SET	Most Western languages can be represented with each character stored in a single byte. Other languages—for instance Kanji—require multiple bytes per character.
NATIONAL LANGUAGE SUPPORT	National Language Support (NLS) allows Oracle to adapt to variations in languages and national conventions. NLS allows the language of error messages, the format of dates and currencies, and the character set to be adjusted.
NESTED LOOPS JOIN	A join method in which each row of the outer table is read. For each row, a lookup of the inner table is undertaken. This best suits joins where the inner table is accessed via an index lookup.
NESTED TABLE	An Oracle8 *collection* type in which a column is defined as containing an embedded ("nested") table.
NLS	See *National Language Support.*
NULL VALUES	Null values indicate that a value is missing, unknown, or inapplicable. The use of null values extends the normal two-valued logic to a three-valued logic.
OBJECT IDENTIFIER	A unique system-generated number associated with every row of an object table.
OBJECT TYPE	Complex datatypes that include both attributes and methods.
OBJECT VIEW	A view that maps relational data to an Oracle object type.
OID	See *Object Identifier.*

Table 11–1 Terms *(Continued)*

Term	Description
OLAP	On-Line Analytical Processing. On-line analytical processing involves the real-time manipulation of large quantities of data, generally for the purpose of facilitating business decisions. OLAP databases are typified by large data volumes and infrequent, long-running queries.
OLTP	On-Line Transaction Processing. OLTP databases typically have a very high rate of update and query activity. OLTP is typified by high rates of index lookups, single-row modifications, and frequent commits.
OPS	See *Oracle Parallel Server.*
OPTIMISTIC LOCKING STRATEGY	A locking strategy based on the assumption that a row is unlikely to be changed by another session between the time the row is queried and the time it is modified. Optimistic locking minimizes the lock duration, but requires that the transaction be aborted if the row is changed by another session.
OPTIMIZER	See *Query Optimizer.*
ORACLE PARALLEL SERVER	An advanced Oracle configuration in which more than one instance opens a single Oracle database. The advantages of OPS are possible scalability and fault tolerance.
ORATAB	A file present on UNIX systems, usually in the */etc* or */var/opt/oracle* directories, which list Oracle instances present on the host, their *ORACLE_HOME* directory, and a flag to indicate if they should be auto-started.
ORB	Object Request Broker. A component of the CORBA architecture which co-ordinates requests for distributed objects.
	Oracle8i includes a Java-based CORBA 2.0 Object Request Broker (ORB).
OUTER JOIN	A join in which rows are returned from one of the tables, even if there is no matching row in the other table. This is achieved in Oracle using the "(+)" operator in the WHERE clause.

Table 11–1 Terms *(Continued)*

Term	Description
OVERLOADING	Overloading refers to the practice of defining functions and procedures that have the same name, but which differ in the number or types of arguments. This allows for the development of routines that perform the same logical function on different datatypes.
PACKAGE	A group of related functions, procedures, and declarations. Packages allow the interface to be declared separately from the implementation, thus providing some degree of encapsulation of program code.
PARALLEL EXECUTION	The execution of an SQL operation using multiple processes or threads. This improves performance when there are multiple disk devices or CPUs available. In Oracle7, only queries and certain DDL operations can be executed in parallel. In Oracle8, DDL may also be executed in parallel under specific circumstances.
PARALLEL QUERY	See *Parallel Execution*.
PARSING	The process of preparing a SQL statement for execution. This involves checking the statement for syntax errors, checking for a matching statement in the *shared pool*, and determining the optimal execution plan. Parsing can contribute significantly to the processing overhead, especially in OLTP environments.
PARTITION	Partitioned objects are stored in multiple *segments*. This allows for objects to be spread across tablespaces and provides many maintenance and performance advantages for very large tables and indexes.
PGA	Program Global Area. An area of memory in the server process that contains stack space and—depending on whether the server is shared or dedicated—session-specific information.
PMON PROCESS	See *Process Monitor Process*.
PRIMARY KEY	The column or columns that uniquely identify a row in a table. Primary key constraints prevent duplicate values for primary keys and allow referential integrity enforcement for tables with corresponding *foreign keys*.

Table 11-1 Terms *(Continued)*

Term	Description
PROCESS	A unit of execution in a multi-processing environment. A process will typically execute a specific program and will have a unique and private allocation of memory. The operating system will determine the process's access to resources such as CPU, physical memory, and disk.
PROCESS MONITOR PROCESS	The Process Monitor (or PMON).
QMN PROCESS	See *Queue Monitor Process.*
QUERY OPTIMIZER	That part of the Oracle program which determines how the data required by a SQL statement will be retrieved. Among other things, the optimizer determines if any indexes will be used and the order in which tables will be joined.
QUEUE MONITOR PROCESS	An Oracle process that monitors queues used by the advanced queuing facility.
RAID	Redundant Array of Independent Disks. RAID is commonly used to describe the configuration of multiple physicals disks into one or more logical disks. RAID 0 is commonly referred to as "striping" and RAID 1 as "mirroring." The other popular RAID configuration, RAID 5, stripes data across multiple drives while storing sufficient parity information on all drives to allow data to be recovered should any single drive fail.
RANDOM I/O	I/O in which a specific disk block is accessed directly. This is typical of the I/O that results from indexed lookups.
RDBMS	Relational Database Management System.
RECO PROCESS	See *Recoverer Process.*
RECOVERER PROCESS	An Oracle background process that performs resolution of failed distributed transactions.
RECURSIVE SQL	SQL that is generated by Oracle to retrieve *data dictionary* or other information which is required to *parse* or execute an SQL statement. Recursive SQL is generated only when the required information is not found in the *row cache*.

Table 11–1 Terms *(Continued)*

Term	Description
RECURSIVE TRANSACTION	A *transaction* that is generated by Oracle to process an SQL statement. Recursive transactions typically update the *data dictionary*.
REDO LOGS	Oracle files that are used to record all changes made to objects with a database. When a COMMIT is issued, the changes made within the transaction are recorded in the redo log. The redo log can be used to restore the transaction in the event of a system failure.
REF	A REF datatype stores a pointer to an object row. The REF datatype contains the *object identifier* and—optionally—the *ROWID* of the object row.
REFERENTIAL INTEGRITY	Referential integrity ensures that *foreign keys* correctly map to *primary keys*. A referential integrity constraint will prevent the insert or update of foreign keys for which there are no matching primary keys, and will either prevent the deletion of primary keys if foreign keys exist or delete these foreign key rows (delete cascade).
RESULT SETS	The output from a SQL query. Results sets have the same tabular construction as tables. Results sets may also be created during intermediate SQL operations.
ROLLBACK SEGMENTS	Rollback segments store the contents of a row before it is modified by a DML (UPDATE, INSERT, DELETE) statement. This information is used in the event of a ROLLBACK, to provide a consistent view of the table for queries which commenced before the transaction was committed and to record the eventual success of a transaction.
ROW CACHE	A cache within the SGA that holds *data dictionary* information.
ROW LEVEL LOCKING	In general, Oracle only ever locks a row that is modified by a DML statement. Page, block, or table locks are not normally applied, and read locks are never applied.
ROWID	The ROWID uniquely identifies a row by its physical location. The ROWID of a row—if known—is the fastest way to access the row. An index includes the ROWIDs for rows matching specific key values, thus providing quick access to these rows.
SAVEPOINT	A savepoint provides a point to which a transaction can be reverted without rolling back the entire transaction.

Table 11–1 Terms *(Continued)*

Term	Description
SCHEMA	A collection of database objects that are logically related. In Oracle, a schema is synonymous with a database account.
SCN	See *System Change Number*.
SEGMENT	An object within an Oracle database that consumes storage. Examples are tables, indexes, rollback segments, temporary segments, and clusters.
SEMI-JOIN	A join that returns rows from a table which have matching rows in a second table, but which does not return multiple rows if there are multiple matches. This is usually expressed in Oracle using a WHERE EXISTS subquery.
SEQUENCE GENERATOR	An Oracle sequence generator returns unique numbers that are often used to populate primary keys. Oracle sequence generators are non-blocking and are independent of transactions.
SEQUENTIAL I/O	I/O in which multiple disk or database blocks are read in sequence. This is typical of the I/O which results from full table scans.
SERIAL EXECUTION	The execution of an SQL statement using a single process or thread. This requires that each stage of the SQL operation be processed one after the other. Compare with *parallel execution*.
SERVER PROCESS	See *Shadow Process*.
SGA	An area of Oracle shared memory that is available to all server processes. It contains cached data, shared SQL statements, message areas, and other shared structures.
SHADOW PROCESS	In many environments, the Oracle server program runs in a separate process from the client program. This "server" process is referred to as the shadow process.
SHARED GLOBAL AREA	See *SGA*.
SHARED POOL	An area of the SGA that stores parsed SQL statements, data dictionary information, and some session information.
SHARED SERVER	A shared MTS (multi-threaded server) process that performs database operations on behalf of multiple client programs.

Table 11–1 Terms *(Continued)*

Term	Description
SMON PROCESS	See *System Monitor Process.*
SMP	Symmetric Multi-processing. An SMP machine contains multiple, identical CPUs. The SMP architecture dominates mid-range UNIX computers and is increasingly popular on Microsoft NT systems.
SNAPSHOT	A table that is defined as the results of a query—typically one which replicates data from a remote site. Snapshots are often used as a means of replicating data, but can also be used to store regularly refreshed aggregate or summary data. In Oracle8i, snapshots and *materialized views* are synonymous.
SNMP	Simple Network Management Protocol. A protocol that allows services on the network to be identified and reports status information. Oracle databases can be located and queried using the SNMP protocol.
SNP PROCESS	See *Job Queue Process.*
SORT-MERGE	Sort-merge is one of the algorithms that Oracle can use to join two tables. When applying the sort-merge algorithm, Oracle sorts each table (or the *result set* from a previous operation) on the column values used to join the two tables. Oracle then merges the two sorted result sets into one.
SQL_TRACE	The SQL_TRACE facility allows SQL statements and execution statistics to be recorded to a trace file for diagnostic or tuning purposes. The trace file may be formatted by the TKPROF utility.
SQLJ	SQLJ is a standard API that allows SQL statements to be embedded in Java programs. These SQL statements are translated to JDBC calls before execution by the SQLJ translator.
STANDBY DATABASE	Standby databases replicate a primary database and can provide a "fall-over" in the event that the primary database fails. Standby databases are implemented by forwarding *redo logs* to the standby database as they complete in the primary database. These logs are then applied to the standby database so the database remains one log file, or more "behind" the primary database.

Table 11–1 Terms *(Continued)*

Term	Description
STAR JOIN	The STAR schema is a way of organizing relational data. It is very popular in data warehouses. In a STAR schema, business data is stored in one or more large tables, referred to as "fact" tables. These tables can be joined to multiple smaller "dimension" tables, which contain the more static details. A join of these tables is referred to as a star join.
STRIPING	A familiar term for *RAID 0*. Striping involves spreading data evenly across a number of disks, thus allowing higher data transfer rates than would otherwise be possible.
SYSTEM CHANGE NUMBER	The System Change Number (SCN) is a global number that is updated whenever a *transaction* commits. The SCN is recorded in *rollback segments* and in data blocks. It allows Oracle to determine if data has changed since a query commenced, and to locate the appropriate rollback segment block to reconstruct the block as it was before the query commenced.
SYSTEM GLOBAL AREA	See *SGA*.
SYSTEM MONITOR	The system monitor process is responsible for performing instance recovery at startup, for cleaning up *temporary segments*, and for coalescing free space within tablespaces.
TABLE SCAN	A full table scan involves reading every block allocated to a table up to the table's *high-water mark*. This is the default access path for a query where there are no appropriate indexes on the table or when the cost-based optimizer determines that index paths will be less efficient than a table scan.
TABLESPACE	A structure that houses database *segments*. A tablespace is comprised of one or more data files. Neither segments nor data files may span tablespaces, although *partitioned* objects (which are comprised of multiple segments) may be housed in multiple tablespaces.
TEMPORARY SEGMENT	A segment created within the *tablespace* assigned as TEMPORARY to the session which is used to support large sorts and intermediate result sets.

Table 11-1 Terms *(Continued)*

Term	Description
TRANSACTION	A set of DML (UPDATE, DELETE, or INSERT) operations that succeed or fail as a unit. A transaction is successfully terminated by the COMMIT statement or aborted with the ROLLBACK statement.
TRIGGER	A PL/SQL stored program that is executed when specified events occur. Prior to Oracle8i, these events were always DML on database tables; but from Oracle8i onwards, the events may also be DDL events or database-wide events such as startup or shutdown.
TRUNCATE	Truncate involves rapidly removing all rows from a table. Rather than issuing a transaction to delete the rows, Oracle simply marks all blocks as unused.
TWO-PHASE COMMIT	Two-phase commit terminates a distributed *transaction*. In the first phase, all nodes prepare the commit. In the second phase, all nodes confirm that they are ready to commit and proceed to commit the transaction.
TWO-TASK	Oracle's two-task architecture provides separation between client programs and the database server programs. In the two-task architecture, Oracle client programs cannot access the SGA or data files directly. Instead, they communicate with a server process or thread which performs these services on their behalf.
UNION	A set operation in which the results of two queries which return result sets with the same structure are concatenated.
VARRAY	A type of *collection*. A varray is a fixed-sized array of simple datatypes that can be stored in within a database column.
VIEW	Views are often referred to as "stored queries" or "virtual tables." A view is presented to the user of a database as a table, but is defined as the result set of a specified query.

Internet Resources

I've tried to include the most frequently required Oracle information in this book, but obviously not everything could be included. When you need more information than you can find in these pages, you may want to refer to the more cumbersome, but clearly more comprehensive, Oracle on-line documentation set. When you can't find the answer in the documentation set, the Internet is your next-best friend. In this appendix, I've listed the Oracle Websites that I believe are most useful.

The Oracle Technology Network

```
http://technet.oracle.com/
```

This site contains perhaps the most extensive and authoritative Oracle technical information available on the Web. It includes full cross-version and cross-platform Oracle documentation sets, technical bulletins, discussion papers, code samples, downloadable software, and more.

You need to register to get access to member services, but the registration is free.

Oracle Support Services

```
http://www.oracle.com/support/
```

If you have an Oracle support account, you can access the Oracle support metalink site, which offers on-line documentation and bulletins, support forums, and patch downloads

Oracle Usenet Newsgroups

```
News:comp.databases.oracle.tools
News:comp.databases.oracle.misc
News:comp.databases.oracle.misc
```

Thousands of Oracle developers world-wide maintain a continual dialogue on these Internet newsgroups. These newsgroups are a great source of general information and a great place to cry for help if you feel you are getting nowhere with some problem.

Deja News Power Search

```
http://www.dejanews.com/home_ps.shtml/
```

Chances are that if you have a problem or query, it has already been asked and answered on the Oracle usenet newsgroups. DejaNews allows you to search a huge archive of newsgroups, including the comp.databases.oracle.*newsgroups.

The Database Domain

```
http://www.dbdomain.com/
```

This site has Oracle articles, software downloads, Web-based training, and links. There are both member-only and free sections.

RevealNet Pipelines

http://www.revealnet.com/pipeline.htm

RevealNet's pipelines offer hints and tips for DBAs and PL/SQL developers, together with on-line discussion forums.

OraPub

http://www.europa.com/~orapub/papers/pmain.htm

This site includes many useful articles on Oracle administration, performance tuning, and capacity management.

International Oracle User Group

http://www.ioug.org/

If you are a member of IOUG, you can get access to utilities, news, and archives of the IOUG select magazine.

Hayden Worthington, Inc.

http://www.mindspring.com/~hayden/

This site has an interesting archive of Oracle performance management documentation and tools.

The Oracle Underground FAQ

http://www.onwe.co.za/frank/faq.htm

In addition to an extensive set of answers to frequently asked questions, this site has probably the most extensive set of links to other Websites.

Oracle Magazine

```
http://www.oramag.com/
```

This site has an archive of Oracle's own *Oracle Magazine*.

Oreview

```
http://www.oreview.com/
```

Oreview has a convoluted lineage which began with *Oracle Technical Journal* in 1996. You can find each on-line issue archived here.

The Ultimate Software Consultants (TUSC)

```
http://www.tusc.com/tusc/document.html
```

TUSC has a large collection of documents and presentations prepared by their Oracle consultants.

Index

B

E

G

H

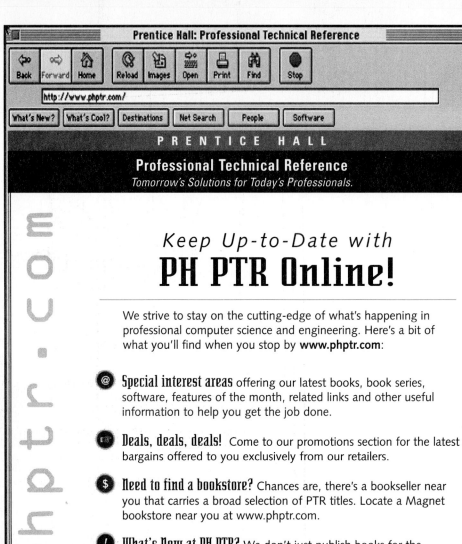